The Essential Guide to
MS-DOS® 5 Programming

The Essential Guide to MS-DOS 5 Programming

Peter G. Aitken

PUBLISHED BY
Microsoft Press
A Division of Microsoft Corporation
One Microsoft Way
Redmond, Washington 98052-6399

Copyright © 1992 by Peter G. Aitken

All rights reserved. No part of the contents of this book may be reproduced or transmitted in any form or by any means without the written permission of the publisher.

Library of Congress Cataloging-in-Publication Data
Aitken, Peter G.
    The essential guide to MS-DOS 5 programming / Peter Aitken.
       p.   cm.
    Includes index.
    ISBN 1-55615-471-2
    1. Operating systems (Computers) 2. MS-DOS (Computer file)
I. Title.
QA76.76.O63A37   1992
005.4'46--dc20   92-810
                                                                               CIP

Printed and bound in the United States of America.

1 2 3 4 5 6 7 8 9   AGAG   6 5 4 3 2 1

Distributed to the book trade in Canada by Macmillan of Canada, a division of Canada Publishing Corporation.

Distributed to the book trade outside the United States and Canada by Penguin Books Ltd.

Penguin Books Ltd., Harmondsworth, Middlesex, England
Penguin Books Australia Ltd., Ringwood, Victoria, Australia
Penguin Books N.Z. Ltd., 182–190 Wairau Road, Auckland 10, New Zealand

British Cataloging-in-Publication Data available.

AT®, IBM®, and PS/2® are registered trademarks and PC/XT™ is a trademark of International Business Machines Corporation. Intel® is a registered trademark of Intel Corporation. Microsoft®, MS-DOS®, and QuickC® are registered trademarks and Microsoft QuickBasic™ is a trademark of Microsoft Corporation.

Acquisitions Editor: Michael Halvorson
Project/Technical Editor: Mary O. DeJong
Manuscript Editor: Barbara Olsen Browne

To Maxine, with love

CONTENTS

INTRODUCTION xi

CHAPTER 1
Overview: What Is MS-DOS? 1

CHAPTER 2
The CPU: Memory, Registers, and Interrupts 15

CHAPTER 3
Calling Interrupts from Basic 27

CHAPTER 4
Calling Interrupts from C 33

CHAPTER 5
The Keyboard 41

CHAPTER 6
Mouse Programming 83

CHAPTER 7
Screen Display 153

CHAPTER 8
Disks: The Basics 207

CHAPTER 9
Disks: Files and Records 221

CHAPTER 10
Disk Management and Directories 281

CHAPTER 11
Serial and Parallel Ports 311

CHAPTER 12
Memory Management 337

CHAPTER 13
Miscellaneous MS-DOS Services 375

APPENDIX A
MS-DOS and BIOS Interrupt Services 393

APPENDIX B
The ASCII and IBM Extended Character Sets 405

INDEX 409

ACKNOWLEDGMENTS

This book owes a great deal to the people at Microsoft Press. In particular, I thank Mike Halvorson, who developed the original idea for the book, and Mary DeJong, who skillfully shepherded the book from rough manuscript to finished product. I also thank Barbara Browne, who edited the book, and Debbie Kem, Barb Runyan, Shawn Peck, Lisa Iversen, Lisa Sandburg, Peggy Herman, and everyone else who had a hand in preparing this book for printing.

INTRODUCTION

The IBM Personal Computer, with all of its descendants and clones, is certainly the most widely used computer in history. Of the millions of PCs in operation, the vast majority use MS-DOS, Microsoft's disk operating system. As a result, tens of thousands of people write programs that run under MS-DOS. Anyone reading this book is probably a member of that group.

You might have professional training in computer science and work as a programmer for a corporation, university, or government agency. Or you might be self-taught and write programs for your own use and entertainment. Whatever your programming skills and experience, it's a safe bet that you make the effort to obtain the programming tools and knowledge required to write robust, high-performance programs and that you work hard to make your programs as good as possible. If this is the case, you're the type of person this book is intended for.

Any application program works with MS-DOS to perform the tasks you want done. Together they handle screen display, keyboard input, file management, and more. MS-DOS provides services, or software routines, that serve as an interface between your program and the computer hardware. You might not be aware of it, but you access these services indirectly whenever you use any of your programming language's built-in features, such as Basic's PRINT statement or C's *printf()* function. Many programmers don't know that they can also access these MS-DOS services directly. Direct access can provide significant advantages in terms of program speed, size, and flexibility. And that's what this book teaches you: how to access MS-DOS services directly from your programs.

Readers of this book should be familiar with PCs and should have a beginning knowledge of either Basic or C. No additional knowledge or experience is assumed.

The first two chapters of the book provide some information about MS-DOS and your computer hardware. I have tried to keep the technical detail to a reasonable level and present the information you need for effective MS-DOS programming without overwhelming you. These two chapters make no pretense of being a complete reference to MS-DOS or to PC hardware. If you want to learn more, consult one of the many technical reference books available.

The third and fourth chapters deal with programming techniques: how you access MS-DOS services from your Basic and C programs. If you use only Basic or only C, you can skip one or the other of these chapters.

The remainder of the book is divided into chapters that are based on specific programming topics: the keyboard, the screen, disk files, and so on. There's no need to read these chapters in order, so you can skip around if you prefer. For example, if your immediate need is to learn how to access disk files in your program, you can turn immediately to Chapter 8 without reading Chapters 5 through 7 first.

I believe that demonstrations are an effective teaching tool, so each chapter contains programs that demonstrate how to use the MS-DOS services being discussed. This is a "bilingual" book—it includes demonstration programs in both Basic and C. Why is this? And why did I select these two languages?

The need to use more than one language seemed obvious from the start. This is an MS-DOS programming book, and not a C programming book, a Basic programming book, or even a Pascal, Fortran, or assembly language programming book! It was clear that limiting the coverage to a single language would have excluded too many potential readers.

Equally clear was that I couldn't include all popular languages. If I had tried, you would have needed a wheelbarrow to take the book home from the store! The best compromise was to use the two most popular programming languages, which are Basic and C. Between these two languages, I felt that the material in this book would be accessible to the great majority of people programming for the MS-DOS environment. Even if neither Basic nor C is your preferred language, it's likely that you know the fundamentals of one of them and will be able to translate the material in this book into your preferred language.

I used Microsoft QuickBasic version 4.5 and Microsoft QuickC version 2.5 to develop the demonstration programs. The Basic source code is compatible with the Microsoft Basic Professional Development System version 7.1, and the C source code is compatible with the Microsoft C compiler versions 6 and later. You can also run most of the C programs with Borland Turbo C and Turbo C++. Note that MS-DOS QBasic—the Basic interpreter that comes with MS-DOS 5—does not support software interrupts, so you cannot use it to access MS-DOS services directly.

Rather than gather all reference information at the end of the book, I have opted to place reference entries for MS-DOS services at the end of the chapter in which they're discussed. Thus, for example, the reference entries for the MS-DOS keyboard services are at the end of Chapter 5, and the reference entries for the screen display services are at the end of Chapter 7. You can find a complete list of all MS-DOS services covered in the book—arranged in numeric order and by category—in Appendix A.

This book's title refers specifically to MS-DOS version 5, but you won't be left out if you use an earlier version of MS-DOS. It's true that MS-DOS 5 offers many significant enhancements over earlier versions, but these enhancements are not directly relevant to the programming topics that this book covers. You'll be okay with MS-DOS 3 or later. If you use a version that's earlier than version 3, it's time to upgrade!

SPECIAL OFFER
Companion Disk for
THE ESSENTIAL GUIDE TO MS-DOS® 5 PROGRAMMING

Microsoft Press has created a companion disk for *The Essential Guide to MS-DOS 5 Programming*. This disk, available in 5¼-inch and 3½-inch format, contains the 60 programs presented in the book. You can use code fragments from the companion disk for commercial or personal purposes without infringing on the copyright of the book.

Domestic Ordering Information:
To order, use the special reply card in the back of the book. If the card has already been used, please send $19.95, plus sales tax in the following states if applicable: AZ, CA, CO, CT, DC, FL, GA, HI, ID, IL, IN, IA, KS, KY, ME, MD, MA, MI, MN, MO, NE, NV, NJ, NM, NY, NC, OH, OK, PA, RI, SC, TN, TX, VA, WA, WV, WI. Microsoft reserves the right to correct tax rates and/or collect the sales tax assessed by additional states as required by law, without notice. Please add $2.50 per disk set for domestic postage and handling charges. Mail your order to: **Microsoft Press, Attn: Companion Disk Offer, 21919 20th Ave. SE, Box 3011, Bothell, WA 98041-3011**. Specify 5¼-inch or 3½-inch format. Payment must be in U.S. funds. You may pay by check or money order (payable to Microsoft Press) or by American Express, VISA, or MasterCard; please include credit card number, expiration date, and cardholder signature. Allow 2–3 weeks for delivery.

Foreign Ordering Information (within the U.K. and Canada, see below):
Follow procedures for domestic ordering. Add $15.00 per disk set for foreign postage and handling.

U.K. Ordering Information:
Send your order in writing along with £17.95 (includes VAT) to: Microsoft Press, 27 Wrights Lane, London W8 5TZ. You may pay by check or money order (payable to Microsoft Press) or by American Express, VISA, MasterCard, or Diners Club; please include credit card number, expiration date, and cardholder signature. Specify 5¼-inch or 3½-inch format.

Canadian Ordering Information:
Send your order in writing along with $26.95 (includes GST) to: Macmillan Canada, Attn: Microsoft Press Department, 164 Commander Blvd., Agincourt, Ontario, Canada M1S 3C7. You may pay by check or money order (payable to Microsoft Press) or by VISA or MasterCard; please include credit card number, expiration date, and cardholder signature. Specify 5¼-inch or 3½-inch format.

Microsoft Press Companion Disk Guarantee:
If a disk is defective, a replacement disk will be sent. Please send the defective disk and your packing slip (or copy) to: Microsoft Press, Consumer Sales, One Microsoft Way, Redmond, WA 98052-6399.

CHAPTER 1

Overview: What Is MS-DOS?

This book's goal is to teach you how to use MS-DOS to enhance the power, speed, and flexibility of your programs. First you need to know exactly what MS-DOS is and what its components are. That's the purpose of this chapter, and I suggest you read it even if you already have some knowledge of MS-DOS. In addition, at the end of the chapter you'll take a brief look at what MS-DOS programming can do for your programs—an appetizer, if you will, for things to come.

A Look at MS-DOS

The term *DOS* is an acronym for *disk operating system.* MS-DOS is Microsoft Corporation's disk operating system for personal computers. The name indicates that the operating system is loaded into your computer's memory from a disk (either a floppy disk or a hard disk).

MS-DOS is software—a collection of instructions that tell the computer hardware what to do. In this sense, MS-DOS is like an application program that you write in Basic, C, or any other computer language. The difference is that an application program is intended to perform a specific task, such as word processing, database management, or numerical analysis. In contrast, MS-DOS is designed to operate your computer hardware—hence the name *operating system.*

Let's look a bit more closely at what MS-DOS does for you. One of its main functions is to act as an interface between you and the computer hardware. You see this relationship most clearly when you are at the MS-DOS prompt, which is the *C>* (or, on computers with floppy disk drives only, *A>*) that is displayed on the screen. These are only some of the tasks you can accomplish by entering a command at this prompt:

- Display the contents of the disk's current directory with the Dir command
- Copy a file from one disk to another with the Copy command
- Format a disk with the Format command
- Clear the screen with the Cls command
- Display and set the computer clock's time with the Time command

When you execute commands such as these, MS-DOS does the work. MS-DOS is intimately involved in nearly everything you do with your computer. Without MS-DOS (or some other operating system), your computer would be little more than an expensive paperweight!

Even more relevant to the subject of this book is MS-DOS's other main function: serving as an interface between application programs and the computer hardware. Let me illustrate with an example. Almost any program you write will need to display information on the screen. In Basic you'll probably use the PRINT statement to display information, and in C you'll likely use the *printf()* function. Neither PRINT nor *printf()*, however, accesses the display hardware directly; rather, both use MS-DOS to perform the requested display action. The statement or function need only send the proper command to MS-DOS, and MS-DOS takes care of communicating with the hardware.

Figure 1-1 illustrates the relationships among the user, the application programs, MS-DOS, and the computer hardware. The dotted line between the application programs and the computer hardware shows that programs can interact directly with the computer hardware without making use of MS-DOS. (Direct interaction with hardware is a risky business, however. If the user changes the system's hardware, the program might not work.)

As an analogy, say you need to make some photocopies. Instead of going to the copy machine yourself, suppose you tell your assistant to make the copies. Your assistant is like MS-DOS, serving as an interface between you and the hardware. You can still get the photocopies made even if you know nothing about operating the copy machine—and with some of today's copy machines, as with computer hardware, there's a lot to know!

When you are programming with a high-level language, such as C or Basic, you're working through the compiler. You write the source code, and the

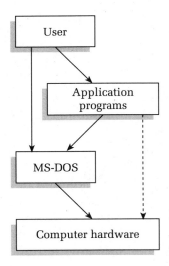

FIGURE 1-1.
The operating system's main function is to serve as an interface between the user and the computer hardware and between the application programs and the computer hardware.

compiler translates it into machine language. For almost every high-level language statement or function that uses the computer hardware, the resulting machine language code is actually a command to the operating system and not a command directly to the hardware.

A Brief History of MS-DOS

As I write this book, MS-DOS is about 10 years old. If you've been involved with PCs for a while, you know that MS-DOS has evolved over the years, starting in 1981 at version 1, and is currently at version 5. Each new version of MS-DOS has added capabilities, yet has remained *backward compatible* with the previous version. That is, each new MS-DOS version has retained all the capabilities and commands of the previous version while adding some new ones.

MS-DOS had its beginnings in 1980 when a fellow named Tim Paterson wrote an operating system named 86-DOS for the line of computers manufactured by Seattle Computer Products. These computers used the same 8086 central processing unit (CPU) that was to be used in IBM's new line of personal computers. At the time, IBM was looking—through Microsoft—for an operating system for its PCs. Microsoft purchased the rights to 86-DOS from Seattle Computer Products and, with modifications, released it as MS-DOS 1.

IBM shipped MS-DOS 1, renamed PC-DOS, with its PCs. Most versions of MS-DOS since then have had a corresponding version of PC-DOS. If you are using a personal computer made by IBM, you probably have PC-DOS; if you are using one of the many PC clones, you probably have MS-DOS. The two versions are like vanilla and French vanilla ice cream—they're essentially identical. The programs we develop in this book will work under both versions.

The first version of MS-DOS (and PC-DOS) was only one of three operating systems available for IBM PCs: The others were Digital Research's CP/M-86 and SofTech Microsystem's p-System. Primarily because of software and programming language support provided by Microsoft and IBM, MS-DOS soon became the operating system of choice for PCs.

Over the years, MS-DOS has undergone great changes. Figure 1-2 lists the major versions of MS-DOS, their introduction dates, and the major enhancements provided by each upgrade. You'll notice that the new features are, for the most part, related to hardware changes.

Some minor versions have been omitted from the list. For example, MS-DOS version 2.11 is version 2.1 with bug fixes, and version 4.01 is version 4.0 with bug fixes. Also, remember that this list includes only the major

Version	Date	Major new features
1.0	August 1981	Original MS-DOS for IBM PC; single-sided disks only
1.25	May 1982	Support for double-sided disks
2.0	March 1983	Support for hierarchical file structure and hard disks (PC/XT)
2.1	October 1983	Support for the PCjr and the Portable PC
3.0	August 1984	Support for the PC/AT and high-density disks
3.1	March 1985	Support for networking
3.2	December 1985	Support for 3.5-inch disks
3.3	April 1987	Support for the IBM PS/2 line of computers; generalized code page (font) support
4.0	June 1988	Integration of enhanced memory capability; visual shell; support for hard disks larger than 32 megabytes
5.0	June 1991	Improved memory management, improved visual shell, support for larger disk partitions

FIGURE 1-2.
Release dates and enhancement features of major MS-DOS versions.

changes that were introduced with each version. Most new versions included many improvements and modifications. Anyone familiar with only version 1.0 of MS-DOS would hardly recognize today's MS-DOS!

Microsoft released version 5 of MS-DOS just as I started to write this book. This is a major new release and has been widely hailed in the computer industry. If you're using MS-DOS 5, you might be wondering what great new programming services it offers you. If you haven't upgraded to version 5, you might be worrying about what programming capabilities you're missing.

Surprisingly, the answer to both questions is "not much." When you take a minute to think about it, this answer makes perfect sense. From the beginning, MS-DOS has had to provide the basics, interfacing between application programs and the computer hardware. Even with version 1, MS-DOS provided services for your program to access the keyboard, disk drives, and so on. Because this book is written for beginning to intermediate programmers, it deals primarily with services that have been available in MS-DOS since before version 5.

You don't need MS-DOS 5 to use this book. If you are using MS-DOS 3 or later, you can write programs using the operating system services covered in this book. Even MS-DOS 2.0 supports most of these services—but if you're using a version of MS-DOS that's earlier than 3, I recommend an upgrade.

This does not mean that you have wasted the money you spent upgrading to MS-DOS 5! Although it does not offer much in the way of new operating system services, MS-DOS 5 offers many significant advantages. One of those advantages is its improved memory management, which makes more memory available to your programs.

A Closer Look at MS-DOS 5 Enhancements

MS-DOS 5 takes up significantly less *user memory* than does its predecessor. This change is important because a PC can have a maximum of 640 KB of user memory (sometimes called *conventional memory*), and the amount available to your application programs is what's left after MS-DOS and its associated device drivers have been loaded. MS-DOS's decreased appetite for user memory was achieved in two ways.

First, MS-DOS itself is smaller, even though it is completely backward compatible with earlier versions. Because it's smaller, MS-DOS takes up less user memory, leaving more for application programs to use. This additional memory lets you run larger applications and also provides a greater amount of memory for your programming tools: the editor, the compiler, and so on.

Second, MS-DOS can perform some tricks that let it load portions of itself into *high memory*. This high memory area is available on most 80286, 80386, and 80486 machines and is located in the first 64 KB above the 1 MB mark in memory. Normally, the high memory area goes unused. If your system has high memory, you can instruct MS-DOS to load portions of its code there, resulting in less code loaded into user memory.

MS-DOS 5 can also make use of *upper memory blocks* (*UMBs*), which are regions of unused memory that many computers have above 640 KB (specifically, between 640 KB and 1 MB). If you load device drivers at boot time—for example, to interface with a mouse, hard disk, or network—MS-DOS can place the driver code in UMBs instead of in user memory. Again, the result is more user memory left for application programs.

MS-DOS 5 sports a new visual shell, which is a menu-driven interface that makes it easy to perform MS-DOS commands and to switch between programs. The MS-DOS visual shell is a task switcher, which means that you can switch from one application to another without exiting the first application. Task switching can be useful to programmers who like to work with a stand-alone editor such as Brief. You can switch almost instantly from your editor to your compiler, speeding the process of program development.

Speaking of editors, MS-DOS 5 also includes a full-screen text editor that replaces the clunky (and unlamented!) EDLIN line editor. This new editor is a stripped-down version of the editor that's provided with the Microsoft QuickBasic and Microsoft QuickC programming environments. It is not by any means a specialized programming editor, but it serves well for simple tasks such as editing batch files.

One new feature that I think users will especially appreciate is the addition of a /? switch to all MS-DOS commands. Include the /? switch when you enter the command, and a screen of help information is displayed. No more thumbing through your MS-DOS manual to find out how to format a 360-KB disk in a 1.2-MB drive!

Several small utilities have been added that are hardly earthshaking but that do manage to make daily computer use easier in little ways. My favorite is DOSKEY, which is a utility that manages a buffer that saves your MS-DOS commands. With a couple of keystrokes, you can recall any command that you used earlier, edit the command if necessary, and reuse it. This approach can be a huge time-saver when you're performing repetitive command line actions such as compiling and linking programs. DOSKEY's more sophisticated capabilities include defining and running macros.

The Components of MS-DOS

MS-DOS has an internal structure that you need to understand if you, as a programmer, are to take full advantage of the operating system. The structure of MS-DOS is hierarchical, consisting of three layers that separate the user and the application programs from the computer hardware. These layers are the BIOS (basic input/output system), the DOS kernel, and the command processor.

The BIOS

The lowest layer of MS-DOS is the BIOS. (By "lowest," I mean the layer that interacts most directly with the hardware.) As its name implies, the BIOS is concerned primarily with input and output. The BIOS contains the drivers, or software interfaces, for the following five hardware devices:

- The console (keyboard and display)
- A generic line printer
- The auxiliary device (usually a serial port)

- The computer's clock (date and time)
- The boot disk device

Because these device drivers are built into the BIOS, they are called *resident* device drivers.

A portion of the BIOS is specific to each individual model of computer and is provided by the computer manufacturer. This part of the BIOS, called the ROM BIOS, is contained in read-only memory (ROM) chips located on the computer motherboard (the computer's main circuit board). The ROM BIOS serves as an interface to the computer hardware both at boot time (when the computer is turned on) and while the computer is operating. At the hardware end, the ROM BIOS is designed to set up the interfaces to the specific hardware devices installed in a particular computer. At the software end, the ROM BIOS presents a standardized interface to other software that uses the devices.

After the ROM BIOS finishes its initialization, your computer gives control to a second portion of the BIOS, which is read into random access memory (RAM) from a disk file. In MS-DOS, this file is named IO.SYS; in PC-DOS, it is named IBMBIO.COM. Despite the difference in names, IO.SYS and IBMBIO.COM serve the same function. In this book, I will use the name "IO.SYS." The file IO.SYS has the hidden and system file attributes, which means that you won't see the file in your directory listing (unless you have MS-DOS 5 and use the /ah switch with the Dir command or you use a utility program, such as XTREE, that displays hidden filenames). IO.SYS loads the five resident device drivers, completing the work begun by the ROM BIOS. In addition, IO.SYS initializes and loads into memory the DOS kernel, installable device drivers, and the command processor.

MS-DOS has the ability to use installable drivers, which are hardware drivers that are not a part of the BIOS. You can have MS-DOS load an installable driver at boot time by specifying its name in a Device command in the CONFIG.SYS file. When you add a new peripheral device to your computer, such as a memory board or a disk drive, an installable driver is often included that provides an interface to the new hardware. An installable driver can take the place of an existing BIOS driver, or it can provide an entirely new function. Some installable drivers are supplied with peripheral hardware; some, such as ANSI.SYS and HIMEM.SYS, are supplied as part of the MS-DOS package.

The DOS kernel

The next component of MS-DOS is the *DOS kernel*. The kernel is loaded from disk during the boot procedure. It is contained in a disk file named

MSDOS.SYS (IBMDOS.COM in PC-DOS), which, like IO.SYS, has the hidden and system file attributes. The kernel is the heart of the operating system and is the part with which application programs interact. The kernel provides hardware-independent functions, called *system services,* that are accessed by means of a *software interrupt* (which you'll learn about in Chapter 2). Much of this book is devoted to showing you how your programs can use these system services. The kernel provides services for

- File and directory management
- Memory management
- Character device input and output
- Time and date support
- Program management

The hardware independence of the DOS kernel services is an important point. As a result of this independence, any program running under MS-DOS can use the system services without regard for the specific hardware in use. The kernel relies on the drivers in the BIOS to communicate directly with the hardware, and it's from that arrangement that the hardware independence results.

The command processor

The third component of MS-DOS is the *command processor*. This is the part of MS-DOS that you are interacting with at the familiar *A>* or *C>* prompt. The command processor's job is to carry out commands that the user enters, including the loading and execution of application programs. For example, if you enter *Dir* for a directory listing or *Cls* to clear the screen, it is the command processor that carries out your command. Likewise, if you enter *QC* to run Microsoft QuickC, it's the command processor that loads the QuickC program from disk, turns control over to the program, and then regains control when you exit QuickC.

The default command processor is contained in the file COMMAND.COM, which is loaded into memory at boot time. COMMAND.COM has three modules: the resident, initialization, and transient modules.

The *resident module* remains loaded in memory as long as the computer is turned on. This module of COMMAND.COM processes Ctrl-Break and Ctrl-C key combinations, which cancel whatever the system is doing. It also issues error messages (which are often followed by the infamous "Abort, Retry, Ignore" prompt) and deals with the termination of application programs.

The *initialization module* of COMMAND.COM has only one function: to load and process the commands in the AUTOEXEC.BAT file. After this task is completed, the initialization module is discarded and the memory it used is freed for other purposes.

The final part of COMMAND.COM is the *transient module*. This section is loaded into the high end of user memory. Its tasks include issuing the *A>* or *C>* prompt, reading commands from the keyboard, and executing those commands. When an application program is loaded into memory, it can use the memory occupied by the transient module of COMMAND.COM if necessary. When the program terminates, the resident COMMAND.COM module checks to see whether the transient module is still loaded. If not (that is, if an application program has made use of that memory), the transient module is reloaded from disk.

Strictly speaking, COMMAND.COM is not a part of the operating system but is rather a shell that provides an interface between the user and the operating system. It can be replaced with user-written or commercially available shells by including the Shell command in the CONFIG.SYS file. The vast majority of PC users, however, use COMMAND.COM.

As you've seen, the components of MS-DOS form layers between the computer hardware and the user. At the top of this layered structure is the user interacting with an application program or with the command processor. Below that is the DOS kernel, which in turn uses the BIOS to interact with the hardware. Figure 1-3 illustrates these relationships.

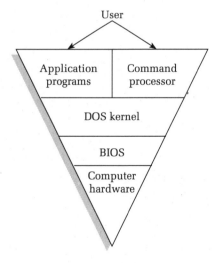

FIGURE 1-3.
The components of MS-DOS form several layers between the user and the computer hardware.

Utility programs

When you purchase MS-DOS, you get a wide variety of utility programs, such as FORMAT, CHKDSK, MORE, SORT, and DEBUG. Because these programs come with MS-DOS, many people think of them as part of MS-DOS. Well, they're not. They are application programs exactly as dBase III, WordPerfect, and Microsoft Excel are. These utility programs run under the operating system and use operating system services to perform their specific tasks.

MS-DOS Services and the Programmer

Why, then, would a programmer need to know a lot about MS-DOS and the services it provides? Doesn't your high-level language compiler handle tasks more or less automatically, making use of MS-DOS services when needed to communicate with the hardware? That's correct, of course, and many creative programmers produce excellent programs without knowing one whit about MS-DOS internals. If you know about MS-DOS services, however, and can access them directly, you have a significant edge—for two reasons.

First, many MS-DOS services are not available from your high-level language. That is, the language has no statements or functions to access certain services. By necessity, MS-DOS contains services for complete control of every aspect of your computer's hardware, but it's impractical and unnecessary to include all of these capabilities in a high-level language such as Basic or C. When implementing a high-level language compiler, the designers must decide which capabilities to include and which to leave out. They are often constrained by the need for compatibility with earlier versions of the language and with national and international standards. As a result, many potentially useful MS-DOS services are omitted.

Second, even if your language can access a particular MS-DOS service, using MS-DOS directly might allow you greater efficiency and flexibility. Statements and functions in a high-level language are written for general use by programmers at all levels of experience. These statements and functions must provide error-checking and control features for all programming situations. Unavoidably, the safety features and the generality of high-level statements and functions result in size and speed penalties—the code is larger and slower than it would be if the safety features were left out.

Please note that this discussion is not meant as a slight against high-level languages. Providing error-checking and general control capabilities is, in fact, one of the main tasks of a high-level language. If, however, you know how to access MS-DOS services directly, you have the option of bypassing your language's built-in statements and functions and executing certain programming tasks in the most efficient manner.

When you access MS-DOS services directly, you'll encounter certain trade-offs. You not only give up your language's error checking, but you sacrifice portability. The term *portability* means the extent to which a program written for one platform (in this case, an IBM PC or compatible running MS-DOS) can be recompiled for use on another platform, such as a Macintosh, a VAX, or a Sun workstation. This issue is a particular concern with the C programming language because C is by design a highly portable language. If you write a program in C using only the language's standard statements and functions, you can make minor modifications to the source code and compile and run the same program on many other platforms. If, however, the program accesses MS-DOS services directly, it is no longer portable. For example, although the *printf()* function is the same in all implementations of C, MS-DOS services are specific to machines running MS-DOS and cannot be used on any other hardware platform.

As a programmer, you'll find yourself in many situations in which a particular programming task can be performed either with a high-level language statement or with an MS-DOS service. Unfortunately, I can make no general statement about which method is preferable. As I've mentioned, trade-offs are associated with either choice. You must make the choice yourself, based on the specifics of the program you're writing. At times, you might want to try both methods to see which works better.

The approach I take in this book is to show you all of the important MS-DOS services. You must decide for yourself when to use specific services in your programs. I will sometimes offer an opinion—based on my own programming experience—about whether MS-DOS services or high-level language statements are preferable for a particular task. This will be only my opinion, however, and I strongly advise you to experiment for yourself.

MS-DOS Services: What's Available

At the start of this chapter, I promised a brief look at what MS-DOS programming can do for your programs. Here is the promised list:

- Determine the total capacity and space available on a disk drive
- Read and modify the attributes (read only, hidden, archive, and system) of any disk file
- Determine the state of the keyboard's "lock keys" (Num Lock, Insert, Caps Lock, and so on)

- Toggle the MS-DOS verify flag (which, when on, causes MS-DOS to check whether data was written correctly to disk)
- Determine how much, if any, expanded memory is installed
- Adjust the keyboard repeat rate
- Set the screen cursor's position and size
- Scroll a text window on the screen
- Create a new disk directory

Remember, this list is just a sampling! You'll learn about these and many other MS-DOS services throughout this book.

CHAPTER 2

The CPU: Memory, Registers, and Interrupts

This is a programming book, and not a hardware book. Nevertheless, you need to know something about your computer hardware in order to make the best use of the MS-DOS services that are the book's main topic. You also need to be familiar with decimal, binary, and hexadecimal numeric notation because they are all commonly used in programming. Let's start with numeric notation.

Decimal Notation

The number system that we use in everyday life is the *decimal* system. This is a base-10 system, which means that it has 10 digits—0 through 9. Each place in a decimal number represents a specific power of 10. The first place (at the far right) represents 10 to the 0 power; the second place represents 10 to the 1 power, and so on. Remembering that any number to the 0 power equals 1 and that any number to the 1 power equals itself, we can construct the following example:

```
1042 (decimal)
 ││││
 │││└─────── 2 * 10⁰ = 2 * 1    =    2 (decimal)
 ││└──────── 4 * 10¹ = 4 * 10   =   40
 │└───────── 0 * 10² = 0 * 100  =    0
 └────────── 1 * 10³ = 1 * 1000 = 1000
                              Total = 1042
```

Binary Notation

Binary notation is a base-2 number system, which means that it uses two digits: 0 and 1. Each place in a binary number represents a power of 2. Let's look at a binary number in detail:

```
1011 (binary)
 ││││
 │││└─────── 1 * 2⁰ = 1 * 1 = 1 (decimal)
 ││└──────── 1 * 2¹ = 1 * 2 = 2
 │└───────── 0 * 2² = 0 * 4 = 0
 └────────── 1 * 2³ = 1 * 8 = 8
                      Total = 11
```

Binary notation is useful in programming because it parallels the way in which data is actually stored inside a computer. Each digit in a binary number can be either 0 or 1, representing the off or on states of the bits (the smallest units of information in a computer) in the system's memory and registers.

Hexadecimal Notation

Hexadecimal notation is a base-16 system and requires 16 digits. The ten digits 0 through 9 have their familiar values, and the letters A through F are used to represent the decimal values 10 through 15, respectively. Let's look at a hexadecimal number in detail:

```
8BF1 (hexadecimal)
 │││└──────── 1 * 16⁰ =  1 * 1    =     1 (decimal)
 ││└───────  15 * 16¹ = 15 * 16   =   240
 │└────────  11 * 16² = 11 * 256  =  2816
 └─────────   8 * 16³ =  8 * 4096 = 32768
                               Total = 35825
```

$$8BF1 \text{ (hexadecimal)}$$
$$1 * 16^0 = 1 * 1 = 1 \text{ (decimal)}$$
$$15 * 16^1 = 15 * 16 = 240$$
$$11 * 16^2 = 11 * 256 = 2816$$
$$8 * 16^3 = 8 * 4096 = \underline{32768}$$
$$\text{Total} = 35825$$

You might have noticed a close relationship between hexadecimal and binary notation. This relationship is due to the fact that 16, the base of the hexadecimal system, is a power of 2 (2 to the fourth power equals 16). Each hexadecimal digit corresponds to a group of four binary digits. You can see this correspondence most easily with the decimal values 0 through 15. These values, and no more, can be represented by a single hexadecimal digit or by four binary digits, as Figure 2-1 shows.

Decimal	Binary	Hexadecimal
0	0000	0
1	0001	1
2	0010	2
3	0011	3
4	0100	4
5	0101	5
6	0110	6
7	0111	7
8	1000	8
9	1001	9
10	1010	A
11	1011	B
12	1100	C
13	1101	D
14	1110	E
15	1111	F

FIGURE 2-1.
Decimal values 0 through 15 and their corresponding binary and hexadecimal representations.

The same relationship holds for longer numbers: Each hexadecimal digit can be represented by four binary digits, as the following illustration demonstrates:

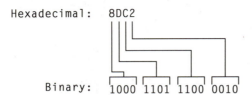

Because of this relationship, you can easily convert from binary to hexadecimal notation and vice versa. This relationship also makes hexadecimal notation suitable for use in your programs. Hexadecimal notation is particularly valuable when you need to express a large value, which can be cumbersome in binary notation. As you'll see, hexadecimal notation is frequently used in discussions of memory addressing. In the text of this book, I'll append the letter H to hexadecimal numbers so that you can distinguish between hexadecimal and binary numbers.

Memory Addressing

Your computer's CPU (central processing unit) works with data stored in memory. This data consists of both the instructions that make up the program and the text or number data that the program manipulates. Memory also holds instructions that are part of the DOS kernel and the BIOS. (As we have seen, some of this memory is read-only memory, or ROM.) How does the CPU access data in memory?

Memory in a PC consists of a large number of individual storage locations. Each location, which can hold 1 byte (8 bits) of data, has a unique numeric address that distinguishes it from all other memory locations. All memory in a PC is organized in sequential order, starting at address 0 and extending to $n-1$ (in a computer with n bytes of memory installed).

To access a particular memory location in an IBM PC with an 8088 microprocessor (the CPU chip used by the original IBM PC), the CPU specifies the location's address as a 20-bit binary value. The computer's memory circuits interpret this 20-bit value and make the corresponding memory location available to the CPU, which can then either read data from or write data to that memory address. Note that a 20-bit binary number can specify 2^{20}, or 1,048,576, different addresses. This amount of memory is called 1 megabyte, or 1 MB. Note also that each address in 1 MB of memory can be specified conveniently in hexadecimal notation in the range 00000H through FFFFFH.

Microprocessors developed after the 8088, such as the 80286, can use more than 20 bits to specify a memory location and can therefore access memory above 1 MB. Memory at addresses above FFFFFH—which MS-DOS can access only by means of special device drivers—is called *extended memory*. Extended memory is often used for disk caches, RAM disks, print spoolers, and the like. It can also be configured as *expanded memory*, which some programs can use for data storage (expanded memory is discussed further in Chapter 12). Extended and expanded memory is not relevant to the present discussion, so we will limit ourselves to memory below FFFFFH.

The memory between 00000H and FFFFFH is used for many tasks; it contains both the BIOS and the DOS kernel, as well as application programs and program data. Figure 2-2 on the following page illustrates how memory is organized in a computer that has 1 MB of memory. The figure shows memory organization after the computer has booted and MS-DOS has loaded but before any user programs are executed. It does not show MS-DOS loaded into the high memory area, which is an option with MS-DOS 5.

Some of the labels in Figure 2-2 might need explaining. The area labeled "Buffers, drivers" is used for disk buffers that are set up by MS-DOS (controlled by the Buffers command in CONFIG.SYS) and for any installable device drivers, such as RAM disks, that are installed with the Device command in CONFIG.SYS. The area labeled "Reserved, unused" is used for the memory associated with certain peripheral devices, such as video adapters. Much memory in this area often goes unused. On computers with an 80386 or higher microprocessor, this unused memory can be reclaimed for device drivers by using the Loadhigh command available with MS-DOS version 5 (or using similar commands provided with some third-party memory managers such as QEMM386). The area labeled "Interrupt vector table" is explained later in this chapter in the section titled "Interrupts."

The CPU manipulates memory addresses by using *registers*. A register is a data storage location that is internal to the CPU chip. Each register is 16 bits, which means that it can specify 2^{16}, or 65,536 (64 KB), memory addresses. How, then, can 20-bit addresses up to 1 MB be manipulated? The solution to this problem is the use of *segmented memory addressing*, which uses two registers to hold an address. Here's how it works.

One register is called the *segment register*. The 16-bit value in the segment register is multiplied automatically by 16. The original range of 0 through 65,535 (0 to 64 KB) is thereby expanded to 0 through 1,048,575 (0 to 1 MB). The resulting addresses are limited to 16-byte increments, of course, but as you'll see, this is OK.

The second register is called the *offset register*. The value in this register is not changed but is used to create the 20-bit address by simply adding it to

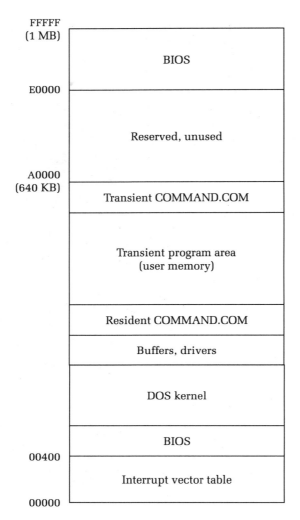

FIGURE 2-2.
Memory organization in a typical computer that has 1 MB of memory.

the value obtained by multiplying the segment register by 16, as shown schematically here (all values are in hexadecimal notation):

Segment register value	2BFCH
Multiplied by 16	2BFC0H
Offset register value	01C2H
Final 20-bit address	2C182H

Here's another way to look at the segmented memory addressing scheme: The segment register points to the base of a 64-KB segment of memory, and the offset register points to a specific address within that 64-KB segment.

Any way you look at it, the result is an address that can be used to access any location in the processor's 1 MB of address space.

For the remainder of this book, I use hexadecimal notation for all addresses. A segmented address is typically written in the form *segment:offset*, where *segment* is the segment value, and *offset* is the offset value, as in the address 2BFCH:01C2H.

CPU Registers

The CPU (central processing unit) is your computer's main chip—its heart and brain, you might say. If you're using an IBM PC, PC/AT, PS/2, or one of the many clones that are available, your CPU is a member of the Intel 80x86 family. It might be an 8088, 8086, 80286, 80386, or even (if you're lucky!) an 80486. By the time you read this, the 80586 might be available as well. How can a programmer keep track of all these CPUs?

The answer is that you don't have to. Because they're members of the same family, these chips all share a certain base-level of compatibility. Each new chip adds features, power, and speed, of course, but even the latest, hottest 80x86 chip retains a foundation of compatibility with the lowly 8088. It is for the 8088 level that most people write because it is normally important that the resulting programs can run on all PCs.

MS-DOS programming doesn't require an in-depth knowledge of CPU internals, so I'm going to explain them in only the most basic terms. You do need to know about the CPU registers, which are used to access MS-DOS services. Every 80x86 CPU contains 14 separate registers, each of which is 16 bits in size (that is, each register can hold a 16-bit binary value). The registers fall into four categories: general purpose, segment, offset, and flags. Each register (except the flags register) is referred to by a two-letter code. Figure 2-3 lists the registers and their categories.

Register	Category	Use
AX	General purpose	Various
BX	General purpose	Various
CX	General purpose	Various
DX	General purpose	Various
CS	Segment	Code segment
DS	Segment	Data segment
ES	Segment	Extra segment

(continued)

FIGURE 2-3.
The 80x86 CPU registers.

FIGURE 2-3. *continued*

Register	Category	Use
SS	Segment	Stack segment
BP	Offset	Base pointer
SP	Offset	Stack pointer
SI	Offset	Source index
DI	Offset	Destination index
IP	Offset	Instruction pointer
Flags	Flags	Status flags

General-purpose registers

The general-purpose registers are the registers you deal with most when accessing MS-DOS services. You place values in one or more registers before calling the service. In some cases, you also retrieve results from one or more registers after the service has completed its task.

Each of the four general-purpose registers—AX, BX, CX, and DX—contains 16 bits, or 2 bytes. The right 8 bits of a register are called the *low byte*. The left 8 bits are the *high byte*. At times, you need to access these two bytes individually. The low and high bytes of the AX register can be accessed as two 8-bit registers named AL and AH (L for low, H for high). The 8-bit registers for the other general-purpose registers can be similarly accessed with BL and BH, CL and CH, and DL and DH, as illustrated in Figure 2-4.

Segment registers

The segment registers are used in memory addressing, which was described earlier in this chapter. Because MS-DOS uses four segment registers, four distinct memory segments can be accessed at once. The following list defines these registers and describes their uses when a program is executing:

- CS is the code segment register. It contains the address of the memory segment that holds the currently executing program code.

- DS is the data segment register. It contains the address of the memory segment that holds the program's data.

- SS is the stack segment register. It contains the address of the stack segment, which is used for temporary data storage—for example, when programs pass arguments to functions.

- ES is the extra segment register. It contains the address of the extra segment, which is used for various purposes, most frequently to hold additional data.

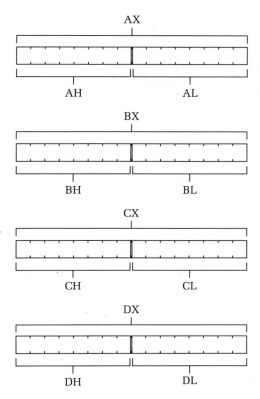

FIGURE 2-4.
The low and high bytes of each general-purpose register can be addressed individually.

Offset registers

MS-DOS uses five offset registers, which, as described earlier, are used in addressing memory. Each offset register is paired with one of the four segment registers.

- BP is the base pointer register and is paired with the SS (stack segment) register. It is most often used to access data on the stack.

- SP is the stack pointer register and is also paired with the SS (stack segment) register. It contains the address of the current location in the stack.

- SI is the source index register and is paired with the DS segment register. It is often used to point to the source address during data transfers.

- DI is the destination index register and is paired with the ES segment register. It is often used to point to the destination address during data transfers.

- IP is the instruction pointer register and is paired with the CS segment register. It contains the address of the statement that will be executed next.

Every time it accesses memory, the CPU uses one of the segment:offset pairs. For example, CS:IP points to the memory location of the next program instruction to be executed, and SS:SP points to the top of the stack. But we're getting into more detail than you need. For the purposes of this book, the above introduction will suffice. Remember, it's primarily the general-purpose registers that you use to access MS-DOS services.

Flags register

The flags register differs from the other registers, and here's how: Although it contains two bytes of data, the flags register is used as a collection of single bits, or flags. Each of the flags, which can be set to either 0 or 1, conveys specific information. Only nine of the register's sixteen bits are used in the 80x86 processors. Six of these bits are status flags that report on the internal status of the CPU, and three are control flags that are used to control certain aspects of the way the CPU functions.

Of these flags, you need be concerned with only the carry flag. This is the first bit (that is, at position 0) in the flags register. The CPU uses the carry flag during arithmetic operations to signal whether an addition operation has produced a carry, or a subtraction operation has produced a borrow. This flag is also used by many MS-DOS services to signal an error. If the service executes without an error, it sets the flag to 0; if an error has occurred, it sets the flag to 1. When your program calls an MS-DOS service that uses the carry flag to signal an error, the flag must be checked. You'll see how to check this flag in Chapters 3 and 4.

Interrupts

Interrupts are an important feature of the 80x86 family of processors. An *interrupt* is a special signal to the CPU that causes it to suspend temporarily whatever it is doing and transfer control to an *interrupt handler,* or *interrupt service routine* (sometimes called an "ISR"). The interrupt handler is a routine that takes appropriate action based on the cause of the interrupt and then returns control to the original suspended process. PCs have 256 available interrupts, numbered from 00H through FFH.

One of the main purposes of interrupts is to allow the CPU to respond to external events, such as keyboard input. (Although the keyboard is part of the computer system, it is external to the CPU.) Without interrupts, your CPU would have two options:

1. Sit and wait for a key to be pressed. The CPU will certainly detect any input, but it can't get anything else done in the meantime.

2. Perform some other task, branching every so often to see if a key has been pressed. This method is called *polling* and was frequently used in early CPUs that did not have interrupt capability. It lets the CPU get some work done while waiting for a key press, but it wastes time when it branches to check for input.

Let's look at an analogy. Imagine that you're hosting a party and you must greet guests at the door. Option 1 would have you sitting by the door waiting for guests to arrive—not much fun for you because you'll miss the party! Option 2 has you running to the door every few minutes to see if someone has arrived. It's better than option 1, perhaps, but it's still not much fun.

Being immensely clever, you install a doorbell. Congratulations! You have just invented the interrupt. You can enjoy the party, confident that the doorbell will alert you every time a guest arrives. You waste no time, and every guest is greeted properly. We can now add a third option to the above list:

3. Perform various tasks, being interrupted whenever the user presses a key.

Now that you know what an interrupt is, we can look at the different interrupt types. PCs have three categories of interrupts:

- An *internal interrupt* is generated internally by the CPU when certain conditions or errors occur during operation. For example, attempting to divide by 0 generates an internal interrupt. Internal interrupts are of little concern to programmers.

- An *external hardware interrupt* is generated by a peripheral hardware device, such as the keyboard, serial port, or disk drive. This type of interrupt is used almost every time the computer interacts with a peripheral device. Programmers can manipulate external hardware interrupts to maximize control over peripheral devices, but doing so is not the subject of this book.

- A *software interrupt* is generated by a program, and not by hardware. Most programming languages allow you to issue software interrupts—in Microsoft QuickBasic, you can call the INTERRUPT and INTERRUPTX subprograms; in Microsoft QuickC, the *int86()*, *int86x()*, *intdos()*, and *intdosx()* functions. It is by means of software interrupts that your programs can gain access to MS-DOS services, and making use of such access is the focus of this book.

You might be wondering exactly how the interrupt mechanism works (if you're not wondering, you can skip ahead!). When an interrupt occurs, execution must jump to the interrupt handler. To do so, the processor must know the handler's address. The segment:offset address of each interrupt handler is stored in an area of memory called the *interrupt vector table*. This table is located at the bottom of memory, as you saw in Figure 2-2.

When an interrupt occurs, the following happens:

1. The address of the currently executing process (contained in the CS:IP registers) is saved on the stack.

2. The address of the interrupt handler is obtained from the interrupt vector table and placed in the CS:IP registers. This action transfers execution to the handler.

3. The interrupt handler saves the *system context* on the stack. The system context is any information about what the state of the computer was when it was interrupted: values of registers, flags, and anything else that the interrupt handler might modify.

4. The interrupt handler then goes about its business, performing whatever tasks are necessary to respond to the interrupt.

5. When finished, the interrupt handler restores the system context from the stack. Finally, execution is transferred back to the original task that was interrupted. This is accomplished by obtaining the address that was first saved and placing it back in the CS:IP registers.

This is a superficial account of interrupt processing; it is intended only as an introduction. You'll learn more about interrupt processing throughout the book.

MS-DOS Services vs. BIOS Services

You've seen how the DOS kernel and the BIOS are two separate but related components of MS-DOS. Some of the operating system services that we talk about in this book are provided by the DOS kernel, usually via interrupt 21H (which is typically called Int 21H). Other services, accessed via interrupts other than 21H, are provided directly by the BIOS. Some programming books make a distinction between the Int 21H MS-DOS services and the BIOS services. This distinction is of no practical significance to us. In the remainder of this book, I refer to all MS-DOS operating system services, whether in the kernel or in the BIOS, as *MS-DOS services* or *MS-DOS interrupt service routines* (*ISRs*).

CHAPTER 3

Calling Interrupts from Basic

The Basic compiler market is dominated by Microsoft. Microsoft QuickBasic version 4.5 was used to write the Basic programs I've included in this book and is probably used by the majority of Basic programmers who are reading this book. The Basic Professional Development System (Basic PDS) version 7.1 is Microsoft's "heavyweight" Basic, which includes advanced features for professional programmers. Fortunately, these two Basics are compatible and use the same methods for calling software interrupts. The material in this chapter is applicable to either of these Basic products.

The INTERRUPT and INTERRUPTX Subprograms

You call either the INTERRUPT or the INTERRUPTX subprogram to issue a software interrupt from a Basic program. To use either of these subprograms, your program must first use the $INCLUDE metacommand to instruct the compiler to include the file QB.BI (in QuickBasic) or QBX.BI (in Basic PDS). These files contain the declarations of the subprograms and the data structures they use. If you're programming in either the QuickBasic or the Basic PDS integrated environment, you must also load the default Quick library (QB.QLB or QBX.QLB) by starting the integrated environment with the /l switch. If you're not using the integrated environment and are compiling from the command line, you must explicitly link your program with either the QB.LIB or the QBX.LIB library. These Quick libraries and link libraries contain the subprograms INTERRUPT and INTERRUPTX. When either of the subprograms is called, code contained in the library is executed. The declarations of the Basic software interrupt subprograms are as follows:

```
DECLARE SUB INTERRUPT (intnum AS INTEGER, inregs AS RegType,
                outregs AS RegType)

DECLARE SUB INTERRUPTX (intnum AS INTEGER, inregs AS RegTypeX,
                outregs AS RegTypeX)
```

For both subprograms, *intnum* contains the number of the software interrupt to be called. The other two arguments are data structures that are used to pass data to (*inregs*) and receive data from (*outregs*) the MS-DOS interrupt service routine that the program called.

The *RegType* and *RegTypeX* Data Structures

You can see that the declarations for INTERRUPT and INTERRUPTX are identical except for the data type of the second and third arguments: INTERRUPT uses *RegType*, and INTERRUPTX uses *RegTypeX*. Both of these types are data structures that are defined by TYPE...END TYPE statements in the QB.BI file, as shown below:

```
TYPE RegType
      ax    AS INTEGER
      bx    AS INTEGER
      cx    AS INTEGER
      dx    AS INTEGER
      bp    AS INTEGER
      si    AS INTEGER
      di    AS INTEGER
      flags AS INTEGER
END TYPE


TYPE RegTypeX
      ax    AS INTEGER
      bx    AS INTEGER
      cx    AS INTEGER
      dx    AS INTEGER
      bp    AS INTEGER
      si    AS INTEGER
      di    AS INTEGER
      flags AS INTEGER
      ds    AS INTEGER
      es    AS INTEGER
END TYPE
```

If you examine these data structures, you'll see that each has an element of type INTEGER that corresponds to one of the CPU registers. The difference is that *RegTypeX* has elements for the ES and DS registers and *RegType* does not. You'll also notice that neither data structure has members for the IP, SP, CS, and SS registers. That's just as well because you don't need access to these registers, and if you could manipulate them, you might inadvertently lose all data on the stack or cause all sorts of other problems.

Although the QB.BI and QBX.BI files define the types *RegType* and *RegTypeX*, they do not declare any instances (variables) of those types. Your program must do so with a statement like the following:

```
DIM inRegs AS RegType, outRegs AS RegType
```

Of course, you can use names other than *inRegs* and *outRegs* if you want, but these two names are descriptive and have become unofficial standards for interrupt calls.

Accessing the byte registers

You learned in Chapter 2 that the general-purpose registers AX, BX, CX, and DX can each be treated as a pair of single-byte registers: AX as AL and AH, and so on. Some of the MS-DOS services return information in the byte registers. QuickBasic provides no direct access to the individual bytes, but they can be extracted as shown below using the AND logical operator and the integer division operator (\):

```
lowByte = register AND &HFF
highByte = register \ 256
```

Using AX as an example, we can extract the byte values in AL and AH as follows:

```
al% = outRegs.ax AND &HFF
ah% = outRegs.ax \ 256
```

Extracting individual bits from registers

At times, you'll need to extract individual bits from registers. Remember that the rightmost bit is bit 0. You can extract any individual bit using the following general method:

Nth bit = (register \ (2 ^ N)) AND 1

Again using AX as an example, the following program statements show how to extract the first four bits:

```
axBit0% = outRegs.ax AND 1
axBit1% = (outRegs.ax \ 2) AND 1
axBit2% = (outRegs.ax \ 4) AND 1
axBit3% = (outRegs.ax \ 8) AND 1
```

Testing the carry flag

You will probably need to extract a single bit from a register only when you want to test the carry flag in the flags register. You learned in Chapter 2 that the carry flag, which is the first bit in the flags register, is used by some MS-DOS services to signal an error. On return from the service routine, the carry flag is set (equal to 1) if an error occurred and clear (equal to 0) if no error occurred. Using the technique learned in the preceding section, you can test this flag as follows:

```
IF (outRegs.flags AND 1) THEN
    ' Flag is set; error occurred
ELSE
    ' Flag is not set; no error occurred
END IF
```

ASCIIZ strings

An ASCIIZ string is simply a string of characters that is terminated by a byte whose ASCII value is 0. When you pass text information to an MS-DOS service, you must be sure the text is in an ASCIIZ string. To convert a

QuickBasic variable-length string to an ASCIIZ string, tack a zero byte on the end using the concatenation operator (+), as shown here:

```
ASCIIZString$ = oldString$ + CHR$(0)
```

Why is it necessary to tack on the zero byte? You pass a string to an MS-DOS service by passing the address of the string's first character, which tells the service where the string begins. The terminating zero byte tells the service where the string ends. Because the value 0 is not used to code any character, there's no chance of confusing the end marker with a character.

Calling an Interrupt

To call an interrupt from QuickBasic, follow these steps:

1. Use the metacommand $INCLUDE to include the QB.BI or QBX.BI file in your program.
2. Declare the variables *inRegs* and *outRegs*.
3. Load the elements of *inRegs* with the register values required by the interrupt. To use a register's current value, load the corresponding element with −1.
4. Call INTERRUPT or INTERRUPTX, passing the interrupt number as the first argument and *inRegs* and *outRegs* as the second and third arguments.
5. Read the values in the elements of *outRegs* to obtain any information returned by the interrupt service routine. When appropriate, check the carry flag to detect an error condition.

It's that simple! Let's take a look at an example. Int 21H provides access to many MS-DOS services. When you call Int 21H, the service is specified by values that the calling program places in the registers. For example, to call Int 21H Function 30H, call Int 21H with the value 30H in the AH register (and 0 in the AL register). This service returns the number of the MS-DOS version being run on the system. The information is returned in registers AL and AH: AL contains the major version number, and AH contains the minor version number (multiplied by 100).

For example, if you're running MS-DOS 3.3, the service returns the following values:

```
AL = 3
AH = 30
```

To obtain the final version number, you combine the two values as follows:

```
version = AL + AH / 100
```

Of course, you can obtain your MS-DOS version number by entering *ver* at the MS-DOS prompt. Using Int 21H Function 30H, however, gives your programs access to this information. You'll often encounter times when your program needs to obtain the number of the version of MS-DOS in use.

The program in Listing 3-1 illustrates the use of Int 21H Function 30H. This program is a simple one, intended to whet your appetite and to illustrate how simple it is to call an MS-DOS service. When you run the program, it displays your MS-DOS version number on the screen.

```
' Uses Int 21H Function 30H to obtain the MS-DOS version number

' $INCLUDE: 'QB.BI'

DECLARE FUNCTION DosVersion! ()

DIM SHARED inRegs AS RegType, outRegs AS RegType

' Begin execution
PRINT "Your system is running MS-DOS version "; DosVersion!

END

FUNCTION DosVersion!
    ' Returns the MS-DOS version number

    inRegs.ax = &H3000      'AL equals 0; AH equals 30H

    CALL INTERRUPT(&H21, inRegs, outRegs)

    ' The major version number is in AL, and the minor
    ' version number is in AH
    major = outRegs.ax AND &HFF
    minor = outRegs.ax \ 256

    ' Combine major and minor to form the MS-DOS version number
    DosVersion! = major + minor / 100
END FUNCTION
```

LISTING 3-1.
Using Int 21H Function 30H to obtain the MS-DOS version number.

You'll notice that in this demonstration program the call to the MS-DOS service was isolated within a Basic function. The main program calls the function without any knowledge of how the function works. This is, of course, in keeping with the tenets of structured programming, which call for code and data to be isolated in independent modules as much as possible. Throughout this book, I emphasize structured programming principles— they are indispensable for developing applications that are robust and easy to maintain.

CHAPTER 4

Calling Interrupts from C

Numerous C compilers are available for the PC, and they all should provide a method by which a program can issue software interrupts. The methods that most compilers use are similar to those of the Microsoft C compiler, which I used when writing the demonstration programs in this book. The bulk of this chapter is devoted to showing you how to call interrupts in Microsoft C, with a smaller section at the end devoted to Borland's Turbo C. If you use neither the Microsoft C nor the Turbo C compiler, you should still be able to run the programs in this book with few or no modifications. Be sure to check your compiler documentation for details.

Calling Interrupts from Microsoft C

Microsoft actually markets two C compilers for the MS-DOS environment: C and QuickC. The "big" C compiler, called the Microsoft C Professional Development System, was in version 6 at this writing but might be in version 7 by the time you read this. I used Microsoft QuickC version 2.5 to compile and test the book's C demonstration programs. These two Microsoft C compilers differ in areas such as code optimization and programming tools. They are, however, almost completely language compatible, which means that, in almost every case, a program written for one will correctly compile with the other.

The *int86()* and *int86x()* functions

Microsoft C has two library functions that are used to issue software interrupts: *int86()* and *int86x()*. Both of these functions require that you include in your program the header file DOS.H by using the #include directive. The prototypes for these functions are shown below:

```
int int86(int, union REGS *, union REGS *);
int int86x(int, union REGS *, union REGS *, struct SREGS *);
```

Because some readers might be a bit rusty at interpreting C function prototypes, I'll go over these in detail. Look first at *int86()*:

- The first argument passed to this function is an integer. The value of this argument specifies the number of the interrupt to be called.

- The second argument is a pointer to type REGS. REGS is a union that is defined in DOS.H. The values in this union are placed in the CPU registers before the MS-DOS service is called.

- The third argument is also a pointer to type REGS. Note that this argument is of the same type as the second argument; it isn't the same instance. The values in the CPU registers are placed in this argument after the call to the service.

Look now at *int86x()*. The first three arguments to this function are the same as for *int86()*. The difference between these functions lies in the function's fourth argument. The fourth argument to *int86x()* is a pointer to type SREGS. SREGS is a structure that is defined in DOS.H. The values in this structure are placed in the CPU segment registers when the service is called. When execution returns from the service, the contents of the CPU segment registers are placed in this structure.

Both of these functions return the value of the AX register. This value can also be accessed through the function's third parameter. Because so many services return data in AX, having the function return this value directly to the calling program often simplifies programming. If an error occurs during the service routine, the global variable *doserrno* is set to the corresponding error code.

You can see that the functions *int86()* and *int86x()* allow your C program to call any software interrupt, passing data to the CPU registers before the call and reading data from the registers after the call. The only difference between these two functions is that *int86x()* provides access to the segment registers and *int86()* does not.

The *intdos()* and *intdosx()* functions

You can use two additional C functions, called *intdos()* and *intdosx()*, to call software interrupts. Their prototypes are shown here:

```
int intdos(union REGS *, union REGS *);
int intdosx(union REGS *, union REGS *, struct SREGS *);
```

Note that these prototypes are identical to the prototypes for *int86()* and *int86x()*, with one exception: The integer argument is missing. That's because these functions work exactly as do *int86()* and *int86x()*, except that the program cannot specify the interrupt number—these functions always call Int 21H. The call in the format

```
x = intdos(...)
```

is exactly equivalent to the following call:

```
x = int86(0x21, ...)
```

Likewise, the call

```
x = intdosx(...)
```

is equivalent to the following call:

```
x = int86x(0x21, ...)
```

Why does C include separate functions for calling Int 21H? A large number of the MS-DOS services are accessed via Int 21H, and using these dedicated functions can simplify programming (if only slightly). You might remember from Chapter 2 that, strictly speaking, all MS-DOS services are accessed via Int 21H. (Other interrupts access BIOS services.) Remember also that this book uses the terms *MS-DOS services* and *MS-DOS interrupt service routines* to refer generically to all MS-DOS and BIOS services.

The REGS and SREGS Types

The data structures that the C interrupt functions use are defined in DOS.H. Type REGS is used to pass data to and return data from the software interrupt services. REGS is a union composed of two structures, as follows:

```
struct WORDREGS {
    unsigned int ax;
    unsigned int bx;
    unsigned int cx;
    unsigned int dx;
    unsigned int si;
    unsigned int di;
    unsigned int cflag;
    };

struct BYTEREGS {
    unsigned char al, ah;
    unsigned char bl, bh;
    unsigned char cl, ch;
    unsigned char dl, dh;
    };

union REGS {
    struct WORDREGS x;
    struct BYTEREGS h;
    };
```

Remember that a union is a data structure in which data items that have different names—and possibly different types—occupy overlapping memory storage space. In the case of REGS, the two items are the structures WORDREGS and BYTEREGS. WORDREGS contains seven type *int* members, each corresponding to one of the CPU registers. Because an integer contains 2 bytes, as does each CPU register, the *int* type is ideal for representing registers.

BYTEREGS contains eight type *char* members, each of which holds one byte. In the union REGS, these eight type *char* members occupy the same storage space as do the first four type *int* members of WORDREGS. You can access that storage space by referring to either the type *int* members of WORDREGS or the type *char* members of BYTEREGS. This arrangement, which is illustrated in Figure 4-1, allows you to access the 2-byte word registers AX, BX, CX, and DX, as well as the byte registers AL, AH, BL, and so on. The example in that figure is based on the assumption that you have declared an instance of type REGS named *reg*. Notice that single-byte access to the registers SI and DI is not possible.

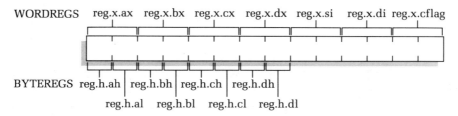

FIGURE 4-1.
The type REGS union allows you to access either the 2-byte registers or the 1-byte registers.

Note that one of the members in REGS is called *cflag*. This member does not correspond to the entire CPU flags register; it corresponds to only the carry flag. As mentioned earlier, some MS-DOS services use the carry flag to signal an error. The flag is set (equal to 1) when an error has occurred and clear (equal to 0) otherwise. When appropriate, your program should test the *cflag* member upon return from an MS-DOS service and take appropriate action if it is set. If *cflag* is set, you can find out more about the error by checking the global variable *doserrno*, which is set to the error code that corresponds to the error.

The structure type SREGS is used by *int86x()* and *intdosx()* to pass and retrieve the segment register values. This structure is defined in DOS.H as follows:

```
struct SREGS {
    unsigned int es;
    unsigned int cs;
    unsigned int ss;
    unsigned int ds;
    };
```

Even though SREGS contains members that correspond to all four segment registers, use only DS and ES when you call MS-DOS services. Unless you know exactly what you're doing, you do not want to alter your C program's CS or SS registers! Doing so changes the address of the code segment and stack segment and would almost surely crash your system.

The header file DOS.H only defines REGS and SREGS. Your program must declare instances (variables) of those types for use by the interrupt functions. The names *inregs* and *outregs* are usually used for the type REGS unions and the name *segregs* for the type SREGS structure. In most cases, the declaration should be outside the *main()* function so that the data objects will be global in scope:

```
union REGS inregs, outregs;
struct SREGS segregs;
    ⋮
main()
{
    ⋮
```

Calling an interrupt from Microsoft C: A summary

To summarize the information presented so far in this chapter, here are the steps you must take to call a software interrupt from a C program:

1. Use the #include directive to include the header file DOS.H in your program.

2. Declare two instances of type REGS named *inregs* and *outregs* (or any other names you like).

3. If you will be using either *int86x()* or *intdosx()*, declare an instance of SREGS (the name is typically *segregs*).

4. Load the members of *inregs* (and, if necessary, *segregs*) with whatever values are needed by the MS-DOS service.

5. Call the interrupt using the appropriate function.

6. If the MS-DOS service uses the carry flag to signal an error, test *outregs.x.cflag* to determine whether an error has occurred. If one has, examine the value of the global variable *doserrno*, which provides information about the error.

7. If the service succeeds, it returns the value in the AX register. If the service returns data in other registers, obtain the values in the registers by accessing the members of *outregs*.

It's time for an example. Int 21H provides access to many MS-DOS services. The specific service is specified by values that the calling program places in the CPU registers. Function 30H, which is called by placing the value 30H in AH before calling Int 21H, returns the system's MS-DOS version number. The service returns the version number, with the major version number in the AL register and the minor version number in AH. For MS-DOS 3.3, for example, the service returns the value 3 in AL and 30 in AH. The final version number is obtained by combining the two:

$$\text{version} = AL + AH / 100$$

Of course, you can obtain your MS-DOS version number by entering *ver* at the MS-DOS prompt. Using Int 21H Function 30H, however, gives your programs access to this information. As you'll see later in this book, you'll encounter times when your program needs to obtain the number of the version of MS-DOS in use.

The program in Listing 4-1 illustrates how to obtain the MS-DOS version number by using Int 21H Function 30H. This program is a simple one and is intended only to illustrate the procedures for calling an MS-DOS service from a C program. When you run the program, it displays your MS-DOS version number on the screen.

```c
/* Demonstrates Int 21H Function 30H, which gets the */
/* MS-DOS version number */

#include <stdio.h>
#include <dos.h>

/* Declare the register unions */
union REGS inregs, outregs;

/* Function prototype */
float dosversion(void);

main()
{
    printf("Your system is running MS-DOS version %.1f", dosversion());
}

float dosversion(void)
{
    /* Returns the MS-DOS version number */

    inregs.h.ah = 0x30;
    intdos(&inregs, &outregs);     /* Call Int 21H Function 30H */

    return (outregs.h.al + outregs.h.ah / 100.0);
}
```

LISTING 4-1.
Using Int 21H Function 30H to obtain the MS-DOS version number.

In this program, the MS-DOS service call is encapsulated within a C function. This method of programming follows principles of structured programming, which isolates in functions code and data for specific program tasks. Throughout this book, I emphasize structured programming principles—they are indispensable for developing applications that are robust and easy to maintain.

Calling Interrupts in Turbo C

The Borland Turbo C compiler calls software interrupts in a manner almost identical to that of the Microsoft C compilers. Turbo C has the same four functions—*int86()*, *int86x()*, *intdos()*, and *intdosx()*—that were described earlier in this chapter. It also has the WORDREGS, BYTEREGS, and SREGS structures as well as the REGS union. In Turbo C, however, the WORDREGS structure (and therefore the REGS union) has one additional member that permits access to the entire CPU flags register. The Turbo C definition of WORDREGS reads as follows:

```
struct WORDREGS {
    unsigned int ax, bx, cx, dx, si, di, cflag, flags;
};
```

The last structure member, *flags*, is not present in the Microsoft version of the WORDREGS structure. This difference has no bearing upon the C programs in this book, although having access to all of the flags can provide additional flexibility in some programming situations.

The bottom line is that if you're using Turbo C (or Turbo C++, which can be used for C as well as for C++ programs), you can access MS-DOS services exactly as shown in this book. In fact, the great majority of the book's C demonstration programs compile and run fine using Turbo C or Turbo C++ version 2—I've tested most of them. One exception is Listing 6-4, which is the graphics mode mouse demonstration program. This program does not work with Turbo C because the Borland and Microsoft graphics libraries are different.

CHAPTER 5

The Keyboard

Perhaps the most crucial aspect of any program is the manner in which it interacts with the user. Information must be passed between the user and the program in a clear, logical, and efficient manner. This transfer of information from the program to the user is accomplished primarily via the screen display, which you'll read about in Chapter 7. Input from the user to the program comes primarily via the keyboard, which is the subject of this chapter. Using the mouse, however, is becoming more and more common as a method of input and is the subject of Chapter 6.

You'll read about many MS-DOS services in this chapter and the chapters that follow. To find out more about a particular service, see the reference section at the end of each chapter. The reference entries are listed there in numeric order.

Every computer has a keyboard, and it's a rare program indeed that doesn't make some use of input from the keyboard. Both C and Basic have keyboard input routines that are adequate for most situations. By going directly to MS-DOS, however, you'll gain significant advantages, including additional control over keyboard input, smaller executable program size, and faster response. Before looking at the MS-DOS services for keyboard access, you need to understand how the keyboard works.

Keyboard Basics

Over the years, PCs have used three different keyboard designs, and all three are still in common use:

- The 83-key keyboard that was supplied with the original IBM PC and PC/XT has ten function keys that are usually grouped at the left.

- The 84-key PC/AT keyboard that was introduced with the PC/AT is essentially identical to the 83-key IBM PC keyboard, with the addition of the Sys Req key.

- The enhanced 101-key keyboard has 12 function keys positioned along its top, and separate arrow and editing keys.

All three types of keyboard operate in the same way, although the later models include some keys and capabilities not found in the earlier models. The keyboard is not simply a collection of switches; it has a degree of "intelligence." Here's how the keyboard works.

When you press a key, the keyboard generates a unique 1-byte scan code that identifies the key. Bit 7 (the leftmost bit) of the scan code is always 0. When you release the key, another unique scan code is generated. For any key, the release scan code is the press scan code with bit 7 set to 1. These scan codes have no relationship to the keyboard character's ASCII codes—they simply represent the position of the key on the keyboard. Figure 5-1 on the following page diagrams the three types of keyboards and includes the press scan codes of each key.

In addition to the corresponding scan code, the keyboard also generates a call to Int 09H (the keyboard interrupt) each time the user presses or releases a key. Execution passes to the ROM BIOS keyboard interrupt service routine, which reads the scan code from the keyboard. The ROM BIOS interprets the scan code and then takes one of three actions:

- If the ROM BIOS detects Ctrl-Break, Sys Req (Alt-Sys Req on the 101-key keyboard), or Shift-PrtSc (Shift-PrintScreen on the 101-key keyboard), it generates another interrupt request. All three of these key combinations are processed by other parts of the BIOS and do not concern us here.

- If the user presses one of the Ctrl, Alt, Shift, or "lock" keys, the ROM BIOS sets a specific bit in the keyboard flag byte. When the user releases the key, the corresponding bit is cleared. The "lock" keys are Scroll Lock, Num Lock, Caps Lock, and Insert. I'll discuss the keyboard flags shortly.

- Otherwise, the ROM BIOS interprets the scan code and places a 2-byte code in the keyboard buffer. For character keys, the first byte of the code is the character's ASCII code and the second byte is the key's scan code. For noncharacter keys (for example, function keys and arrow keys), the first byte of the code is 0 and the second byte— the scan code—identifies the key. (The latter are called *extended key codes* and are included in the upcoming discussion.)

It is possible for a program to interact with the keyboard by calling Int 09H. In fact, this is how "pop-up," or terminate-and-stay-resident (TSR), programs such as SideKick work. These programs replace the BIOS keyboard interrupt handler with their own interrupt handler. Each time the user presses a key, the interrupt handler examines it to see if it's the key or key combination that signals the program to pop up. If so, the program pops up and is ready for use. If not, the scan code is passed to the regular keyboard handler routine for processing in the normal way.

We will not, however, program the keyboard at the Int 09H level. The keyboard service routines that MS-DOS contains provide sufficient flexibility for almost any programming need.

Hexadecimal scan codes for a PC keyboard

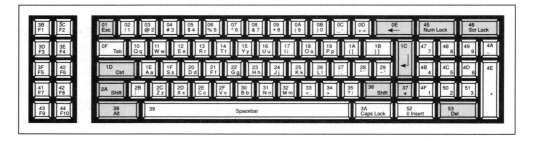

Hexadecimal scan codes for a PC/AT keyboard

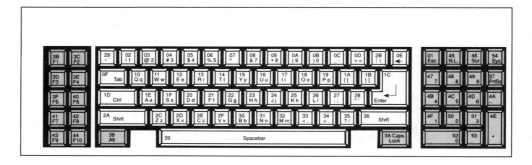

Hexadecimal scan codes for an enhanced keyboard

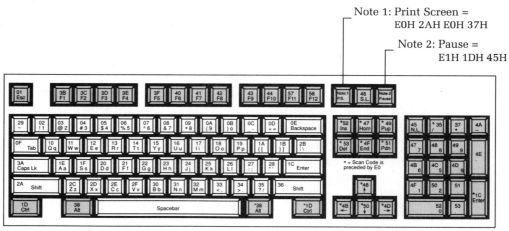

FIGURE 5-1.
The three types of keyboards and their scan codes.

Keyboard Input

When using MS-DOS services for keyboard input, you have a choice between the Int 21H DOS kernel services and the Int 16H BIOS services. The main difference between these two groups is that the Int 21H services are sensitive to input redirection and the Int 16H services are not.

What is input redirection?

Most input and output functions—MS-DOS functions as well as those that are part of C or Basic—do not interact directly with the hardware. Rather, they receive input from *stdin* and send output to *stdout*, which are names that, by default, refer to the keyboard and the display screen devices, respectively. Thus, input functions such as the C *scanf( )* function and the Basic INPUT statement normally receive input from the keyboard, and output functions such as *printf( )* and PRINT normally send output to the screen.

The operating system permits both input and output to be redirected, which means that the names *stdin* and *stdout*, or either one individually, become associated temporarily with a different physical device. For example, *stdin* could be associated with a disk file, and *stdout* could be linked with a printer. Based on this scenario, a program would take its input from a disk file instead of from the keyboard and would send output to the printer instead of to the screen. In certain applications, redirection can be an extremely useful tool. For information about the MS-DOS redirection commands, see your MS-DOS documentation.

The Int 21H keyboard input services are sensitive to input redirection, and those input services that display the input on the screen are sensitive to output redirection. The Int 16H keyboard services, however, ignore redirection. Keep this difference in mind when deciding which interrupt to use in your programs.

Ctrl-C and Ctrl-Break

Users often press the Ctrl-C or the Ctrl-Break key combination to interrupt an ongoing process. You need to understand how these combinations work in order to use the MS-DOS keyboard input services correctly.

When you press Ctrl-C, 03H (the ASCII code for Ctrl-C) is placed in the keyboard buffer like any other character. When MS-DOS reads Ctrl-C from the buffer, it calls Int 23H. The default handler for Int 23H terminates the active process and returns control to the parent process—usually, the program then terminates, and the MS-DOS prompt returns.

A similar process occurs when you press Ctrl-Break, which causes Int 1BH to be called. This interrupt places a Ctrl-C in the keyboard buffer ahead of any other waiting characters. As before, Int 23H is executed when this character is read. Thus, Ctrl-C and Ctrl-Break are equivalent except that Ctrl-C is read only after any previous characters in the buffer are read, and Ctrl-Break gets immediate action by being placed at the front of the line.

Strictly speaking, the response to a Ctrl-Break (or Ctrl-C) keystroke is not always immediate. MS-DOS maintains a break flag for which the default setting is 0, which means that MS-DOS checks for a Ctrl-Break only during certain input/output (I/O) operations. If you use C or Basic I/O functions or statements when the break flag is set to 0, Ctrl-Break is detected only when your program does either of the following:

- Sends data to the screen, printer, or communications port
- Reads data from the keyboard or communications port

If the break flag is set to 1, MS-DOS checks for a Ctrl-Break every time an MS-DOS service is called—including not only the I/O operations mentioned above but also disk operations, memory allocation, and so on. With the break flag set, therefore, users are able to interrupt a program's operation more readily by pressing Ctrl-Break (for example, if execution becomes stuck in a program loop that doesn't involve any I/O operations).

When programming, keep in mind two questions. The first is "What happens when the system responds to a Ctrl-C or Ctrl-Break?" The default handler simply terminates the currently executing program and returns control to the MS-DOS command processor. This action can cause data loss—for example, any information that has not yet been saved on disk will be lost. To avoid this problem, you can write and install your own Int 23H handler so that a Ctrl-Break causes execution to branch to your code rather than to the MS-DOS default handler. You would usually write such a handler in assembly language, which is beyond the scope of this book.

The second question is "When does the system respond to Ctrl-C or Ctrl-Break?" You have some control over the system's response. You can select MS-DOS input services based on whether they respond to Ctrl-Break. The following section, titled "Character Input," covers the MS-DOS keyboard input services. You can also control the state of the MS-DOS break flag by using Int 21H Function 33H. This service lets you query the state of the break flag and set or clear it. Later in the chapter, Listings 5-1 and 5-2 demonstrate the use of Int 21H Function 33H.

Here's a note to Basic users: When you are creating an EXE file from within the QuickBasic or Basic PDS integrated environment, selecting the Produce Debug Code option from the Make EXE File dialog box tells the resulting program to check for a Ctrl-Break after executing each line (and to activate other debugging features). If you're compiling from the command line, you can achieve the same effect by using the /D compiler switch. Using this switch, however, results in a larger, slower program.

Character Input

MS-DOS offers several services for character input. By *character input,* I mean that the service reads input one keystroke at a time from the keyboard buffer—somewhat like the Basic INKEY$ statement and the C *getch()* function. You can use the MS-DOS character input services when your program is looking for single keystrokes, such as a function key, a cursor-pad editing key, and the like. With a little programming, you can also use them to read lines of text.

Int 21H character input services

You can access four character input services via Int 21H. Figure 5-2 summarizes these services, which differ in terms of whether they wait for input, whether they echo the input to the screen, and whether they respond to Ctrl-C and Ctrl-Break.

Int 21H service	Waits for input?	Responds to Ctrl-Break?	Echoes character?
01H	Yes	Yes	Yes
06H	No	No	No
07H	Yes	No	No
08H	Yes	Yes	No

FIGURE 5-2.
The Int 21H character input services and their characteristics.

When using any of these four MS-DOS input services, keep in mind that these services all return the corresponding ASCII value for standard characters. If the user has entered an extended character (for example, a function key or an Alt-[letter] key combination), the services return the value 0. You must then read the next character in the keyboard buffer to obtain the extended character's scan code.

The programs in Listings 5-1 and 5-2 demonstrate (in Basic and C respectively) how to use Int 21H Function 08H for character and line input. Using Int 21H Function 01H would be the same except that the program would not have to echo characters explicitly because the service would do it. In addition, using Int 21H Function 07H would be the same except for its lack of response to Ctrl-Break. The programs also show how to use Int 21H Function 33H to query and set the break flag. See the reference section at the end of this chapter to learn what values to place in the registers before calling these MS-DOS interrupt service routines and to learn what registers to examine for return values.

When running these programs, try pressing the Backspace key while you enter the line of text. You'll see that doing so does not delete the last character as you might expect but instead displays a small square with a diamond in the middle. This demonstrates that to MS-DOS and the BIOS the Backspace key is only another key and has no special meaning. Backspace has an ASCII value of 08H, and the small square is the display character that corresponds to ASCII 08H. The fact that Backspace deletes the last character when you enter data at the MS-DOS prompt and in response to an INPUT statement or *scanf()* function is a feature of the MS-DOS command interpreter and of the Basic and C languages.

```
' Using Int 21H Function 33H to query and set the break flag
' and Int 21H Function 08H for keyboard input

' INCLUDE: 'QB.BI'

DIM SHARED inRegs AS RegType, outRegs AS RegType


' Begin execution

' Get the status of the break flag
inRegs.ax = &H3300            ' AL = 0H; AH = 33H
CALL INTERRUPT(&H21, inRegs, outRegs)

oldflag% = (outRegs.dx AND &HFF)

' Turn the break flag off
inRegs.ax = &H3301            ' AL = 01H; AH = 33H
inRegs.dx = 0
CALL INTERRUPT(&H21, inRegs, outRegs)


' The following section of the program reads one character input
' by the user. If that character is ASCII 13 (Enter), the loop
' terminates. If it's 0, an extended key has been pressed and a
' second character is read. This second character is the extended
' key's scan code. If the first character is neither 13 nor 0, it's
' a standard key, and the ASCII value is displayed.
```

LISTING 5-1. *(continued)*
Demonstration in Basic of using Int 21H Function 33H to query and set the break flag and of using Int 21H Function 08H to read characters and lines of text.

LISTING 5-1. *continued*

```
CLS
PRINT "Press any key; press Enter when done."

DO
    ' Read a character
    inRegs.ax = &H800
    CALL INTERRUPT(&H21, inRegs, outRegs)

    ' Look for Enter
    IF (outRegs.ax AND &HFF) = 13 THEN EXIT DO

    IF (outRegs.ax AND &HFF) = 0 THEN
        ' Read the next character
        inRegs.ax = &H800
        CALL INTERRUPT(&H21, inRegs, outRegs)
        scan% = outRegs.ax AND &HFF
        PRINT "You pressed an extended key that has a scan code of ";
        PRINT scan%
    ELSE
        ascval% = outRegs.ax AND &HFF
        PRINT "You pressed a nonextended key that has an ASCII value of ";
        PRINT ascval%
    END IF
LOOP WHILE (1)


' The next part of the program uses the MS-DOS service to read a
' line of text one character at a time. Non-ASCII characters are
' discarded, and input terminates when Enter is pressed.

CLS
PRINT "Now type a line of text, and then press Enter."
PRINT

buffer$ = ""

DO
    ' Read a character
    inRegs.ax = &H800
    CALL INTERRUPT(&H21, inRegs, outRegs)

    ' Look for Enter
    IF (outRegs.ax AND &HFF) = 13 THEN EXIT DO

    ' If an extended key was pressed, call the service again to remove
    ' the scan code from the keyboard buffer
    IF (outRegs.ax AND &HFF) = 0 THEN
        inRegs.ax = &H800
        CALL INTERRUPT(&H21, inRegs, outRegs)
```

(continued)

LISTING 5-1. *continued*

```
        ' Otherwise, it's a standard ASCII character
        ' Echo it and add it to the string
        ELSE
            PRINT CHR$(outRegs.ax AND &HFF);
            buffer$ = buffer$ + CHR$(outRegs.ax AND &HFF)
        END IF
LOOP WHILE (1)

PRINT
PRINT "You entered: "; buffer$

' Restore the original status of the break flag
inRegs.ax = &H3301
inRegs.dx = oldflag%
CALL INTERRUPT(&H21, inRegs, outRegs)

END
```

```c
/* Using Int 21H Function 33H to query and set the break flag */
/* and Int 21H Function 08H for keyboard input */

#include <stdio.h>
#include <dos.h>


/* Declare the register unions */
union REGS inregs, outregs;

void clearscreen(void);

main()
{
    char oldflag, buf[80];
    int count = 0;

    /* Get the status of the break flag */
    inregs.h.ah = 0x33;
    int86(0x21, &inregs, &outregs);

    oldflag = outregs.h.dl;

    /* Turn the break flag off */
    inregs.x.ax = 0x3301;      /* AL = 01H; AH = 33H */
    inregs.x.dx = 0;
    int86(0x21, &inregs, &outregs);
```

LISTING 5-2. *(continued)*
Demonstration in C of using Int 21H Function 33H to query and set the break flag and of using Int 21H Function 08H to read characters and lines of text.

LISTING 5-2. *continued*

```
/* The following section of the program reads one character input
   by the user. If that character is ASCII 13 (Enter), the loop
   terminates. If it's 0, an extended key has been pressed and a
   second character is read. This second character is the extended
   key's scan code. If the first character is neither 13 nor 0, it's
   a standard key, and the ASCII value is displayed. */

clearscreen();
puts("Press any key; press Enter when done.");

do
    {
    /* Read a character */
    inregs.h.ah = 0x8;
    int86(0x21, &inregs, &outregs);

    /* Look for Enter */
    if (outregs.h.al == 13)
        break;

    if (outregs.h.al == 0)
        {
        /* Read the next character */
        inregs.h.ah = 0x8;
        int86(0x21, &inregs, &outregs);
        printf("You pressed an extended key that has a scan code of %d.\n",
            outregs.h.al);
        }
    else
        {
        printf("You pressed a nonextended key that has an ACSII value ");
        printf("of %d.\n", outregs.h.al);
        }
    }
while (1);

/* The next part of the program uses the MS-DOS service to read a
   line of text one character at a time. Non-ASCII characters are
   discarded, and input terminates when Enter is pressed. */

clearscreen();
puts("Now type a line of text, and then press Enter.");

do
    {
    /* Read a character */
    inregs.h.ah = 0x8;
    int86(0x21, &inregs, &outregs);
```

(continued)

LISTING 5-2. *continued*

```c
            /* If Enter is pressed, tack a terminating null character */
            /* on the string and exit the loop */
            if (outregs.h.al == 13)
                {
                buf[count] = 0;
                break;
                }

            /* If an extended key was pressed, call the service again */
            /* to remove the scan code from the keyboard buffer */
            if (outregs.h.al == 0)
                {
                inregs.h.ah = 0x8;
                int86(0x21, &inregs, &outregs);
                }

            /* Otherwise, it's a standard ASCII character */
            /* Echo the character and add it to the string */
            else
                {
                putch(outregs.h.al);
                buf[count++] = outregs.h.al;
                }
            }
        while (1);

        /* Display the entire string */
        printf("\n\nYou entered: %s", buf);

        /* Restore the original status of the break flag */
        inregs.x.ax = 0x3301;
        inregs.h.dl = oldflag;
        int86(0x21, &inregs, &outregs);
}

void clearscreen(void)
{
    int x;

    for (x = 0; x < 25; x++)
        printf("\n");
}
```

Int 16H Function 00H—BIOS character input

If you are willing to forgo the ability to redirect input, you can bypass MS-DOS and go directly to the BIOS keyboard input routine, which is accessed via Int 16H Function 00H. You'll want to keep several factors in mind when considering this method.

Because Int 16H Function 00H is not sensitive to redirection of input, using it for character input means that input will come from the keyboard at all times. You can use this service to ensure that responses to error messages come from the user. For example, a program could use Int 21H input services for most of its input, permitting data to be read from either the keyboard or, with redirection, from a disk or another device. If an error occurred (for example, a problem with the disk), the program could display an error message on the screen and accept the user's response by using Int 16H Function 00H.

Int 16H Function 00H has this advantage: With a single call, it returns both the ASCII character code and the scan code. This capability enables the program to read extended keys using a single call, rather than the two calls required with the Int 21H character input services.

The Int 16H services, however, are dependent on compatibility with the IBM PC BIOS. This issue is not usually a problem, but be aware that these calls will not work on some older machines, such as the Hewlett-Packard TouchScreen and the Wang Professional Computer.

Perhaps the most serious drawback to Int 16H Function 00H is that it can cause problems when certain pop-up (TSR) utilities are installed. Unless you know in advance the environment in which your program will be executing, you should probably avoid using this service.

The programs in Listings 5-3 and 5-4 demonstrate how to use Int 16H Function 00H for reading both single characters and lines of text.

```
' Using Int 16H Function 00H to read a character from
' the keyboard

' $INCLUDE: 'QB.BI'
DIM SHARED inRegs AS RegType, outRegs AS RegType


' Begin execution

CLS
PRINT "Press any key for a display of its ASCII code and"
PRINT "scan code. Press Enter when done."

DO
    ' Read a character
    inRegs.ax = 0
    CALL INTERRUPT(&H16, inRegs, outRegs)
```

LISTING 5-3. *(continued)*
Demonstration of using Int 16H Function 00H in Basic for keyboard input.

LISTING 5-3. *continued*

```
        ' AL contains the ASCII code, AH contains the scan code
        PRINT "ASCII code = ", outRegs.ax AND &HFF
        PRINT "Scan code = ", outRegs.ax \ 256
        PRINT
    LOOP UNTIL (outRegs.ax AND &HFF) = 13        ' Loop until Enter is pressed

    CLS

    PRINT "Type a line of text, and then press Enter."
    PRINT

    DO
        ' Read a character
        CALL INTERRUPT(&H16, inRegs, outRegs)

        ' If the character is Enter, exit the loop. Otherwise, echo
        ' the character to the screen, and add it to the string.

        IF (outRegs.ax AND &HFF) = 13 THEN
            EXIT DO
        ELSE
            buffer$ = buffer$ + CHR$(outRegs.ax AND &HFF)
            PRINT CHR$(outRegs.ax AND &HFF);
        END IF
    LOOP WHILE (1)

    ' Display the line of text
    PRINT
    PRINT "You entered: "; buffer$

    END
```

```c
/* Using Int 16H Function 00H to read a character from */
/* the keyboard */

#include <stdio.h>
#include <dos.h>

/* Declare the register unions */
union REGS inregs, outregs;

void clearscreen(void);

main()
{
    char buf[80];
    int count = 0;

    clearscreen();
```

LISTING 5-4. *(continued)*
Demonstration of using Int 16H Function 00H in C for keyboard input.

LISTING 5-4. *continued*

```c
    puts("Press any key for a display of its ASCII code and");
    puts("scan code. Press Enter when done.");

    do
        {
        /* Read a character */
        inregs.x.ax = 0;
        int86(0x16, &inregs, &outregs);

        printf("\nASCII code = %d", outregs.h.al);
        printf("\nScan code = %d", outregs.h.ah);
        }
    while (outregs.h.al != 13);    /* Loop until Enter is pressed */

    clearscreen();

    puts("Type a line of text, and then press Enter.");

    do
        {
        /* Read a character */
        inregs.x.ax = 0;
        int86(0x16, &inregs, &outregs);

        /* If the character is Enter, add the null character to the */
        /* string, and exit the loop. Otherwise, echo the character to */
        /* the screen, and add it to the string. */

        if (outregs.h.al == 13)
            {
            buf[count] = 0;
            break;
            }
        else
            {
            buf[count++] = outregs.h.al;
            putch(outregs.h.al);
            }
        }
    while (1);

    /* Display the line of text */
    printf("\n\nYou entered %s", buf);
}

void clearscreen(void)
{
    int x;

    for (x = 0; x < 25; x++)
        printf("\n");
}
```

Line Input

MS-DOS includes only one service—Int 21H Function 0AH—that reads a single line of input from *stdin* and places it in a user-defined buffer. This service is not used often because it lacks flexibility. For example, it does not enable a program to respond to an extended key while a line is being input. You can easily develop a more flexible line input routine by using the character input services to fill a buffer one character at a time. You'll find the reference for Int 21H Function 0AH at the end of this chapter, but I doubt you'll use this service much.

Checking Input Status

At times, you might want to find out whether a character is available in the buffer of the input device yet not want to remove the character from the buffer. You can do so by using Int 21H Function 0BH. This service does not wait for a character to be input but instead returns immediately to the calling program, letting it know whether a character is in the buffer. You can use this service to implement a simple form of multitasking—this is possible because in most situations a computer can process keyboard input much faster than a person can type. If you use one of the standard character input services, such as Int 21H Function 08H, your computer spends a lot of time waiting between keystrokes. By using Int 21H Function 0BH, you can check for a character and, when a character is available, process it. Otherwise, the program can be doing other tasks, as illustrated in Figure 5-3.

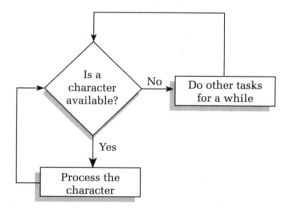

FIGURE 5-3.
Performing other tasks while waiting for input.

The programs in Listings 5-5 and 5-6 demonstrate how to use Int 21H Function 0BH to allow your program to perform some other task while waiting for input. In these programs, the "other task" is nothing that's actually useful: Program-generated characters are simply displayed at one screen location while input (most likely from the keyboard) is displayed at another location.

```
' Using Int 21H Function 0BH to determine whether a character
' is in the input buffer

' $INCLUDE: 'QB.BI'

DIM SHARED inRegs AS RegType, outRegs AS RegType


' Begin execution
CLS

position% = 1
code% = 32
ch$ = " "

DO
    ' Check the input buffer
    inRegs.ax = &HB00
    CALL INTERRUPT(&H21, inRegs, outRegs)

    ' If the input buffer contains a character, get it and echo it in
    ' the upper left of the screen. If not, display the next ASCII
    ' character in the sequence in the center of the screen.

    IF (outRegs.ax AND &HFF) <> 0 THEN
        ch$ = INKEY$
        LOCATE 1, position%
        PRINT ch$;
        position% = position% + 1
    ELSE
        LOCATE 15, 39
        PRINT CHR$(code%)
        code% = code% + 1
        IF code% > 125 THEN code% = 32
    END IF
LOOP UNTIL ch$ = CHR$(13)     ' Exit the loop when the user presses Enter

END
```

LISTING 5-5.
Demonstration of using Int 21H Function 0BH in Basic to determine whether a character is in the input buffer.

Listing 5-6 shows the C demonstration program. It includes a function named *locate()*, which uses an MS-DOS service to position the cursor at a specified screen location. But I'm getting ahead of myself here—we do not look at MS-DOS screen services until Chapter 7. Because C has no equivalent function, I used this method. For now, don't worry about how *locate()* positions the screen cursor at the specified position. You'll learn all about the MS-DOS service that performs this task in Chapter 7.

```c
/* Using Int 21H Function 0BH to determine whether a character */
/* is in the input buffer */

#include <stdio.h>
#include <dos.h>

/* Declare the register unions */
union REGS inregs, outregs;

/* Functions for clearing the screen and */
/* for setting the screen cursor position */
void clearscreen(void);
void locate(char, char);


main()
{
    char pos1 = 1, code = 32, ch;

    /* Clear the screen */
    clearscreen();

    do
        {
        /* Check the input buffer */
        inregs.h.ah = 0xB;
        int86(0x21, &inregs, &outregs);

        /* If the input buffer contains a character, get it and echo it
           in the upper left of the screen. If not, display the next ASCII
           character in the sequence in the center of the screen. */

        if (outregs.h.al != 0)
            {
            locate(pos1++, 1);
            ch = getch();
            putchar(ch);
            }
```

LISTING 5-6.   *(continued)*
Demonstration of using Int 21H Function 0BH in C to determine whether a character is in the input buffer.

LISTING 5-6. *continued*

```
        else
            {
            locate(39, 15);
            putchar(code++);
            if (code > 125)
                code = 32;
            }
        }                       /* Exit when user presses Enter */
    while (ch != 13);

    clearscreen();
}
void locate(char x, char y)
{
    inregs.h.ah = 0x02;
    inregs.h.dh = y - 1;
    inregs.h.dl = x - 1;
    inregs.h.bh = 0;

    int86(0x10, &inregs, &outregs);
}
void clearscreen(void)
{
    int x;

    for (x = 0; x < 25; x++)
        printf("\n");
}
```

Flushing the Input Buffer

The input buffer (often called the type-ahead buffer) can be a great convenience, but at times it can be dangerous. When a program is querying the user about an important task, for example, you don't want an old keystroke left over in the buffer to be misinterpreted as the response! You should empty the buffer first to ensure that the program gets the correct response—the one that was entered after the program's prompt. Some of the MS-DOS utility programs use this technique—you might have noticed, for example, that Format will not accept typed-ahead keystrokes.

Int 21H Function 0CH flushes the input buffer and then calls one of the input services. The programs in Listings 5-7 and 5-8 demonstrate the use of this service. Each program loops for eight seconds, allowing you to place some characters in the input buffer by pressing some keys. Then you are prompted for a response of Y or N. Using Int 21H Function 0CH ensures that the program reads your actual response and not the earlier keystrokes.

```basic
' Using Int 21H Function 0CH to flush the input buffer before
' accepting input

' $INCLUDE: 'QB.BI'

DIM SHARED inRegs AS RegType, outRegs AS RegType


' Begin execution

CLS

' Pause awhile
FOR i% = 1 TO 8
    timer1% = VAL(RIGHT$(TIME$, 2))         ' Get current number of seconds
    PRINT "Looping..."
    DO
        timer2% = VAL(RIGHT$(TIME$, 2))
    LOOP WHILE (timer2% < timer1% + 1)      ' Loop until 1 second elapses
NEXT i%

PRINT
PRINT "Erase all files on disk (Y or N)? "

' Flush buffer then use input service 01H
inRegs.ax = &HC01
CALL INTERRUPT(&H21, inRegs, outRegs)

' Convert the ASCII value to a character
ch$ = CHR$(outRegs.ax AND &HFF)

IF UCASE$(ch$) = "N" THEN
    LOCATE 12, 1                            ' Move cursor to next row
    PRINT "Good choice!"
ELSE
    PRINT "Say bye-bye to all your data..."
    SLEEP 2
    PRINT "Just kidding!"
END IF

END
```

LISTING 5-7.
Demonstration of using Int 21H Function 0CH in Basic to flush the input buffer before accepting input.

```c
/* Using Int 21H Function 0CH to flush the input buffer */
/* before accepting input */

#include <stdio.h>
#include <dos.h>

/* Declare the register unions */
union REGS inregs, outregs;

void clearscreen(void);

main()
{
    int i;
    char ch;
    long timer1, timer2, ltime;

    clearscreen();

    /* Pause awhile */
    for (i = 1; i < 8; i++)
        {
        timer1 = time(&ltime);          /* Get time */
        printf("Looping...\n");
        do
            timer2 = time(&ltime);
        while (timer2 < timer1 + 1);    /* Loop until 1 second elapses */
        }

    puts("\nErase all files on disk (Y or N)? ");

    /* Flush the buffer, and then use input service 01H */
    inregs.x.ax = 0xC01;
    int86(0x21, &inregs, &outregs);

    ch = outregs.h.al;

    if (ch == 'N' || ch == 'n')
        puts("\nGood choice!");
    else
        {
        puts("\nSay bye-bye to all your data...");
        puts("Just kidding!");
        }
}
```

LISTING 5-8. *(continued)*
Demonstration of using Int 21H Function 0CH in C to flush the input buffer before accepting input.

LISTING 5-8. *continued*

```
void clearscreen(void)
{
    int x;

    for (x = 0; x < 25; x++)
        printf("\n");
}
```

The Keyboard Flags

The ROM BIOS maintains a set of keyboard flags that reflect the status of the Ctrl, Shift, Alt, and "lock" keys. For Ctrl, Shift, and Alt, the flags byte indicates whether they are currently being pressed. For the "lock" keys (Scroll Lock, Num Lock, Caps Lock, and Insert), the flags byte indicates whether they are set to "on" or "off."

The BIOS uses the keyboard flags when processing keystrokes because the keyboard scan codes do not take into account whether any of these special keys are pressed. For example, pressing the g key sends a scan code of 22, regardless of whether the Shift, Caps Lock, or other special key is active. The BIOS checks the keyboard flags when processing a scan code. If you press the g key, the BIOS places 103 (the ASCII code for g) in the keyboard buffer. If you press the g key while holding down one of the Shift keys, the BIOS places 71 (the ASCII code for G) in the keyboard buffer.

Your program can read the keyboard flags by calling Int 16H Function 02H or Int 16H Function 12H. The difference between these two services is that Function 02H works with all keyboards, but Function 12H works only with enhanced keyboards. Function 12H, however, provides more detailed information, as you can see by examining the reference entries for these two interrupt services in the "Keyboard Service Reference" at the end of this chapter. Eight status flags (contained in one byte) are available for regular keyboards and sixteen flags for enhanced keyboards. See either Int 16H reference entry for more information about the meanings of the individual bits in the flags byte.

The keyboard flags are commonly used to enable your program to detect unusual key combinations. Your program can use such combinations to ensure that the user does not trigger potentially dangerous program actions. For example, you could require a user to press Ctrl-Shift, a key combination that's unlikely to be pressed by mistake, in order to exit the program without saving data.

It's time to demonstrate how your program can read the keyboard flags. The Basic program in Listing 5-9 and the C program in Listing 5-10 show how to read the keyboard flags using Int 16H Function 02H. These programs also show how to require a key combination for exiting the program—to exit either program, you must press both Shift keys at the same time.

Because these programs use Int 16H Function 02H, they can run on any system, regardless of the type of keyboard installed. It would be easy to modify the programs so that they use Int 16H Function 12H to sense the enhanced keyboard flags. In fact, making that modification would provide an excellent programming exercise for you (if you have an enhanced keyboard, that is!).

```
DECLARE SUB kbFlags ()

' Using Int 16H Function 02H to read the keyboard flags

' $INCLUDE: 'QB.BI'

DIM SHARED inRegs AS RegType, outRegs AS RegType

' Declare a structure to hold the values of the flags
TYPE Keyboard
    insert AS INTEGER
    capsLock AS INTEGER
    numLock AS INTEGER
    scrollLock AS INTEGER
    alt AS INTEGER
    ctrl AS INTEGER
    leftShift AS INTEGER
    rightShift AS INTEGER
END TYPE

DIM kb AS Keyboard


' Begin execution

CLS
PRINT "Demonstration of using Int 16H Function 02H to read the keyboard flags."
PRINT
PRINT "Press the Ctrl, Alt, Shift, and lock keys."
PRINT "Then press both Shift keys at the same time to exit."

' Set up an infinite loop
DO WHILE (1)

    ' Call the flags subprogram
    kbFlags
```

LISTING 5-9. *(continued)*
Demonstration of using Int 16H Function 02H in Basic to read the keyboard flags.

LISTING 5-9. *continued*

```
' If both Shift keys are pressed, exit the loop
IF (kb.leftShift AND kb.rightShift) THEN EXIT DO

' Otherwise, print the status of the keys
LOCATE 10, 1, 0

IF kb.insert THEN
    PRINT "Insert"
ELSE
    PRINT "      "
END IF

IF kb.capsLock THEN
    PRINT "Caps Lock"
ELSE
    PRINT "         "
END IF

IF kb.numLock THEN
    PRINT "Num Lock"
ELSE
    PRINT "        "
END IF

IF kb.scrollLock THEN
    PRINT "Scroll Lock"
ELSE
    PRINT "           "
END IF


IF kb.alt THEN
    PRINT "Alt"
ELSE
    PRINT "   "
END IF

IF kb.ctrl THEN
    PRINT "Ctrl"
ELSE
    PRINT "    "
END IF

IF kb.leftShift THEN
    PRINT "Left Shift"
ELSE
    PRINT "          "
END IF
```

(continued)

LISTING 5-9. *continued*

```
        IF kb.rightShift THEN
            PRINT "Right Shift"
        ELSE
            PRINT "            "
        END IF
LOOP

CLS

END

SUB kbFlags
    ' Returns the keyboard flags in a type Keyboard structure

    SHARED kb AS Keyboard

    ' Call the keyboard flags service
    inRegs.ax = &H200
    CALL INTERRUPT(&H16, inRegs, outRegs)

    ' Extract the bits of the flag byte
    kb.insert = outRegs.ax \ 128
    kb.capsLock = (outRegs.ax AND &H40) \ 64
    kb.numLock = (outRegs.ax AND &H20) \ 32
    kb.scrollLock = (outRegs.ax AND &H10) \ 16
    kb.alt = (outRegs.ax AND &H8) \ 8
    kb.ctrl = (outRegs.ax AND &H4) \ 4
    kb.leftShift = (outRegs.ax AND &H2) \ 2
    kb.rightShift = (outRegs.ax AND 1)
END SUB
```

```c
/* Using Int 16H Function 02H to read the keyboard flags */

#include <stdio.h>
#include <dos.h>

/* Declare the register unions */
union REGS inregs, outregs;

/* Declare a bit field structure to hold the values of the flags */
typedef struct {
    unsigned rightshift : 1;
    unsigned leftshift  : 1;
    unsigned ctrl       : 1;
    unsigned alt        : 1;
    unsigned scrollock  : 1;
```

LISTING 5-10. *(continued)*
Demonstration of using Int 16H Function 02H in C to read the keyboard flags.

LISTING 5-10. *continued*

```c
        unsigned numlock    : 1;
        unsigned capslock   : 1;
        unsigned insert     : 1;
} keyboard;

union {
    keyboard bd;
    int i;
} key;

/* Function prototypes */
int kbflags(void);
void clearscreen(void);
void locate(char, char);

main()
{
    clearscreen();
    puts("\n\nDemonstration of using Int 16H function 02H to read the");
    puts("keyboard flags. Press the Ctrl, Alt, Shift, or lock keys.");
    puts("Then press both Shift keys at the same time to exit.");


    /* Set up an infinite loop */
    do
        {

        /* Call the keyboard flags function */
        kbflags();

        /* If both Shift keys are pressed, exit the loop; */
        /* otherwise, print the flags byte in hexadecimal format. */

        if (key.bd.rightshift && key.bd.leftshift)
            break;
        else
            {
            locate(1, 25);
            printf("The keyboard flag byte equals %X", key.i);

            /* Flush the keyboard buffer */
            inregs.x.ax = 0xC00;
            int86(0x21, &inregs, &outregs);
            }
        }
    while (1);

} /* End of main() */
```

(continued)

LISTING 5-10. *continued*

```c
int kbflags(void)
{
    /* Reads the keyboard flags byte into a union of type key */
    /* The function's return value is the value in the AX register */

    int result;

    /* Call the keyboard flags service */
    inregs.h.ah = 0x02;
    result = int86(0x16, &inregs, &outregs);

    key.i = outregs.h.al;
    return result;
}

void clearscreen(void)
{
    int x;

    for (x = 0; x < 25; x++)
        printf("\n");
}

void locate(char x, char y)
{
    inregs.h.ah = 0x02;
    inregs.h.dh = y - 1;
    inregs.h.dl = x - 1;
    inregs.h.bh = 0;

    int86(0x10, &inregs, &outregs);
}
```

Setting the Keyboard Delay and Repeat Rate

All PC keyboards have a built-in repeat, or "typematic," feature. When you hold a character key down for some period of time, the character begins to be repeated. You can control both the delay time and the repeat rate for the character keys by using the MS-DOS service Int 16H Function 03H.

The ability to change the keyboard delay time and repeat rate can be useful. With this feature, you can write programs that allow users to customize the keyboard settings to suit their preferences. For example, users who use the typematic feature often might want to decrease the delay time and increase the repeat rate. You can also write a utility program that sets the keyboard to the desired rate before the user starts an application program. In fact, the programs in Listings 5-11 and 5-12 do exactly that if you remove the call at the end of each program that resets the keyboard to moderate settings.

```
DECLARE SUB kbRepeat (rate%, delay%)

' Using Int 16H Function 03H to change the keyboard
' repeat rate and delay time

' $INCLUDE: 'QB.BI'

DIM SHARED inRegs AS RegType, outRegs AS RegType


' Begin execution

DO
    CLS

    PRINT "Enter a repeat rate between 0 (fastest) and 31 (slowest): ";
    INPUT x%
    PRINT "Enter a delay value between 0 (shortest) and 3 (longest): ";
    INPUT y%
    PRINT "Try out some keys! Hit q to quit, s to start over."
    PRINT

    kbRepeat x%, y%       ' Call the kbRepeat subprogram

    k$ = INKEY$
    DO WHILE (LCASE$(k$) <> "q" AND LCASE$(k$) <> "s")
        PRINT k$;
        k$ = INKEY$
    LOOP

LOOP UNTIL (LCASE$(k$) = "q")

' Reset to typical settings
kbRepeat 10, 1

END

SUB kbRepeat (rate%, delay%)
    ' Sets the keyboard repeat rate and delay time

    ' rate% = 00H sets fastest rate
    '         1FH sets slowest rate
    '         Any other sets rate to 10 per second

    ' delay% = 0 sets delay time to 250 msec
    '          1 sets delay time to 500 msec
    '          2 sets delay time to 750 msec
    '          Any other sets delay time to 1000 msec
```

LISTING 5-11. *(continued)*
Demonstration of using Int 16H Function 03H in Basic to modify the keyboard repeat rate and delay time.

LISTING 5-11. *continued*

```
    inRegs.ax = &H305

    IF delay% >= 0 AND delay% <= 2 THEN
        inRegs.bx = (delay% * &H100)
    ELSE
        inRegs.bx = &H300
    END IF

    IF rate% >= 0 AND rate <= &H1F THEN
        inRegs.bx = inRegs.bx + rate%
    ELSE
        inRegs.bx = inRegs.bx + &HC
    END IF

    CALL INTERRUPT(&H16, inRegs, outRegs)

END SUB
```

```c
/* Using Int 16H Function 03H to set the keyboard */
/* repeat rate and delay time */

#include <stdio.h>
#include <dos.h>

/* Declare the register unions */
union REGS inregs, outregs;

void kbrepeat(int, int);
void clearscreen(void);

main()
{
    int rate, delay;
    char ch;

    do
        {
        clearscreen();

        printf("Enter a repeat rate between 0 (fastest) and 31 (slowest): ");
        scanf("%d", &rate);
        printf("Enter a delay value between 0 (shortest) and 3 (longest): ");
        scanf("%d", &delay);
        puts("Try out some keys! Hit q to quit, s to start over.");
```

LISTING 5-12. *(continued)*
Demonstration of using Int 16H Function 03H in C to modify the keyboard repeat rate and delay time.

LISTING 5-12. *continued*

```
            kbrepeat(rate, delay);

            do
                ch = getche();
            while (ch != 'q' && ch != 's');

            }
        while (ch != 'q');

        kbrepeat(10, 1);
}

void kbrepeat(int rate, int delay)
{
/* Sets the keyboard repeat rate and delay time */

/* rate% = 00H sets fastest rate
            1FH sets slowest rate
            Any other sets rate to 10 per second

   delay% = 0 sets delay time to 250 msec
            1 sets delay time to 500 msec
            2 sets delay time to 750 msec
            Any other sets delay time to 1000 msec */


    inregs.x.ax = 0x305;

    if (delay >= 0 && delay <= 2)
        inregs.h.bh = delay;
    else
        inregs.h.bh = 3;

    if (rate >= 0 && rate <= 0x1F)
        inregs.h.bl = rate;
    else
        inregs.h.bl = 0xC;

    int86(0x16, &inregs, &outregs);
}

void clearscreen(void)
{
    int x;

    for (x = 0; x < 25; x++)
        printf("\n");
}
```

Placing a Character in the Keyboard Buffer

Much of this chapter has dealt with explaining how to use various MS-DOS services to get characters out of the keyboard buffer. MS-DOS also has a service that lets you put a character in the buffer. This service can be useful when you want program-generated data to appear as if it were coming from the keyboard. For example, keyboard enhancers and other utilities can insert characters in the keyboard buffer so that application programs respond as if all of the characters were input by the user. Int 16H Function 05H actually places both a character and a scan code in the keyboard buffer, exactly mimicking the action of the keyboard itself. You can use this service only with PC/AT and enhanced keyboards.

The programs in Listings 5-13 and 5-14 demonstrate how to put characters in the keyboard buffer. Note that these programs perform no error checking. In a commercial program, you would need to check the carry flag after each call to Int 16H Function 05H to ensure that the character was put in the buffer successfully.

```
' Using Int 16H Function 05H to put characters in the
' keyboard buffer

' $INCLUDE: 'QB.BI'

DIM SHARED inRegs AS RegType, outRegs AS RegType


' Begin execution

CLS

' Use Int 21H Function 0CH to flush keyboard buffer without
' accepting input
inRegs.ax = &HC00
CALL INTERRUPT(&H21, inRegs, outRegs)

' Put the character and scan codes for "Hello!" in the buffer
inRegs.ax = &H500
inRegs.cx = (35 * &H100) + ASC("H")
CALL INTERRUPT(&H16, inRegs, outRegs)

inRegs.ax = &H500
```

LISTING 5-13.
Demonstration of using Int 16H Function 05H in Basic to put characters in the keyboard buffer.

(continued)

LISTING 5-13. *continued*

```
    inRegs.cx = (18 * &H100) + ASC("e")
    CALL INTERRUPT(&H16, inRegs, outRegs)

    inRegs.ax = &H500
    inRegs.cx = (38 * &H100) + ASC("l")
    CALL INTERRUPT(&H16, inRegs, outRegs)

    inRegs.ax = &H500
    inRegs.cx = (38 * &H100) + ASC("l")
    CALL INTERRUPT(&H16, inRegs, outRegs)

    inRegs.ax = &H500
    inRegs.cx = (24 * &H100) + ASC("o")
    CALL INTERRUPT(&H16, inRegs, outRegs)

    inRegs.ax = &H500
    inRegs.cx = (33 * &H100) + ASC("!")
    CALL INTERRUPT(&H16, inRegs, outRegs)

    ' Put the Enter character in the buffer
    inRegs.ax = &H500
    inRegs.cx = (&H1C * &H100) + 13
    CALL INTERRUPT(&H16, inRegs, outRegs)

    ' Read and display the contents of the keyboard buffer
    INPUT k$

    PRINT
    PRINT "The input taken from the keyboard buffer was: "; k$

    END
```

```
/* Using Int 16H Function 05H to put characters in the */
/* keyboard buffer */

#include <stdio.h>
#include <dos.h>

/* Declare the register unions */

union REGS inregs, outregs;

void clearscreen(void);
```

LISTING 5-14. *(continued)*
Demonstration of using Int 16H Function 05H in C to put characters in the input buffer.

LISTING 5-14. *continued*

```c
main()
{
    char buf[80];

    clearscreen();

    /* Use Int 21H Function 0CH to flush the keyboard buffer without */
    /* accepting input */
    inregs.x.ax = 0xC00;
    int86(0x21, &inregs, &outregs);

    /* Put the character and scan codes for "Hello!" in the buffer */
    inregs.x.ax = 0x500;
    inregs.h.ch = 35;
    inregs.h.cl = 'H';
    int86(0x16, &inregs, &outregs);

    inregs.x.ax = 0x500;
    inregs.h.ch = 18;
    inregs.h.cl = 'e';
    int86(0x16, &inregs, &outregs);

    inregs.x.ax = 0x500;
    inregs.h.ch = 38;
    inregs.h.cl = 'l';
    int86(0x16, &inregs, &outregs);

    inregs.x.ax = 0x500;
    inregs.h.ch = 38;
    inregs.h.cl = 'l';
    int86(0x16, &inregs, &outregs);

    inregs.x.ax = 0x500;
    inregs.h.ch = 24;
    inregs.h.cl = 'o';
    int86(0x16, &inregs, &outregs);

    inregs.x.ax = 0x500;
    inregs.h.ch = 33;
    inregs.h.cl = '!';
    int86(0x16, &inregs, &outregs);

    /* Put an Enter character in the buffer */
    inregs.x.ax = 0x500;
    inregs.h.ch = 0x1C;
    inregs.h.cl = 13;
    int86(0x16, &inregs, &outregs);
```

(continued)

LISTING 5-14. *continued*

```
    /* Read and display the contents of the keyboard buffer */
    gets(buf);
    printf("\n\nThe input taken from the keyboard buffer was %s", buf);
}

void clearscreen(void)
{
    int x;

    for (x = 0; x < 25; x++)
        printf("\n");
}
```

Keyboard Service Reference

The remainder of this chapter contains reference entries for the MS-DOS keyboard services. Each entry lets you know what the service does, what values to place in the CPU registers before calling the service, what values the service returns, and any important facts about the service.

Int 16H   Function 00H
Read character from keyboard

Action:	Reads a character and its scan code from the keyboard
Call with:	AH = 00H
Returns:	AH = keyboard scan code AL = ASCII character code
Notes:	This service waits for a character if none are in the keyboard buffer. It does not respond to Ctrl-C or Ctrl-Break and is not sensitive to input redirection.

Int 16H   Function 02H
Read keyboard flags

Action:	Returns the status of the keyboard flags

Call with:	AH = 02H
Returns:	AL = the keyboard flags
	Each bit in the flags byte corresponds to one of the Ctrl, Shift, Alt, or "lock" keys. A bit value of 1 means the key is pressed or turned on.

Bit number	Corresponding key
0	Right Shift
1	Left Shift
2	Ctrl
3	Alt
4	Scroll Lock
5	Num Lock
6	Caps Lock
7	Insert

Notes:	This service enables your program to distinguish between the right and left Shift keys.

Int 16H   Function 03H
Set keyboard repeat

Action:	Sets the rate and the delay time for the keyboard repeat
Call with:	AH = 03H AL = 05H BH = delay time (see "Notes") BL = repeat rate (see "Notes")
Returns:	Nothing
Notes:	The delay time is the amount of time a key must be pressed before it begins to repeat. Specify one of the four available delay values by placing one of the following values in the BH register:

BH	Delay (milliseconds)
00H	250
01H	500
02H	750
03H	1000

The Keyboard

Specify the repeat rate by placing a value in the BL register. The following values are available:

BL	Repeat rate (characters per second)	BL	Repeat rate (characters per second)
00H	30.0	10H	7.5
01H	26.7	11H	6.7
02H	24.0	12H	6.0
03H	21.8	13H	5.5
04H	20.0	14H	5.0
05H	18.5	15H	4.6
06H	17.1	16H	4.3
07H	16.0	17H	4.0
08H	15.0	18H	3.7
09H	13.3	19H	3.3
0AH	12.0	1AH	3.0
0BH	10.9	1BH	2.7
0CH	10.0	1CH	2.5
0DH	9.2	1DH	2.3
0EH	8.6	1EH	2.1
0FH	8.0	1FH	2.0

Int 16H Function 05H
Place character and scan code

Action: Places a character and a scan code in the keyboard buffer

Call with: AH = 05H
CH = keyboard scan code
CL = ASCII character code

Returns: On success:
AL = 00H
Carry flag = 0

On failure (buffer full):
AL = 01H
Carry flag = 1

Notes: The character and scan code combination that this service puts in the keyboard buffer is placed behind any other characters that are already waiting in the buffer.

If input has been redirected, the characters that this service places will not be detected by input services that read from the redirected *stdin*.

This service works only on PC/AT and enhanced keyboards.

Int 16H   Function 12H
Get enhanced keyboard flags

Action: Returns the status of the enhanced keyboard flags

Call with: AH = 12H

Returns: AX = the keyboard flags

Each bit in the flag word (2 bytes) corresponds to one of the Ctrl, Shift, Alt, or "lock" keys. A bit value of 1 means the key is pressed or turned on.

Bit number	Corresponding key
0	Right Shift
1	Left Shift
2	Either Ctrl
3	Either Alt
4	Scroll Lock
5	Num Lock
6	Caps Lock
7	Insert
8	Left Ctrl
9	Left Alt
10	Right Ctrl
11	Right Alt
12	Scroll Lock pressed
13	Num Lock pressed
14	Caps Lock pressed
15	SysRq pressed

Notes: This service can distinguish between the left and right Shift, Ctrl, and Alt keys. In addition to checking whether the Scroll Lock, Num Lock, and Caps Lock keys are turned on or off, this service can check whether any of these keys is currently being pressed.

Int 21H   Function 01H
Character input with echo

Action: Reads a character from *stdin* and echoes it to *stdout*; responds to Ctrl-C and Ctrl-Break; waits until a character is available

Call with: AH = 01H

Returns: AL = ASCII character code

Notes: If *stdin* is not redirected, this service responds to the Ctrl-C or Ctrl-Break key combination by issuing Int 23H. If *stdin* is redirected, it responds to Ctrl-C or Ctrl-Break by issuing Int 23H only if the break flag is set to 1.

Int 21H   Function 06H
Direct I/O without echo

Action: Reads a character from *stdin*; does not filter input, allowing input of all possible characters and control codes; ignores Ctrl-C and Ctrl-Break; does not wait if no character is available

Call with: AH = 06H
DL = FFH

Returns: If a character is available:
Zero flag = 0
AL   = ASCII character code

If no character is available:
Zero flag = 1

Notes: Use this service when your program needs to have access to all possible keystrokes without interference from MS-DOS. This service is the same as Int 21H Function 07H except that it does not wait for a character if one is not immediately available.

You cannot use this service in C because the REGS union does not provide access to the zero flag.

In addition to performing character input, this service can also perform character output, as explained in Chapter 7.

Int 21H   Function 07H
Direct character input without echo

Action:	Reads a character from *stdin*; does not filter input, allowing input of all possible characters and control codes; ignores Ctrl-C and Ctrl-Break; waits until a character is available
Call with:	AH = 07H
Returns:	AL = ASCII character code
Notes:	Use this service when your program needs to have access to all possible keystrokes without interference from MS-DOS. This service is the same as Int 21H Function 06H except that it will wait until a character is available.

Int 21H   Function 08H
Character input without echo

Action:	Reads a character from *stdin*; responds to Ctrl-C and Ctrl-Break; waits until a character is available
Call with:	AH = 08H
Returns:	AL = ASCII character code
Notes:	This service is the same as Int 21H Function 01H except that it does not echo the input.

Int 21H   Function 0AH
Read line from *stdin*

Action:	Reads a line of input from the standard input—up to and including a carriage return—and places it in a user-designated buffer
Call with:	AH = 0AH DS = segment of buffer DX = offset of buffer

The Keyboard

Returns:	Nothing
Notes:	The first byte of the user-designated buffer must contain a value *n* in the range 1 through 255 that specifies the maximum number of characters to be read. If *n* − *1* characters are input, subsequent characters are ignored until the user enters a carriage return.
	Upon return from this service, the second byte of the user-designated buffer contains the number of characters actually read (excluding the carriage return). Actual data begins at position 3 in the buffer.
	Extended keys (for example, function keys) are each stored in 2 bytes.
	If *stdin* is not redirected, this service responds to the Ctrl-C or Ctrl-Break key combination by issuing Int 23H. If *stdin* is redirected, it responds to Ctrl-C or Ctrl-Break by issuing Int 23H only if the break flag is set to 1.

Int 21H   Function 0BH
Check input status

Action:	Determines whether a character is available from the standard input device
Call with:	AH = 0BH
Returns:	AL = 00H if no character is available = FFH if at least one character is available
Notes:	This service is sensitive to input redirection.
	If a character is available when this service is called, the character is not read. The character remains available in the buffer for reading by Int 21H Function 08H or by another character input service.
	If *stdin* is not redirected, this service responds to the Ctrl-C or Ctrl-Break key combination by issuing Int 23H. If *stdin* is redirected, it responds to Ctrl-C or Ctrl-Break by issuing Int 23H only if the break flag is set to 1.

Int 21H   Function 0CH
Flush input buffer and then input a character

Action: Clears the input buffer and then calls one of the character input services

Call with: AH = 0CH
AL = number of input service to call (01H, 06H, 07H, or 08H)

Returns: AL = ASCII character code

Notes: This service is sensitive to redirection. Its response to Ctrl-C and Ctrl-Break depends on the input service specified. If a nonvalid input service number is passed in AL, the service simply flushes the input buffer and returns to the calling program.

Int 21H   Function 33H
Get or set break flag

Action: Queries or modifies the state of the MS-DOS break flag

Call with: To query break flag:
   AH = 33H
   AL = 00H

To set break flag:
   AH = 33H
   AL = 01H
   DL = 00H to turn break flag off
      = 01H to turn break flag on

Returns: DL = 00H if break flag is off
   = 01H if break flag is on

Notes: The break flag status affects all programs, and if your program changes the break flag's setting, that setting remains in effect even after your program terminates. For this reason, you should save the break flag's status before changing it and then restore the original break flag setting before terminating your program.

The Keyboard

CHAPTER 6

Mouse Programming

Using a mouse is becoming more and more common on PC systems. Although people often have opposing views of mice—some love 'em and some hate 'em—there's no doubt that a mouse can make certain operations much easier. The Microsoft Basic and C integrated programming environments make use of a mouse but offer no support for using a mouse in your programs. Fortunately, it's not too difficult to include mouse support in a Basic or C program, and this chapter shows you how.

Any program that interacts with the mouse does so by means of the *mouse driver*, which is a small program that comes with your mouse. It is loaded into memory, usually at boot time. Once loaded, the mouse driver monitors the activity of the mouse continually. This monitoring goes on in the background, so it has no effect on any program you might be running.

When a program wants to make use of the mouse, it queries the mouse driver by means of a software interrupt, Int 33H. A program uses various Int 33H services to obtain information about the mouse, such as position, movement, and button status. You call Int 33H in your programs in the same way you call MS-DOS services: Place the function number in a CPU register, and call the interrupt. Upon return, the service has placed the requested information in one or more CPU registers. The mouse driver handles all of the complex interactions with the mouse hardware. The mouse driver also handles the display and movement of the mouse cursor, or pointer, on your screen.

Strictly speaking, the mouse driver is not a part of MS-DOS. Rather, it's an installable device driver. Because it is such a common PC accessory, however, and the ability to program a mouse is so generally useful, I feel justified in including mouse programming in an MS-DOS programming book.

The de facto default for mouse drivers is the Microsoft mouse driver. Several other companies make mice, but they all come with a Microsoft-compatible driver and can be used with programs that support the Microsoft standard. Some of these non-Microsoft mice have extra features not found in the Microsoft mouse, such as a third button or higher resolution. When you use these mice with their Microsoft-compatible driver (which you must do in order for them to work with the programs in this chapter), these extra features are not available.

You can use a mouse in either text mode or graphics mode. Each addressable position on a screen in text mode can contain a character; each position in graphics mode can contain a pixel (the smallest element that can be displayed on the screen). Mouse programming differs slightly between these two modes, so I cover the modes separately in this chapter. Even if you're interested only in graphics mode programming, however, you need to read the section that explains text mode programming because some of the mouse services discussed there are also used in graphics mode. But before we get into text mode programming, let's take a quick look at the mouse services.

Mouse Services

The Int 33H mouse services can be divided into two categories. *Control services* modify the operation of the mouse but do not return any information to the calling program. *Inquiry services* return information about the mouse status to the program, usually in registers BX, CX, and DX and occasionally also in register AX. All services require that you place the function number in AX before calling Int 33H. Some services also require other parameters, which you must place in other registers.

Figure 6-1 summarizes a subset of the available mouse services. At the end of this chapter, you'll find a more detailed reference to these Int 33H services. The *Microsoft Mouse Programmer's Reference,* 2d edition (Microsoft Press, 1991), contains a complete discussion of all the mouse services. This book covers those services that you will use most often.

Service	Type	Action
00H	Control	Initialize mouse
01H	Control	Display mouse cursor
02H	Control	Hide mouse cursor
03H	Inquiry	Get button and position status
04H	Control	Set mouse cursor position
05H	Inquiry	Get button press information
06H	Inquiry	Get button release information
07H	Control	Set horizontal cursor movement limits
08H	Control	Set vertical cursor movement limits
09H	Control	Define graphics mode cursor shape
0AH	Control	Define text mode cursor shape
0BH	Inquiry	Get mouse movement information
0CH	Control	Define event handler
0DH	Control	Turn light-pen emulation on
0EH	Control	Turn light-pen emulation off
0FH	Control	Set ratio of mouse motion to screen pixels
10H	Control	Set cursor exclusion area

FIGURE 6-1. *(continued)*
Microsoft mouse Int 33H services.

FIGURE 6-1. *continued*

Service	Type	Action
13H	Control	Set double-speed threshold
15H	Inquiry	Get buffer size for mouse driver state
16H	Inquiry	Save mouse driver state
17H	Control	Restore mouse driver state
1AH	Control	Set mouse sensitivity
1BH	Inquiry	Get mouse sensitivity
1CH	Control	Set mouse interrupt rate
1DH	Control	Select display page for mouse cursor
1EH	Inquiry	Get display page for mouse cursor
21H	Control	Reset mouse driver
2AH	Inquiry	Get cursor hot spot

Text Mode Mouse Programming

When your video system is in text mode, the screen is divided into a matrix of character cells. You don't actually see these cells, of course, but they define the positions at which text and other characters can be displayed. They also define the movement of the mouse cursor: The cursor can be positioned at one cell or at its neighbor cell, but it cannot be between cells. As you move the mouse, the cursor "jumps" from cell to cell. (Remember, the mouse driver handles moving the cursor in response to mouse movement.)

Mouse cursor position

Even though the mouse cursor is limited to jumping between character cells, the mouse driver keeps track of its position in a grid of pixels called the *virtual screen*. No matter what display hardware you have or what video mode you are in, most virtual screens have 640 pixels horizontally and 200 pixels vertically. In fact, all standard text modes use a 640x200 virtual screen. The upper left corner of the screen has pixel coordinates (0, 0), and the lower right corner has pixel coordinates (639, 199).

When you query the mouse driver about the mouse cursor's position, therefore, its answer is in virtual screen pixels. In text mode, you are interested in which character cell the cursor is positioned on. You must translate the cursor's location from pixels to character cells. The standard text mode screen has 80 columns and 25 rows of character cells. Because the typical screen's pixel dimensions are 640 by 200, a quick division reveals that the size of each character cell is 8 pixels by 8 pixels. To convert from pixels to rows and columns, use the following formulas, in which the result of the division operation is truncated to return an integer:

text column = INT ((horizontal pixel) / 8) + 1
text row = INT ((vertical pixel) / 8) + 1

Displaying and hiding the mouse cursor

Even when it is not displayed, the mouse cursor has a position on the screen, and the driver keeps track of that position. The mouse driver maintains a counter that determines whether the mouse cursor is displayed. If the counter has a value of 0, the cursor is displayed; if it has a value less than 0, the cursor is hidden. Int 33H Functions 00H and 21H initialize this counter to –1 when they reset the values maintained by the mouse driver.

Calls to Int 33H Function 01H, which shows the mouse cursor, increment the counter if it has a value less than 0 and have no effect if it has a value of 0. Calls to Int 33H Function 02H, which hides the mouse cursor, always decrement the counter by 1. If you call Int 33H Function 02H two or more times without an intervening call to Int 33H Function 01H, the counter has a value of –2 or even lower. If this situation occurs, a single call to Int 33H Function 01H does not display the cursor because the counter still has a value less than 0.

Mouse drivers prior to version 7.02, which are still used by many people, do not offer a way to read the state of the display counter. Therefore, the program has no direct way to tell at any moment whether the cursor is displayed or hidden. To be sure that the cursor is displayed when needed, your program can take either of two approaches:

- Maintain a display flag that indicates whether the cursor is displayed. When you want to hide the cursor, call Int 33H Function 02H only if this flag indicates that the cursor is displayed. Doing so prevents the display counter from having a value less than –1.

- Call Int 33H Function 01H multiple times when you want to display the cursor. Doing so ensures that the display counter is incremented sufficiently to reach 0. Because the counter cannot be incremented above 0, a single call to Int 33H Function 02H is always sufficient to hide the cursor.

The programs later in this chapter demonstrate both these approaches. Using the first method—maintaining a display flag—can create one problem: Under certain circumstances, the display counter might be decremented and the cursor turned off without your program knowing it. (For example, Int 33H Function 10H decrements the counter.) If this problem crops up, the program cursor display flag does not reflect the state of the cursor accurately.

Versions 7.02 and later of the mouse driver provide the ability to read the state of the mouse driver display counter. This is done with Int 33H Function 2AH, which returns several items of information about the mouse status including the display counter state. See the reference entry for this service at the end of the chapter for further information.

To determine whether your mouse driver supports Int 33H Function 2AH, check the version number that the device driver displays when it is installed at boot time. Note, however, that if you're writing programs for distribution, you cannot be sure what mouse driver will be in use, and you should therefore maintain a display flag in your program rather than depending on Int 33H Function 2AH.

Text mode mouse cursor types

When programming a mouse in text mode, keep in mind that the mouse can control two different types of cursors. The *hardware cursor* is displayed by the video adapter, and the *software cursor* is displayed by the mouse driver. When you use a mouse in either the Basic or the C integrated programming environment, you see both cursors. The hardware cursor is the blinking underline or block cursor that moves in response to the arrow keys and marks the location in your source code where editing operations will occur. The software cursor is the block cursor that moves when you move the mouse.

When the mouse driver is initialized, the default cursor type for the mouse is the software cursor. To switch to the hardware cursor, call Int 33H Function 0AH after placing 01H in the BX register. When the mouse uses the hardware cursor, only the one cursor is visible on the screen, and that cursor moves in response to mouse movement. It also moves in response to program commands that move the cursor.

The hardware cursor normally marks the screen location where text output will appear (for example, with a PRINT statement or the *printf()* function). When the mouse controls the hardware cursor position, however, moving the hardware cursor using the mouse does not move the text output position. Rather, text appears at the place where the cursor was located when the mouse driver first took control of it.

If you want to control the text display position using the mouse, follow these steps, which are the same whether the mouse is controlling the hardware cursor or the software cursor:

1. Move the mouse cursor to the position on the screen for text output.

2. Determine the location of the mouse cursor by calling Int 33H Function 03H, 05H, or 06H.

3. Move the text output location to the mouse cursor location. In Basic, you do so using the LOCATE statement. C has no equivalent function, so you must use an MS-DOS screen service—several programs in Chapter 5 demonstrated this approach using the *locate()* function. Chapter 7 explains more about using MS-DOS screen services.

Most applications use the software cursor. Using this cursor lets you have two cursors visible: the hardware cursor to mark the text entry position and the software cursor for making menu selections and performing other tasks (as in the Basic and C integrated programming environments). If you've switched to a hardware cursor, you can go back to a software cursor by calling Int 33H Function 0AH after placing 0H in the BX register.

Mouse cursor appearance

The appearance of the mouse cursor—hardware or software—is controlled by the values in registers CX and DX when you call Int 33H Function 0AH. Thus, you specify both the type and the appearance of the mouse cursor by calling one service.

When you use the hardware cursor, you can control only the size and position of the rectangular cursor within the character cell. You do this by specifying the start and stop scan lines that the mouse cursor uses. A character cell contains a certain number of scan lines: The top scan line is number 0, and the bottom scan line is number 7 for all graphics display adapters. For monochrome text-only display adapters, the bottom scan line is number 13. Before you call Int 33H Function 0AH to specify a hardware cursor, place 01H in the BX register and place the values for the top and bottom cursor scan lines in CX and DX, respectively. For example, on graphics adapters, placing 6 in CX and 7 in DX produces an underline cursor, and placing 0 in CX and 7 in DX produces a full-block cursor.

You have much more control over the appearance of a software cursor. When you call Int 33H Function 0AH to specify a software cursor, you pass the *cursor mask* in DX and the *screen mask* in CX. The cursor mask determines the appearance of the cursor itself, and the screen mask determines the appearance of characters on the screen when the cursor covers them.

How the cursor and screen masks operate need not concern us here. One of the following sets of cursor and screen masks handles most situations perfectly well:

- The cursor can be a user-specified character that covers the character cell on which it's positioned. (The underlying character, if any, does not show through.) To get these characteristics, call Int 33H Function 0AH with 0000H in CX and 00nnH in DX, where nn is the desired character's ASCII code in hexadecimal notation. For example, for a dollar sign cursor (great for financial programs!), place 0024H in DX.

- The cursor can be a rectangle that allows any underlying character to show through in reverse video. For these characteristics, call Int 33H Function 0AH with 77FFH in CX and 7700H in DX.

Mouse movement

At times, you might need information about mouse movement, as distinct from information about the mouse cursor. Mouse movement refers to the physical movement of the mouse itself and is measured in *mickeys*. One mickey equals approximately ½₀₀ inch. You get mouse movement information by calling Int 33H Function 0BH, which returns the amount of horizontal movement in the CX register and the amount of vertical movement in DX. The mickey values returned reflect the total movement of the mouse since the last call to this service or since the mouse was initialized. These values are always in the range –32,768 through 32,767. Positive values indicate movement down or to the right, and negative values indicate movement up or to the left.

Restricting mouse cursor movement

You can restrict mouse cursor movement in two ways. The first is a true restriction. By calling Int 33H Functions 07H and 08H, which restrict the horizontal and vertical cursor positions respectively, you can define a rectangular screen region outside of which the cursor will not move. This capability can be quite useful—for example, you can restrict the cursor to an active menu region.

The second method is not a true restriction. By calling Int 33H Function 10H, you can define a mouse cursor exclusion area. The mouse cursor is not actually prevented from going inside the defined area, but if the cursor enters the exclusion area, it is hidden exactly as if Int 33H Function 02H had been called. When you want to display the cursor again, simply call Int 33H Function 01H.

User-defined mouse event handler

The mouse inquiry services—those that return information about the mouse's status—are *polling* services. The program must specifically call the service to ask, or poll, the mouse driver for information. In the absence of a program request for information from the mouse driver, the program remains unaware of mouse activity.

The service that can create an exception to this rule is Int 33H Function 0CH, which defines a *mouse event handler*. A mouse event handler is a section of program code that is executed whenever a specified mouse event occurs. When you call Int 33H Function 0CH, you pass to it the address of the mouse event handler code and an integer that specifies the mouse events to be trapped. You can trap mouse movement and the pressing or releasing of either button.

After you install a mouse event handler by calling Int 33H Function 0CH, your program can then go about its business without having to inquire about the mouse's status. As soon as the mouse driver detects the specified mouse event, it transfers execution to the mouse event handler. The mouse driver then passes to the mouse event handler information about the current status of the mouse: its button status, its position, and the event that caused the call. This arrangement allows your program to respond to the mouse without having to poll the mouse driver constantly.

The capabilities of the mouse event handler are limited. Most important, it cannot perform any I/O, MS-DOS, or BIOS calls. In most situations, the purpose of the mouse event handler is to save a record of the mouse event to which the program can respond later. If you define a mouse event handler for your program, be sure to call Int 33H Function 00H to reset the mouse before the program ends so that the mouse driver will no longer call the event handler.

Defining a mouse event handler is, unfortunately, difficult in Basic. Although Basic uses code addresses internally, they are not accessible to the programmer, as they are in C. Thus, you cannnot obtain the address of a mouse event handler written in Basic to pass to the mouse driver. You can, however, write a mouse event handler in assembly language and load it into your Basic program—but that is beyond the scope of this book.

Text mode demonstration programs

The programs in Listings 6-1 and 6-2 demonstrate mouse programming in text mode. Each program declares a data structure that holds information about the mouse. When a mouse inquiry service is called, it loads into the data structure the information that the mouse driver returns. Each program reads information from the data structure and acts accordingly.

Both programs use structured programming, isolating each mouse driver call into a subprogram (Basic) or a function (C). You can use these subprograms and functions in your own programs—place them in a separate library for easy access. Note that the demonstration programs do not contain subprograms and functions for all of the mouse services this chapter discusses but only for the more frequently used ones. Furthermore, the demonstration parts of the programs do not use all of the subprograms and functions in the listings. By examining the way in which the programs call and use mouse services, you should be able to write code quickly for any other mouse service that your own programs might need.

The demonstration programs include two useful routines. The *ClearButtons* routine sets all of the mouse driver's button press and release counters to 0. Call *ClearButtons* when you want to ensure that your program does not respond to an "old" button press or release. The *WaitClick* routine allows your program to pause until the user presses a specified mouse button. You pass to *WaitClick* a constant that specifies which button to wait for (left, right, either, or both). *WaitClick* then displays a message on the screen and loops until the specified button is pressed and released.

```
DEFINT A-Z

DECLARE SUB ClearButtons ()
DECLARE SUB MsLightPenOn ()
DECLARE SUB MsLightPenOff ()
DECLARE SUB MsMovement ()
DECLARE SUB MsBtnPress (button%)
DECLARE SUB MsBtnRelease (button%)
DECLARE SUB MsSetTextCrsr (cursorType%, scan1%, scan2%)
DECLARE SUB MsSetHRange (leftCol%, rightCol%)
DECLARE SUB MsSetVRange (upperRow%, lowerRow%)
DECLARE SUB MsGetStatus ()
DECLARE SUB MsShowCrsr ()
DECLARE SUB MsHideCrsr ()
DECLARE SUB MsInit ()
DECLARE SUB MsMoveCrsr (row%, col%)
DECLARE SUB Mouse (a%, b%, c%, d%)
DECLARE SUB MsExclude (topLeftx%, topLefty%, BtmRtx%, BtmRty%)
DECLARE SUB WaitClick (button%)

' $INCLUDE: 'QB.BI'

CONST YES = 1, NO = 0
```

LISTING 6-1. *(continued)*
Demonstration of using text mode mouse services in Basic.

LISTING 6-1. *continued*

```
' Constants for the mouse buttons
CONST LEFT = 0, RIGHT = 1, BOTH = 2, EITHER = 3

' Constants for cursor types
CONST HARDCURSOR = 1, SOFTCURSOR = 0

' Declare a data type to hold mouse information
TYPE MouseData
    exists AS INTEGER           ' Greater than 0 if mouse exists
    cursorDisplay AS INTEGER    ' 1 if cursor displayed, 0 if hidden
    btnStatus AS INTEGER        ' Current button status (up or down)
    btnClicks AS INTEGER        ' Times button has been clicked
    column AS INTEGER           ' Mouse cursor column position
    row AS INTEGER              ' Mouse cursor row position
    hMovement AS INTEGER        ' Horizontal mouse movement
    vMovement AS INTEGER        ' Vertical mouse movement
END TYPE

DIM rodent AS MouseData


' Begin execution

CLS

' See whether mouse is installed
MsInit

IF rodent.exists THEN
    PRINT "A Microsoft-compatible mouse is installed."
    CALL WaitClick(EITHER)
    CLS
ELSE
    PRINT "The program did not detect a mouse."
    PRINT "A mouse and a Microsoft-compatible driver"
    PRINT "must be installed to run this program."
    PRINT
    PRINT "Press any key to exit."
    WHILE INKEY$ = "": WEND
    END
END IF

' Move the mouse cursor to the top center of the screen and display it
CALL MsMoveCrsr(1 * 8, 40 * 8)
MsShowCrsr

LOCATE 1, 1
PRINT "This is the mouse cursor movement demonstration."
PRINT "Click the left button to hide the cursor."
PRINT "Click the right button to display the cursor again."
PRINT "Click both buttons to continue."
```

(continued)

LISTING 6-1. *continued*

```
    DO
        MsGetStatus

        ' Display the mouse cursor's current row and column position
        LOCATE 6, 1
        column% = (rodent.column / 8) + 1
        row% = (rodent.row / 8) + 1
        PRINT "Column ="; column%, "Row ="; row%

        ' rodent.btnStatus = 0 if no button was pressed
        '                  = 1 if the left button was pressed
        '                  = 2 if the right button was pressed
        '                  = 3 if both buttons were pressed

        SELECT CASE rodent.btnStatus
            CASE 1
                MsHideCrsr
            CASE 2
                MsShowCrsr
            CASE 3
                EXIT DO
        END SELECT
    LOOP

    ' Hide the mouse cursor
    MsHideCrsr

    CLS
    PRINT "Now using the hardware cursor with scan lines 6 and 7."

    ' Activate the hardware cursor, and be sure it's displayed
    CALL MsSetTextCrsr(HARDCURSOR, 6, 7)
    MsShowCrsr
    CALL WaitClick(EITHER)

    ' Modify hardware cursor to use scan lines 0 through 7
    CLS
    CALL MsSetTextCrsr(HARDCURSOR, 0, 7)
    MsShowCrsr

    PRINT "Now using the hardware cursor with scan lines 0 through 7."
    CALL WaitClick(EITHER)

    ' Demonstrate the software cursor with a program-defined
    ' character (dollar sign on black background)
    CLS

    PRINT "Demonstrating a user-defined software cursor."
    CALL MsSetTextCrsr(SOFTCURSOR, 0, &H724)
    CALL WaitClick(EITHER)
```

(continued)

LISTING 6-1. *continued*

```
' Return to a rectangular software cursor
CALL MsSetTextCrsr(SOFTCURSOR, &H77FF, &H7700)

' Restrict the mouse cursor movement to a defined region of the screen
CLS

PRINT "Mouse cursor movement is now restricted to a"
PRINT "region in the center of the screen."
PRINT "Click the left button to continue."

ClearButtons
CALL MsSetHRange(25 * 8, 55 * 8)
CALL MsSetVRange(10 * 8, 15 * 8)

DO
    CALL MsBtnRelease(LEFT)
    MsGetStatus

    ' Display the mouse cursor's current row and column position
    LOCATE 6, 1
    column% = rodent.column / 8
    row% = rodent.row / 8
    PRINT "Column ="; column%, "Row ="; row%
LOOP UNTIL rodent.btnClicks > 0

' Demonstrate text entry
CLS
PRINT "Move the mouse cursor to the desired text entry location,"
PRINT "and click the left button."
PRINT "Type some text, and press Enter."
PRINT "Click the right button to continue."

' Display the mouse cursor and clear any waiting button clicks
MsShowCrsr
ClearButtons

' Restrict the mouse cursor movement to the lower 18 rows and
' left 60 columns so that input will not overwrite information
' on the screen and will not try to extend past the right edge
CALL MsSetVRange(6 * 8, 24 * 8)
CALL MsSetHRange(0, 60 * 8)

DO
    CALL MsBtnRelease(LEFT)
    IF rodent.btnClicks > 0 THEN
        col% = rodent.column / 8
        row% = rodent.row / 8
        LOCATE row% + 1, col% + 2
```

(continued)

LISTING 6-1. *continued*

```
            INPUT ": ", temp$
            MsShowCrsr
            ClearButtons
        END IF
        CALL MsBtnRelease(RIGHT)
LOOP UNTIL rodent.btnClicks > 0

' Cancel the movement restriction
CALL MsSetVRange(0 * 8, 24 * 8)
CALL MsSetHRange(0, 79 * 8)

' Demonstrate a mouse cursor exclusion area
CLS
PRINT "A cursor exclusion area is now defined in the lower right"
PRINT "corner of the screen. If you move the cursor there,"
PRINT "it will be hidden."
PRINT "Click both buttons to continue."

CALL MsMoveCrsr(1 * 8, 1 * 8)
CALL MsExclude(400, 150, 639, 199)

DO
    MsGetStatus

    ' Display the mouse cursor's current row and column position
    LOCATE 5, 1
    col% = (rodent.column / 8) + 1
    row% = (rodent.row / 8) + 1
    PRINT "Column ="; col%, "Row ="; row%
    IF rodent.btnStatus = 3 THEN EXIT DO
LOOP

' Reset the mouse to its default state
MsInit

CLS
PRINT "This ends the text mode mouse demonstration program."
END

' *******************************
' These are the mouse subprograms
' *******************************

SUB ClearButtons
    ' Resets the mouse driver's internal press and release
    ' counters to 0 for both buttons

    CALL Mouse(&H5, LEFT, 0, 0)
    CALL Mouse(&H5, RIGHT, 0, 0)
```

(continued)

LISTING 6-1. *continued*

```
        CALL Mouse(&H6, LEFT, 0, 0)
        CALL Mouse(&H6, RIGHT, 0, 0)
END SUB     ' End of ClearButtons

SUB Mouse (a, b, c, d)
    ' Places parameters in CPU registers and calls Int 33H

    DIM inRegs AS RegType, outRegs AS RegType

    ' Place values in CPU registers
    inRegs.ax = a
    inRegs.bx = b
    inRegs.cx = c
    inRegs.dx = d

    ' Call the mouse service
    CALL INTERRUPT(&H33, inRegs, outRegs)

    ' Get values from CPU registers
    a = outRegs.ax
    b = outRegs.bx
    c = outRegs.cx
    d = outRegs.dx
END SUB     ' End of Mouse

SUB MsBtnPress (button)
    SHARED rodent AS MouseData

    a = &H5
    b = button
    c = 0
    d = 0

    ' Call Int 33H Function 05H to get button press information
    CALL Mouse(a, b, c, d)

    rodent.btnStatus = a
    rodent.btnClicks = b
    rodent.column = c
    rodent.row = d
END SUB     ' End of MsBtnPress

SUB MsBtnRelease (button)
    SHARED rodent AS MouseData

    a = &H6
    b = button
    c = 0
    d = 0

    ' Call Int 33H Function 06H to get button release information
    CALL Mouse(a, b, c, d)
```

(continued)

LISTING 6-1. *continued*

```
        rodent.btnStatus = a
        rodent.btnClicks = b
        rodent.column = c
        rodent.row = d
END SUB    ' End of MsBtnRelease

SUB MsExclude (topLeftx, topLefty, BtmRtx, BtmRty)
    ' Defines a mouse cursor exclusion area for which the corners
    ' are specified in pixels.
    ' This subprogram doesn't use the Mouse subprogram because
    ' it needs to access the SI and DI registers.

    DIM inRegs AS RegType, outRegs AS RegType

        inRegs.ax = &H10
        inRegs.cx = topLeftx
        inRegs.dx = topLefty
        inRegs.si = BtmRtx
        inRegs.di = BtmRty

    ' Call Int 33H Function 10H to set cursor exclusion area
    CALL INTERRUPT(&H33, inRegs, outRegs)
END SUB    ' End of MsExclude

SUB MsGetStatus
    ' Returns mouse status at the time of the call.
    ' rodent.column and rodent.row give mouse cursor position.
    ' rodent.btnStatus = 0 if no button was pressed
    '                  = 1 if left button was pressed
    '                  = 2 if right button was pressed
    '                  = 3 if both buttons were pressed

    SHARED rodent AS MouseData

    a = &H3

    ' Call Int 33H Function 03H to get mouse status
    CALL Mouse(a, b, c, d)

        rodent.btnStatus = b
        rodent.column = c
        rodent.row = d
END SUB    ' End of MsGetStatus

SUB MsHideCrsr
    ' Hides the mouse cursor if it is displayed

    SHARED rodent AS MouseData
```

(continued)

LISTING 6-1. *continued*

```
        IF rodent.cursorDisplay = YES THEN
            CALL Mouse(&H2, 0, 0, 0)
            rodent.cursorDisplay = NO
        END IF
END SUB     ' End of MsHideCrsr

SUB MsInit
    ' If a mouse is installed, initializes mouse and
    ' sets rodent.exists to 1. If no mouse is installed,
    ' sets rodent.exists to 0

    SHARED rodent AS MouseData

    a = &H0

    CALL Mouse(a, 0, 0, 0)
    rodent.exists = a
END SUB     ' End of MsInit

SUB MsLightPenOff
    ' Turns light-pen emulation off

    CALL Mouse(&HE, 0, 0, 0)
END SUB     ' End of MsLightPenOff

SUB MsLightPenOn
    ' Turns light-pen emulation on (the default when the
    ' mouse is initialized)

    CALL Mouse(&HD, 0, 0, 0)
END SUB     ' End of MsLightPenOn

SUB MsMoveCrsr (row, col)
    ' Moves the mouse cursor to the screen position specified
    ' by the parameters

    CALL Mouse(&H4, 0, col, row)
END SUB     ' End of MsMoveCrsr

SUB MsMovement
    ' Reports the net movement of the mouse (not the mouse cursor)
    ' since the last call to this subprogram

    SHARED rodent AS MouseData

    CALL Mouse(&HB, b, c, d)
    rodent.hMovement = c
    rodent.vMovement = d
END SUB     ' End of MsMovement
```

(continued)

LISTING 6-1. *continued*

```
SUB MsSetHRange (leftCol, rightCol)
    ' Restricts horizontal mouse cursor movement to the screen
    ' region between leftcol and rightcol. If the cursor is
    ' outside this range, it is moved inside

    CALL Mouse(&H7, 0, leftCol, rightCol)
END SUB    ' End of MsSetHRange

SUB MsSetTextCrsr (cursorType, scan1, scan2)
    ' Sets the text cursor type.
    ' If cursorType = 0, the software cursor is set, and scan1 and
    ' scan2 specify the screen and cursor masks.
    ' If cursorType = 1, the hardware cursor is set, and scan1 and
    ' scan2 specify the start and stop scan lines for the cursor.

    CALL Mouse(&HA, cursorType, scan1, scan2)
END SUB

SUB MsSetVRange (upperRow, lowerRow)
    ' Restricts vertical mouse cursor movement to the screen
    ' region between upperRow and lowerRow. If the cursor is
    ' outside this range, it is moved inside

    CALL Mouse(&H8, 0, upperRow, lowerRow)
END SUB    ' End of MsSetVRange

SUB MsShowCrsr
    SHARED rodent AS MouseData

    ' Call Int 33H Function 01H five times to display the
    ' cursor and increment the display counter
    FOR i% = 1 TO 5
        CALL Mouse(&H1, 0, 0, 0)
    NEXT i%

    rodent.cursorDisplay = YES
END SUB    ' End of MsShowCrsr

SUB WaitClick (button)
    ' Pauses until the specified mouse button is pressed and released
    ' If button = 0, left button
    ' If button = 1, right button
    ' If button = 2, both buttons
    ' If button = 3, either button

    SHARED rodent AS MouseData
    DIM whichbtn(3) AS STRING
```

(continued)

LISTING 6-1. *continued*

```
    whichbtn(0) = "the left button"
    whichbtn(1) = "the right button"
    whichbtn(2) = "both buttons"
    whichbtn(3) = "any button"

    rodent.btnStatus = 0

    PRINT "Click "; whichbtn(button); " to continue."

    DO
        MsGetStatus
    LOOP UNTIL rodent.btnStatus = 0

    IF button < 3 THEN
        DO
            MsGetStatus
        LOOP UNTIL rodent.btnStatus = (button + 1)
    ELSE
        DO
            MsGetStatus
        LOOP UNTIL rodent.btnStatus > 0
    END IF

    ' Wait for button release
    DO
        MsGetStatus
    LOOP UNTIL rodent.btnStatus = 0
END SUB     ' End of WaitClick
```

```c
/* Demonstration of using text mode mouse services */

#include <stdio.h>
#include <dos.h>

/* Define a macro to simplify calling Int 33H */
#define MouseCall int86(0x33, &inregs, &outregs)

/* Constants for button and cursor definitions */
#define LEFT 0
#define RIGHT 1
#define BOTH 2
#define EITHER 3
#define SOFTCURSOR 0
#define HARDCURSOR 1
```

LISTING 6-2. *(continued)*
Demonstration of using text mode mouse services in C.

LISTING 6-2. *continued*

```c
/* Declare the register unions */
union REGS inregs, outregs;

/* Declare a structure to hold mouse information */
struct mousedata {
    int exists;              /* Greater than 0 if mouse exists */
    int cursor_display;      /* 1 if cursor displayed, 0 if hidden */
    int btnstatus;           /* Current button status (up or down) */
    int btnclicks;           /* Times button has been clicked */
    int column;              /* Mouse cursor column position */
    int row;                 /* Mouse cursor row position */
    int hmovement;           /* Horizontal mouse movement */
    int vmovement;           /* Vertical mouse movement */
} rodent;

/* Function prototypes */
void clearscreen(void);
void clearbuttons(void);
int ms_btnpress(int button);
void ms_exclude(int topleftx, int toplefty, int btmrtx, int btmrty);
int ms_getstatus(void);
void ms_hidecrsr(void);
int ms_init(void);
void ms_lightpenoff(void);
void ms_lightpenon(void);
void ms_movecrsr(int row, int col);
void ms_movement(void);
void ms_sethrange(int leftcol, int rightcol);
void ms_setvrange(int upperrow, int lowerrow);
void ms_settextcrsr(int cursortype, int scan1, int scan2);
void ms_showcrsr(void);
void waitclick(int button);
void locate(char x, char y);

main()
{
    int flag;
    char temp[80];
    char col, row;

    /* Clear the screen, and initialize the mouse */
    ms_init();
    clearscreen();

    /* See whether a mouse was detected */
    if (rodent.exists)
        {
        locate(1, 1);
        puts("A Microsoft-compatible mouse is installed.");
```

(continued)

LISTING 6-2. *continued*

```c
        waitclick(EITHER);
        clearscreen();
        }
    else
        {
        locate(1, 1);
        puts("The program did not detect a mouse.");
        puts("A mouse and a Microsoft-compatible driver");
        puts("must be installed to run this program.\n");
        puts("Press any key to exit");
        getch();
        exit();
        }

    /* Move the mouse cursor to the top center of the screen, */
    /* and display it */
    clearscreen();
    ms_movecrsr(1 * 8, 40 * 8);
    ms_showcrsr();

    locate(1, 1);
    puts("This is the mouse cursor movement demonstration.");
    puts("Click the left button to hide the cursor.");
    puts("Click the right button to display the cursor again.");
    puts("Click both buttons to continue.");

    flag = 1;
    clearbuttons();

    do
        {
        ms_getstatus();

        /* Display the mouse cursor's current row and column position */
        locate(1, 6);
        printf("Column = %d ", (rodent.column / 8 + 1));
        printf("Row = %d ", (rodent.row / 8) + 1);

        /* rodent.btnstatus = 0 if no button was pressed
                           = 1 if the left button was pressed
                           = 2 if the right button was pressed
                           = 3 if both buttons were pressed */

        switch (rodent.btnstatus)
            {
            case 1:
                ms_hidecrsr();
                break;
```

(continued)

LISTING 6-2. *continued*

```
            case 2:
                ms_showcrsr();
                break;
            case 3:
                flag = 0;
                ms_movecrsr(8, 8);
                ms_showcrsr();
                break;
        }
    } while (flag);

/* Clear the screen, and hide the cursor */
clearscreen();
ms_hidecrsr();

/* Modify the hardware cursor to use scan lines 0 through 7 */
ms_settextcrsr(HARDCURSOR, 0, 7);
ms_showcrsr();

locate(1, 1);
puts("Now using the hardware cursor with scan lines 0 through 7.");
waitclick(EITHER);

clearscreen();

/* Switch to a hardware cursor with scan lines 6 and 7 */
locate(1, 1);
ms_settextcrsr(HARDCURSOR, 6, 7);
ms_showcrsr();

locate(1, 1);
puts("Now using the hardware cursor with scan lines 6 and 7.");
waitclick(EITHER);

clearscreen();

/* Demonstrate the software cursor with a program-defined */
/* character (dollar sign on black background) */
ms_settextcrsr(SOFTCURSOR, 0, 0x724);
ms_showcrsr();

locate(1, 1);
puts("Demonstrating a user-defined software cursor.");
waitclick(EITHER);

/* Return to a rectangular software cursor */
ms_settextcrsr(SOFTCURSOR, 0x77FF, 0x7700);
```

(continued)

LISTING 6-2. *continued*

```c
/* Restrict the mouse cursor movement to the center of the screen */
ms_hidecrsr();
clearscreen();

locate(1, 1);
puts("The mouse cursor is now restricted to a");
puts("region in the center of the screen.");
puts("Click the left button to continue.");

clearbuttons();
ms_sethrange(25 * 8, 55 * 8);
ms_setvrange(10 * 8, 15 * 8);
ms_showcrsr();

do
    {
    ms_btnrelease(LEFT);
    ms_getstatus();

    /* Display the mouse cursor's current row and column position */
    locate(1, 6);
    printf("Column = %d ", (rodent.column / 8 + 1));
    printf("Row = %d", (rodent.row / 8 + 1));
    } while (rodent.btnclicks <= 0);

/* Demonstrate text entry */
ms_hidecrsr();
clearscreen();

locate(1, 1);
puts("Move the mouse cursor to the desired text entry");
puts("location and click the left button.");
puts("Type some text, and press Enter.");
puts("Click the right button to continue.");

/* Display the mouse cursor, and clear any waiting button clicks */
ms_showcrsr();
clearbuttons();

/* Restrict the mouse cursor movement to the lower 18 rows and */
/* left 60 columns so that input will not overwrite information */
/* on the screen and will not try to extend past the right edge */
ms_setvrange(6 * 8, 24 * 8);
ms_sethrange(0, 60 * 8);

do
    {
    ms_btnrelease(LEFT);
```

(continued)

LISTING 6-2. *continued*

```c
            if (rodent.btnclicks > 0)
                {
                col = (rodent.column / 8) + 2;
                row = (rodent.row / 8) + 1;
                locate(col, row);
                printf(": ");
                gets(temp);
                ms_showcrsr();
                clearbuttons();
                }

        ms_btnrelease(RIGHT);
        } while (rodent.btnclicks <= 0);

/* Cancel the movement restriction */
ms_setvrange(0, 24 * 8);
ms_sethrange(0, 79 * 8);

/* Demonstrate a mouse cursor exclusion area */
ms_hidecrsr();
clearscreen();

locate(1, 1);
ms_showcrsr();
ms_exclude(400, 150, 639, 199);

puts("A cursor exclusion area is defined in the lower right");
puts("corner of the screen. If you move the mouse cursor there,");
puts("it will be hidden.");
puts("Click both buttons to continue.");

ms_movecrsr(8, 8);

do
    {
    ms_getstatus();

    /* Display the cursor's current row and column position */
    locate(1, 5);
    printf("Column = %d   ", (rodent.column / 8 + 1));
    printf("Row = %d", (rodent.row / 8 + 1));
    } while (rodent.btnstatus != 3);

/* Reset the mouse to its default state */
ms_init();
clearscreen();
locate(1, 1);
puts("End of text mode mouse demonstration.");

}   /* End of main() */
```

(continued)

LISTING 6-2. *continued*

```c
/************************************/
/* These are the mouse functions    */
/************************************/

void clearbuttons(void)
{
    /* Resets the mouse driver's internal press and release */
    /* counters to 0 for both buttons */

    inregs.x.ax = 0x05;
    inregs.x.bx = LEFT;
    MouseCall;

    inregs.x.ax = 0x05;
    inregs.x.bx = RIGHT;
    MouseCall;

    inregs.x.ax = 0x06;
    inregs.x.bx = LEFT;
    MouseCall;

    inregs.x.ax = 0x06;
    inregs.x.bx = RIGHT;
    MouseCall;
}   /* End of clearbuttons() */

int ms_btnpress(int button)
{
    /* Returns button press information about the specified button */

    inregs.x.ax = 0x05;
    inregs.x.bx = button;

    MouseCall;

    rodent.btnstatus = outregs.x.ax;
    rodent.btnclicks = outregs.x.bx;
    rodent.column = outregs.x.cx;
    rodent.row = outregs.x.dx;

    return outregs.x.bx;
}   /* End of ms_btnpress() */

int ms_btnrelease(int button)
{
    /* Returns button release information about the specified button */

    inregs.x.ax = 0x06;
    inregs.x.bx = button;
```

(continued)

LISTING 6-2. *continued*

```c
    MouseCall;

    rodent.btnstatus = outregs.x.ax;
    rodent.btnclicks = outregs.x.bx;
    rodent.column = outregs.x.cx;
    rodent.row = outregs.x.dx;

    return outregs.x.bx;
}   /* End of ms_btnrealease() */

void ms_exclude(int topleftx, int toplefty, int btmrtx, int btmrty)
{
    /* Defines a mouse cursor exclusion area for which the corners */
    /* are specified in pixels */

    inregs.x.ax = 0x10;
    inregs.x.cx = topleftx;
    inregs.x.dx = toplefty;
    inregs.x.si = btmrtx;
    inregs.x.di = btmrty;

    MouseCall;
}   /* End of ms_exclude() */

int ms_getstatus(void)
{
    /* Returns mouse status at the time of the call.
       rodent.column and rodent.row give mouse cursor position.
       rodent.btnstatus = 0 if no button was pressed
                        = 1 if left button was pressed
                        = 2 if right button was pressed
                        = 3 if both buttons were pressed */

    inregs.x.ax = 0x03;

    MouseCall;

    rodent.btnstatus = outregs.x.bx;
    rodent.column = outregs.x.cx;
    rodent.row = outregs.x.dx;

    return outregs.x.bx;
}   /* End of ms_getstatus() */

void ms_hidecrsr(void)
{
    /* Hides the mouse cursor if it is displayed */
```

(continued)

LISTING 6-2. *continued*

```c
        if (rodent.cursor_display)
            {
            inregs.x.ax = 0x02;
            MouseCall;
            }
}   /* End of ms_hidecrsr() */

int ms_init(void)
{
    /* If a mouse is installed, initializes mouse and  */
    /* sets rodent.exists to 1. If no mouse is installed, */
    /* sets rodent.exists to 0. */

    inregs.x.ax = 0;

    MouseCall;

    rodent.exists = outregs.x.ax;
    return outregs.x.ax;
}   /* End of ms_init() */

void ms_lightpenoff(void)
{
    /* Turns light-pen emulation off */

    inregs.x.ax = 0x0E;
    MouseCall;
}   /* End of ms_lightpenoff() */

void ms_lightpenon(void)
{
    /* Turns light-pen emulation on (the default when the */
    /* mouse is initialized) */

    inregs.x.ax = 0x0D;
    MouseCall;
}   /* End of ms_lightpenon() */

void ms_movecrsr(int row, int col)
{
    /* Moves the mouse cursor to the screen position specified */
    /* in pixels by the parameters */

    inregs.x.ax = 0x04;
    inregs.x.cx = col;
    inregs.x.dx = row;

    MouseCall;
}   /* End of ms_movecrsr() */
```

(continued)

LISTING 6-2. *continued*

```c
void ms_movement(void)
{
    /* Reports the net movement of the mouse (not the mouse cursor) */
    /* since the last call to this function */

    inregs.x.ax = 0x0B;

    MouseCall;

    rodent.hmovement = outregs.x.cx;
    rodent.vmovement = outregs.x.dx;
}   /* End of ms_movement() */

void ms_sethrange(int leftcol, int rightcol)
{
    /* Restricts horizontal mouse cursor movement to the screen */
    /* region between leftcol and rightcol. If the cursor is */
    /* outside this range, it is moved inside. */

    inregs.x.ax = 0x07;
    inregs.x.cx = leftcol;
    inregs.x.dx = rightcol;

    MouseCall;
}   /* End of ms_sethrange() */

void ms_setvrange(int upperrow, int lowerrow)
{
    /* Restricts vertical mouse cursor movement to the screen */
    /* region between upperrow and lowerrow. If the cursor is */
    /* outside the range, it is moved inside. */

    inregs.x.ax = 0x08;
    inregs.x.cx = upperrow;
    inregs.x.dx = lowerrow;

    MouseCall;
}   /* End of ms_setvrange() */

void ms_settextcrsr(int cursortype, int scan1, int scan2)
{
    /* Sets the text cursor type.
       If cursortype = 0, the software cursor is set, and scan1 and
       scan2 specify the screen and cursor masks.
       If cursortype = 1, the hardware cursor is set, and scan1 and
       scan2 specify the start and stop scan lines for the cursor. */

    inregs.x.ax = 0x0A;
    inregs.x.bx = cursortype;
    inregs.x.cx = scan1;
    inregs.x.dx = scan2;
```

(continued)

LISTING 6-2. *continued*

```c
    MouseCall;
}   /* End ms_settextcrsr() */

void ms_showcrsr(void)
{
    /* Displays the mouse cursor */

    int i, counter;

    /* Call Int 33H Function 02AH to get the value of the */
    /* display counter */
    inregs.x.ax = 0x2A;
    MouseCall;
    counter = inregs.x.ax;

    /* Call Int 33H Function 01H as many times as needed to display */
    /* the mouse cursor */
    for (i = 1; i < counter; i++)
        {
        inregs.x.ax = 0x01;
        MouseCall;
        }

    rodent.cursor_display = 1;
}   /* End of ms_showcrsr() */

void waitclick(int button)
{
    /* Pauses until the specified mouse button is pressed
        and released.
        If button = 0, left button
        If button = 1, right button
        If button = 2, both buttons
        If button = 3, either button */

    /* Define strings for screen messages */
    char *whichbtn[4] = { "the left button",
                          "the right button",
                          "both buttons",
                          "any button" };

    printf("Click %s to continue.", whichbtn[button]);

    rodent.btnstatus = 0;

    do
        ms_getstatus();
    while (rodent.btnstatus != 0);
```

(continued)

LISTING 6-2. *continued*

```
    if (button < 3)
        {
        do
            ms_getstatus();
        while (rodent.btnstatus != button+1);
        }
    else
        {
        do
            ms_getstatus();
        while (rodent.btnstatus <= 0);
        }

    /* Wait for the button release */
    do
        ms_getstatus();
    while (rodent.btnstatus != 0);
}   /* End of waitclick() */

void clearscreen(void)
{
    int x;

    for (x = 0; x < 25; x++)
        printf("\n");
}   /* End of clearscreen() */

void locate(char x, char y)
{
    inregs.h.ah = 0x02;
    inregs.h.dh = y-1;
    inregs.h.dl = x-1;
    inregs.h.bh = 0;

    int86(0x10, &inregs, &outregs);
}   /* End of locate() */
```

Graphics Mode Mouse Programming

Mouse programming in graphics mode is much like programming in text mode. You use the same services to initialize the mouse, detect cursor position and button presses and releases, define an event handler, measure mouse motion, and so on.

In two respects, however, mouse programming in graphics mode is different from text mode programming. First, in graphics mode, you have almost complete freedom to design any cursor shape you want. You can use any image that can be designed within a 16-by-16-pixel region of the screen.

Second, cursor movement differs. Rather than being constrained to jumping between character cells, as in text mode programming, the graphics mode mouse cursor moves over the screen smoothly, pixel by pixel.

The accuracy with which the graphics mode cursor can point to a screen location is limited only by the screen's pixel resolution (which, you will remember, depends on the size of the virtual screen—most often 640 pixels horizontal by 200 pixels vertical).

The virtual screen sizes for the most frequently used graphics modes are listed in Figure 6-2.

Mode	Adapter(s)	Virtual screen size
04H, 05H, 06H	CGA, EGA, MCGA, VGA	640×200
0DH, 0EH	EGA, VGA	640×200
0FH, 10H	EGA, VGA	640×350
11H	MCGA, VGA	640×480
12H	VGA	640×480
13H	MCGA, VGA	640×200

FIGURE 6-2.
Virtual screen dimensions for commonly used graphics screen modes.

Defining the graphics mode cursor

In graphics mode, the mouse driver uses its default cursor shape unless you define a new cursor by calling Int 33H Function 09H. The default graphics mode cursor is an arrow that points upward and to the left, which is fine for most applications. Defining other cursor shapes, however, gives you greater programming control. For example, your program could display a different cursor shape depending on the specific task being done—you could use an I-beam cursor to indicate text entry mode, an hourglass cursor to signal to the user to wait, and so on.

The graphics mode cursor is defined by two 32-byte (256-bit) arrays, each of which contains 1 bit for each pixel in the 16-by-16-pixel cursor. The first 32-byte array is called the *cursor mask;* it defines the appearance of the cursor. The second array is called the *screen mask;* it defines the appearance of the screen image under the cursor. The mouse driver uses the bits of both masks when it displays the cursor. The bits in each mask correspond to the pixels in the cursor in a one-to-one fashion: The 16 bits in the first 2 bytes of a mask correspond to the 16 pixels that make up the top row of the cursor, and so on.

Your program needs two masks to ensure that the cursor is always visible. A white cursor is fine except on a white background, where it will not be visible. You can use the screen mask to be sure that the cursor always has a black border and will therefore be visible against any background. Figure 6-3 shows how the bits in the cursor mask and the screen mask are combined to create the displayed cursor. A bit value of 1 in the displayed cursor turns the pixel on (white); a value of 0 turns the pixel off (black).

Screen mask bit	Cursor mask bit	Displayed bit
0	0	0
0	1	1
1	0	Underlying bit not changed
1	1	Underlying bit inverted

FIGURE 6-3.
How the bits in the cursor mask and the screen mask are combined to create the displayed graphics mode cursor.

The best way to design cursor and screen masks is to use two 16-by-16-grids on graph paper. Fill in the squares needed for the desired shape, and then convert each 16-square row to a 16-bit binary number (1 for a filled-in square and 0 for an empty one). Finally, convert each 16-bit binary number to a hexadecimal value for use in the program. The demonstration programs in Listing 6-3 and Listing 6-4 show you how to design screen and cursor masks. One of the mask patterns—the one for the pointing hand—is accompanied by program comments that show the binary representation of the pixel pattern for both the cursor mask and the screen mask.

The graphics mode cursor also has a *hot spot,* which is the single pixel within the cursor that defines the screen location to which the cursor is pointing. The hot spot, which you specify when you call Int 33H Function 09H, is defined in terms of its vertical and horizontal position relative to the upper left corner of the cursor's 16-by-16-pixel area. A hot spot of (0, 0) refers to the upper left pixel in the cursor's 16-by-16 area. Although the allowable vertical and horizontal range for the hot spot is –127 through 128, you will most often use a value in the range 0 through 15. (Note that in CGA, 320-by-200, four-color graphics mode the horizontal range is 0 through 7.) The mouse driver's default graphics mode cursor has its hot spot at the tip of the arrow, which is location (1, 1). To determine the current hot spot setting, use Int 33H Function 2AH.

Graphics mode demonstration programs

Listings 6-3 and 6-4 present the graphics mode mouse demonstration programs. They concentrate on those tasks that are unique to graphics mode: They use Int 33H Function 09H to define the cursor shape and Int 33H Function 0FH to modify the mickeys-to-pixels ratio (which specifies how far the cursor moves on the screen when the mouse is moved). These programs also use a number of the functions that were developed in the text mode demonstrations earlier in this chapter. To run these programs, you must have a graphics display system that can operate in CGA, 640-by-200, two-color graphics mode (which is screen mode 2 in Basic and video mode _HRESBW in C).

```
DEFINT A-Z

DECLARE SUB MsSetRatio (horizontal, vertical)
DECLARE SUB MsSetGrCrsr (xHot, yHot)
DECLARE SUB MsSetCrsrMask (shape)
DECLARE SUB WaitClick (button)
DECLARE SUB MsShowCrsr ()
DECLARE SUB MsInit ()
DECLARE SUB Mouse (a, b, c, d)
DECLARE SUB MsPosition ()

' $INCLUDE: 'QB.BI'

CONST YES = 1, NO = 0, LEFT = 0, RIGHT = 1, BOTH = 2, EITHER = 3

' Define the constants for the different graphics cursor shapes
CONST HAND = 1, CHECK = 2, LEFTARROW = 3, CROSS = 4, IBEAM = 5

' Define the array to hold the graphics cursor masks
DIM mouseCrsrMask(32) AS INTEGER

' Define a structure to hold information that the mouse subprograms
' return and use
TYPE MouseData
    exists AS INTEGER          ' Greater than 0 if mouse exists
    cursorDisplay AS INTEGER   ' 1 if cursor displayed, 0 if hidden
    btnStatus AS INTEGER       ' Current button status (up or down)
    btnClicks AS INTEGER       ' Times button has been clicked
    column AS INTEGER          ' Mouse cursor column position
    row AS INTEGER             ' Mouse cursor row position
    hMovement AS INTEGER       ' Horizontal mouse movement
    vMovement AS INTEGER       ' Vertical mouse movement
END TYPE
```

LISTING 6-3. *(continued)*
Demonstration of graphics mode mouse programming in Basic.

LISTING 6-3. *continued*

```
DIM rodent AS MouseData


' Begin execution

CLS

' See whether a mouse is installed
MsInit

IF rodent.exists THEN
    PRINT "A Microsoft-compatible mouse is installed."
    CALL WaitClick(EITHER)
    CLS
ELSE
    PRINT "The program did not detect a mouse."
    PRINT "A mouse and a Microsoft-compatible driver"
    PRINT "must be installed to run this program."
    PRINT
    PRINT "Press any key to exit."
    WHILE INKEY$ = "": WEND
    END
END IF

' Set the screen to mode 2 (CGA, 640-by-200, two-color)
SCREEN 2

' Display a filled box in the center of the screen
LINE (210, 90)-(450, 170), 1, BF

LOCATE 1, 1
PRINT "Click the left mouse button to cycle through the cursor shapes."

MsShowCrsr
LOCATE 3, 1
PRINT "This is the default arrow cursor."
PRINT
WaitClick (LEFT)

CALL MsSetCrsrMask(CHECK)
CALL MsSetGrCrsr(1, 1)
MsShowCrsr
LOCATE 3, 1
PRINT "This is the check mark cursor.      "
PRINT
WaitClick (LEFT)

CALL MsSetCrsrMask(LEFTARROW)
CALL MsSetGrCrsr(1, 1)
MsShowCrsr
```

(continued)

LISTING 6-3. *continued*

```
     LOCATE 3, 1
     PRINT "This is the left-pointing arrow cursor."
     PRINT
     WaitClick (LEFT)

     CALL MsSetCrsrMask(IBEAM)
     CALL MsSetGrCrsr(1, 1)
     MsShowCrsr
     LOCATE 3, 1
     PRINT "This is the I-beam cursor.          "
     PRINT
     WaitClick (LEFT)

     CALL MsSetCrsrMask(HAND)
     CALL MsSetGrCrsr(1, 1)
     MsShowCrsr
     LOCATE 3, 1
     PRINT "This is the pointing-hand cursor."
     PRINT
     WaitClick (LEFT)

     CALL MsSetCrsrMask(CROSS)
     CALL MsSetGrCrsr(1, 1)
     MsShowCrsr
     LOCATE 3, 1
     PRINT "This is the cross cursor.           "
     PRINT
     WaitClick (LEFT)

     MsInit
     CLS
     MsShowCrsr

     LOCATE 1, 1
     PRINT "The effect of setting different mickey-to-pixel ratios."
     PRINT "At each setting, move the mouse, and observe the mouse cursor"
     PRINT "movement. Click the left button to change the settings."

     LOCATE 5, 1
     PRINT "Horizontal 8, vertical 16 (the default)."
     PRINT
     WaitClick (LEFT)

     CALL MsSetRatio(3, 3)
     LOCATE 5, 1
     PRINT "Horizontal = 3, vertical = 3.           "
     PRINT
     WaitClick (LEFT)
```

(continued)

LISTING 6-3. *continued*

```
    CALL MsSetRatio(20, 4)
    LOCATE 5, 1
    PRINT "Horizontal = 20, vertical = 4."
    PRINT
    WaitClick (LEFT)

    CALL MsSetRatio(4, 20)
    LOCATE 5, 1
    PRINT "Horizontal = 4, vertical = 20."
    PRINT
    WaitClick (LEFT)

    CALL MsSetRatio(30, 30)
    LOCATE 5, 1
    PRINT "Horizontal = 30, vertical = 30."
    PRINT
    WaitClick (LEFT)

    SCREEN 0

    PRINT "This ends the graphics mode mouse demonstration."

    END

' **********************************
' These are the program's subprograms
' **********************************

SUB Mouse (a, b, c, d) STATIC

    DIM inRegs AS RegTypeX, outRegs AS RegTypeX
    SHARED mouseCrsrMask() AS INTEGER

    ' For Int 33H Function 09H, register ES must equal
    ' register DS. DS is the default data segment, so we
    ' can get its value by using VARSEG.

    IF a = &H9 THEN
        inRegs.es = VARSEG(mouseCrsrMask(1))
    END IF

    ' Place values in CPU registers
    inRegs.ax = a
    inRegs.bx = b
    inRegs.cx = c
    inRegs.dx = d

    ' Call the mouse service
    CALL INTERRUPTX(&H33, inRegs, outRegs)
```

(continued)

LISTING 6-3. *continued*

```
    ' Get values from CPU registers
    a = outRegs.ax
    b = outRegs.bx
    c = outRegs.cx
    d = outRegs.dx
END SUB    ' End of Mouse

SUB MsInit
    ' If a mouse is installed, initializes the mouse and
    ' sets rodent.exists to 1.  If no mouse is installed,
    ' sets rodent.exists to 0.

    SHARED rodent AS MouseData

    a = &H0
    CALL Mouse(a, 0, 0, 0)
    rodent.exists = a
END SUB    ' End of MsInit

SUB MsPosition
    ' Returns the mouse status at the time of the call.
    ' rodent.column and rodent.row give the mouse cursor position.
    ' rodent.btnStatus = 0 if no button was pressed
    '                  = 1 if left button was pressed
    '                  = 2 if right button was pressed
    '                  = 3 if both buttons were pressed

    SHARED rodent AS MouseData

    a = &H3

    ' Call Int 33H Function 03H to get mouse status
    CALL Mouse(a, b, c, d)

    rodent.btnStatus = b
    rodent.column = c
    rodent.row = d
END SUB    ' End of MsPosition

SUB MsSetCrsrMask (shape)
    ' Places a screen mask and a cursor mask in the array mouseCrsrMask.
    ' A subsequent call to MsSetGrCrsr will change the cursor to the
    ' one defined by the masks.

    ' The following constants must be defined in the calling program
    ' and can be passed to this subprogram as arguments:
    '
    '            CHECK          -> check mark
    '            LEFTARROW      -> left-pointing arrow
```

(continued)

LISTING 6-3. *continued*

```
    '                   CROSS           -> cross
    '                   IBEAM           -> I-beam
    '                   HAND            -> pointing hand

    SHARED mouseCrsrMask() AS INTEGER

    SELECT CASE shape
        CASE CHECK

            ' screen mask
            mouseCrsrMask(1) = &HFFF0
            mouseCrsrMask(2) = &HFFE0
            mouseCrsrMask(3) = &HFFC0
            mouseCrsrMask(4) = &HFF81
            mouseCrsrMask(5) = &HFF03
            mouseCrsrMask(6) = &H607
            mouseCrsrMask(7) = &HF
            mouseCrsrMask(8) = &H1F
            mouseCrsrMask(9) = &HC03F
            mouseCrsrMask(10) = &HF07F
            mouseCrsrMask(11) = &HFFFF
            mouseCrsrMask(12) = &HFFFF
            mouseCrsrMask(13) = &HFFFF
            mouseCrsrMask(14) = &HFFFF
            mouseCrsrMask(15) = &HFFFF
            mouseCrsrMask(16) = &HFFFF

            ' cursor mask
            mouseCrsrMask(17) = &H0
            mouseCrsrMask(18) = &H6
            mouseCrsrMask(19) = &HC
            mouseCrsrMask(20) = &H18
            mouseCrsrMask(21) = &H30
            mouseCrsrMask(22) = &H60
            mouseCrsrMask(23) = &H70C0
            mouseCrsrMask(24) = &H1080
            mouseCrsrMask(25) = &H700
            mouseCrsrMask(26) = &H0
            mouseCrsrMask(27) = &H0
            mouseCrsrMask(28) = &H0
            mouseCrsrMask(29) = &H0
            mouseCrsrMask(30) = &H0
            mouseCrsrMask(31) = &H0
            mouseCrsrMask(32) = &H0

        CASE LEFTARROW

            ' screen mask
            mouseCrsrMask(1) = &HFE1F
            mouseCrsrMask(2) = &HF01F
```

(continued)

LISTING 6-3. *continued*

```
            mouseCrsrMask(3)  = &H0
            mouseCrsrMask(4)  = &H0
            mouseCrsrMask(5)  = &H0
            mouseCrsrMask(6)  = &HF01F
            mouseCrsrMask(7)  = &HFE1F
            mouseCrsrMask(8)  = &HFFFF
            mouseCrsrMask(9)  = &HFFFF
            mouseCrsrMask(10) = &HFFFF
            mouseCrsrMask(11) = &HFFFF
            mouseCrsrMask(12) = &HFFFF
            mouseCrsrMask(13) = &HFFFF
            mouseCrsrMask(14) = &HFFFF
            mouseCrsrMask(15) = &HFFFF
            mouseCrsrMask(16) = &HFFFF

            ' cursor mask
            mouseCrsrMask(17) = &H0
            mouseCrsrMask(18) = &HC0
            mouseCrsrMask(19) = &H7C0
            mouseCrsrMask(20) = &H7FFE
            mouseCrsrMask(21) = &H7C0
            mouseCrsrMask(22) = &HC0
            mouseCrsrMask(23) = &H0
            mouseCrsrMask(24) = &H0
            mouseCrsrMask(25) = &H0
            mouseCrsrMask(26) = &H0
            mouseCrsrMask(27) = &H0
            mouseCrsrMask(28) = &H0
            mouseCrsrMask(29) = &H0
            mouseCrsrMask(30) = &H0
            mouseCrsrMask(31) = &H0
            mouseCrsrMask(32) = &H0

        CASE CROSS

            ' screen mask
            mouseCrsrMask(1)  = &HFC3F
            mouseCrsrMask(2)  = &HFC3F
            mouseCrsrMask(3)  = &HFC3F
            mouseCrsrMask(4)  = &H0
            mouseCrsrMask(5)  = &H0
            mouseCrsrMask(6)  = &H0
            mouseCrsrMask(7)  = &HFC3F
            mouseCrsrMask(8)  = &HFC3F
            mouseCrsrMask(9)  = &HFC3F
            mouseCrsrMask(10) = &HFFFF
            mouseCrsrMask(11) = &HFFFF
            mouseCrsrMask(12) = &HFFFF
            mouseCrsrMask(13) = &HFFFF
```

(continued)

LISTING 6-3. *continued*

```
        mouseCrsrMask(14) = &HFFFF
        mouseCrsrMask(15) = &HFFFF
        mouseCrsrMask(16) = &HFFFF

        ' cursor mask
        mouseCrsrMask(17) = &H0
        mouseCrsrMask(18) = &H180
        mouseCrsrMask(19) = &H180
        mouseCrsrMask(20) = &H180
        mouseCrsrMask(21) = &H7FFE
        mouseCrsrMask(22) = &H180
        mouseCrsrMask(23) = &H180
        mouseCrsrMask(24) = &H180
        mouseCrsrMask(25) = &H0
        mouseCrsrMask(26) = &H0
        mouseCrsrMask(27) = &H0
        mouseCrsrMask(28) = &H0
        mouseCrsrMask(29) = &H0
        mouseCrsrMask(30) = &H0
        mouseCrsrMask(31) = &H0
        mouseCrsrMask(32) = &H0
    CASE IBEAM

        ' screen mask
        mouseCrsrMask(1) = &HFFFF
        mouseCrsrMask(2) = &HFFFF
        mouseCrsrMask(3) = &HFFFF
        mouseCrsrMask(4) = &HFFFF
        mouseCrsrMask(5) = &HFFFF
        mouseCrsrMask(6) = &HFFFF
        mouseCrsrMask(7) = &HFFFF
        mouseCrsrMask(8) = &HFFFF
        mouseCrsrMask(9) = &HFFFF
        mouseCrsrMask(10) = &HFFFF
        mouseCrsrMask(11) = &HFFFF
        mouseCrsrMask(12) = &HFFFF
        mouseCrsrMask(13) = &HFFFF
        mouseCrsrMask(14) = &HFFFF
        mouseCrsrMask(15) = &HFFFF
        mouseCrsrMask(16) = &HFFFF

        ' cursor mask
        mouseCrsrMask(17) = &HF00F
        mouseCrsrMask(18) = &HC30
        mouseCrsrMask(19) = &H240
        mouseCrsrMask(20) = &H240
        mouseCrsrMask(21) = &H180
        mouseCrsrMask(22) = &H180
        mouseCrsrMask(23) = &H180
```

(continued)

LISTING 6-3. *continued*

```
            mouseCrsrMask(24) = &H180
            mouseCrsrMask(25) = &H180
            mouseCrsrMask(26) = &H180
            mouseCrsrMask(27) = &H180
            mouseCrsrMask(28) = &H180
            mouseCrsrMask(29) = &H240
            mouseCrsrMask(30) = &H240
            mouseCrsrMask(31) = &HC30
            mouseCrsrMask(32) = &HF00F

        CASE HAND

            ' screen mask
            mouseCrsrMask(1)  = &HE1FF      ' Binary 1110000111111111
            mouseCrsrMask(2)  = &HE1FF      ' Binary 1110000111111111
            mouseCrsrMask(3)  = &HE1FF      ' Binary 1110000111111111
            mouseCrsrMask(4)  = &HE1FF      ' Binary 1110000111111111
            mouseCrsrMask(5)  = &HE1FF      ' Binary 1110000111111111
            mouseCrsrMask(6)  = &HE000      ' Binary 1110000000000000
            mouseCrsrMask(7)  = &HE000      ' Binary 1110000000000000
            mouseCrsrMask(8)  = &HE000      ' Binary 1110000000000000
            mouseCrsrMask(9)  = &H0         ' Binary 0000000000000000
            mouseCrsrMask(10) = &H0         ' Binary 0000000000000000
            mouseCrsrMask(11) = &H0         ' Binary 0000000000000000
            mouseCrsrMask(12) = &H0         ' Binary 0000000000000000
            mouseCrsrMask(13) = &H0         ' Binary 0000000000000000
            mouseCrsrMask(14) = &H0         ' Binary 0000000000000000
            mouseCrsrMask(15) = &H0         ' Binary 0000000000000000
            mouseCrsrMask(16) = &H0         ' Binary 0000000000000000

            ' cursor mask
            mouseCrsrMask(17) = &H1E00      ' Binary 0001111000000000
            mouseCrsrMask(18) = &H1200      ' Binary 0001001000000000
            mouseCrsrMask(19) = &H1200      ' Binary 0001001000000000
            mouseCrsrMask(20) = &H1200      ' Binary 0001001000000000
            mouseCrsrMask(21) = &H1200      ' Binary 0001001000000000
            mouseCrsrMask(22) = &H13FF      ' Binary 0001001111111111
            mouseCrsrMask(23) = &H1249      ' Binary 0001001001001001
            mouseCrsrMask(24) = &H1249      ' Binary 0001001001001001
            mouseCrsrMask(25) = &H1249      ' Binary 0001001001001001
            mouseCrsrMask(26) = &H9001      ' Binary 1001000000000001
            mouseCrsrMask(27) = &H9001      ' Binary 1001000000000001
            mouseCrsrMask(28) = &H9001      ' Binary 1001000000000001
            mouseCrsrMask(29) = &H8001      ' Binary 1000000000000001
            mouseCrsrMask(30) = &H8001      ' Binary 1000000000000001
            mouseCrsrMask(31) = &H8001      ' Binary 1000000000000001
            mouseCrsrMask(32) = &HFFFF      ' Binary 1111111111111111
    END SELECT
END SUB      ' End of MsSetCrsrMask
```

(continued)

LISTING 6-3. *continued*

```
SUB MsSetGrCrsr (xHot, yHot)
    ' Sets the graphics cursor to the pattern defined
    ' in the array MouseCrsrMask()

    SHARED mouseCrsrMask() AS INTEGER

    CALL Mouse(&H9, xHot, yHot, VARPTR(mouseCrsrMask(1)))
END SUB

SUB MsSetRatio (horizontal, vertical)
    ' Calls Int 33H Function 0FH to set the mickeys-per-pixel mouse cursor
    ' movement ratio

    CALL Mouse(&HF, 0, horizontal, vertical)
END SUB

SUB MsShowCrsr
    SHARED rodent AS MouseData

    ' Call Int 33H Function 01H to display the mouse cursor
    FOR i = 1 TO 5
        CALL Mouse(&H1, 0, 0, 0)
    NEXT i
    rodent.cursorDisplay = YES
END SUB    ' End of MsShowCrsr

SUB WaitClick (button)
    ' Pauses until the specified mouse button is pressed and released.
    ' If button = 0, left button
    ' If button = 1, right button
    ' If button = 2, both buttons
    ' If button = 3, either button

    SHARED rodent AS MouseData

    DIM whichbtn(3) AS STRING
    whichbtn(0) = "the left button"
    whichbtn(1) = "the right button"
    whichbtn(2) = "both buttons"
    whichbtn(3) = "any button"

    rodent.btnStatus = 0

    PRINT "Click "; whichbtn(button); " to continue."

    DO
        MsPosition
    LOOP UNTIL rodent.btnStatus = 0
```

(continued)

LISTING 6-3. *continued*

```
    IF button < 3 THEN
        DO
            MsPosition
        LOOP UNTIL rodent.btnStatus = (button + 1)

    ELSE
        DO
            MsPosition
        LOOP UNTIL rodent.btnStatus > 0
    END IF

    ' Wait for the button release
    DO
        MsPosition
    LOOP UNTIL rodent.btnStatus = 0
END SUB    ' End of WaitClick
```

```c
/* Graphics mode mouse demonstration */

#include <stdio.h>
#include <dos.h>
#include <graph.h>

/* Define a macro for calling mouse services */
#define MouseCall int86(0x33, &inregs, &outregs)

#define LEFT 0
#define RIGHT 1
#define BOTH 2
#define EITHER 3
#define SOFTCURSOR 0
#define HARDCURSOR 1
#define HAND 1
#define CHECK 2
#define LEFTARROW 3
#define CROSS 4
#define IBEAM 5

/* Define the array to hold the graphics cursor masks */
int mousecrsrmask[32];

/* Declare the register unions */
union REGS inregs, outregs;
```

LISTING 6-4. *(continued)*
Demonstration of graphics mode mouse programming in C.

LISTING 6-4. *continued*

```c
/* Define a structure to hold information that the mouse functions */
/* return and use */

struct mousedata {
    int exists;         /* Greater than 0 if mouse exists */
    int cursor_display; /* 1 if cursor displayed, 0 if hidden */
    int btnstatus;      /* Current button status (up or down) */
    int btnclicks;      /* Times button has been clicked */
    int column;         /* Mouse cursor column position */
    int row;            /* Mouse cursor row position */
    int hmovement;      /* Horizontal mouse movement */
    int vmovement;      /* Vertical mouse movement */
} rodent;

int ms_init(void);
/* Function prototypes */
void ms_showcrsr(void);
void waitclick(int button);
void ms_setcrsrmask(int shape);
void ms_setgrcrsr(int xhot, int yhot);
void locate(char x, char y);
void clearscreen(void);
int ms_getstatus(void);
void ms_setratio(int horizontal, int vertical);

main()
{

    /* See whether a mouse is installed */
    ms_init();
    clearscreen();

    if (rodent.exists)
        {
        locate(1, 1);
        puts("A Microsoft-compatible mouse is installed.");
        waitclick(EITHER);
        clearscreen();
        }
    else
        {
        clearscreen();
        locate(1, 1);
        puts("The program did not detect a mouse.");
        puts("A mouse and a Microsoft-compatible driver");
        puts("must be installed to run this program.\n");
        puts("Press any key to exit.");
        getch();
        exit();
        }
```

(continued)

LISTING 6-4. *continued*

```c
    /* Set the screen to mode _HRESBW (CGA, 640-by-200, two-color) */
    _setvideomode(_HRESBW);

    /* Draw a filled box in the center of the screen */
    _rectangle(_GFILLINTERIOR, 200, 60, 440, 140);

    _settextposition(1,1);
    puts("Click the left mouse button to cycle through the cursor shapes.");

    ms_showcrsr();
    _settextposition(3,1);
    puts("This is the default arrow cursor.");
    waitclick(LEFT);

    ms_setcrsrmask(CHECK);
    ms_setgrcrsr(1,1);
    ms_showcrsr();
    _settextposition(3,1);
    puts("This is the check mark cursor.          ");
    waitclick(LEFT);

    ms_setcrsrmask(LEFTARROW);
    ms_setgrcrsr(1,1);
    ms_showcrsr();
    _settextposition(3,1);
    puts("This is the left-pointing arrow cursor.");
    waitclick(LEFT);

    ms_setcrsrmask(IBEAM);
    ms_setgrcrsr(1,1);
    ms_showcrsr();
    _settextposition(3,1);
    puts("This is the I-beam cursor.              ");
    waitclick(LEFT);

    ms_setcrsrmask(HAND);
    ms_setgrcrsr(1,1);
    ms_showcrsr();
    _settextposition(3,1);
    puts("This is the pointing-hand cursor.");
    waitclick(LEFT);

    ms_setcrsrmask(CROSS);
    ms_setgrcrsr(1,1);
    ms_showcrsr();
    _settextposition(3,1);
    puts("This is the cross cursor.       ");
    waitclick(LEFT);

    ms_init();
    _clearscreen(_GCLEARSCREEN);
    ms_showcrsr();
```

(continued)

LISTING 6-4. *continued*

```
        /* Demonstrate different mickey-to-pixel ratios */

        _settextposition(1,1);
        puts("The effect of setting different mickey-to-pixel ratios.");
        puts("At each setting, move the mouse, and observe the mouse cursor");
        puts("movement. Click the left button to change the settings.");

        _settextposition(5,1);
        puts("Horizontal; 8, vertical 16 (the default).");
        waitclick(LEFT);

        ms_setratio(3,3);
        _settextposition(5,1);
        puts("Horizontal 3, vertical 3              ");
        waitclick(LEFT);

        ms_setratio(20,4);
        _settextposition(5,1);
        puts("Horizontal 20, vertical 4");
        waitclick(LEFT);

        ms_setratio(4,20);
        _settextposition(5,1);
        puts("Horizontal 4, vertical 20");
        waitclick(LEFT);

        ms_setratio(30,30);
        _settextposition(5,1);
        puts("Horizontal 30, vertical 30");
        waitclick(LEFT);

        /* Shut down and exit */
        ms_init();
        _setvideomode(_DEFAULTMODE);
        puts("This ends the graphics mode mouse demonstration.");

}       /* End of main() */

/*****************************************/
/* The program's functions start here    */
/*****************************************/

int ms_init(void)
{
    /* If a mouse is installed, initializes the mouse and */
    /* sets rodent.exists to 1. If no mouse is installed, */
    /* sets rodent.exists to 0. */

    inregs.x.ax = 0;

    MouseCall;
```

(continued)

LISTING 6-4. *continued*

```c
        rodent.exists = outregs.x.ax;
        return outregs.x.ax;
}       /* End of ms_init() */

void ms_showcrsr(void)
{

        /* Displays the mouse cursor */

        int i, counter;

        /* Call Int 33H Function 2AH to get the value of the */
        /* display counter */
        inregs.x.ax = 0x2A;
        MouseCall;
        counter = inregs.x.ax;

        /* Call Int 33H Function 01H as many times as needed to display */
        /* the mouse cursor */
        for (i = 1; i < counter; i++)
            {
            inregs.x.ax = 0x01;
            MouseCall;
            }

        rodent.cursor_display = 1;
}       /* End of ms_showcrsr() */

void waitclick(int button)
{
        /* Pauses until the specified mouse button is pressed
           and released.
           If button = 0, left button
           If button = 1, right button
           If button = 2, both buttons
           If button = 3, either button */

        /* Define strings for screen messages */
        char *whichbtn[4] = { "the left button",
                              "the right button",
                              "both buttons",
                              "any button" };

        printf("Click %s to continue.", whichbtn[button]);

        rodent.btnstatus = 0;

        do
            ms_getstatus();
        while (rodent.btnstatus != 0);
```

(continued)

LISTING 6-4. *continued*

```c
        if (button < 3)
            {
            do
                ms_getstatus();
            while (rodent.btnstatus != button + 1);
            }
        else
            {
            do
                ms_getstatus();
            while (rodent.btnstatus <= 0);
            }

        /* Wait for the button release */
        do
            ms_getstatus();
        while (rodent.btnstatus != 0);
    }   /* End of waitclick() */

void ms_setcrsrmask(int shape)
{
    /* Places a screen mask and a cursor mask in the array mouseCrsrMask. */
    /* A subsequent call to ms_setgrcrsr will change the cursor to the */
    /* one defined by the masks. */

    /* The following constants must be defined in the calling program
       and can be passed to this function as the arguments:
                    CHECK           -> check mark
                    LEFTARROW       -> left-pointing arrow
                    CROSS           -> cross
                    IBEAM           -> I-beam
                    HAND            -> pointing hand      */

    switch (shape)
    {

    case CHECK:

        /* screen mask */
        mousecrsrmask[0]  = 0xFFF0;
        mousecrsrmask[1]  = 0xFFE0;
        mousecrsrmask[2]  = 0xFFC0;
        mousecrsrmask[3]  = 0xFF81;
        mousecrsrmask[4]  = 0xFF03;
        mousecrsrmask[5]  = 0x607;
        mousecrsrmask[6]  = 0xF;
        mousecrsrmask[7]  = 0x1F;
        mousecrsrmask[8]  = 0xC03F;
        mousecrsrmask[9]  = 0xF07F;
        mousecrsrmask[10] = 0xFFFF;
```

(continued)

LISTING 6-4. *continued*

```c
        mousecrsrmask[11] = 0xFFFF;
        mousecrsrmask[12] = 0xFFFF;
        mousecrsrmask[13] = 0xFFFF;
        mousecrsrmask[14] = 0xFFFF;
        mousecrsrmask[15] = 0xFFFF;

        /* cursor mask */
        mousecrsrmask[16] = 0x0;
        mousecrsrmask[17] = 0x6;
        mousecrsrmask[18] = 0xC;
        mousecrsrmask[19] = 0x18;
        mousecrsrmask[20] = 0x30;
        mousecrsrmask[21] = 0x60;
        mousecrsrmask[22] = 0x70C0;
        mousecrsrmask[23] = 0x1080;
        mousecrsrmask[24] = 0x700;
        mousecrsrmask[25] = 0x0;
        mousecrsrmask[26] = 0x0;
        mousecrsrmask[27] = 0x0;
        mousecrsrmask[28] = 0x0;
        mousecrsrmask[29] = 0x0;
        mousecrsrmask[30] = 0x0;
        mousecrsrmask[31] = 0x0;
        break;

    case LEFTARROW:

        /* screen mask */
        mousecrsrmask[0] = 0xFE1F;
        mousecrsrmask[1] = 0xF01F;
        mousecrsrmask[2] = 0x0;
        mousecrsrmask[3] = 0x0;
        mousecrsrmask[4] = 0x0;
        mousecrsrmask[5] = 0xF01F;
        mousecrsrmask[6] = 0xFE1F;
        mousecrsrmask[7] = 0xFFFF;
        mousecrsrmask[8] = 0xFFFF;
        mousecrsrmask[9] = 0xFFFF;
        mousecrsrmask[10] = 0xFFFF;
        mousecrsrmask[11] = 0xFFFF;
        mousecrsrmask[12] = 0xFFFF;
        mousecrsrmask[13] = 0xFFFF;
        mousecrsrmask[14] = 0xFFFF;
        mousecrsrmask[15] = 0xFFFF;

        /* cursor mask */
        mousecrsrmask[16] = 0x0;
        mousecrsrmask[17] = 0xC0;
        mousecrsrmask[18] = 0x7C0;
        mousecrsrmask[19] = 0x7FFE;
```

(continued)

LISTING 6-4. *continued*

```
            mousecrsrmask[20] = 0x7C0;
            mousecrsrmask[21] = 0xC0;
            mousecrsrmask[22] = 0x0;
            mousecrsrmask[23] = 0x0;
            mousecrsrmask[24] = 0x0;
            mousecrsrmask[25] = 0x0;
            mousecrsrmask[26] = 0x0;
            mousecrsrmask[27] = 0x0;
            mousecrsrmask[28] = 0x0;
            mousecrsrmask[29] = 0x0;
            mousecrsrmask[30] = 0x0;
            mousecrsrmask[31] = 0x0;
            break;

    case CROSS:

            /* screen mask */
            mousecrsrmask[0] = 0xFC3F;
            mousecrsrmask[1] = 0xFC3F;
            mousecrsrmask[2] = 0xFC3F;
            mousecrsrmask[3] = 0x0;
            mousecrsrmask[4] = 0x0;
            mousecrsrmask[5] = 0x0;
            mousecrsrmask[6] = 0xFC3F;
            mousecrsrmask[7] = 0xFC3F;
            mousecrsrmask[8] = 0xFC3F;
            mousecrsrmask[9] = 0xFFFF;
            mousecrsrmask[10] = 0xFFFF;
            mousecrsrmask[11] = 0xFFFF;
            mousecrsrmask[12] = 0xFFFF;
            mousecrsrmask[13] = 0xFFFF;
            mousecrsrmask[14] = 0xFFFF;
            mousecrsrmask[15] = 0xFFFF;

            /* cursor mask */
            mousecrsrmask[16] = 0x0;
            mousecrsrmask[17] = 0x180;
            mousecrsrmask[18] = 0x180;
            mousecrsrmask[19] = 0x180;
            mousecrsrmask[20] = 0x7FFE;
            mousecrsrmask[21] = 0x180;
            mousecrsrmask[22] = 0x180;
            mousecrsrmask[23] = 0x180;
            mousecrsrmask[24] = 0x0;
            mousecrsrmask[25] = 0x0;
            mousecrsrmask[26] = 0x0;
            mousecrsrmask[27] = 0x0;
            mousecrsrmask[28] = 0x0;
```

(continued)

LISTING 6-4. *continued*

```c
            mousecrsrmask[29] = 0x0;
            mousecrsrmask[30] = 0x0;
            mousecrsrmask[31] = 0x0;
            break;

    case IBEAM:

            /* screen mask */
            mousecrsrmask[0] = 0xFFFF;
            mousecrsrmask[1] = 0xFFFF;
            mousecrsrmask[2] = 0xFFFF;
            mousecrsrmask[3] = 0xFFFF;
            mousecrsrmask[4] = 0xFFFF;
            mousecrsrmask[5] = 0xFFFF;
            mousecrsrmask[6] = 0xFFFF;
            mousecrsrmask[7] = 0xFFFF;
            mousecrsrmask[8] = 0xFFFF;
            mousecrsrmask[9] = 0xFFFF;
            mousecrsrmask[10] = 0xFFFF;
            mousecrsrmask[11] = 0xFFFF;
            mousecrsrmask[12] = 0xFFFF;
            mousecrsrmask[13] = 0xFFFF;
            mousecrsrmask[14] = 0xFFFF;
            mousecrsrmask[15] = 0xFFFF;

            /* cursor mask */
            mousecrsrmask[16] = 0xF00F;
            mousecrsrmask[17] = 0xC30;
            mousecrsrmask[18] = 0x240;
            mousecrsrmask[19] = 0x240;
            mousecrsrmask[20] = 0x180;
            mousecrsrmask[21] = 0x180;
            mousecrsrmask[22] = 0x180;
            mousecrsrmask[23] = 0x180;
            mousecrsrmask[24] = 0x180;
            mousecrsrmask[25] = 0x180;
            mousecrsrmask[26] = 0x180;
            mousecrsrmask[27] = 0x180;
            mousecrsrmask[28] = 0x240;
            mousecrsrmask[29] = 0x240;
            mousecrsrmask[30] = 0xC30;
            mousecrsrmask[31] = 0xF00F;
            break;

    case HAND:

            /* screen mask */
            mousecrsrmask[0] = 0xE1FF;       /* 1110000111111111 */
            mousecrsrmask[1] = 0xE1FF;       /* 1110000111111111 */
            mousecrsrmask[2] = 0xE1FF;       /* 1110000111111111 */
```

(continued)

LISTING 6-4. *continued*

```
            mousecrsrmask[3] = 0xE1FF;       /* 1110000111111111 */
            mousecrsrmask[4] = 0xE1FF;       /* 1110000111111111 */
            mousecrsrmask[5] = 0xE000;       /* 1110000000000000 */
            mousecrsrmask[6] = 0xE000;       /* 1110000000000000 */
            mousecrsrmask[7] = 0xE000;       /* 1110000000000000 */
            mousecrsrmask[8] = 0x0;          /* 0000000000000000 */
            mousecrsrmask[9] = 0x0;          /* 0000000000000000 */
            mousecrsrmask[10] = 0x0;         /* 0000000000000000 */
            mousecrsrmask[11] = 0x0;         /* 0000000000000000 */
            mousecrsrmask[12] = 0x0;         /* 0000000000000000 */
            mousecrsrmask[13] = 0x0;         /* 0000000000000000 */
            mousecrsrmask[14] = 0x0;         /* 0000000000000000 */
            mousecrsrmask[15] = 0x0;         /* 0000000000000000 */

            /* cursor mask */
            mousecrsrmask[16] = 0x1E00;      /* 0001111000000000 */
            mousecrsrmask[17] = 0x1200;      /* 0001001000000000 */
            mousecrsrmask[18] = 0x1200;      /* 0001001000000000 */
            mousecrsrmask[19] = 0x1200;      /* 0001001000000000 */
            mousecrsrmask[20] = 0x1200;      /* 0001001000000000 */
            mousecrsrmask[21] = 0x13FF;      /* 0001001111111111 */
            mousecrsrmask[22] = 0x1249;      /* 0001001001001001 */
            mousecrsrmask[23] = 0x1249;      /* 0001001001001001 */
            mousecrsrmask[24] = 0x1249;      /* 0001001001001001 */
            mousecrsrmask[25] = 0x9001;      /* 1001000000000001 */
            mousecrsrmask[26] = 0x9001;      /* 1001000000000001 */
            mousecrsrmask[27] = 0x9001;      /* 1001000000000001 */
            mousecrsrmask[28] = 0x8001;      /* 1000000000000001 */
            mousecrsrmask[29] = 0x8001;      /* 1000000000000001 */
            mousecrsrmask[30] = 0x8001;      /* 1000000000000001 */
            mousecrsrmask[31] = 0xFFFF;      /* 1111111111111111 */
            break;
    }

}   /* End of ms_setcrsrmask() */

void ms_setgrcrsr(int xhot, int yhot)
{
    /* Sets the graphics cursor to the pattern defined */
    /* in the array mousecrsrmask[], and the hot spot to */
    /* xhot, yhot */

    inregs.x.ax = 0x09;
    inregs.x.bx = xhot;
    inregs.x.cx = yhot;
    inregs.x.dx = (int)mousecrsrmask;
```

(continued)

LISTING 6-4. *continued*

```c
    MouseCall;
}   /* End of ms_setgrcrsr() */

void ms_setratio(int horizontal, int vertical)
{

    /* Sets the mickeys-per-pixel movement ratio for the mouse cursor*/

    inregs.x.ax = 0x000F;
    inregs.x.cx = horizontal;
    inregs.x.dx = vertical;

    MouseCall;
}   /* End of ms_setratio() */

int ms_getstatus(void)
{
/* Obtains the mouse status at the time of the call.
   rodent.column and rodent.row give the mouse cursor position.
   rodent.btnstatus = 0 if no button was pressed
                    = 1 if left button was pressed
                    = 2 if right button was pressed
                    = 3 if both buttons were pressed */

    inregs.x.ax = 0x03;

    MouseCall;

    rodent.btnstatus = outregs.x.bx;
    rodent.column = outregs.x.cx;
    rodent.row = outregs.x.dx;

    return outregs.x.bx;
}   /* End of ms_getstatus() */

void locate(char x, char y)
{
    inregs.h.ah = 0x02;
    inregs.h.dh = y-1;
    inregs.h.dl = x-1;
    inregs.h.bh = 0;

    int86(0x10, &inregs, &outregs);
}   /* End of locate() */

void clearscreen(void)
{
    int x;

    for (x = 0; x < 25; x++)
        printf("\n");
}   /* End of clearscreen() */
```

Mouse Programming

Mouse Service Reference

The remainder of this chapter provides reference entries for the Int 33H mouse service calls that you will likely use most often. With the exception of Function 2AH, which is available with versions 7.2 and later, these services are available with versions 6 and later of the Microsoft Mouse Driver. When you review the mouse service reference entries, keep in mind that the mouse driver differentiates between pressing a mouse button and releasing it. Also note that two types of information can be reported by the inquiry services: current mouse information and mouse history information. Current mouse information is the state of the mouse at the time the service is called—for example, whether the left button is currently down. Mouse history information reflects what has been done with the mouse in the recent past—for example, how many times the left button has been pressed since the last call to this service. You use both types of information when adding support for the mouse in a program.

Remember that mouse cursor position is always specified in terms of screen pixels according to the virtual screen in effect. The virtual screen dimensions are 640 horizontally and 200 vertically for all text modes and most graphics modes. See Figure 6-2 earlier in the chapter for details on virtual screen sizes for all commonly used graphics modes.

Note that some mouse services refer to a center button. This reference is relevant only with Microsoft-compatible three-button mice (for example, the Logitech mouse).

Int 33H   Function 00H
Reset mouse and get status

Action: Determines whether a mouse is available and, if it is, initializes the mouse driver

Call with: AX = 0000H

Returns: If a mouse is installed:
    AX = nonzero
    BX = number of mouse buttons

    If a mouse is not installed:
    AX = 0000H

Notes: The following list shows how a call to this service initializes the mouse driver. The references in parentheses following each item specify the Int 33H service or services that control the specific item.

- Mouse cursor hidden (services 01H, 02H, 10H, and 2AH)
- Mouse cursor located at screen center (services 03H and 04H)
- Mouse cursor located on display page 0 (services 1DH and 1EH)
- Mouse cursor shape set to reverse block (text mode) or default arrow (graphics mode) (services 09H and 0AH)
- User-installed mouse event handler (if any) disabled (services 0CH and 14H)
- Light-pen emulation enabled (services 0DH and 0EH)
- Mickeys-to-pixels ratio set to 8:8 horizontal and 16:8 vertical (service 0FH)
- Double-speed threshold set to 64 mickeys per second (service 13H)
- Cursor position limits set to entire screen (services 07H and 08H)

Int 33H Function 01H
Show mouse cursor

Action: Displays the mouse cursor on the screen

Call with: AX = 0001H

Returns: Nothing

Notes: Calling this service cancels any cursor exclusion area previously set using Int 33H Function 10H.

The mouse driver maintains a counter whose value determines whether the mouse cursor is displayed. If the counter has a value of 0, the cursor is displayed; if the counter has a value less than 0, the cursor is hidden. Calls to this service increment the counter by 1 if it has a value less than 0 and have no effect on the counter if it has a value of 0. Calls to Int 33H Function 02H (which hides the mouse cursor) always decrement the counter by 1. If a program makes two consecutive calls to Int 33H Function 02H, the counter has a value of –2. It then takes two calls to Int 33H Function 01H to increment the counter to 0 and to display the cursor. A program can read the value of the counter by calling Int 33H Function 2AH, which is available in versions 7.02 and later of the Microsoft Mouse Driver.

Int 33H Function 02H
Hide mouse cursor

Action: Removes the mouse cursor from the screen

Call with: AX = 0002H

Returns: Nothing

Notes: Even when the mouse cursor is hidden, the mouse driver tracks its position.

This service decrements the counter whose value determines whether the mouse cursor is displayed. See "Notes" for Int 33H Function 01H.

Int 33H Function 03H
Get mouse cursor position and button status

Action: Returns the current mouse cursor position and button status

Call with: AX = 0003H

Returns: BX = button status; a bit with a value of 1 indicates that the corresponding button is down:

    Bit 0   = left button
    Bit 1   = right button
    Bit 2   = center button
    Bits 3–15 reserved

CX = horizontal (*x*) coordinate in pixels
DX = vertical (*y*) coordinate in pixels

Notes: The position is returned in virtual screen pixels in all display modes. The upper left corner of the screen is position (0, 0), and the lower right corner of the screen is most often position (639, 199). See Figure 6-2 in this chapter for details on virtual pixel coordinates for various graphics modes.

Int 33H   Function 04H
Set mouse cursor position

Action: Moves the mouse cursor to the specified screen position

Call with: AX = 0004H
    CX = horizontal coordinate
    DX = vertical coordinate

Returns: Nothing

Notes: The coordinates are specified in virtual screen pixels; the horizontal coordinate range is most often 0 through 639, and the vertical coordinate range is most often 0 through 199. See Figure 6-2 in this chapter for details on virtual pixel coordinates for various graphics modes.

If the specified new cursor position is outside the limits that were defined with Int 33H Functions 07H and 08H, the cursor is positioned as close to the new position as possible within the limits.

Int 33H   Function 05H
Get button press information

Action: Reports on the status and number of presses for a specified button and on the mouse position when the button was last pressed

Call with: AX = 0005H
    BX = button to query:
        0 = left
        1 = right
        2 = center

Returns: AX = button status; a bit with a value of 1 indicates that the corresponding button is down:
    Bit 0   = left button
    Bit 1   = right button
    Bit 2   = center button
    Bits 3–15   reserved

BX = button press counter
CX = horizontal (x) coordinate, in pixels, of last button press
DX = vertical (y) coordinate, in pixels, of last button press

Mouse Programming

Notes:	After the service returns, AX contains the current state of all mouse buttons. BX contains the number of times the user pressed the specified button since the last time the program called this service for that button (or since the mouse driver was initialized or reset).
	If the specified button is down, CX and DX contain the current mouse cursor position. If the specified button is not down, CX and DX report the cursor's position the last time the user pressed the specified button.
	Int 33H Function 06H works in the same way as does this service except that it returns information about button releases.

Int 33H Function 06H
Get button release information

Action:	Reports on the status and number of releases for a specified button and on the mouse position when the button was last pressed

Call with:	AX = 0006H
	BX = button to query:
	    0 = left
	    1 = right
	    2 = center

Returns:	AX = button status; a bit with a value of 1 indicates that the corresponding button is down:
	    Bit 0 = left button
	    Bit 1 = right button
	    Bit 2 = center button
	    Bits 3–15 reserved
	BX = button release counter
	CX = horizontal (x) coordinate, in pixels, of last button release
	DX = vertical (y) coordinate, in pixels, of last button release

Notes:	After the service returns, AX contains the current state of all mouse buttons. BX contains the number of times the user released the specified button since the last time the program called this service for that button (or since the mouse driver was initialized or reset).
	If the specified button is down, CX and DX contain the current mouse cursor position. If the specified button is not down, CX and DX report the cursor's position the last time the user released the specified button.

Int 33H Function 05H works in the same way as does this service except that it returns information about button presses.

Int 33H Function 07H
Set horizontal limits for mouse cursor

Action:	Sets left and right horizontal limits for mouse cursor movement
Call with:	AX = 0007H CX = minimum (left) horizontal coordinate in pixels DX = maximum (right) horizontal coordinate in pixels
Returns:	Nothing
Notes:	If the value in CX is greater than the value in DX, this service swaps the two values. After you set horizontal limits using this service, you cannot use the mouse or Int 33H Function 04H to move the mouse cursor beyond the limits. If the mouse cursor lies outside the specified area when this service is called, the mouser cursor is moved into the area. Your program must pass pixel coordinates to this service. To use text column coordinates, multiply them by 8. For example, to restrict horizontal movement to the area between column 4 and column 40, you would call this service with 32 in the CX register and 320 in DX.

Int 33H Function 08H
Set vertical limits for mouse cursor

Action:	Sets upper and lower vertical limits for mouse cursor movement
Call with:	AX = 0008H CX = minimum (upper) vertical coordinate in pixels DX = maximum (lower) vertical coordinate in pixels
Returns:	Nothing

Mouse Programming

Notes:	If the value in CX is greater than the value in DX, this service swaps the two values.
	After you set vertical limits using this service, you cannot use the mouse or Int 33H Function 04H to move the mouse cursor beyond the limits.
	If the mouse cursor lies outside the specified area when this service is called, the mouse cursor is moved into the area.
	Your program must pass pixel coordinates to this service. To use text column coordinates, multiply them by 8. For example, to restrict vertical movement to the area between row 5 and row 10, you would call this service with 40 in the CX register and 80 in DX.

Int 33H   Function 09H
Set graphics mode cursor shape

Action:	Defines the shape, color, and hot spot of the graphics mode cursor
Call with:	AX = 0009H BX = horizontal hot spot offset CX = vertical hot spot offset ES = segment of buffer containing the cursor masks DX = offset of cursor buffer containing the cursor masks
Returns:	Nothing
Notes:	The graphics mode cursor image is a 16-by-16-pixel area on the screen that is defined by a 64-byte buffer passed to this service. The bits in the screen mask, which is contained in the first 32 bytes of the buffer, are first combined with the existing screen image by using logical AND operations. The bits in the cursor mask, which is contained in the second 32 bytes, are then combined with the resulting values by using XOR operations to get the final displayed image.
	The hot spot of the cursor is relative to the upper left corner of the cursor image. In display modes 4 and 5, the value of the horizontal offset must be even. Most often the horizontal and vertical values of the hot spot range from 0 through 15. Use Int 33H Function 2AH to read the current hot spot.

Int 33H Function 0AH
Set text mode cursor shape

Action: Defines the shape and attributes of the text mode mouse cursor

Call with: AX = 000AH
BX = cursor type:
 0 = software cursor
 1 = hardware cursor

if BX = 0
 CX = screen mask value
 DX = cursor mask value

if BX = 1
 CX = starting scan line for cursor
 DX = ending scan line for cursor

Returns: Nothing

Notes: See the section "Mouse cursor appearance" early in this chapter for information about setting the mouse cursor appearance in text mode.

Int 33H Function 0BH
Read mouse motion counters

Action: Returns the net mouse movement that has occurred since the last call to this service or since the mouse was initialized

Call with: AX = 000BH

Returns: CX = horizontal mouse movement
DX = vertical mouse movement

Notes: Movement is measured in mickeys, with one mickey equal to approximately 1/200 inch. Positive mickey values represent movement down or to the right; negative mickey values represent movement up or to the left. These values reflect actual mouse movement, not mouse cursor movement.

Int 33H   Function 0CH
Set user-defined mouse event handler

Action: Specifies the mouse event that the program should trap and the offset and address of the code that the mouse driver will execute when the specified event occurs

Call with: AX = 000CH
CX = event mask:

Bit(s)	Meaning (if set)
0	Mouse cursor movement
1	Left button pressed
2	Left button released
3	Right button pressed
4	Right button released
5	Center button pressed
6	Center button released
7–15	Reserved (must be 0)

ES = segment of mouse event handler code
DX = offset of mouse event handler code

Returns: Nothing

Notes: This service sets up an event handler that the mouse driver calls when and if the mouse driver detects the mouse event specified by the event mask. When the handler begins executing, the following information is in the CPU registers:

AX = mouse event flags (that is, the event mask)
BX = current button state:

Bit(s)	Meaning (if set)
0	Left button down
1	Right button down
2	Center button down
3–15	Reserved

CX = horizontal cursor pixel position
DX = vertical cursor pixel position
SI = current vertical mickey count
DI = current horizontal mickey count
DS = data segment of mouse driver

To disable calls to the handler, either call this service with an event mask of 0 or call Int 33H Function 00H.

The event handler code must be called with a far call and terminated with a far return.

Int 33H   Function 0DH
Enable light-pen emulation

Action:	Enables light-pen emulation by the mouse
Call with:	AX = 000DH
Returns:	Nothing
Notes:	When light-pen emulation is on, a program that is looking for light-pen input interprets the mouse's position as the light pen's position. When both mouse buttons are pressed, the program interprets the situation as "pen down."

Int 33H   Function 0EH
Disable light-pen emulation

Action:	Disables light-pen emulation by the mouse
Call with:	AX = 000EH
Returns:	Nothing
Notes:	See Int 33H Function 0DH for information.

Int 33H   Function 0FH
Set mickeys-to-pixels ratio

Action:	Specifies the number of mickeys of mouse movement required for eight pixels of mouse cursor movement

Call with:	AX = 000FH CX = horizontal mickeys (1 through 32,767; default = 8) DX = vertical mickeys (1 through 32,767; default = 16)
Returns:	Nothing
Notes:	The values that are placed in CX and DX specify the number of mickeys—approximately 1/200 inch—that the mouse must move to cause the mouse cursor to move eight pixels (or one character cell). Smaller values result in greater cursor movement for a given mouse movement. The default values require 3.2 inches horizontal and 2 inches vertical mouse movement to move the cursor over the entire screen.

Int 33H Function 10H
Set mouse cursor exclusion area

Action:	Defines a screen area in which the mouse cursor is hidden
Call with:	AX = 0010H CX = *x*-coordinate of upper left corner DX = *y*-coordinate of upper left corner SI = *x*-coordinate of lower right corner DI = *y*-coordinate of lower right corner
Returns:	Nothing
Notes:	When the user moves the mouse cursor within a defined exclusion area, the mouse cursor is hidden. This service decrements the counter whose value determines whether the mouse cursor is displayed, exactly as if Int 33H Function 02H had been called. Calling Int 33H Function 00H or 01H cancels any defined exclusion area.

Int 33H Function 13H
Set double-speed threshold

Action:	Specifies the mouse movement speed at which cursor movement is doubled
Call with:	AX = 0013H DX = threshold speed in mickeys per second

Returns:	Nothing
Notes:	When the double-speed threshold is exceeded, cursor movement relative to mouse movement doubles, which allows the user to make large mouse cursor movements more efficiently. To effectively disable movement doubling, set a large threshold (for example, 12,000). The default doubling threshold is 64 mickeys per second.

Int 33H   Function 15H
Get buffer size for saving mouse driver state

Action:	Determines the size of the buffer needed to store the mouse driver's state retrieved by a call to Int 33H Function 16H
Call with:	AX = 0015H
Returns:	BX = required buffer size in bytes
Notes:	See "Notes" for Int 33H Function 16H.

Int 33H   Function 16H
Save mouse driver state

Action:	Saves the current state of the mouse driver in a user-allocated buffer
Call with:	AX = 0016H ES = segment of buffer DX = offset of buffer
Returns:	Nothing
Notes:	First the program must call Int 33H Function 15H to determine the size of the buffer. The calling program must allocate the buffer. A program should call this service before executing a child process (with Int 21H Function 4BH) that might use the mouse. After execution returns from the child process, use Int 33H Function 17H to restore the mouse driver state.

Mouse Programming

Int 33H Function 17H
Restore mouse driver state

Action:	Restores a previously saved mouse driver state
Call with:	AX = 0017H ES = segment of buffer DX = offset of buffer
Returns:	Nothing
Notes:	This service restores a mouse driver state that was saved previously with Int 33H Function 16H. See "Notes" for that service for more information.

Int 33H Function 1AH
Set mouse sensitivity

Action:	Specifies the mickeys–to–cursor movement sensitivity and also sets the mouse threshold speed for cursor movement doubling
Call with:	AX = 001AH BX = horizontal mickey sensitivity (0 through 100) CX = vertical mickey sensitivity (0 through 100) DX = double-speed threshold sensitivity (0 through 100)
Returns:	Nothing
Notes:	This service combines the actions of Int 33H Functions 0FH and 13H. The values placed in BX and CX specify the sensitivity of the cursor to mouse movement. These values don't specify a particular mickeys-to-pixels ratio. Instead, they offer programmers an intuitive range from which to choose mouse sensitivity. Smaller values result in greater cursor movement for a given mouse movement. When the double-speed threshold is exceeded, cursor movement relative to mouse movement doubles, which allows the user to make large mouse cursor movements more efficiently. The value placed in DX doesn't specify a particular double-speed threshold. A value of 0 results in a low double-speed threshold; a value of 50, the default double-speed threshold of 64 mickeys per second; and a value of 100, a high double-speed threshold.

Int 33H Function 1BH
Get mouse sensitivity

Action: Returns the current values of the vertical and horizontal mickey-to-pixel ratios and the speed threshold for doubling of cursor motion

Call with: AX = 001BH

Returns: BX = current horizontal mickey sensitivity
CX = current vertical mickey sensitivity
DX = current double-speed threshold sensitivity

Notes: See "Notes" for Int 33H Function 1AH for further information about these settings.

Int 33H Function 1CH
Set mouse driver interrupt rate

Action: Sets the rate at which mouse driver queries mouse hardware

Call with: AX = 001CH
BX = interrupt rate:

Bit(s)	Meaning (if set)
0	No interrupts
1	30 interrupts per second
2	50 interrupts per second
3	100 interrupts per second
4	200 interrupts per second
5–15	Reserved (0)

Returns: Nothing

Notes: This service is available only with the InPort mouse.

The higher interrupt rates provide better resolution in graphics mode but might slow program performance.

If more than one bit in BX is set, the service uses the rightmost set bit (the lowest-order set bit).

Mouse Programming   **149**

Int 33H   Function 1DH
Set mouse cursor display page

Action:	Specifies the video display page for the mouse cursor
Call with:	AX = 001DH BX = display page number
Returns:	Nothing
Notes:	The number of available display pages depends on the display mode. See the reference entry for Int 10H Function 05H in Chapter 7.

Int 33H   Function 1EH
Get mouse cursor display page

Action:	Returns the current mouse cursor display page
Call with:	AX = 001EH
Returns:	BX = current display page
Notes:	For information about this service, see "Notes" for Int 33H Function 1DH.

Int 33H   Function 21H
Reset mouse driver

Action:	Resets the mouse driver and returns its status
Call with:	AX = 0021H

Returns:	If mouse available:
	    AX = FFFFH
	    BX = number of buttons
	If mouse not available:
	    AX = 0021H

Notes: Unlike Int 33H Function 00H, this service does not initialize the mouse hardware. However, like Int 33H Function 00H, this service initializes the mouse software.

Int 33H Function 2AH
Get cursor hot spot

Action: Returns graphics cursor hot spot coordinates, mouse display counter state, and mouse type

Call with: AX = 002AH

Returns: AX = cursor display counter state
BX = horizontal hot spot
CX = vertical hot spot
DX = mouse type (see "Notes")

Notes This service is available with Microsoft Mouse Driver versions 7.02 and later.

If the cursor display counter is 0, the cursor is visible on the screen. If it is less than 0, the cursor is hidden. Calls to Int 33H Function 01H increment the counter by 1 if it is less than 0, and have no effect if it is 0. Calls to Int 33H Function 02H decrement the counter by 1.

The hot spot coordinates are relative to the upper left corner of the cursor block, and specify the exact pixel to which the graphics cursor is pointing. To set the hot spot coordinates, use Int 33H Function 09H.

The mouse type can be one of six values:

Value	Type
0	No mouse
1	Bus mouse
2	Serial mouse
3	InPort mouse
4	IBM mouse
5	Hewlett-Packard mouse

Mouse Programming

CHAPTER 7

Screen Display

The screen display is what most people notice first about a program. An attractive, well-designed screen display can make a program a pleasure to use. Conversely, a poorly designed screen display can make using a program real torture! It's for good reason, therefore, that programmers typically spend a great deal of time on programming the screen display. This chapter explains how you can use MS-DOS services for display programming.

Before we get into the details of MS-DOS display services, you need to know a little about the way your video system operates. A computer's video system is made up of a monitor and a display adapter. As you know, the monitor displays output. The display adapter is a piece of hardware (an add-on card that you place in your computer) that controls the monitor. This section introduces the video systems most commonly found on PCs.

Screens, Pixels, and Video Adapters

If you look closely at any PC display, you'll see that the image is made up of thousands of small dots. Each dot is called a *pixel,* which is short for *picture element.* Your display adapter controls each pixel, turning it on or off and, on color systems, determining the pixel's color. The image that you view on the screen is the visual composite of all the screen pixels. Thus, to display a particular image on the screen, your program must see to it that the correct pattern of pixels is illuminated.

All PC display adapters are *memory mapped,* which means that they have a section of random access memory (RAM) that is devoted to the screen display. This memory has various names: video RAM, video buffer, refresh buffer, and display buffer. (In this discussion, we use *video RAM.*) Dedicated hardware on the display adapter scans the video RAM continually and converts the data in the memory into the appropriate pixel pattern, which it then sends to the monitor. To display an image, therefore, a program must write the appropriate data to video RAM. You'll see how to do so in this chapter.

Each type of PC display adapter has a specific maximum resolution, which refers to the number of pixels it can display. By convention, resolution is referred to in the format $X \times Y$, where X is the number of pixels horizontally, and Y is the number of pixels vertically. The total number of pixels on the screen is, of course, X multiplied by Y. As you would expect, higher resolution displays provide sharper, easier-to-read images.

Over the years, PC video systems have evolved toward higher resolution and a greater number of colors. Most display adapters support a variety of modes that enable you to select the resolution used in your program output. Each mode is defined by its resolution, the number of colors it can display, and whether it displays text or graphics. Later in this chapter, Figure 7-4 lists the modes available on the most common PC display adapters, which are described in the following list:

- The Monochrome Display and Printer Adapter (MDA) was introduced in 1981 with the first IBM PCs. It displays monochrome text only and has no graphics capabilities.
- The Color Graphics Adapter (CGA) was also introduced in 1981. It provides a 16-color text mode and two graphics modes: a 640x200 monochrome mode and a 320x200 4-color mode.
- The Enhanced Graphics Adapter (EGA) was released in 1985. It provides a 16-color text mode and a 640x350 16-color graphics mode.
- The Multi-Color Graphics Array (MCGA) came out in 1987. In addition to 16-color text, this display adapter provides a 640x480 2-color graphics mode and a 320x200 256-color graphics mode.
- The Video Graphics Array (VGA), released in 1987, offers a 16-color text mode, a 640x480 16-color graphics mode, and a 320x200 256-color graphics mode.
- The Hercules products—the Graphics Card (1982), Graphics Card Plus (1986), and InColor Card (1987)—offer MDA compatibility in text modes, but their graphics modes are nonstandard and are not supported directly by MS-DOS or the BIOS.

Text and Graphics Modes

All of the previously listed display adapters can operate in text modes. With the exception of the MDA, all of them can also operate in graphics modes. The next two sections explain the fundamental distinction—in terms of screen output—between these two modes.

Text modes

In text modes, the screen is divided into a matrix of character cells. Most display adapters offer two text modes: one with a matrix of 40 columns by 25 rows and the other (the default) with a matrix of 80 columns by 25 rows. The cells are not visible, of course—they simply mark possible display locations. In each cell, the display adapter can display one of a predefined set of characters. This set includes letters, numerals, punctuation marks, special symbols, and other characters (for a complete list of display characters, see Appendix B). That's all you can do in text mode: display the predefined characters in the matrix of character cells. Each cell is identified by its row and column coordinates; the coordinates of the upper left cell are (0, 0). On a screen that has 80 columns by 25 rows, therefore, the coordinates of the lower right cell are (79, 24).

Like all images on the screen, each character in a text mode is displayed as a pattern of pixels. The pixel pattern for each character is stored in read-only memory (ROM) on the display adapter. As a result, when a program wants to display a certain character, it does not have to specify the character's pixel pattern. Rather, a program need only specify the character's identity (that is, the ASCII code). The display adapter hardware retrieves the corresponding pixel pattern from ROM and displays it on the screen.

As mentioned earlier, PC display adapters are memory mapped. In text modes, each character cell on the screen is represented by 2 adjacent bytes of memory in video RAM. The first, or low-order, byte specifies the character to display. The second byte, called the *attribute byte*, specifies the attributes—how the character is displayed. Bit fields in the attribute byte control such aspects as color and intensity. Figure 7-1 shows the fields in the attribute byte.

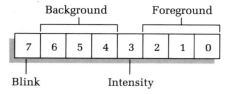

FIGURE 7-1.
The text mode attribute byte.

If the blink bit is set in the attribute byte, the character is displayed blinking. If the intensity bit is set, the character is displayed in high intensity. The effects of the foreground and background fields in the attribute byte depend on whether you use a monochrome text mode or a color text mode. Figure 7-2 lists the effects for monochrome modes, and Figure 7-3 lists the effects for color modes.

In color text modes, the foreground and background fields control the color of the character (foreground) and the color of the character cell (background). You can choose from 8 colors. (This is the number of values that can be specified by a 3-bit field.) Because the attribute byte's intensity bit applies to the foreground, you have 16 choices in foreground colors—the 8 colors of normal intensity plus 8 high-intensity colors. The table shown in Figure 7-3 lists these 16 colors. The table assumes that the default color palette is active.

Character display	Background	Foreground
Normal video	000	111
Reverse video	111	000
None (all black)	000	000
None (all white)*	111	111
Underline	000	001

* VGA only

FIGURE 7-2.
Foreground and background attribute settings for the monochrome text mode (mode number 07H on MDA, EGA, VGA, and Hercules display adapters).

Value (decimal)	Value (binary)	Foreground or background color	Foreground color with intensity bit set
0	000	Black	Gray
1	001	Blue	Bright blue
2	010	Green	Bright green
3	011	Cyan	Bright cyan
4	100	Red	Bright red
5	101	Magenta	Bright magenta
6	110	Brown	Yellow
7	111	White	Bright white

FIGURE 7-3.
Foreground and background attribute byte color settings for color text modes (mode numbers 00H through 03H on CGA, EGA, MCGA, and VGA adapters).

Let's look at some actual attribute bytes and their effects on the display of characters—first for a monochrome display mode:

Attribute byte	Display
00000111	Normal video (white characters on black background)
01110000	Reverse video (black characters on white background)
10000111	Blinking normal video
00001001	Underlined bright white characters on black background

Here are some examples for color text modes:

Attribute byte	Display
00000111	White characters on black background
00010111	White characters on blue background
01000110	Brown characters on red background
11110000	Blinking black characters on white background

Graphics modes

In graphics modes, your program has all of the text display capabilities described earlier in this chapter for text modes. In addition, graphics modes give your program control over each individual pixel on the screen. With the freedom to illuminate any pattern of pixels, a program can display any image you want, from simple circles and lines to the complex patterns required for a graphical user interface such as Microsoft Windows.

As with text modes, a graphics mode screen display is memory mapped. Each pixel on the screen is controlled by the contents of one or more bits in video RAM. How many pixels and colors are available on the screen depends on the display adapter and the screen display mode being used. As you might guess, writing data to video RAM to display a particular graphics image is a complex task.

MS-DOS provides little support for graphics mode programming. A BIOS service (Int 10H Function 0CH) is available for writing a single pixel, but no services are available for more complex drawing tasks. For this reason, I strongly recommend that you use your high-level language's capabilities for graphics programming. Both Microsoft Basic and C include a rich set of commands for creating graphics.

PC display modes

PC display adapters offer a variety of text and graphics display modes. Figure 7-4 lists these modes, showing the resolution and the number of colors for each mode, whether the mode is text or graphics, and the supporting display adapters. The list shows resolution in terms of character cells for text mode and pixels for graphics mode. Recently developed display adapters, such as the Super VGA, also support a variety of text and graphics modes and might use modes not listed here. See your display adapter documentation for more information.

If you examine Figure 7-4 closely, you'll notice that each higher-resolution display adapter can usually emulate the modes of the lower-resolution

Display mode	Resolution	Colors	Text or graphics	Adapters
00H	40x25	16*	T	CGA, EGA, MCGA, VGA
01H	40x25	16	T	CGA, EGA, MCGA, VGA
02H	80x25	16*	T	CGA, EGA, MCGA, VGA
03H	80x25	16	T	CGA, EGA, MCGA, VGA
04H	320x200	4	G	CGA, EGA, MCGA, VGA
05H	320x200	4*	G	CGA, EGA, MCGA, VGA
06H	640x200	2	G	CGA, EGA, MCGA, VGA
07H	80x25	2†	T	MDA, EGA, and VGA
0DH	320x200	16	G	EGA and VGA
0EH	640x200	16	G	EGA and VGA
0FH	640x350	2†	G	EGA and VGA
10H	640x350	n‡	G	EGA and VGA
11H	640x480	2	G	MCGA and VGA
12H	640x480	16	G	VGA
13H	320x200	256	G	MCGA and VGA

* Color burst is disabled if you use a composite monitor with a CGA display adapter, improving the appearance of green or amber displays. Otherwise, modes 00H and 01H are equivalent, as are modes 02H and 03H and modes 04H and 05H.

† Monochrome monitor.

‡ Four colors are available in mode 10H on an EGA display adapter that has 64 KB of installed video RAM. Sixteen colors are available on an EGA display adapter that has 128 KB or more of RAM and on a VGA display adapter.

FIGURE 7-4.
Display modes available on PC video systems.

display adapters. Thus, all CGA modes are also available on EGA and VGA adapters, and the EGA modes are available on VGA adapters.

You can set the current display mode using the service Int 10H Function 00H. To read the current display mode, use Int 10H Function 0FH. Note that the display mode numbers used by the BIOS do not correspond to the values used to set modes with the SCREEN statement in Basic. For example, to set display mode 06H in Basic, you would use the SCREEN statement with a parameter of 2.

Display Pages

Most display adapters have more installed video RAM than is needed to hold a full screen of information. The video RAM, therefore, is divided into a number of *display pages,* each of which can hold the data required for a full screen display. The number of pages available depends on the display adapter and the current display mode.

At any given moment, the screen displays the data in a single display page, called the *active display page*. By default, this is display page 0. Your program can change the active display page by calling Int 10H Function 05H. When you change display pages, the screen switches immediately to display the data in the newly active page. Switching pages has no effect on the information in any page. To determine which display page is active, use Int 10H Function 0FH. For more information about this service, see the reference entry for Int 10H Function 0FH in the reference section at the end of this chapter.

You can use multiple display pages to good advantage in your programs. As you'll see in this chapter, you can write to any valid display page, even when it is not active. For example, your program can write text to an inactive display page without affecting the active display and then display the new text immediately by calling Int 10H Function 05H.

Cursor Control in Text Mode Display Pages

Every text mode display page has a cursor, which is a blinking underline or rectangle that marks the location where text will be displayed. Clearly, you must be able to control the location of the cursor if you are to design text mode screen displays. In addition, you might also want to change the appearance of the cursor to signal program status to the user. For example, the Microsoft Basic and C integrated environment editors use an underline cursor for insert editing and a block cursor for overstrike editing.

Note that a cursor exists for every valid display page, even when that page is not the active one. You can modify the location of the cursor on inactive display pages, but you cannot modify the cursor's appearance.

To modify the appearance of the cursor on the active display page, use Int 10H Function 01H. You can change only the rectangular cursor's size and its position in the character cell. You do this by specifying the start and stop scan lines that the cursor uses. A character cell contains a certain number of scan lines: The top scan line is number 0, and the bottom scan line is number 7. If you specified 6 for the start scan line and 7 for the stop scan line, the cursor would be an underline character. See the reference section at the end of this chapter for more information about Int 10H Function 01H.

To change the position of the cursor on any display page, use Int 10H Function 02H. To get the position and scan lines of the cursor on any display page, use Int 10H Function 03H.

When programming in Microsoft Basic, keep in mind two considerations, both of which relate to cursor position. The first consideration is relatively minor. The Basic cursor-related statements, such as LOCATE, assign coordinates (1, 1) to the character cell at the upper left of the screen. In contrast, the BIOS assigns coordinates (0, 0) to that cell. For the same screen position, therefore, the BIOS coordinates are always one number lower (for both the *x*-coordinate and the *y*-coordinate) than the Basic coordinates.

The second consideration is more serious. The BIOS keeps a record of the cursor position. Microsoft Basic is different from C (and from most other languages) because it maintains its own record of cursor position in parallel with the BIOS record. When you display text using the Basic output statements, such as PRINT, the output appears at the screen position indicated by Basic's record of the cursor position.

Here's where the problem arises. If Basic modifies the cursor position (for example, with a PRINT or a LOCATE statement), both the Basic and the BIOS cursor position records are updated. If you modify the cursor position using Int 10H Function 02H, however, only the BIOS cursor position record is updated. Basic's cursor position record still indicates the position of the cursor as it was before the call to Int 10H Function 02H, and that's where Basic's output statements will display text. In contrast, the BIOS output services, such as Int 10H Function 0EH, use the position indicated by the BIOS cursor position record.

The bottom line is that if you're going to use Int 10H Function 02H in Basic to move the cursor, you must also use the Int 10H text output services. And, if you want to use the Basic text output statements, you must use the LOCATE statement to control the cursor position.

Demonstration Programs for BIOS Display Services

The programs in Listings 7-1 and 7-2 demonstrate most of the topics covered so far in this chapter. When you run these programs, note the difference between the high-level language text output statements. In Basic, the PRINT statement always sends text to display page 0, even if the program has made another page active. In C, however, the *puts()* and *printf()* functions send output to the currently active page. Later in this chapter, you'll learn how to use MS-DOS output services to write text on any display page.

```
DEFINT A-Z

DECLARE SUB SetDisplayPage (page)
DECLARE FUNCTION GetDisplayPage ()
DECLARE FUNCTION GetDisplayMode ()

' $INCLUDE: 'QB.BI'

DIM SHARED inRegs AS RegType, outRegs AS RegType


' Begin execution

CLS

PRINT "Your video system is in display mode"; GetDisplayMode
PRINT "Display page"; GetDisplayPage; "is active."

LOCATE 4, 1

PRINT "Press any key to continue."
WHILE INKEY$ = "": WEND

PRINT
PRINT "Press a key to make display page 1 active. (It will be blank.)"
PRINT "Then press any key to return to this page."

WHILE INKEY$ = "": WEND

CALL SetDisplayPage(1)

' The following PRINT statements write to page 0, even though page 1
' is active
PRINT
PRINT "Now display page 0 is active again."
PRINT
PRINT "Press any key to end the program."

WHILE INKEY$ = "": WEND
CALL SetDisplayPage(0)
WHILE INKEY$ = "": WEND

END

FUNCTION GetDisplayMode
    ' Calls Int 10H Function 0FH to get the current display mode

    inRegs.ax = &HF00
    CALL INTERRUPT(&H10, inRegs, outRegs)
```

LISTING 7-1. *(continued)*
Demonstration of a number of BIOS display services in Basic.

LISTING 7-1. *continued*

```
    GetDisplayMode = outRegs.ax AND &HFF
END FUNCTION

FUNCTION GetDisplayPage
    ' Calls Int 10H Function 0FH to get the current display page

    inRegs.ax = &HF00
    CALL INTERRUPT(&H10, inRegs, outRegs)

    GetDisplayPage = outRegs.bx \ 256
END FUNCTION

SUB SetDisplayPage (page)
    ' Calls Int 10H Function 05H to set the current display page

    inRegs.ax = &H500 + page
    CALL INTERRUPT(&H10, inRegs, outRegs)
END SUB
```

```c
/* Demonstrates a number of BIOS display services */

#include <stdio.h>
#include <dos.h>

/* Declare the register unions */
union REGS inregs, outregs;

/* Function prototypes */
void clearscreen(void);
int get_video_mode(void);
int get_display_page(void);
void set_display_page(int page);

main()
{
    clearscreen();

    printf("Your video system is in display mode %d.", get_video_mode());
    printf("\nDisplay page %d is active.", get_display_page());

    puts("\n\nPress any key to continue.\n\n");
    getch();

    puts("Press any key to make display page 1 active. (It will be blank.)");
    puts("Then press any key to return to this display page.");
```

LISTING 7-2. *(continued)*
Demonstration of a number of BIOS display services in C.

LISTING 7-2. *continued*

```c
        getch();
        set_display_page(1);

        /* The following output is written to display page 1 */
        puts("\n\nDisplay page 1 is now active.");
        puts("\n\nPress any key to return to page 0.");

        getch();
        clearscreen();
        set_display_page(0);
        puts("\n\nPress any key to end the program.");
        getch();

        clearscreen();
}   /* End of main() */

int get_video_mode(void)
{
    /* Returns the current video mode */

    inregs.x.ax = 0XF00;
    int86(0X10, &inregs, &outregs);
    return(outregs.h.al);
}

int get_display_page(void)
{
    /* Returns the current display page */

    inregs.x.ax = 0XF00;
    int86(0X10, &inregs, &outregs);
    return(outregs.x.bx >> 8);
}

void set_display_page(int page)
{
    /* Sets the active display page */

    inregs.x.ax = 0X500 + page;
    int86(0X10, &inregs, &outregs);
}

void clearscreen(void)
{
    int x;

    for (x = 0; x < 25; x++)
        printf("\n");
}
```

Screen Output Using
MS-DOS and BIOS Display Services

When using operating system services to write text to the screen display, you have two choices. The MS-DOS display services, which you access via Int 21H, operate correctly on any system that runs MS-DOS, regardless of the level of IBM hardware compatibility. These services, however, execute relatively slowly. The BIOS display services, which you access via Int 10H, are much more efficient than the MS-DOS services. They do, however, require IBM hardware compatibility. Fortunately, compatibility is not as serious an issue as it used to be. With rare exceptions, the PC "clones" that are so common today have excellent IBM hardware compatibility.

Note that the MS-DOS display services do not let you control the value of the attribute byte. If output goes to the screen (it is not redirected), the text is displayed using whatever attributes the corresponding character cells already have. In contrast, some of the BIOS display services provide control of the attribute byte.

Another difference between the MS-DOS and BIOS display services involves cursor control. The MS-DOS services update the cursor position for you. After an MS-DOS service displays one or more characters, the screen cursor is positioned immediately after the last character. When the output reaches the right edge of the screen, it wraps to the start of the next line. In most cases, the BIOS display services provide no cursor updating—your program must update the cursor position explicitly.

A final difference between the MS-DOS and BIOS display services is related to display pages. The MS-DOS display services always send output to the active display page, but some of the BIOS display services allow you to send output to any valid display page.

MS-DOS display services

To use MS-DOS services to display a string of one or more characters on the screen, use Int 21H Function 40H. This is one of MS-DOS's *handle* services. A handle is a numeric identifier that MS-DOS assigns to an input or output (I/O) device. MS-DOS can associate a handle with a disk file, the keyboard, a serial port, the display screen, and so on. As you'll see later in this book, you can use the handle-based I/O services for input and output with all of these devices.

At present, however, we're interested in the display screen. When a program runs, MS-DOS assigns handles for the standard devices. Standard output (*stdout*) is assigned handle 1, and standard error (*stderr*) is assigned handle 2. Standard output can be redirected and is by default the screen. Standard error cannot be redirected and is always the screen. Your program can use these two handles immediately after MS-DOS assigns them, without any special program action.

When you call Int 21H Function 40H, you pass to it the handle of the device that will accept the output, the number of characters to output, and the address of the program buffer that holds the characters. If the service succeeds, it returns with the carry flag clear and the number of bytes transferred in AX. If the service fails, it sets the carry flag and returns an error code in AX.

MS-DOS also has two services that write a single character to the standard output (and are therefore sensitive to output redirection). They differ in how they handle Ctrl-C. Int 21H Function 02H writes one character to standard output and responds to Ctrl-C. If the keyboard detects a Ctrl-C after this service completes, it issues Int 23H. Int 21H Function 06H, however, does not respond to Ctrl-C. Note that your programs can also use Int 21H Function 06H for keyboard input, as explained in Chapter 5.

The programs in Listings 7-3 and 7-4 demonstrate Int 21H Functions 40H and 02H. (Using Int 21H Function 06H is essentially the same as using Function 02H.) Basic programmers should note that you use the SADD statement to obtain the offset address of a variable-length string. If you want to display a fixed-length string using Int 21H Function 40H, you obtain its address using VARPTR. For both variable-length and fixed-length strings, VARSEG obtains the segment address.

```
DEFINT A-Z

'$INCLUDE: 'QB.BI'

DIM SHARED inRegs AS RegTypeX, outRegs AS RegTypeX


' Begin execution
msg1$ = "Displayed using Int 21H Function 40H."
msg2$ = "Displayed using Int 21H Function 02H."

CLS

PRINT "Press any key to display a message using Int 21H Function 40H."
PRINT

WHILE INKEY$ = "": WEND
```

LISTING 7-3. *(continued)*
Demonstration of the Int 21H display services in Basic.

LISTING 7-3. *continued*

```
        inRegs.ax = &H4000
        inRegs.bx = 1                       ' Handle for standard output
        inRegs.cx = LEN(msg1$)

        ' Get segment and offset addresses of the string
        inRegs.ds = VARSEG(msg1$)
        inRegs.dx = SADD(msg1$)

        ' Display the string
        CALL INTERRUPTX(&H21, inRegs, outRegs)

        LOCATE 5, 1

        PRINT "Press any key to display a string using Int 21H Function 02H."
        PRINT

        WHILE INKEY$ = "": WEND

        ' Loop one time for each character in the string
        FOR i = 1 TO LEN(msg2$)
            inRegs.ax = &H200

            ' Place the next character in the DL register
            inRegs.dx = ASC(MID$(msg2$, i, 1))

            ' Display the character
            CALL INTERRUPTX(&H21, inRegs, outRegs)
        NEXT

        PRINT : PRINT
        PRINT "Press any key to exit."

        WHILE INKEY$ = "": WEND

        CLS

        END
```

```c
/* Demonstrates Int 21H display services */

#include <stdio.h>
#include <dos.h>

/* Declare the register unions */
union REGS inregs, outregs;
```

LISTING 7-4.
Demonstration of the Int 21H display services in C.

(continued)

LISTING 7-4. *continued*

```c
/* Function prototype */
void clearscreen(void);

main()
{
    char *msg1 = "Displayed using Int 21H Function 40H.";
    char *msg2 = "Displayed using Int 21H Function 02H.";
    char *p;
    int count;

    clearscreen();

    printf("Press any key to display a message using ");
    printf("Int 21H Function 40H.\n ");

    getch();

    inregs.x.ax = 0X4000;
    inregs.x.bx = 1;
    inregs.x.cx = strlen(msg1);
    inregs.x.dx = (int)msg1;

    /* We can assume that register DS already contains the segment */
    /* address of the data segment. If this were not the case, we  */
    /* would need to declare a type SREGS structure, put the segment */
    /* of the string in DS, and use int86x().  */

    /* Display the string */
    int86(0X21, &inregs, &outregs);


    printf("\n\nPress any key to display a message using");
    printf("Int 21H Function 02H.\n");

    getch();

    /* p points to the first letter of msg2 */
    p = msg2;

    /* Loop one time for each character in the string */
    for (count = 1; count <= strlen(msg2); count++)
        {
        inregs.x.ax = 0X200;

        /* Place the next character in the DL register */
        inregs.h.dl = *p++;

        /* Display the character */
        int86(0X21, &inregs, &outregs);
        }
```

(continued)

LISTING 7-4. *continued*

```
    printf("\n\nPress any key to exit.");
    getch();
}

void clearscreen(void)
{
    int x;

    for (x = 0; x < 25; x++)
        printf("\n");
}
```

BIOS display services

You can choose from three BIOS display services, each of which outputs a single character to the screen. All of them permit the program to specify to which display page the output is going. These are the display services:

- Int 10H Function 09H writes a character-and-attribute pair to the screen and does not update the cursor position.

- Int 10H Function 0AH writes a character to the screen using the existing attributes and does not update the cursor position.

- Int 10H Function 0EH writes a character to the screen and updates the cursor position. In text modes, the service uses the existing attributes. In graphics modes, the service can specify the foreground color.

You'll want to use the BIOS display services if you need the ability to write characters to any display page. Choosing among the three services, however, presents a quandary. If you want attribute control, you must use Int 10H Function 09H. But if you use that service, your program has to update the cursor position by using Int 10H Function 02H. If you want automatic cursor position updating, you must use Int 10H Function 0AH. If you use that service, however, you have no control over the attributes. What's the solution to this dilemma? First use Int 10H Function 09H to write to the cursor location a space character (ASCII 20H) that has the desired attribute. Then use Int 10H Function 0AH to write the desired character to the same location and update the cursor position. The demonstration programs in Listings 7-5 and 7-6 use this approach.

The programs in Listings 7-5 and 7-6 use two of the BIOS display services to create a function that displays strings. You can use this function to display any string on the screen. If the string exceeds the right edge of the screen, the function displays the extra characters on the next line. You can specify the cursor position and the attributes to be used for display, or you can use the current values. The programs also contain a function that uses Int 10H Function 02H to set the screen cursor position. You'll find more details about these functions in the programs' comments.

```
DEFINT A-Z

DECLARE SUB DisplayString (x$, row, col, fg, bg, blink)
DECLARE SUB SetCursorPos (col, row, page)

' $INCLUDE: 'QB.BI'

DIM SHARED inRegs AS RegType, outRegs AS RegType


' Begin execution

CLS

' Display a string eight times, each time with different attributes
FOR i = 1 TO 8
    CALL DisplayString("MS-DOS Programming!", i, i, i + 1, i, i MOD 2)
NEXT i

WHILE INKEY$ = "": WEND

CLS

END

SUB DisplayString (x$, row, col, fg, bg, blink)
    ' x$ is the string to be displayed.
    ' The string is displayed on display page 0.

    ' row and col are text coordinates of the desired display location.
    ' If either row or col is less than 0, the subprogram uses the current
    ' cursor position.

    ' Use fg and bg to specify the foreground (0 through 15) and background
    ' (0 through 7) attributes. The blink parameter controls blinking
    ' (if blink = 0, no blinking; if blink > 0, blinking). If any of these
    ' three arguments are less than 0, the string is displayed using the
    ' position's current attributes.


    ' Check for an empty string
    IF LEN(x$) = 0 THEN EXIT SUB
```

LISTING 7-5. *(continued)*
Demonstration of using the BIOS display services to display strings in Basic.

LISTING 7-5. *continued*

```
        ' Construct the attribute byte if requested
        IF (fg >= 0) AND (bg >= 0) AND (blink >= 0) THEN

            ' Set bit 7 if blinking requested
            IF (blink > 0) THEN
                attribute = &H80
            ELSE
                attribute = 0
            END IF

            ' Specify the background color in bits 4 through 6
            attribute = attribute OR ((bg * 16) AND &H70)

            ' Specify the foreground color in bits 0 through 2
            attribute = attribute OR (fg AND &HF)

        ELSE
            attribute = -1
        END IF

        ' Set the cursor position if requested
        IF (row >= 0) AND (col >= 0) THEN
            CALL SetCursorPos(col, row, 0)
        END IF

        ' Display the string
        FOR i = 1 TO LEN(x$)

            ' If the attributes are changing, use Int 10H Function 09H
            ' to write a space character that has the desired attributes
            IF (attribute >= 0) THEN
                inRegs.ax = &H920
                inRegs.bx = attribute
                inRegs.cx = 1
                CALL INTERRUPT(&H10, inRegs, outRegs)
            END IF

            ' Use Int 10H Function 0EH to write the character
            inRegs.ax = &HE00 + ASC(MID$(x$, i, 1))
            inRegs.bx = 0
            CALL INTERRUPT(&H10, inRegs, outRegs)
        NEXT i
    END SUB

    SUB SetCursorPos (col, row, page)
        ' Sets the cursor position on the specified display page

        inRegs.ax = &H200
        inRegs.bx = page * 256          ' Place the page number in BH
        inRegs.dx = (row * 256) + col   ' Place row in DH and col in DL

        CALL INTERRUPT(&H10, inRegs, outRegs)
    END SUB
```

```c
/* Displaying strings using the BIOS display services */

#include <stdio.h>
#include <dos.h>

/* Declare the register unions */
union REGS inregs, outregs;

/* Function prototypes */
void clearscreen(void);
void display_string(char *p, int row, int col, int fg, int bg, int blink);
void set_cursor_pos(int col, int row, int page);

main()
{
    int i;
    char *msg = "MS-DOS Programming!";

    clearscreen();

    /* Display a string eight times, each time with different attributes */
    for (i = 1; i < 9; i++)
        display_string(msg, i, i, i+1, i, i%2);

    getch();

    clearscreen();
}

void display_string(char *p, int row, int col, int fg, int bg, int blink)
{
    /* p points to the string to be displayed.
       The string is displayed on display page 0.

       row and col are text coordinates of the desired display location.
       If either row or col is less than 0, the function uses the current
       cursor position.

       Use fg and fb to specify the foreground (0 through 15) and background
       (0 through 7) attributes. The blink parameter controls blinking (if
       blink = 0, no blinking; if blink > 0, blinking). If any of these three
       arguments are less than 0, the string is displayed using the position's
       current attributes. */

    int count, length, attribute = 0;
    char *p1;

    /* Check for an empty string */
    if (strlen(p) == 0)
        return;
```

LISTING 7-6. *(continued)*
Demonstration of using the BIOS display services to display strings in C.

LISTING 7-6. *continued*

```c
    /* Construct the attribute byte if requested */
    if ((fg >= 0) && (bg >= 0) && (blink >= 0))
        {
        /* Set bit 7 if blinking requested */
        if (blink > 0)
            attribute = 0X80;

        /* Specify the background color in bits 4 through 6 */
        attribute = attribute | ((bg * 16) & 0X70);

        /* Specify the foreground color in bits 0 through 2 */
        attribute = attribute | (fg & 0XF);
        }
    else
        attribute = -1;

    /* Set the cursor position if requested */
    if ((row >= 0) && (col >= 0))
        set_cursor_pos(col, row, 0);

    /* Display the string */
    length = strlen(p);
    p1 = p;

    for (count = 1; count <= length; count++)
        {
        /* If the attributes are changing, use Int 10H Function 09H */
        /* to write a space character that has the desired attributes */
        if (attribute >= 0)
            {
            inregs.x.ax = 0X920;
            inregs.x.bx = attribute;
            inregs.x.cx = 1;
            int86(0X10, &inregs, &outregs);
            }

        /* Use Int 10H Function 0EH to write the character */
        inregs.x.ax = 0XE00 + *p1++;
        inregs.x.bx = 0;
        int86(0X10, &inregs, &outregs);
        }
}

void set_cursor_pos(int col, int row, int page)
{
    /* Sets cursor position on the specified display page */
    /* to the indicated position */
```

(continued)

LISTING 7-6. *continued*

```
    inregs.x.ax = 0X200;
    inregs.h.bh = page;
    inregs.h.dh = row;
    inregs.h.dl = col;

    int86(0X10, &inregs, &outregs);
}

void clearscreen(void)
{
    int x;

    for (x = 0; x < 25; x++)
        printf("\n");
}
```

Miscellaneous Video Functions

The MS-DOS display services also allow your programs to perform a number of other important tasks that we haven't yet discussed, such as reading the data in video RAM and clearing and scrolling windows. This section covers some of those miscellaneous display services.

Reading data from video RAM

In addition to writing data (characters and attributes) to video RAM, your programs can read data from video RAM. By reading the data in video RAM, a program can determine the character and the attributes at a specific location on any display page. The BIOS provides a service to do this task: Int 10H Function 08H. Listings 7-7 and 7-8 demonstrate this service.

Scrolling and clearing windows

Two BIOS services enable a program to scroll or clear a text mode window. Int 10H Function 06H scrolls the window up, and Int 10H Function 07H scrolls it down. Either service can be used to clear a window.

In this context, the term *window* simply means any rectangular screen region. When a program scrolls a window up, lines at the top of the window disappear, and blank lines that have the specified attributes appear at the bottom of the window. The converse applies when a program scrolls a window down. Text that scrolls out of the window is lost—it does not reappear if you scroll the window in the opposite direction. When a program uses either of these services to clear a window, blank lines that have the specified attribute fill the entire window.

The programs in Listings 7-7 and 7-8 demonstrate window scrolling and clearing. The *Scroll* subprogram in Listing 7-7 and the *scroll()* function in Listing 7-8 let the program specify the scrolling direction, the window coordinates, the number of lines scrolled, and the attribute to use for the new lines. If a negative attribute argument is passed, the program uses the current screen attribute as the cursor position (which is obtained using Int 10H Function 08H). For the sake of demonstration, the programs scroll the window one line at a time.

```
DEFINT A-Z

DECLARE SUB Scroll (direction, lines, x1, y1, x2, y2, attr)
DECLARE FUNCTION GetDisplayPage ()
DECLARE FUNCTION GetAttribute ()

' $INCLUDE: 'QB.BI'

DIM SHARED inRegs AS RegType, outRegs AS RegType

' Constants for the scrolling direction
CONST UP = 1, DOWN = 0


' Begin execution

CLS
PRINT "Scrolling demonstration. Press any key to continue."
WHILE INKEY$ = "": WEND
CLS

' Fill the screen with asterisks (*)
FOR i = 1 TO 2000
    PRINT "*";
NEXT i

' Put some text in a rectangular area
FOR i = 8 TO 17
    FOR j = 25 TO 65
        LOCATE i, j
        PRINT CHR$(i + 57);
    NEXT j
NEXT i

' Scroll down five lines, one line at a time
FOR i = 1 TO 5
    CALL Scroll(DOWN, 1, 24, 7, 64, 16, 39)
    SLEEP (1)
NEXT i
```

LISTING 7-7. *(continued)*
Demonstration of scrolling screen windows using Int 10H Functions 06H and 07H in Basic.

LISTING 7-7. *continued*

```
' Scroll up four lines, one line at a time
FOR i = 1 TO 4
    CALL Scroll(UP, 1, 24, 7, 64, 16, 23)
    SLEEP (1)
NEXT i

WHILE INKEY$ = "": WEND
CLS

END

FUNCTION GetAttribute
    ' Returns the current attributes at the cursor position
    ' on the current display page

    inRegs.ax = &H800
    inRegs.bx = GetDisplayPage * 256

    CALL INTERRUPT(&H10, inRegs, outRegs)

    GetAttribute = outRegs.ax \ 256
END FUNCTION

FUNCTION GetDisplayPage
    ' Returns the number of the currently active display page

    inRegs.ax = &HF00
    CALL INTERRUPT(&H10, inRegs, outRegs)

    GetDisplayPage = outRegs.bx \ 256
END FUNCTION

SUB Scroll (direction, lines, x1, y1, x2, y2, attr)
    ' Scrolls or clears a text mode window.

    ' Clears the window if lines equals 0. If lines is greater
    ' than 0, scrolls the window the number of lines specified.

    ' direction must equal UP or DOWN. (These constants must be defined
    ' in the calling program.)

    ' x1 and y1 are the text coordinates of the window's upper
    ' left corner.
    ' x2 and y2 are the text coordinates of the window's lower
    ' right corner.

    ' attr specifies the attributes to be used for the entire
    ' window (if cleared) or for new lines scrolling in at the top
    ' or bottom of the window (if scrolled). If attr is less than 0,
    ' the subprogram uses the attributes at the current cursor position.
```

(continued)

LISTING 7-7. *continued*

```
    IF attr < 0 THEN
        attr = GetAttribute
    END IF

    IF direction = UP THEN
        inRegs.ax = &H600 + lines
    ELSE
        inRegs.ax = &H700 + lines
    END IF

    inRegs.bx = attr * 256
    inRegs.cx = y1 * 256 + x1
    inRegs.dx = y2 * 256 + x2

    ' Scroll or clear the window
    CALL INTERRUPT(&H10, inRegs, outRegs)
END SUB
```

```c
/* Demonstration of scrolling and clearing windows */

#include <stdio.h>
#include <dos.h>

/* Declare the register unions */
union REGS inregs, outregs;

/* Constants for the scrolling direction */
#define UP 1
#define DOWN 0

/* Function prototypes */
void clearscreen(void);
int get_display_page(void);
int get_attribute(void);
void set_cursor_pos(int col, int row, int page);
void scroll(int direction, int lines, int x1, int y1,
            int x2, int y2, int attr);

main()
{
    int i, j;

    clearscreen();
    puts("Scrolling demonstration. Press any key to continue.");
    getch();
```

LISTING 7-8. *(continued)*
Demonstration of scrolling and clearing screen windows using Int 10H Functions 06H and 07H in C.

LISTING 7-8. *continued*

```
    /* Fill the screen with asterisks (*) */
    for (i = 1; i <= 2000; i++)
        putch('*');

    /* Put some text in a rectangular area */
    for (i = 7; i < 17; i++)
        for (j = 24; j < 65; j++)
            {
            set_cursor_pos(j, i, 0);
            putch(i + 58);
            }

    set_cursor_pos(30, 3, 0);
    puts("Press any key to continue.");

    /* Scroll down five lines, one line at a time */
    for (i = 1; i < 6; i++)
        {
        scroll(DOWN, 1, 24, 7, 64, 16, 39);
        getch();
        }

    /* Scroll up four lines, one line at a time */
    for (i = 1; i < 5; i++)
        {
        scroll(UP, 1, 24, 7, 64, 16, 23);
        getch();
        }

    clearscreen();
}

void set_cursor_pos(int col, int row, int page)
{
    /* Sets the text screen cursor on the specified display page */
    /* to the indicated position */

    inregs.x.ax = 0X200;
    inregs.h.bh = page;
    inregs.h.dh = row;
    inregs.h.dl = col;

    int86(0X10, &inregs, &outregs);
}

int get_attribute(void)
{
    /* Returns the current attributes at the cursor */
    /* position on the current display page */
```

(continued)

LISTING 7-8. *continued*

```c
        inregs.x.ax = 0X800;
        inregs.h.bh = get_display_page();
        int86(0X10, &inregs, &outregs);

        return(outregs.h.ah);
}

int get_display_page(void)
{
        /* Returns the number of the currently active display page */

        inregs.x.ax = 0XF00;
        int86(0X10, &inregs, &outregs);

        return(outregs.h.bh);
}

void scroll(int direction, int lines, int x1, int y1, int x2,
            int y2, int attr)
{
        /* Scrolls or clears a text mode window.

           Clears the window if lines equals 0. If lines is greater
           than 0, scrolls the window the number of lines specified.

           direction must equal UP or DOWN. (These constants must be defined
           in the calling program.)

           x1 and y1 are the text coordinates of the window's upper
           left corner.
           x2 and y2 are the text coordinates of the window's lower
           right corner.

           attr specifies the attributes to be used for the entire window
           (if cleared) or for new lines scrolling in at the top or bottom
           of the window (if scrolled). If attr is less than 0, the subprogram
           uses the attributes at the current cursor position. */

        /* Get the current attributes if requested */
        if (attr < 0)
            attr = get_attribute();

        if (direction == UP)
            inregs.h.ah = 0X6;
        else
            inregs.h.ah = 0X7;

        inregs.h.al = lines;
        inregs.h.bh = attr;
        inregs.h.ch = y1;
```

(continued)

LISTING 7-8. *continued*

```
    inregs.h.cl = x1;
    inregs.h.dh = y2;
    inregs.h.dl = x2;

    /* Scroll or clear the window */
    int86(0X10, &inregs, &outregs);
}

void clearscreen(void)
{
    /* Clears the entire screen and moves the cursor to (0, 0) */

    int page;

    scroll(UP, 0, 0, 0, 80, 25, 7);
    page = get_display_page();
    set_cursor_pos(0, 0, page);
}
```

Using ANSI.SYS to Control the Screen Display

Another way to control the screen display is to use the installable device driver called ANSI.SYS, which comes with MS-DOS. You must install ANSI.SYS at boot time using the statement

   DEVICE=C:\DOS\ANSI.SYS

in your CONFIG.SYS file (assuming that the file ANSI.SYS is in the DOS directory). After ANSI.SYS is installed, a program can perform certain screen control operations (for example, clear the screen, set foreground and background colors, and control cursor position) by embedding commands to the device driver in the output.

The commands that ANSI.SYS responds to are called *escape sequences* because they begin with the escape character, 1BH. When ANSI.SYS detects an escape sequence in the text that a program is sending to the screen, the device driver intercepts it, interprets it, and sends the appropriate command to the video hardware. The program passes all other text to the display unchanged. If ANSI.SYS is not installed, escape sequences receive no special treatment and are displayed like other text. As a result, ANSI.SYS must always be installed if a program that is designed to use ANSI.SYS is to function properly.

ANSI.SYS intercepts only output that MS-DOS sends to the screen (for example, via Int 21H). It does not detect output that a BIOS service sends (for example, Int 10H Function 0AH). Because Basic's output statements (such as

PRINT) do not use MS-DOS to send output to the screen, you cannot use them with ANSI.SYS to control the screen. Listing 7-9 includes a subprogram named *StringOut* that uses Int 21H Function 40H to display a string. You can use this subprogram in Basic programs to send escape sequences to ANSI.SYS.

But before looking at the demonstration programs in Listings 7-9 and 7-10, you'll want to review the table in Figure 7-5, which lists the escape sequences that the MS-DOS ANSI.SYS driver supports. Note that ANSI.SYS treats the upper left corner of the screen as cursor position (1, 1), but the BIOS treats it as (0, 0). The word *Esc* in this table represents a character that has the value 1BH. Numbers must be sent to the device driver as ASCII characters, not as values.

Escape sequence	Action	
Esc[2J	Clear the screen, and move the cursor to (1, 1).	
Esc[K	Clear from the cursor to the end of the line.	
Esc[*row*;*col*H	Move the cursor to row *row* (1 through 25) and column *col* (1 through 80).	
Esc[*n*A	Move the cursor up *n* rows.	
Esc[*n*B	Move the cursor down *n* rows.	
Esc[*n*C	Move the cursor right *n* columns.	
Esc[*n*D	Move the cursor left *n* columns.	
Esc[s	Save the current cursor position.	
Esc[u	Return the cursor to the saved position.	
Esc[6n	Send the current cursor position to standard input in the format *Esc*[*row*;*col*R.	
Esc[*n*m	Specify character attributes:	
	n	**Attribute**
	0	No special attributes
	1	High intensity
	2	Low intensity
	3	Italic
	4	Underline
	5	Blink
	6	Rapid blink
	7	Reverse video
	8	Hidden text (no display)
	30	Black foreground

(continued)

FIGURE 7-5.
The escape sequences supported by the MS-DOS device driver ANSI.SYS.

FIGURE 7-5. *continued*

Escape sequence	Action	
Esc[*nm (cont.)*	*n*	**Attribute**
	31	Red foreground
	32	Green foreground
	33	Yellow foreground
	34	Blue foreground
	35	Magenta foreground
	36	Cyan foreground
	37	White foreground
	40	Black background
	41	Red background
	42	Green background
	43	Yellow background
	44	Blue background
	45	Magenta background
	46	Cyan background
	47	White background
Esc[=*n*h	Set display mode (you can terminate this escape sequence with either an h or an l):	
	n	***Display Mode***
	0	40x25, 16-color text*
	1	40x25, 16-color text
	2	80x25, 16-color text*
	3	80x25, 16-color text
	4	320x200, 4-color graphics
	5	320x200, 4-color graphics*
	6	640x200, 2-color graphics
	14	640x200, 16-color graphics (EGA, VGA)†
	15	640x350, 2-color graphics (EGA, VGA)†
	16	640x350, 16-color graphics (EGA, VGA)†
	17	650x480, 2-color graphics (MCGA, VGA)†
	18	640x480, 16-color graphics (VGA)†
	19	320x200, 256-color graphics (MCGA, VGA)†
Esc[=7h	Enable line wrap.	
Esc[=7l	Disable line wrap.	

* Color burst off
† MS-DOS 4.0 and later

The programs in Listings 7-9 and 7-10 demonstrate how to use ANSI.SYS for control of the screen display.

```
DEFINT A-Z

' $INCLUDE: 'QB.BI'

DECLARE SUB StringOut (x$)

DIM SHARED inRegs AS RegTypeX, outRegs AS RegTypeX


' Begin execution

CLS

PRINT "The following text was displayed using Int 21H Function 40H."
PRINT "Press any key to continue."
PRINT
FOR i = 1 TO 20
    CALL StringOut("MS-DOS Programming ")
NEXT i

WHILE INKEY$ = "": WEND

' Clear the screen, and move the cursor to (1, 1) by sending an escape
' sequence to ANSI.SYS
x$ = CHR$(&H1B) + "[2J"
CALL StringOut(x$)
CALL StringOut("Screen cleared and cursor moved by ANSI.SYS.")

PRINT "Press any key to continue."
WHILE INKEY$ = "": WEND

' Move the cursor to (10, 10)
x$ = CHR$(&H1B) + "[10;10H"
CALL StringOut(x$)

' Set background to red and foreground to black
x$ = CHR$(&H1B) + "[41m" + CHR$(&H1B) + "[30m"
CALL StringOut(x$)

' Display another message
CALL StringOut("Press any key to continue.")
WHILE INKEY$ = "": WEND

' Return the attributes to white on black
x$ = CHR$(&H1B) + "[40m" + CHR$(&H1B) + "[37m"
CALL StringOut(x$)
```

(continued)

LISTING 7-9.
Demonstration of sending escape sequences to ANSI.SYS to control the screen display in Basic.

LISTING 7-9. *continued*

```
    CLS

    END

    SUB StringOut (x$)
        ' Displays a string at the current cursor position
        ' using Int 21H Function 40H

        inRegs.ax = &H4000
        inRegs.bx = 1
        inRegs.cx = LEN(x$)
        inRegs.ds = VARSEG(x$)
        inRegs.dx = SADD(x$)

        CALL INTERRUPTX(&H21, inRegs, outRegs)
    END SUB
```

```c
/* Using ANSI.SYS for controlling the screen display */

#include <stdio.h>
#include <dos.h>
#include <string.h>

/* Declare the register unions */
union REGS inregs, outregs;

/* Function prototype */
void clearscreen(void);

char buf[20];
char esc[2] = {27, 0};
main()
{
    /* Clear the screen by sending an escape sequence to ANSI.SYS */
    clearscreen();

    printf("Screen cleared and cursor moved by ANSI.SYS.\n");
    printf("Press any key to continue.");
    getch();

    /* Move the cursor to (10, 10) */
    strcpy(buf, esc);
    strcat(buf, "[10;10H");
    printf(buf);            /* Send the escape sequence */
```

LISTING 7-10. *(continued)*
Demonstration of sending escape sequences to ANSI.SYS to control the screen display in C.

LISTING 7-10. *continued*

```
    /* Set background to red and foreground to black */
    strcpy(buf, esc);
    strcat(buf, "[41m");
    strcat(buf, esc);
    strcat(buf, "[30m");
    printf(buf);            /* Send the escape sequence */

    /* Display another message */
    printf("Press any key to continue.");
    getch();

    /* Return attributes to white on black */
    strcpy(buf, esc);
    strcat(buf, "[40m");
    strcat(buf, esc);
    strcat(buf, "[37m");
    printf(buf);            /* Send the escape sequence */

    clearscreen();
}

void clearscreen(void)
{
    /* Clear the screen, and move the cursor to (1, 1) by sending */
    /* an escape sequence to ANSI.SYS */

    strcpy(buf, esc);
    strcat(buf, "[2J");
    printf(buf);            /* Send the escape sequence */
}
```

Detecting Video Hardware

When you write a program that will be run on a variety of different systems, it is useful for the program to be able to determine what video hardware is installed so that the program can make the best use of the available colors and the screen resolution. Some programs obtain this information by asking the user to enter it. This method does not work, however, if the user doesn't know what hardware is in use. It's best if the program itself can detect the installed video hardware.

To understand how a program can detect video hardware, you must understand the three-layered structure of the video portion of the BIOS. The oldest video BIOS layer is the CGA/MDA BIOS, which was a part of the original IBM PC. The next layer is the EGA BIOS, which is a part of EGA video adapters. And the newest layer is the VGA/MCGA BIOS, which is a part of VGA and MCGA adapters. Each subsequent video BIOS is a superset of the previous BIOS. Thus, the VGA/MCGA BIOS contains the EGA BIOS plus additional services. Likewise, the EGA BIOS contains the CGA/MDA BIOS plus additional services. Each BIOS layer contains its own hardware detection services, so we can take the following approach:

1. Call the VGA/MCGA BIOS hardware detection service, Int 10H Function 1AH. If the BIOS supports this service, it provides information about which adapter (VGA or MCGA) and monitor are installed.

2. If the VGA/MCGA BIOS is not present, call the EGA BIOS hardware detection service, Int 10H Function 12H. If this service is supported, you know that an EGA adapter is present. The service returns information about the monitor (whether it is color or monochrome).

3. If the EGA BIOS is not present, call the CGA/MDA BIOS hardware detection service, Int 11H. Bits 4 and 5 of the value in the AX register returned by this service tell the program whether a CGA or an MDA adapter is installed. If the service detects neither adapter, your program should return the message "unknown."

The programs in Listings 7-11 and 7-12 demonstrate how to use video BIOS services to detect the installed video hardware. One unavoidable shortcoming of this technique is that when a CGA display adapter is detected, the program cannot determine whether it's connected to a color or a monochrome (composite) monitor. If it detects a CGA display adapter, you might want your program to ask the user which type of monitor is in use so that the program can set screen colors accordingly. Please note that the "highest video mode" reported by the programs in Listings 7-11 and 7-12 corresponds to the BIOS video mode values, as listed in Figure 7-4.

```
DEFINT A-Z

DECLARE FUNCTION DisplayHardware$ ()

' $INCLUDE: 'QB.BI'

' Define a structure to hold information about the video hardware
TYPE DisplayInfo
      adapter AS STRING * 10
      maxMode AS INTEGER
      maxX AS INTEGER
      maxY AS INTEGER
      maxColor AS INTEGER
END TYPE
```

LISTING 7-11. *(continued)*
Demonstration of using video BIOS services to detect the installed video hardware in Basic.

LISTING 7-11. *continued*

```
DIM display AS DisplayInfo

' Call the hardware detection services
display.adapter = DisplayHardware$

' Assign values to the members of the display data structure.
' display.maxColor equals the total number of available
' colors. Because colors are numbered starting at 0, this
' number is one greater than the maximum color number that
' can be used.

SELECT CASE display.adapter
    CASE "MDA       "
        display.maxMode = 0
        display.maxX = 0
        display.maxY = 0
        display.maxColor = 2
    CASE "CGA       "
        display.maxMode = 6
        display.maxX = 639
        display.maxY = 199
        display.maxColor = 2
    CASE "Color EGA "
        display.maxMode = 16
        display.maxX = 639
        display.maxY = 349
        display.maxColor = 16
    CASE "Mono EGA  "
        display.maxMode = 15
        display.maxX = 639
        display.maxY = 349
        display.maxColor = 2
    CASE "Color VGA "
        display.maxMode = 18
        display.maxX = 639
        display.maxY = 479
        display.maxColor = 16
    CASE "Mono VGA  ", "Mono MCGA "
        display.maxMode = 17
        display.maxX = 639
        display.maxY = 479
        display.maxColor = 2
    CASE "Color MCGA"
        display.maxMode = 19
        display.maxX = 319
        display.maxY = 199
        display.maxColor = 256
```

(continued)

LISTING 7-11. *continued*

```
        CASE "Unknown   "
            display.maxMode = 0
            display.maxX = 0
            display.maxY = 0
            display.maxColor = 0
END SELECT

' Display the video information on the screen
CLS

PRINT "The installed display adapter is "; display.adapter
PRINT "The highest-resolution display mode ="; display.maxMode
PRINT "The maximum graphics x-coordinate ="; display.maxX
PRINT "The maximum graphics y-coordinate ="; display.maxY
PRINT "The maximum number of colors ="; display.maxColor

END

FUNCTION DisplayHardware$
    ' This function uses video BIOS services to detect the
    ' video hardware installed. The function returns one of
    ' the following strings:

    '   MDA         Monochrome Display and Printer Adapter
    '   CGA         Color Graphics Adapter
    '   Color EGA   Enhanced Graphics Adapter with color monitor
    '   Mono EGA    Enhanced Graphics Adapter with monochrome monitor
    '   Color VGA   Video Graphics Array with color monitor
    '   Mono VGA    Video Graphics Array with monochrome monitor
    '   Color MCGA  Multi-Color Graphics Array with color monitor
    '   Mono MCGA   Multi-Color Graphics array with monochrome monitor
    '   Unknown     unknown adapter type

    DIM inRegs AS RegType, outRegs AS RegType

    ' Call the VGA/MCGA BIOS hardware detection service
    inRegs.ax = &H1A00
    CALL INTERRUPT(&H10, inRegs, outRegs)

    ' Isolate the AL and BL registers
    outRegs.ax = outRegs.ax AND &HFF
    outRegs.bx = outRegs.bx AND &HFF

    ' If AL = 1AH, the VGA/MCGA BIOS was found and the
    ' value in BL indicates the hardware.

    IF outRegs.ax = &H1A THEN
        SELECT CASE outRegs.bx
            CASE 1
                DisplayHardware = "MDA"
```

(continued)

LISTING 7-11. *continued*

```
            CASE 2
                DisplayHardware = "CGA"
            CASE 4
                DisplayHardware = "Color EGA"
            CASE 5
                DisplayHardware = "Mono EGA"
            CASE 7
                DisplayHardware = "Mono VGA"
            CASE 8
                DisplayHardware = "Color VGA"
            CASE &HB
                DisplayHardware = "Mono MCGA"
            CASE &HA, &HC
                DisplayHardware = "Color MCGA"
            CASE ELSE
                DisplayHardware = "CGA"
        END SELECT
        EXIT FUNCTION
END IF

' Execution reaches this point if the program didn't find
' the VGA/MCGA BIOS.

' Call the EGA BIOS equipment service
inRegs.ax = &H1200
inRegs.bx = &H10
CALL INTERRUPT(&H10, inRegs, outRegs)

' If BX has been changed, an EGA BIOS is present, and the value
' in BH tells us whether a color or monochrome monitor is
' attached.

IF outRegs.bx <> &H10 THEN
    IF (outRegs.bx \ 256) = 0 THEN
        DisplayHardware = "Color EGA"
    ELSE
        DisplayHardware = "Mono EGA"
    END IF
    EXIT FUNCTION
END IF

' Execution reaches this point if the program found neither the
' VGA/MCGA nor the EGA BIOS.

' Call the CGA BIOS Interrupt
CALL INTERRUPT(&H11, inRegs, outRegs)
' Isolate bits 4 and 5 of AL to determine the type of adapter
outRegs.ax = outRegs.ax AND &H30
```

(continued)

LISTING 7-11. *continued*

```
      SELECT CASE outRegs.ax
          CASE &H10, &H20
              DisplayHardware = "CGA"
          CASE &H30
              DisplayHardware = "MDA"
          CASE ELSE
              DisplayHardware = "Unknown"
      END SELECT
END FUNCTION    ' End of DisplayHardware$
```

```c
/* Using BIOS services to detect the installed video hardware */

#include <stdio.h>
#include <dos.h>

/* Constants for the adapter types */
#define UNKNOWN     0
#define MDA         1
#define CGA         2
#define COLOR_EGA   3
#define MONO_EGA    4
#define COLOR_VGA   5
#define MONO_VGA    6
#define COLOR_MCGA  7
#define MONO_MCGA   8

/* Declare the register unions */
union REGS inregs, outregs;

/* Define a structure to hold information about the video hardware */
struct display_info {
    int max_mode;
    int max_color;
    int max_x;
    int max_y;
    int type;
    char adapter[30];
} display;

/* Function prototypes */
void clearscreen(void);
int display_hardware(void);
```

LISTING 7-12.
Demonstration of using video BIOS services to detect the installed video hardware in C.

(continued)

LISTING 7-12. *continued*

```
main()
{
    clearscreen();

    /* Call the hardware detection services */
    display.type = display_hardware();

    /* Assign values to the members of the display structure. */
    /* display.max_color equals the total number of available */
    /* colors. Because colors are numbered starting at 0, this */
    /* number is one greater than the maximum color number that */
    /* can be used. */

    switch (display.type)
        {
        case MDA:
            strcpy(display.adapter, "Monochrome adapter");
            display.max_mode = 0;
            display.max_x = 0;
            display.max_y = 0;
            display.max_color = 2;
            break;
        case CGA:
            strcpy(display.adapter, "Color Graphics Adapter");
            display.max_mode = 6;
            display.max_x = 639;
            display.max_y = 199;
            display.max_color = 2;
            break;
        case COLOR_EGA:
            strcpy(display.adapter, "Color EGA");
            display.max_mode = 16;
            display.max_x = 639;
            display.max_y = 349;
            display.max_color = 16;
            break;
        case MONO_EGA:
            strcpy(display.adapter, "Monochrome EGA");
            display.max_mode = 15;
            display.max_x = 639;
            display.max_y = 349;
            display.max_color = 2;
            break;
        case COLOR_VGA:
            strcpy(display.adapter, "Color VGA");
            display.max_mode = 18;
            display.max_x = 639;
            display.max_y = 479;
            display.max_color = 16;
            break;
```

(continued)

LISTING 7-12. *continued*

```c
            case MONO_VGA:
                strcpy(display.adapter, "Monochrome VGA");
                display.max_mode = 17;
                display.max_x = 639;
                display.max_y = 479;
                display.max_color = 2;
                break;
            case MONO_MCGA:
                strcpy(display.adapter, "Monochrome MCGA");
                display.max_mode = 17;
                display.max_x = 639;
                display.max_y = 479;
                display.max_color = 2;
                break;
            case COLOR_MCGA:
                strcpy(display.adapter, "Color MCGA");
                display.max_mode = 19;
                display.max_x = 319;
                display.max_y = 199;
                display.max_color = 256;
                break;
            case UNKNOWN:
                strcpy(display.adapter, "Unknown type");
                display.max_mode = 0;
                display.max_x = 0;
                display.max_y = 0;
                display.max_color = 0;
                break;
        }

    /* Display the video information on the screen */
    printf("The installed adapter is %s.", display.adapter);
    printf("\nThe highest resolution display mode = %d.", display.max_mode);
    printf("\nThe maximum graphics x-coordinate = %d.", display.max_x);
    printf("\nThe maximum graphics y-coordinate = %d.", display.max_y);
    printf("\nThe maximum number of colors = %d.\n\n", display.max_color);

}   /* End of main() */

int display_hardware(void)
{
    /* This function uses the video BIOS services to detect the type
       of video hardware installed. It returns an integer value that
       specifies the type of hardware detected. The calling program
       must define the symbolic constants for the adapter types.

       0: unknown type
       1: Monochrome Display and Printer Adapter
       2: Color Graphics Adapter
       3: Enhanced Graphics Adapter with color monitor
```

(continued)

LISTING 7-12. *continued*

```
            4: Enhanced Graphics Adapter with monochrome monitor
            5: Video Graphics Array with color monitor
            6: Video Graphics Array with monochrome monitor
            7: Multi-Color Graphics Array with color monitor
            8: Multi-Color Graphics Array with monochrome monitor */

    /* Call the VGA/MCGA BIOS hardware detection service */
    inregs.x.ax = 0X1A00;
    int86(0X10, &inregs, &outregs);

    /* If AL = 1AH, the VGA/MCGA BIOS was found, and the */
    /* value in BL indicates the hardware. */

    if (outregs.h.al == 0X1A)
        {
        switch (outregs.h.bl)
            {
            case 1:
                return(MDA);
            case 2:
                return(CGA);
            case 4:
                return(COLOR_EGA);
            case 5:
                return(MONO_EGA);
            case 7:
                return(MONO_VGA);
            case 8:
                return(COLOR_VGA);
            case 0XB:
                return(MONO_MCGA);
            case 0XA:
            case 0XC:
                return(COLOR_MCGA);
            default:
                return(CGA);
            }
        }

    /* Execution reaches this point if the program didn't find
       the VGA/MCGA BIOS. */

    /* Call the EGA BIOS equipment service */
    inregs.x.ax = 0X1200;
    inregs.x.bx = 0X10;
    int86(0X10, &inregs, &outregs);

    /* If BX has been changed, an EGA BIOS is present, and the */
    /* value in BH tells us whether a color or a monochrome monitor */
    /* is attached. */
```

(continued)

LISTING 7-12. *continued*

```
        if (outregs.x.bx != 0X10)
            {
            if (outregs.h.bh == 0)
                return(COLOR_EGA);
            else
                return(MONO_EGA);
            }

        /* Execution reaches this point if the program found neither the
           VGA/MCGA nor the EGA BIOS. */

        /* Call the CGA BIOS interrupt */
        int86(0X11, &inregs, &outregs);

        /* Isolate bits 4 and 5 of AL to determine the type of adapter */
        outregs.h.al = outregs.h.al & 0X30;

        switch(outregs.h.al)
            {
            case 0X10:
            case 0X20:
                return(CGA);
            case 0X30:
                return(MDA);
            default:
                return(UNKNOWN);
            }
    }   /* End of display_hardware() */
void clearscreen(void)
    {
    int x;

    for (x = 0; x < 25; x++)
        printf("\n");
    }   /* End of clearscreen() */
```

Display Service Reference

Some MS-DOS display services are supported by only a subset of the common PC video adapters. Each of the service reference entries that follow indicates hardware support as follows:

[all]	All of those listed below
[MDA]	Monochrome Display and Printer Adapter
[CGA]	Color Graphics Adapter
[EGA]	Enhanced Graphics Adapter
[MCGA]	Multi-Color Graphics Array
[VGA]	Video Graphics Array

Int 10H Function 00H [all]
Set display mode

Action: Sets the display mode

Call with: AH = 00H
AL = display mode

Returns: Nothing

Notes: Earlier in the chapter, Figure 7-4 summarized the various display modes and the adapters on which they can be used. Do not attempt to set a display mode on hardware that does not support it.

On the PC/AT and PS/2, bit 7 of AL determines whether the service will clear the display buffer when it sets a new mode. (If bit 7 is set, the buffer is not cleared.) On the PC and PC/XT, this feature is available only when an EGA, MCGA, or VGA adapter is installed.

Int 10H Function 01H [all]
Set cursor appearance

Action: Sets the start and stop scan lines for the cursor in text modes

Call with: AH = 01H
CH = start scan line (in bits 0 through 4)
CL = stop scan line (in bits 0 through 4)

Returns: Nothing

Notes: This cursor is available in text modes only. The program cannot modify the rate of cursor blinking. The following list shows the options for the scan lines:

Display mode	Scan line range	Default start	Default stop
00H – 03H	0 – 7	6	7
07H	0 – 12	11	12

On EGA, MCGA, and VGA monitors, the cursor contains more than eight scan lines. You still specify the cursor start and stop scan lines in the range 0 through 7, and the BIOS remaps the values to the cursor's true dimensions. This process is called *cursor emulation*.

To turn off the cursor, you do not set out-of-range values for the cursor start and stop scan lines. For MDA, CGA, and VGA adapters, you turn off the cursor by calling this service with CH = 20H. You can also hide the cursor by using Int 10H Function 02H to position the cursor off screen (for example, at row 25, column 0).

Int 10H   Function 02H   [all]
Set cursor position

Action:	Positions the cursor on a display page using text coordinates
Call with:	AH = 02H BH = display page DH = row DL = column
Returns:	Nothing
Notes:	The upper left corner of the screen is row 0, column 0. The display mode determines the maximum allowed row and column values:

Display mode	Maximum row	Maximum column
00H	39	24
01H	39	24
02H	79	24
03H	79	24
04H	39	24
05H	39	24
06H	79	24
07H	79	24
0DH	39	24
0EH	79	24
0FH	79	24
10H	79	24
11H	79	29
12H	79	29
13H	39	24

The number of available display pages depends on the installed video hardware and the display mode. (See the reference entry for Int 10H Function 05H for information about display pages.) Each page has its own cursor; this service can set the cursor's position even when the page is not displayed.

Int 10H   Function 03H   [all]
Get cursor position

Action: Returns the current cursor position and the cursor start and stop scan lines

Call with: AH = 03H
                BH = display page

Returns: CH = start scan line
                CL = stop scan line
                DH = cursor row
                DL = cursor column

Notes: The position at the upper left corner of the screen is row 0, column 0.

The number of available display pages depends on the installed video hardware and the display mode. (See the reference entry for Int 10H Function 05H for information about display pages.) Each page has its own cursor; this service can read the cursor's position even when the page is not displayed.

Int 10H   Function 05H   [CGA][EGA][MCGA][VGA]
Set active display page

Action: Sets the active video display page

Call with: AH = 05H
                AL = display page number (see "Notes")

Returns: Nothing

Notes: Which display pages are available depends on the installed video hardware and the current display mode:

Display mode	Adapter	Page range
00H, 01H	CGA, EGA, MCGA, VGA	0 – 7
02H, 03H	CGA	0 – 3
02H, 03H	EGA, MCGA, VGA	0 – 7
07H	EGA, VGA	0 – 7
0DH	EGA, VGA	0 – 7
0EH	EGA, VGA	0 – 3
0FH	EGA, VGA	0 – 1
10H	EGA, VGA	0 – 1

Screen Display   197

Any video adapter/mode combination that is not listed above supports a single display page.

A program can write text and control the cursor on any available display page, regardless of whether the page is currently displayed. See the reference entries for Int 10H Functions 02H, 03H, 09H, and 0AH for information about writing text and positioning the cursor.

Switching active pages has no effect on page contents.

Int 10H   Function 06H   [all]
Clear or scroll window up

Action:	Scrolls a screen window up by a specified number of lines, or clears a screen window to blank lines using a specified attribute
Call with:	AH = 06H AL = number of lines to scroll, or 0 to clear the window BH = attribute to use for the scrolled area or the cleared window CH = upper window row CL = left window column DH = lower window row DL = right window column
Returns:	Nothing
Notes:	With video hardware and modes that support multiple display pages, this service affects only the currently active display page. If AL is greater than 0, the service scrolls the window contents up by the specified number of lines. Text that scrolls past the top of the window is lost. Blank lines that have the attributes specified by BH fill in the bottom of the window.

Int 10H   Function 07H   [all]
Clear or scroll window down

Action:	Scrolls a screen window down by a specified number of lines, or clears a screen window to blank lines using a specified attribute

Call with:	AH = 07H AL = number of lines to scroll, or 0 to clear the window BH = attribute to use for the scrolled area or the cleared window CH = upper window row CL = left window column DH = lower window row DL = right window column
Returns:	Nothing
Notes:	With video hardware and modes that support multiple display pages, this service affects only the currently active display page. If AL is greater than 0, the service scrolls the window contents down by the specified number of lines. Text that scrolls past the bottom of the window is lost. Blank lines that have the attributes specified by BH fill in the top of the window.

Int 10H   Function 08H [all]
Read character and attribute at cursor position

Action:	Reads the character and attribute at the current cursor position
Call with:	AH = 08H BH = display page
Returns:	AH = attribute byte AL = ASCII character code
Notes:	This service can read character/attribute pairs from any supported display page, even if the page is not currently displayed.

Int 10H   Function 09H [all]
Write character and attribute at cursor position

Action:	Writes a character/attribute pair at the current cursor location

Call with:	AH = 09H AL = ASCII character code BH = display page BL = attribute or color CX = repeat factor
Returns:	Nothing
Notes:	Displaying a single character using this service (when CX equals 1) does not move the cursor to the next position; you must do so explicitly using Int 10H Function 02H. If CX is greater than 1, the specified number of characters are displayed in subsequent screen positions. The cursor position does not change; it remains at the location of the first character displayed. In graphics modes, a program can use a repeat factor greater than 1 only if the resulting output does not extend past the end of the current screen row. If the service writes more characters than there are spaces remaining in the current row, unpredictable results can occur. In graphics modes, setting bit 7 of BL causes the service to perform an XOR operation with the written character and the existing display contents. If you set bit 7 and then use this service to write characters, you can "erase" those characters by calling the service again with the same register values. All characters (specified by the value in AL) are displayed. Special characters, such as backspace and linefeed, are not recognized as special and do not affect the cursor position. To write a character without changing the current attribute at the cursor position, use Int 10H Function 0AH.

Int 10H   Function 0AH   [all]
Write character at cursor position

Action:	Writes a single character to the current cursor position and leaves the existing attribute at that position unchanged
Call with:	AH = 0AH AL = ASCII character code BH = display page BL = color (graphics modes only) CX = repeat factor

Returns: Nothing

Notes: Displaying a single character using this service (when CX equals 1) does not move the cursor to the next position; you must do so explicitly using Int 10H Function 02H.

If CX is greater than 1, the specified number of characters are displayed in subsequent screen positions. The cursor position does not change; it remains at the location of the first character displayed.

In graphics modes, a program can use a repeat factor greater than 1 only if the resulting output does not extend past the end of the current screen row. If the service writes more characters than there are spaces remaining in the current row, unpredictable results can occur.

In graphics modes, setting bit 7 of BL causes the service to perform an XOR operation with the written character and the existing display contents. If you set bit 7 and then use this service to write characters, you can "erase" those characters by calling the service again with the same register values.

All characters (specified by the value in AL) are displayed. Special characters, such as backspace and linefeed, are not recognized as special and do not affect the cursor position.

To write a character/attribute pair at the cursor position, use Int 10H Function 09H.

Int 10H   Function 0EH   [all]
Write character, update cursor position

Action: Writes a single character at the current cursor position and updates the cursor position

Call with: AH = 0EH
AL = ASCII character code
BH = display page
BL = foreground color (graphics modes only)

Returns: Nothing

Notes: The value in BL controls character color only in graphics modes. In text modes, the character is displayed using the position's existing attributes.

The service moves the cursor right one space after each character and wraps to the start of the next line if output reaches the right edge of the screen.

Int 10H Function 0FH [all]
Get display mode

Action: Returns the current display mode of the display adapter plus the current screen width and the active display page

Call with: AH = 0FH

Returns: AH = screen width (in character cells)
AL = current display mode (see Figure 7-4)
BH = active display page

Notes: Use this service to obtain information about the display mode that is in effect and the display page that is active when your program starts. You can then use this information to restore the screen to its initial condition when the program is ready to exit.

Int 10H Function 12H [EGA][VGA]
Get configuration information

Action: Returns information about the active video system

Call with: AH = 12H
BL = 10H

Returns: BH = monitor type:
  0 = color
  1 = monochrome

BL = memory on the EGA display adapter:
  00H = 64 KB
  01H = 128 KB
  02H = 192 KB
  03H = 256 KB

Notes: If this service is not supported by your adapter, BX remains unchanged. EGA adapters can be equipped with varying amounts of video RAM. How much video RAM the adapter has affects the number of colors that can be displayed and the number of available display pages.

Int 10H   Function 1AH   [VGA][MCGA]
Get or set display hardware information

Action: Returns information that describes the installed display adapter(s) or updates the BIOS information that describes the installed adapter(s)

Call with: AH = 1AH

To get video information:
  AL = 00H

To set video information:
  AL = 01H
  BH = inactive display code
  BL = active display code

Returns: If service supported:
  AL = 1AH

If called with AL = 00H:
  AL = 1AH
  BH = inactive display code
  BL = active display code

Notes: Some PC systems can have two video systems installed at the same time; the active system is the one that's receiving output. A system with a VGA/MCGA BIOS could have a CGA or an EGA adapter installed as its second video system. As a result, this service can return codes that specify the adapters being used.

The hardware codes are as follows:

Code	Video hardware
00H	None
01H	MDA with monochrome monitor
02H	CGA with color or monochrome monitor
04H	EGA with color monitor
05H	EGA with monochrome monitor
07H	VGA with monochrome monitor
08H	VGA with color monitor
0AH	MCGA with digital color monitor
0BH	MCGA with analog monochrome monitor
0CH	MCGA with analog color monitor

Int 11H [all]
Get equipment information

Action: Returns information about installed equipment from the BIOS

Call with: Nothing

Returns: AX = equipment information:
Bits 4 and 5:
01 or 10 = CGA
11 = MDA

Notes: Upon return, other bits in AX provide information about other system hardware. See the reference section in Chapter 13 for information about the other bits in AX.

Int 21H Function 02H [all]
Character output

Action: Writes a single character to the standard output device

Call with: AH = 02H
DL = ASCII character code

Returns: Nothing

Notes: If Ctrl-C is detected after the character is output, MS-DOS executes Int 23H.

If the standard output (*stdout*) has not been redirected, the service moves the cursor left by one space when a backspace character (08H) is output. If the standard output has been redirected, a backspace character receives no special treatment.

Int 21H   Function 06H   [all]
Direct I/O without echo

Action: Writes a single character to the standard output device

Call with: AH = 06H
DL = ASCII character code (00H through FEH; see "Notes")

Returns: Nothing

Notes: If called using FFH in the DL register, this service reads a character from standard input. (See Chapter 5 for information about character input.)

This service does not respond to Ctrl-C.

Int 21H   Function 40H   [all]
Write characters to file or device

Action: Writes a specified number of characters from a buffer to a file or device specified by a valid handle

Call with: AH = 40H
BX = handle (0 = standard output, 1 = standard error)
CX = number of bytes to write
DS = segment of buffer
DX = offset of buffer

Returns: On success:
   Carry flag = clear
   AX   = number of bytes transferred

On failure:
   Carry flag = set
   AX   = error code

Notes: If the service returns a clear carry flag but the value in AX is less than the value that was passed in CX, a partial transfer has occurred.

Screen Display

CHAPTER 8

Disks: The Basics

Every PC system has at least one floppy disk drive, and most have a hard disk as well. A disk serves as a permanent storage medium for operating system files, programs, and data. It's the last item—the data—that is of most concern to programmers. Most programs that you create will need to write data to a disk file, read data from a disk file, or, most likely, do a combination of the two. MS-DOS provides many services for accessing disk data, and a familiarity with them will be valuable to you. To use these MS-DOS disk services effectively, you should have a basic understanding of how disks operate and how MS-DOS interacts with disks—that's the subject of this chapter. Chapters 9 and 10 discuss the MS-DOS disk services and explain how to use them.

Disks as Mechanical Devices

Every disk consists of one or more rotating platters. The surfaces of each platter are coated with a magnetic recording material. It's here that the data is recorded, as small variations in magnetization of the platter coating. Associated with each side of the platter is a mechanism called a *read-write head*. As the platter rotates, the head skims the surface of the platter and writes information on or reads information from the platter's surface. The head is movable and can be positioned anywhere along the radius of the platter, from near the center to the outside edge.

Each recording surface on a disk (each side of a platter) is divided into a number of concentric *tracks*, and each track is divided into a number of *sectors*. (The sector is the basic unit of disk data storage.) Figure 8-1 illustrates this arrangement. The number of tracks per side and sectors per track varies according to the type of disk.

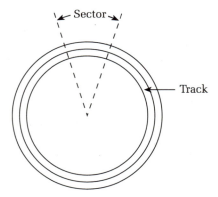

FIGURE 8-1.
The physical recording surface of a disk is divided into tracks and sectors.

We've covered only the most rudimentary information here about the physical structure of disks, but fortunately programmers rarely need to know more details than this. MS-DOS and the BIOS hide the details of disk mechanics from you, allowing application programs (and programmers!) to deal with disks only as *logical devices* that have consistent interfaces.

Disks as Logical Devices

MS-DOS views disks as logical devices, or volumes, that are identified by drive letters. Thus your system might have two floppy disk drives called A: and B: and a hard disk drive called C:. With floppy disks, each logical device always corresponds to one physical drive. With hard disks, a single disk can be divided into two or more logical devices. For example, you could have a single hard disk that's divided into logical devices C: and D:. MS-DOS recognizes each of the logical devices as a separate entity, even though the devices might share the same physical disk.

MS-DOS organizes every logical device according to a specific scheme. This organization, which is the main topic of this chapter, might seem complicated at first glance. It's not all that bad, however, and because it's the same for all drives, you need to learn the organization only once. Understanding the basics of how MS-DOS interacts with disks can help you write better programs.

A lot of diversity exists among PC disks. At the hardware level, you'll find a vast difference between a 360-kilobyte (KB) floppy disk and a 200-megabyte (MB) hard disk. You might therefore think that programming for the two disk types would be a vastly different task. Remember, however, that the aim of MS-DOS is to isolate programs from the system hardware. Nowhere is this aim more obvious than with disk drives. MS-DOS provides an array of disk services, accessed via Int 21H, that permit a program to create, delete, open, close, read, and write disk files without paying any attention to the disk's actual physical characteristics.

Let's take a look at how MS-DOS deals with disks. MS-DOS sees each logical device as a contiguous sequence of logical sectors, starting at sector 0. The size of a logical sector depends on the specifics of the disk, but a sector is typically 512, 1024, or 2048 bytes. MS-DOS keeps track of all the information on the disk in terms of the logical sectors in which the information is stored. MS-DOS keeps this information on the disk in *directories* and *file allocation tables,* as explained in the upcoming sections.

Please note the difference between a physical sector, as discussed earlier, and a logical sector. Physical sectors are the actual sectors on the disk, which are numbered from 0 starting at a certain point on the disk and working around the disk. Logical sectors are often the same size as physical sectors, but they might not be next to each other on the disk. To make data access more efficient, logical sectors that are adjacent according to their numbering might not be physically adjacent on the disk. From now on, the term "sector" will refer to a logical sector unless specified otherwise.

When a program requests an MS-DOS disk service via Int 21H, MS-DOS translates the command into a request for the transfer of information to or from logical disk sectors. For example, if your program asks that the data in a disk file be read into an array, MS-DOS determines where, in terms of logical sectors, that file is stored on the disk and then requests that those sectors be read and transferred to the program.

MS-DOS sends its request for logical sectors to the device driver for the disk. The device driver then translates the request for logical sectors into information about actual physical storage locations on the disk and sends the needed commands to the disk hardware, which performs the necessary read operations. The BIOS contains the device driver for IBM-compatible floppy disks and hard disks. You can load manufacturer-supplied drivers for nonstandard disk hardware at boot time by using a DEVICE statement in your CONFIG.SYS file.

The process by which an application program accesses disk data involves three levels. At the top level, the application program deals with disk data in terms of entire files. At the middle level, MS-DOS deals with disk data in terms of logical sectors. And, at the bottom level, the device driver deals with disk data in terms of physical storage locations (the addresses of the physical sectors) on the disk itself. Figure 8-2 shows this arrangement.

Disk Organization

MS-DOS arranges the information on a disk according to a specific scheme. Some of the data on a disk is about the disk itself: its sector size, the number of tracks, and so on. MS-DOS uses other information—such as directories of filenames and file sizes—to keep track of the data stored on the disk. The organization of an MS-DOS disk is not difficult to understand. Every MS-DOS disk has four major sections: the boot sector, the file allocation table, the root directory, and the files area. The rest of the chapter covers each of these sections in turn.

The boot sector

Logical sector 0 is the *boot sector* on every MS-DOS disk, even on disks that are non-bootable. The boot sector's main purpose is to hold information about the disk's physical characteristics and, as its name implies, to *boot,* or

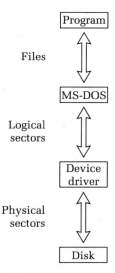

FIGURE 8-2.
The three-level process by which an application program accesses disk data.

start, the computer. Because the boot sector is identical on both bootable and non-bootable disks, you might be wondering how your computer can tell the difference between the two types of disk. This is explained on page 213 in the box entitled "The Boot Procedure." The boot sector has several parts, as Figure 8-3 on page 214 shows.

The first 3 bytes of the boot sector contain a jump instruction that includes the offset to the bootstrap routine. This jump instruction, which transfers execution to the bootstrap routine, must be present in the proper location if MS-DOS is to recognize the disk as a formatted disk.

The next 8 bytes of the boot sector are reserved for *OEM* information. OEM stands for *original equipment manufacturer.* When the disk is formatted, MS-DOS records information here about the computer manufacturer and the MS-DOS version being used.

Following the OEM identification, the boot sector contains the *BIOS parameter block,* which is abbreviated as *BPB.* Although the size of the BPB has changed from version to version of MS-DOS, it has always contained various data about the disk's physical characteristics. The disk driver uses the data in the BPB to translate logical sector requests into physical addresses and to locate the root directory and the file allocation table.

The last component of the boot sector is the *disk bootstrap routine.* This small program is involved in booting the computer when you first turn on the computer or when you reset the computer from the keyboard using the Ctrl-Alt-Del key combination.

Disks: The Basics

The file allocation table

The file allocation table, or *FAT*, keeps track of where on the disk a file is stored. To understand the FAT, you must first understand the way in which MS-DOS allocates disk storage space to files.

MS-DOS assigns storage space in units called *clusters,* or *allocation units.* Each cluster contains a specific number of sectors, which is always a power

---

The Boot Procedure

When you boot (turn on or reset) an 80x86-based microcomputer, you initiate the *boot sequence,* which is a predefined series of events that loads the operating system and leaves your computer ready to use. The computer completes many tasks during the boot sequence, most of which are invisible to the user.

Whether you perform a cold boot by turning on the power or a warm boot by pressing the system reset key combination (Ctrl-Alt-Del), the central processing unit (CPU) begins executing instructions at address FFFFH:0000H. This action on the part of the CPU is independent of MS-DOS or any other software and results from the CPU's design. At address FFFFH:0000H, the ROM BIOS contains a jump instruction that directs execution to the beginning of the hardware test routines and the ROM bootstrap code, both of which are also located in the ROM BIOS.

The hardware test routines, called the POST for "power-on self test," are executed only during a cold boot. These routines check the amount of installed memory, perform a memory test, and test for the availability of peripheral devices. During this phase, the screen often displays information about the size of installed memory and other system parameters. When you perform a warm boot, the POST is skipped, which is why a warm boot is quicker than a cold boot.

From this point on, the sequence is the same for both cold and warm boots. Code in the ROM bootstrap routine sets up portions of the interrupt vector table in low memory, initializes the ROM BIOS tables at 0400H:0000H, and performs other hardware initialization steps. Next the ROM bootstrap routine searches the region of memory between A000H:0000H and F000H:0000H for additional ROM BIOS extensions, such as those found on hard disk controllers and EGA and VGA display adapters. If the code finds any extensions, it initializes them and updates the interrupt vector table.

of 2; the exact value depends on the disk type. For example, a 360-KB floppy disk has 2 sectors per cluster, and a PC/AT hard disk has 4 sectors per cluster. The number of sectors per cluster is defined in the disk's BPB, at offset 0DH. When a file requires multiple clusters, the clusters that MS-DOS assigns to the file might not be in adjacent disk locations—they might be scattered here and there throughout the disk. The FAT keeps a record of exactly which clusters are assigned to each file and which clusters are available for use.

Next the ROM bootstrap routine looks for the disk bootstrap code on sector 0 of the boot disk, searching disk A: first, followed by the hard disk if one is installed. When the routine finds the disk bootstrap, it loads the code into memory and gives the disk bootstrap control.

The disk bootstrap routine looks at the boot disk to locate the files IO.SYS and MSDOS.SYS (on IBM-manufactured systems and some clones, these files are named IBMBIO.COM and IBMDOS.COM).

Note that at this point, the bootstrap routine knows nothing about filenames or other aspects of disk organization. It can find the files IO.SYS and MSDOS.SYS only because they are always stored at specific disk locations. (If those files are not located at the specific locations, the disk is not bootable.) The disk bootstrap routine loads IO.SYS into memory first.

After IO.SYS gains control, it performs certain hardware initialization tasks, and then its SYSINIT portion loads MSDOS.SYS into memory. The MS-DOS Int 21H file services then become available. SYSINIT uses these services to read the CONFIG.SYS file from the boot disk into memory. It then converts the characters in CONFIG.SYS to uppercase and interprets the file, one line at a time, to obtain system configuration information about files, buffers, device drivers, and so on. If CONFIG.SYS is not present on the disk, SYSINIT assigns default values for certain configuration parameters.

After it performs additional initialization tasks, SYSINIT opens the handles for standard input (the keyboard), standard output and standard error (the screen), standard list (the printer), and standard auxiliary (the serial port). Finally, SYSINIT loads COMMAND.COM from the disk and passes control to it.

COMMAND.COM looks for the AUTOEXEC.BAT file. If it finds that file, COMMAND.COM loads it and executes the commands it contains. Your screen then displays the MS-DOS prompt, and you are ready to go!

Offset	Field
00H	Jump instruction to bootstrap routine
03H	OEM name and version (8 bytes)
0BH	Bytes per sector (2 bytes)
0DH	Sectors per allocation unit (1 byte)
0EH	Reserved sectors, starting at 0 (2 bytes)
10H	Number of FATs (1 byte)
11H	Number of root-directory entries (2 bytes)
13H	Total sectors in logical volume (2 bytes)
15H	Media descriptor byte
16H	Number of sectors per FAT (2 bytes)
18H	Sectors per track (2 bytes)
1AH	Number of heads (2 bytes)
1CH	Number of hidden sectors (4 bytes)
20H	Total sectors in logical volume (MS-DOS 4.0 and volume size > 32 MB)
24H	Physical drive number
25H	Reserved
26H	Extended boot signature record (29H)
27H	32-bit binary volume ID
2BH	Volume label (11 bytes)
36H	Reserved (8 bytes)
3EH	Bootstrap routine

Offsets 0BH through 18H comprise the BIOS parameter block (BPB).

FIGURE 8-3.
The structure of the boot sector on an MS-DOS disk.

Each disk's FAT is divided into fields. A FAT field has 12 bits on disks that are formatted with MS-DOS versions 2.x and earlier. With MS-DOS 3.0 and later, a FAT field has either 12 or 16 bits: Disks that contain 4096 or fewer clusters use 12-bit FAT fields, and disks that contain more than 4096 clusters use 16-bit FAT fields.

The first two FAT fields are reserved. The first byte of the reserved fields contains a copy of the *media descriptor byte,* which is also contained in the BPB at offset 15H. This byte identifies the nature of the disk media, as Figure 8-4 shows. Notice that certain codes in this list correspond to multiple media types.

Code	Medium
F8H	Hard disk
F0H	Two-sided, 18-sector, 3.5-inch floppy disk
F9H	Two-sided, 15-sector, 5.25-inch floppy disk Two-sided, 9-sector, 3.5-inch floppy disk
FCH	Two-sided, 9-sector, 5.25-inch floppy disk
FDH	Two-sided, 9-sector, 5.25-inch floppy disk
FEH	Two-sided, 8-sector, 5.25-inch floppy disk
FFH	Two-sided, 8-sector, 5.25-inch floppy disk

FIGURE 8-4.
MS-DOS media descriptor byte codes.

The remainder of the reserved FAT fields (which is 2 or 3 bytes, depending on whether the fields are 12 or 16 bits) always contain the value FFH.

Following the two reserved fields, the FAT contains one field for each cluster on the disk. Each FAT field corresponds directly to a specific cluster. The value stored in a FAT field either indicates the status of the corresponding cluster or points to the next cluster of a file, as shown in Figure 8-5. The hexadecimal digit in parentheses in this figure is present only in 16-bit FAT fields.

Code	Meaning
(0)000H	Cluster available
(F)FF0H–(F)FF6H	Cluster reserved
(F)FF7H	Cluster bad (if not part of chain)
(F)FF8H–(F)FFFH	Last cluster of file
(X)XXXH	Next cluster of file

FIGURE 8-5.
FAT cluster assignment codes.

In MS-DOS, each file has a directory entry that contains the number of the first cluster assigned to the file. The FAT field corresponding to the file's first cluster points to the file's second cluster, the FAT field corresponding to the second cluster points to the third cluster, and so on. The FAT links each cluster of the file to the next cluster, until the FAT field contains the code that indicates the last cluster. In this way, the FAT entries "chain" a file's clusters together so that MS-DOS can access them in the proper order. Likewise, when you create a new file or expand an existing file, MS-DOS uses FAT entries to locate available clusters for assignment to the file.

The root directory

MS-DOS dedicates the disk area that follows the FAT to the *root directory*. The root directory contains entries that describe files, subdirectories (a directory within a directory), and the disk's optional volume label. The size of the root directory—that is, its maximum number of entries—is fixed. For a given disk, the BPB contains this size at offset 11H.

Each entry in the root directory consists of 32 bytes that are divided into specific fields. Figure 8-6 shows a diagram of these fields.

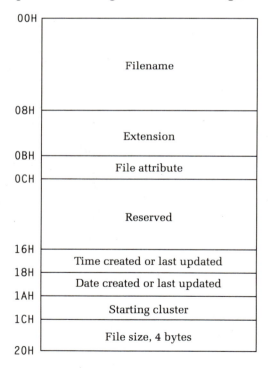

FIGURE 8-6.
The fields in a directory entry.

The first byte in the filename field indicates whether the directory entry is in use. If the first byte is E5H, the entry represents an erased file or subdirectory and is therefore available for reuse. If the first byte is 00H, that entry (and all subsequent entries) has never been used and is available. Any other value in the first byte of the filename field indicates that the entry is in use. Figure 8-7 lists the special meanings of the first byte in the filename field.

Byte	Meaning
00H	Entry has never been used.
E5H	File or subdirectory has been erased, and entry is available.
05H	Entry is in use; the first character of the filename is actually E5H.
2EH	Entry is an alias for the current directory or the parent directory.
Other	Entry is in use; the value is the first character of the filename or subdirectory name.

FIGURE 8-7.
Meanings of the first byte in the filename field of a directory entry.

The terms *alias* and *parent directory* in Figure 8-7 might not be familiar to you. If you display a directory listing of any subdirectory (not the root directory), you see—in addition to the subdirectory's filenames and subdirectory names—the entries . (one period) and .. (two periods). These are aliases. The single period stands for the current directory, and the double period stands for the parent directory (that is, the one immediately above the current directory). These aliases are not present in the root directory but only in subdirectories, which use the same directory entry structure as does the root directory.

The third field in a directory entry is a single byte that describes the entry's attributes. Figure 8-8 lists the meanings of the bits in the attribute byte.

Bit(s)	Meaning (if set)
0	Read-only file; attempts to modify or delete file will fail
1	Hidden file; not included in normal directory listings and searches
2	System file; not included in normal directory listings and searches
3	Volume label; can exist only in root directory
4	Directory; not included in normal searches
5	File that has been modified
6 and 7	Reserved

FIGURE 8-8.
Meanings of the bits in the attribute byte.

Following the attribute byte in the directory entry, a reserved area extends from offset 0CH to 16H. Next are the time and date fields, which are each 2 bytes in size. These fields encode the time and date when the file or subdirectory was created or last modified (based on the system clock). Figures 8-9 and 8-10 show the coding of the time and date fields; values are coded in both fields in binary.

Bits	Contents
0–4	Number of 2-second increments (0 through 29, representing 0 through 58 seconds)
5–10	Number of minutes (0 through 59)
11–15	Number of hours (0 through 23)

FIGURE 8-9.
Coding of the time field in directory entries.

Bits	Contents
0–4	Day of month (1 through 31)
5–8	Month (1 through 12)
9–15	Year (relative to 1980)

FIGURE 8-10.
Coding of the date field in directory entries.

Following the date field, the directory entry contains a 2-byte field that holds the value of the starting cluster in which the corresponding file is stored. This value serves as the entry point into the FAT and allows MS-DOS to locate all of the file's clusters, as explained earlier.

The final field in each directory is the file size. This field contains the size, in bytes, of the corresponding file.

Subdirectories use directory entries that have the same format as the ones used by the root directory. The root directory, however, is different from other directories in several ways. When a disk is formatted, the format program fixes the size and location of the root directory. Thus the root directory has a finite capacity and can hold a certain maximum number of entries and no more. Such a size limit does not apply to subdirectories. Also, on a bootable disk, the first two entries in the root directory are always the BIOS file (IO.SYS or IBMBIO.COM) and the kernel system file (MSDOS.SYS or IBMDOS.COM). Because these files have hidden and system attributes, you don't see them in directory listings.

The files area

Following the root directory, the remainder of the disk is the *files area*. It's here that MS-DOS stores data and program files and subdirectories. The next two chapters show you how to use MS-DOS services to manipulate files and directories.

CHAPTER 9
Disks: Files and Records

A file is a named section of data storage on a physical storage medium, which is usually a floppy disk or a hard disk. A *record* is a portion of file data of a specific size. You use files to store operating system components, program code, configuration information, and more. From the perspective of the programmer, however, the most important use of files is for storing program data. For example, a word processing program stores its documents in files, and a spreadsheet program stores its numerical data in files. When a program stores data in a file, the data is sometimes—but not always—organized as records. This chapter discusses how to use MS-DOS services to read from and write to files.

As a programmer, you need maximum flexibility in using disk files. Although both C and Basic include a wide range of disk access capabilities, by going directly to MS-DOS you might be able to make your programs smaller and give them a speed advantage. Remember, your high-level language's statements and functions are designed for wide applicability, thorough error checking, and maximum flexibility. By working directly with MS-DOS, you can avoid excess and include in your programs only the functionality you need.

A Broad Look at File Manipulation Services

MS-DOS has two independent sets of file manipulation services, called *file control block services* and *handle services*. This dual approach can be traced back to historical factors that need not concern us here. The result of these factors, however, is that for most file-related or record-related tasks that your program might need to perform, MS-DOS provides two distinct services.

If you are to use the file control block (FCB) services, your application program must set up, in its own data space, a data structure called (you guessed it!) a file control block. One FCB is required for each open file. The FCB maintains information about the file and passes the information between the program and MS-DOS. The FCB services present one major disadvantage: They do not support the hierarchical directory structure. All FCB file operations are limited to the current, or default, directory on a given disk.

If you are to use the handle services, your program must pass to MS-DOS a null-terminated (ASCIIZ) string that specifies the drive, path, name, and extension of the file to be created or opened. If this operation is successful, MS-DOS returns to the program a 2-byte identifier, or handle, that subsequent operations use to refer to the file. MS-DOS maintains the information about the file in its own memory areas, and the program cannot directly access this information.

Of course, the question arises: Which set of services should I use? The answer to that question is simple: Use the handle services. You would use the FCB services only to maintain compatibility with MS-DOS version 1.x, which did not support the handle services. It's likely, however, that few if any people are still using such antiquated versions of MS-DOS, so maintaining compatibility with MS-DOS 1.x is not a real concern. Compared with the FCB services, the handle services offer the following advantages:

- Support for the hierarchical directory structure
- No need for the application program to devote memory space for file information
- Support for file locking and file sharing or record locking in network environments
- Support for input and output redirection
- Superior error handling and reporting
- Easier access to individual records within a file

Along with the significant advantages that using the handle services offers come a few, albeit minor, disadvantages. In MS-DOS versions 2.0 through 3.2, a program is limited to a maximum of 20 files that are open concurrently and that use handles. Also, a few tasks require the use of FCB services, such as changing volume labels and accessing directory information directly.

The first part of this chapter covers the FCB services, partly because you might need to use them occasionally and partly because you might encounter them in other programs. Most often, however, your own programs should use the handle services that are covered later in this chapter.

The FCB Services

MS-DOS provides FCB services for all aspects of file manipulation: creating, opening, writing to, reading from, and deleting, among others. Each service, accessed via Int 21H, uses the FCB data structure in some way.

File control blocks

To use the MS-DOS FCB services, you must understand the file control block data structure. Remember, the FCB is an area of program memory that holds information about a file. Your program places some of the information in the FCB, and MS-DOS also places information there when you call the MS-DOS FCB services that open or create a file.

Two varieties of FCB exist: the *normal FCB* and the *extended FCB*. They are quite similar, as the following sections explain.

The normal FCB

The normal FCB is a 37-byte data structure that is divided into 11 fields. Figure 9-1 illustrates the normal FCB fields.

```
Byte offset
   00H  ┌─────────────────────────────────────┐
        │          Drive identifier           │
   01H  ├─────────────────────────────────────┤
        │       Filename (8 characters)       │
   09H  ├─────────────────────────────────────┤
        │       Extension (3 characters)      │
   0CH  ├─────────────────────────────────────┤
        │        Current-block number         │
   0EH  ├─────────────────────────────────────┤
        │            Record size              │
   10H  ├─────────────────────────────────────┤
        │         File size (4 bytes)         │
   14H  ├─────────────────────────────────────┤
        │       Date created or updated       │
   16H  ├─────────────────────────────────────┤
        │       Time created or updated       │
   18H  ├─────────────────────────────────────┤
        │                                     │
        │              Reserved               │
        │                                     │
   20H  ├─────────────────────────────────────┤
        │        Current-record number        │
   21H  ├─────────────────────────────────────┤
        │    Relative-record number (4 bytes) │
        └─────────────────────────────────────┘
```

FIGURE 9-1.
The fields of a normal FCB.

Under most circumstances, the program must fill in only the first three FCB fields, which are listed below:

- The drive identifier is a number that specifies the drive (0 specifies the default drive; 1, the A: drive; 2, the B: drive; and so on). If the program specifies the default drive by placing a 0 for the drive identifier in this field, MS-DOS places the code for the actual current disk drive in this field (after a successful call to a file create or file open service).

- The filename field contains the filename, which is made up of one to eight characters. If the name contains fewer than eight characters, it must be left justified within the field and padded with spaces to achieve a total length of eight characters.

- The extension field contains the file extension, which is made up of one to three characters. Like the filename, the extension must be left justified within the field and padded with spaces if it contains fewer than three characters. For a file that has no extension, use all spaces. You'll find it most convenient to place the filename and the extension in the FCB using Int 21H Function 29H, which takes a string containing both the filename and the extension, separates the two, and places each in its proper FCB field.

MS-DOS fills in the remaining fields in a normal FCB after a successful call to a file create or file open service. The following list describes the remaining fields:

- The file size field indicates, in bytes, the size of the file, as obtained from the file's directory entry. A newly created file's size is 0.

- MS-DOS uses the reserved area of the FCB to store a variety of bookkeeping information about the file. Different versions of MS-DOS keep different kinds of information here. In any case, the program should never modify this information.

- MS-DOS services that perform read and write operations on a file use the current-block number, record size, file size, current-record number, and relative-record number fields. Note that the file open and file create services (Int 21H Functions 0FH and 16H) set the record size to the default of 128 bytes. If your program will use a record size that's different from the default, the program must write the proper record size value to the record size FCB field after the file has been opened or created but before any read or write operations are performed.

- The date and time fields give the date and time that the file was created or last updated. MS-DOS obtains this data from the file's directory entry. As Figures 9-2 and 9-3 show, the FCB date and time fields have the same format as the directory entry date and time fields.

Bits	Contents
0–4	Number of 2-second increments (0 through 29, representing 0 through 58 seconds)
5–10	Number of minutes (0 through 59)
11–15	Number of hours (0 through 23)

FIGURE 9-2.
Coding of the time field in the FCB.

Bits	Contents
0–4	Day of month (1 through 31)
5–8	Month (1 through 12)
9–15	Year (relative to 1980)

FIGURE 9-3.
Coding of the date field in the FCB.

The extended FCB

You must use an extended FCB to manipulate files that have special attributes, including volume labels, directories, and hidden or read-only files. You can also use an extended FCB with regular files, but there is no need to do so. An extended FCB consists of a normal 37-byte FCB plus an additional 7 bytes at the beginning, for a total size of 44 bytes. Figure 9-4 shows the fields of an extended FCB.

```
Byte offset
   00H  +--------------------------------------+
        |                 FFH                  |
   01H  +--------------------------------------+
        |    Reserved (5 bytes, must be zero)  |
   06H  +--------------------------------------+
        |            Attribute byte            |
   07H  +--------------------------------------+
        |           Drive identifier           |
   08H  +--------------------------------------+
        |                                      |
        |      Filename (8 characters)         |
   10H  +--------------------------------------+
        |      Extension (3 characters)        |
   13H  +--------------------------------------+
        |        Current-block number          |
   15H  +--------------------------------------+
        |             Record size              |
   17H  +--------------------------------------+
        |          File size (4 bytes)         |
   1BH  +--------------------------------------+
        |        Date created or updated       |
   1DH  +--------------------------------------+
        |        Time created or updated       |
   1FH  +--------------------------------------+
        |                                      |
        |               Reserved               |
        |                                      |
   27H  +--------------------------------------+
        |         Current-record number        |
   28H  +--------------------------------------+
        |    Relative-record number (4 bytes)  |
        +--------------------------------------+
```

FIGURE 9-4.
The fields of an extended FCB.

Except for the first 7 bytes, the field structure of an extended FCB is identical to that of a normal FCB. An extended FCB's first byte must contain the value FFH. Because this value could never be a valid drive code, it identifies the FCB to MS-DOS as extended rather than normal. The next 5 bytes in the extended FCB are reserved. The seventh byte is the attribute byte, which has the same structure as the file attribute byte that the directory entry maintains. By placing the appropriate attribute byte in this field, you can use the extended FCB to manipulate files that have special attributes.

Now that we've taken a look at the structure of an FCB, let's look at the FCB services and the way programs use them to manipulate files. Figure 9-5 lists the MS-DOS FCB services.

Service	Purpose
Opening and closing	
0FH	Open file
10H	Close file
16H	Create file
Reading and writing	
14H	Sequential read
15H	Sequential write
21H	Random read
22H	Random write
27H	Random block read
28H	Random block write
Miscellaneous	
13H	Delete file
17H	Rename file
1AH	Set disk transfer area address
23H	Obtain file size
24H	Set relative-record number
29H	Parse filename
2FH	Get disk transfer area address

FIGURE 9-5.
MS-DOS Int 21H FCB file manipulation services.

The disk transfer area

The FCB services (and a couple of the handle services) make use of the *disk transfer area,* or *DTA.* The DTA is an area of memory that serves as a buffer between the application program and the disk. When you want to write data to disk, the program must first place the data in the DTA. You then call

The Program Segment Prefix

Whenever you load a program, MS-DOS creates a reserved area of memory that is called the *program segment prefix,* or *PSP*. The PSP is 256 bytes long and immediately precedes the program in memory. The PSP contains information that MS-DOS needs about the program, as well as information that MS-DOS passes to the program. The structure of the PSP is shown in Figure 9-6.

Many components of the PSP have their origin in the first version of MS-DOS, which was intended to emulate the older CP/M operating system in some ways. Some of these components are of no interest to programmers. As you can see in Figure 9-6, other portions of the PSP are reserved, meaning that they are undocumented. Because they are undocumented, however, does not mean that they are unused! A program must not alter these areas. In fact, a program must not alter any part of the PSP below offset 5CH.

At offset 00H, the PSP contains a link to the MS-DOS *process termination handler*. The code in the process termination handler performs any necessary final cleanup tasks when a process (in this case, the program) terminates and then returns control to MS-DOS. At offset 05H, the PSP contains a link to the MS-DOS *function dispatcher,* which performs various services for programs (for example, disk and console access). Note that using the PSP links is not the correct way to access these services. Rather, you should use MS-DOS and BIOS interrupts, as discussed earlier in this book.

The 2 bytes at offset 02H contain the top segment address of the program's allocated block. The program can use this value to determine whether sufficient memory has been allocated to it or whether the program needs more memory from the memory arena.

The region between 0AH and 16H is used to store the contents of the interrupt vectors, which give the addresses of the interrupts for program termination, Ctrl-C handling, and critical-error handling as they existed when the program was loaded. If the program modifies these vectors in the vector table, the original values are restored from the PSP when the program terminates.

At offset 2CH, the PSP contains the segment address of the *environment block*. This is a series of null-terminated ASCIIZ strings that contain information such as the paths set by the PATH statement, the disk location of COMMAND.COM, and so on.

When the program loads, MS-DOS places the length of the *command tail* at offset 80H in the PSP and the contents of the command tail at offset 81H.

The command tail is the last portion—following the program name—of the command line that was used to start the program. Redirection and piping parameters are not included here.

Most of the remainder of the PSP is devoted to the two default file control blocks and the 128-byte default disk transfer area, both of which are discussed in this chapter.

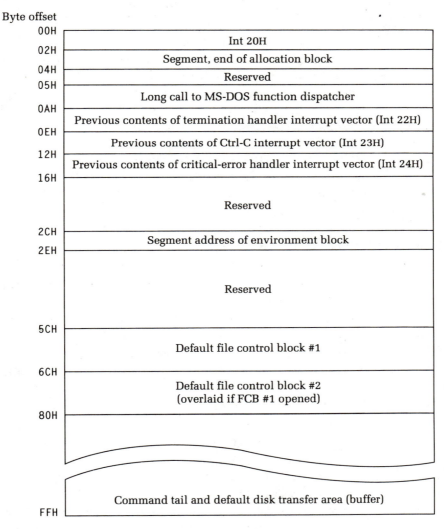

FIGURE 9-6.
The structure of the PSP.

one of the disk write services, which reads the data from the DTA and writes it to the disk. Likewise, when you call a disk read service, MS-DOS places the data that it reads from the disk in the DTA, where your program can access it.

When MS-DOS loads a program, it sets up a default DTA at offset 80H in the *program segment prefix,* or *PSP.* The default DTA size is 128 bytes. If the size of the default DTA is adequate for your program's needs, you need take no further action; the FCB services will use the default DTA.

Be aware, however, that MS-DOS doesn't ascertain the DTA size; it knows only the DTA's starting address. If your program performs disk data transfers that are too large for the DTA size, the data written to the DTA might extend past the end of the DTA and overwrite other information, causing a program crash or other problems. You specify the number of records you want to read or write when you call a read or write FCB service. The size of each record, however, is specified by the record size field in the FCB. It is your program's responsibility, when it needs more memory, to allocate memory for a larger DTA and then use Int 21H Function 1AH to inform MS-DOS of the new DTA address. If your program modifies the DTA address, it should reset the address to the default before terminating. To obtain the current DTA address, call Int 21H Function 2FH.

The default file control blocks

After a program is loaded, the PSP contains two default FCBs that MS-DOS sets up. These are normal FCBs and are located at offsets 5CH and 6CH in the PSP. Looking at the relative addresses of the two default FCBs and remembering the 37-byte size of a normal FCB, it's clear that some overlap occurs between the fields of the two default FCBs. This overlap makes the two default FCBs essentially useless for real file operations; they are provided primarily for backward compatibility with the older CP/M operating system.

You can, however, use the default FCBs for one task. When you start a program, MS-DOS parses the first two parameters in the command line that started the program (excluding any redirection directives) into the filename and extension fields of the default FCBs. MS-DOS does so on the assumption that command line parameters might be filenames. Please note that MS-DOS does not verify that the command line parameters are, in fact, filenames; your program must do so. If your program does accept one or two filenames as command line parameters, however, the program can obtain the names from the default FCBs and copy them directly, without parsing, into FCBs that the program allocates.

FCB read and write methods

The FCB services offer three different file access methods: *sequential access, random record access,* and *random block access.* Each method is most appropriate for a specific type of application. All three access methods are based on the concept of a record, which is a chunk of data whose size is specified in bytes by the FCB's record size field.

Sequential access steps through the file one record at a time, starting at the beginning of the file (at the first record, record 0). The sequential read and write services, Int 21H Functions 14H and 15H, read or write one record of data and then update the current record and current block fields in the FCB. As a result, sequential access services work with the file's records in order. The sequential access method is ideal when you need to read or write an entire file.

Random record access permits direct access to any record in a file, without the need to read all previous records. The relative record field in the FCB—whose value the program must set—specifies the file record accessed for reading or writing. The random record access services, Int 21H Functions 21H and 22H, do not update this field; the program must do so by calling Int 21H Function 24H. Random record access is useful for applications such as database programs that need to read or write fixed-length records at nonsequential locations within a file.

The third method, random block access, combines some features of the sequential access and random record access methods. Using random block access, a program can access any record in a file directly, reading or writing any number of records. After the service finishes, MS-DOS updates the record number to the record following the one last read or written. Using the random block access services (Int 21H Functions 27H and 28H), a program can initiate a sequential read or write operation at any file location. This method is flexible and can be used in many types of applications.

General FCB procedure

Here is an outline of the procedure to follow when you use FCB services for file manipulation.

1. Allocate space for the FCB (normal or extended), and initialize all fields in it to 0.

2. Place the drive code, filename, and file extension in the proper FCB fields. Obtain command line filenames from the default FCBs if appropriate. If you want to do so, use Int 21H Function 29H to place the filename in the FCB.

3. If you're using an extended FCB to manipulate a file that has special attributes, write the corresponding attribute byte to the FCB.

4. Create a new file using Int 21H Function 16H, or open an existing file using Int 21H Function 0FH.

5. If you do not plan to use the default record size of 128 bytes, change the record size field in the FCB to the correct value.

6. If you do not plan to use the default DTA, allocate an appropriate amount of space for the new DTA, and use Int 21H Function 1AH to set the DTA address.

7. When performing random read or write operations, set the relative record field in the FCB to point to the desired record.

8. When writing data to a file, place the data in the DTA, and then call one of the FCB write services. When reading data from a file, call one of the FCB read services, and then read the data from the DTA.

9. Return to Step 7. When file access is complete, close the file using Int 21H Function 10H.

Error handling using FCB services

As you look through the "FCB Service Reference" at the end of this chapter, you'll see that many of the FCB services return an error code in AL. This code, however, is not all that useful. It tells you that an error has occurred, but it provides little if any information about the exact nature of the error. Under MS-DOS 3.0 and later, after an error has occurred, you can call Int 21H Function 59H to obtain additional information about the error. This service, which is covered in detail in Chapter 13, can deal with all types of errors, not only disk-related errors. The codes that the service returns not only indicate the nature of the error but, in many cases, suggest an action that your program can take.

The general procedure for FCB service error handling, therefore, is to test the value that the MS-DOS service returns in AL. If an error has occurred, call Int 21H Function 59H. Based on this service's return values, your program then can take appropriate action.

FCB service demonstration

The programs in Listings 9-1 and 9-2 demonstrate how to use the FCB services. If you examine the reference entries for the various FCB services at the end of this chapter, you'll notice that the services use not only the offset address of the FCB and the data they are working with but also the segment address. In the Basic program, the VARSEG statement obtains the segment address, and the VARPTR statement obtains the offset address.

The C program, however, uses code that might not be familiar to all readers. You can obtain both a segment and an offset only from a *far pointer*. The default pointer type, the *near pointer*, contains only offset information. (A near pointer is assumed to point to either the data segment or the stack segment.) Therefore, in the demonstration program shown in Listing 9-2, the functions are defined to take far pointers as arguments (pointers to the FCB array, to the DTA array, and to the filename). Note that the data items themselves need not be declared as far pointers. When a function receives as an argument a near pointer that is defined as a far pointer (in the function's parameter list), the compiler makes the necessary conversion.

When the function begins executing, it must extract the offset and the segment from the far pointer and place them in the appropriate registers. You accomplish these tasks using the macros FP_OFF and FP_SEG, which are defined in the header file DOS.H. They extract the offset or the segment from a far pointer. Thus, if *fp* is a far pointer, the following expressions evaluate, respectively, as the offset portion and the segment portion of the address to which *fp* points:

```
FP_OFF(fp)
FP_SEG(fp)
```

You'll notice that the programs perform no error checking. The omission is intentional because including error-checking code would have increased the complexity and size of the programs and might have obscured the points I wanted the programs to demonstrate. Most of the FCB services return a value in AL that indicates the outcome of the call, with 0 indicating success and nonzero values indicating other conditions. The Basic and C subprograms and functions in these demonstration programs return the value in AL to the calling program. The demonstration programs ignore this value, but in a real-world application, you would include error-checking code. Chapter 13 presents additional information about error checking.

```
DECLARE FUNCTION CloseFile% (fcb() AS INTEGER)
DECLARE FUNCTION CreateFile% (fcb() AS INTEGER)
DECLARE FUNCTION OpenFile% (fcb() AS INTEGER)
DECLARE FUNCTION ParseFileName% (fcb() AS INTEGER, filename$)
DECLARE FUNCTION ReadRecord% (fcb() AS INTEGER)
DECLARE SUB SetDta (dta() AS INTEGER)
DECLARE FUNCTION WriteRecord% (fcb() AS INTEGER)

' $INCLUDE: 'QB.BI'
```

(continued)

LISTING 9-1.
Demonstration of using the FCB services to create, open, write to, read from, and close a file in Basic.

LISTING 9-1. *continued*

```
DEFINT A-Z

DIM SHARED inRegs AS RegTypeX, outRegs AS RegTypeX


' Begin execution

CLS

' Allocate space for two FCBs and two 128-byte DTAs
DIM fcb1(19) AS INTEGER
DIM fcb2(19) AS INTEGER
DIM dta1(64) AS INTEGER
DIM dta2(64) AS INTEGER

' Place a sequence of numbers in the first DTA buffer
FOR i = 0 TO 63
    dta1(i) = i
NEXT i

' Display data on the screen
PRINT "Original data:"
PRINT

FOR i = 0 TO 63 STEP 4
    PRINT dta1(i), dta1(i + 1), dta1(i + 2), dta1(i + 3)
NEXT i

PRINT "Press any key to continue"
WHILE INKEY$ = "": WEND

' Create an ASCIIZ string that contains the filename
f$ = "testfile.xxx" + CHR$(0)

result = ParseFileName(fcb1(), f$)   ' Parse the filename into the FCB
result = CreateFile(fcb1())          ' Create the file in the current directory

CALL SetDta(dta1())                  ' Set the DTA address to the first buffer
result = WriteRecord(fcb1())         ' Write one record to disk
result = CloseFile(fcb1())           ' Close the file

CALL SetDta(dta2())                  ' Set the DTA to the second buffer
result = ParseFileName(fcb2(), f$)   ' Parse the filename into the second FCB
result = OpenFile(fcb2())            ' Open the file

' Read one record using the default 128-byte record size
result = ReadRecord(fcb2())
result = CloseFile(fcb2())           ' Close the file
```

(continued)

LISTING 9-1. *continued*

```
' Show that the second DTA buffer now contains the data that was
' originally written to the file.

CLS
PRINT "Data read from file:"
PRINT

FOR i = 0 TO 63 STEP 4
    PRINT dta2(i), dta2(i + 1), dta2(i + 2), dta2(i + 3)
NEXT i

END

FUNCTION CloseFile% (fcb() AS INTEGER)
    ' Closes the file associated with the FCB

    inRegs.ax = &H1000
    inRegs.ds = VARSEG(fcb(0))
    inRegs.dx = VARPTR(fcb(0))

    ' Call Int 21H Function 10H to close the file
    CALL INTERRUPTX(&H21, inRegs, outRegs)
    CloseFile = outRegs.ax AND &HFF
END FUNCTION

FUNCTION CreateFile% (fcb() AS INTEGER)
    ' Creates the file specified by the FCB

    inRegs.ax = &H1600
    inRegs.ds = VARSEG(fcb(0))
    inRegs.dx = VARPTR(fcb(0))

    ' Call Int 21H Function 16H to create the file
    CALL INTERRUPTX(&H21, inRegs, outRegs)
    CreateFile = outRegs.ax AND &HFF
END FUNCTION

FUNCTION OpenFile% (fcb() AS INTEGER)
    ' Opens the file specified by the FCB

    inRegs.ax = &HF00
    inRegs.ds = VARSEG(fcb(0))
    inRegs.dx = VARPTR(fcb(0))

    ' Call Int 21H Function 0FH to open the file
    CALL INTERRUPTX(&H21, inRegs, outRegs)
    OpenFile = outRegs.ax AND &HFF
END FUNCTION
```

(continued)

LISTING 9-1. *continued*

```
FUNCTION ParseFileName% (fcb() AS INTEGER, f$)
    ' Places the filename in f$ into the FCB
    ' The parse control flags in AL are all set to 0, except for the first,
    ' which signals that leading separators should be skipped

    inRegs.ax = &H2901
    inRegs.ds = VARSEG(f$)
    inRegs.si = SADD(f$)

    inRegs.es = VARSEG(fcb(0))
    inRegs.di = VARPTR(fcb(0))

    ' Call Int 21H Function 29H to place the filename in the FCB
    CALL INTERRUPTX(&H21, inRegs, outRegs)
    ParseFileName = outRegs.ax AND &HFF
END FUNCTION

FUNCTION ReadRecord% (fcb() AS INTEGER)
    ' Reads a single record from the open file specified
    ' by the FCB

    inRegs.ax = &H1400
    inRegs.ds = VARSEG(fcb(0))
    inRegs.dx = VARPTR(fcb(0))

    ' Call Int 21H Function 14H to read a record
    CALL INTERRUPTX(&H21, inRegs, outRegs)
    ReadRecord = outRegs.ax AND &HFF
END FUNCTION

SUB SetDta (dta() AS INTEGER)
    ' Sets the disk transfer area to the specified program array

    inRegs.ax = &H1A00
    inRegs.ds = VARSEG(dta(0))
    inRegs.dx = VARPTR(dta(0))

    ' Call Int 21H Function 1AH to set the DTA
    CALL INTERRUPTX(&H21, inRegs, outRegs)
END SUB

FUNCTION WriteRecord% (fcb() AS INTEGER)
    ' Writes a single record to the open file specified
    ' by the FCB

    inRegs.ax = &H1500
    inRegs.ds = VARSEG(fcb(0))
    inRegs.dx = VARPTR(fcb(0))

    ' Call Int 21H Function 15H to write a record
    CALL INTERRUPTX(&H21, inRegs, outRegs)
    WriteRecord = outRegs.ax AND &HFF
END FUNCTION
```

```c
/* File access with FCB services */

#include <stdio.h>
#include <dos.h>

/* Declare the register unions */
union REGS inregs, outregs;
struct SREGS segregs;

/* Function prototypes */
int close_file(int _far f[]);
int create_file(int _far f[]);
int open_file(int _far f[]);
int parse_filename(int _far f[], char _far *filename);
int read_record(int _far f[]);
void set_dta(int _far d[]);
int write_record(int _far f[]);
void clearscreen(void);

main()
{
    /* Allocate space for two FCBs and two DTAs */
    int fcb1[19], fcb2[19], dta1[64], dta2[64];
    int i, result;

    /* Allocate and initialize space for a filename */
    char *filename = "testfile.xyz";

    /* Zero all bytes in the FCBs */
    for (i = 0; i < 20; i++)
        {
        fcb1[i] = 0;
        fcb2[i] = 0;
        }

    clearscreen();

    /* Place a sequence of numbers in the first DTA buffer */
    for (i = 0; i < 64; i++)
        dta1[i] = i;

    /* Display data on the screen */
    for (i = 0; i < 64; i += 4)
        printf("%d\t%d\t%d\t%d\n", dta1[i], dta1[i+1], dta1[i+2],
            dta1[i+3]);

    /* Parse the filename into the FCB */
    result = parse_filename(fcb1, filename);
```

LISTING 9-2. *(continued)*
Demonstration of using the FCB services to create, open, write to, read from, and close a file in C.

LISTING 9-2. *continued*

```c
    /* Create the file in the current directory */
    result = create_file(fcb1);

    /* Set the DTA address to the first buffer */
    set_dta(dta1);

    result = write_record(fcb1);    /* Write one record to disk */
    result = close_file(fcb1);      /* Close the file */

    puts("\n\nPress a key to continue...");
    getch();

    /* Set the DTA to the second buffer */
    set_dta(dta2);

    /* Parse the filename into the second FCB */
    result = parse_filename(fcb2, filename);
    result = open_file(fcb2);       /* Open the file again */

    /* Read one record using the default 128-byte record size */
    result = read_record(fcb2);
    result = close_file(fcb2);      /* Close the file */

    /* Show that the second DTA buffer now contains the data that */
    /* was originally written to the file. */

    clearscreen();
    puts("Data read from file:");

    for (i = 0; i < 64; i += 4)
        printf("%d\t%d\t%d\t%d\n", dta2[i], dta2[i+1], dta2[i+2],
            dta2[i+3]);
}   /* End of main() */

int close_file(int _far fcb[])
{
    /* Closes the file associated with the FCB */

    inregs.x.ax = 0X1000;
    inregs.x.dx = FP_OFF(fcb);
    segregs.ds = FP_SEG(fcb);

    /* Call Int 21H Function 10H to close the file */
    int86x(0X21, &inregs, &outregs, &segregs);
    return(outregs.h.al);
}

int create_file(int _far fcb[])
{
```

(continued)

LISTING 9-2. *continued*

```c
    /* Creates the file specified by the FCB */

    inregs.x.ax = 0X1600;
    inregs.x.dx = FP_OFF(fcb);
    segregs.ds = FP_SEG(fcb);

    /* Call Int 21H Function 16H to create the file */
    int86x(0X21, &inregs, &outregs, &segregs);
    return(outregs.h.al);
}

int open_file(int _far fcb[])
{
    /* Opens the file specified by the FCB */

    inregs.x.ax = 0XF00;
    inregs.x.dx = FP_OFF(fcb);
    segregs.ds = FP_SEG(fcb);

    /* Call Int 21H Function 0FH to open the file */
    int86x(0X21, &inregs, &outregs, &segregs);
    return(outregs.h.al);
}

int parse_filename(int _far fcb[], char _far *filename)
{
    /* Places the filename in *filename into the FCB */
    /* The parse control bits in AL are all set to 0 except */
    /* for the first, which signals that leading separators */
    /* should be skipped */

    inregs.x.ax = 0X2901;
    inregs.x.si = FP_OFF(filename);
    segregs.ds = FP_SEG(filename);

    inregs.x.di = FP_OFF(fcb);
    segregs.es = FP_SEG(fcb);

    /* Call Int 21H Function 29H to place the filename in the FCB */
    int86x(0X21, &inregs, &outregs, &segregs);
    return(outregs.h.al);
}

int read_record(int _far fcb[])
{
    /* Reads a single record from the open file specified */
    /* by the FCB */

    inregs.x.ax = 0X1400;
    inregs.x.dx = FP_OFF(fcb);
    segregs.ds = FP_SEG(fcb);
```

(continued)

LISTING 9-2. *continued*

```c
        /* Call Int 21H Function 14H to read a record */
        int86x(0X21, &inregs, &outregs, &segregs);
        return(outregs.h.al);
}

void set_dta(int _far *dta)
{
    /* Sets the disk transfer area to the specified address */

    inregs.x.ax = 0X1A00;
    inregs.x.dx = FP_OFF(dta);
    segregs.ds = FP_SEG(dta);

    /* Call Int 21H Function 1AH to set the DTA */
    int86x(0X21, &inregs, &outregs, &segregs);
}

int write_record(int _far fcb[])
{
    /* Writes a single record to the open file specified */
    /* by the FCB */

    inregs.x.ax = 0X1500;
    inregs.x.dx = FP_OFF(fcb);
    segregs.ds = FP_SEG(fcb);

    /* Call Int 21H Function 15H to write a record */
    int86x(0X21, &inregs, &outregs, &segregs);
    return(outregs.h.al);
}

void clearscreen(void)
{
    int x;

    for (x = 0; x < 25; x++)
        printf("\n");
}
```

The Handle Services

The second method of accessing files is via the handle services. As was mentioned earlier in this chapter, the handle services require only that the program pass to the file create or file open service an ASCIIZ string that specifies the drive, path, name, and extension of the file. The service returns the file handle, a 2-byte identifier that MS-DOS uses to refer to the file in subsequent operations. MS-DOS maintains information about the file internally, where it is not directly available to the program.

Perhaps the major advantage of the handle services over the FCB services is that the handle services support the hierarchical directory structure. Using the handle services also results in simpler programming because MS-DOS maintains the file's information, and the programmer need not be concerned with it. At the beginning of this chapter, I listed the advantages that the handle services offer.

You should be aware that the handle services make no distinction between sequential and random file access. The handle services view any file as a linear sequence of bytes. When you use the handle services, each open file has an associated *file pointer* that defines the location in the file at which the next read or write operation will occur. For sequential and random file access, MS-DOS maintains this pointer. For random block file access, the program must update the file pointer.

Most of the handle services do not use the disk transfer area. The call to the handle read or write services specifies the memory location where your program should read or write the data. Thus, it is easy to transfer data directly between the file and your program's data structures.

The flexibility of the handle services is enhanced by their ability to read from and write to devices other than disk files—for example, the screen, the printer, and the keyboard. When MS-DOS loads a program, it opens and assigns handles to the five standard devices, as described in Figure 9-7.

Device	*Handle*	*Opened to*
Standard input (*stdin*)	0	Keyboard
Standard output (*stdout*)	1	Screen
Standard error (*stderr*)	2	Screen
Standard auxiliary (*stdaux*)	3	Serial port COM1:
Standard printer (*stdprn*)	4	Parallel port LPT1:

FIGURE 9-7.
MS-DOS's five standard devices and their preassigned handles.

The number of handles that can be open at one time is limited. The FILES statement in your CONFIG.SYS file specifies the total number of handles available for all processes. A FILES statement can specify a maximum of 255 handles. If no FILES statement is included in your CONFIG.SYS file, the default value is 8. After you boot MS-DOS, you can change this maximum value only by editing the CONFIG.SYS file and rebooting the computer.

A single executing program can use a maximum of 20 handles at one time, assuming that the system has at least 20 handles available. When the program starts, MS-DOS opens and assigns the 5 preassigned handles listed in Figure 9-7, leaving 15 handles available for files. In MS-DOS versions earlier than 3.3, you cannot change this maximum. Under MS-DOS 3.3 and later, however, you can use Int 21H Function 67H to increase the limit, assuming, of course, that the program has not reached the system's handle limit.

Figure 9-8 lists the handle-based file manipulation services.

Service	Action
Opening and closing	
3CH	Create file
3DH	Open file
3EH	Close file
41H	Delete file
5AH	Create temporary file*
5BH	Create file only if it doesn't already exist*
Reading and writing	
42H	Set file pointer
3FH	Read file
40H	Write file
Miscellaneous	
43H	Get or modify file attributes
45H	Duplicate handle
46H	Redirect handle
56H	Rename file
57H	Get or set file date and time
67H	Set handle count†
68H	Commit file†
6CH	Extended file open‡

* MS-DOS 3.0 and later
† MS-DOS 3.3 and later
‡ MS-DOS 4.0 and later

FIGURE 9-8.
The MS-DOS Int 21H handle-based file manipulation services.

General handle procedure

Here is an outline of the procedure to follow when you use the handle services for file manipulation.

1. Create an ASCIIZ string that contains the filename, including the drive and the path if necessary.

2. Open an existing file using Int 21H Function 3DH or 6CH, or create a new file using Int 21H Function 3CH, 5BH, or 6CH. Save the handle that the service returns.

3. If necessary, set the file pointer position using Int 21H Function 42H. You can set the position relative to the start of the file, the end of the file, or the current pointer position. For sequential read and write operations, MS-DOS maintains the file pointer.

4. Read data from the file using Int 21H Function 3FH, or write data to the file using Int 21H Function 40H. The program must pass to both of these services the file handle, the number of bytes to transfer, and the address of the program memory to use for the transfer.

5. Return to Step 3. When the program completes the file access, close the file using Int 21H Function 3EH.

Error handling using handle services

When the handle services are successful, they return with the carry flag clear. When they encounter an error, they return with the carry flag set. If the carry flag is set, the service returns an error code that provides details about the error. The same error code can also be obtained by calling Int 21H Function 59H, which is discussed in detail in Chapter 13. Figure 9-9 lists the possible error codes. Some of the errors that these codes refer to might not be familiar to you because they deal with aspects of MS-DOS that are beyond the scope of this book.

Code	Meaning
MS-DOS 2.0 and later error codes	
01H	Function number invalid
02H	File not found
03H	Path not found
04H	Too many open files
05H	Access denied
06H	Handle invalid
07H	Arena entries destroyed

FIGURE 9-9. *(continued)*
MS-DOS error codes.

FIGURE 9-9. *continued*

Code	Meaning
08H	Insufficient memory
09H	Arena entry address invalid
0AH	Environment invalid
0BH	Format invalid
0CH	Access code invalid
0DH	Data invalid
0FH	Disk drive invalid
10H	Attempted to remove current directory
11H	Not same device
12H	No more files

Critical error codes

Code	Meaning
13H	Disk write protected
14H	Unknown unit
15H	Drive not ready
16H	Unknown command
17H	Data error (CRC)
18H	Bad request-structure length
19H	Seek error
1AH	Unknown media type
1BH	Sector not found
1CH	Printer out of paper
1DH	Write fault
1EH	Read fault
1FH	General failure

MS-DOS 3.0 and later error codes

Code	Meaning
20H	Sharing violation
21H	File-lock violation
22H	Disk change invalid
23H	FCB unavailable
24H	Sharing buffer exceeded
25H	Code page mismatched
26H	End of file
27H	Disk full
28H–31H	Reserved

(continued)

FIGURE 9-9. *continued*

Code	Meaning
32H	Unsupported network request
33H	Remote machine not listening
34H	Duplicate name on network
35H	Network name not found
36H	Network busy
37H	Device no longer exists on network
38H	NetBIOS command limit exceeded
39H	Error in network adapter hardware
3AH	Incorrect response from network
3BH	Unexpected network error
3CH	Remote adapter incompatible
3DH	Print queue full
3EH	Not enough space for print file
3FH	Print file deleted
40H	Network name deleted
41H	Network access denied
42H	Incorrect network device type
43H	Network name not found
44H	Network name limit exceeded
45H	NetBIOS session limit exceeded
46H	File sharing temporarily paused
47H	Network request not accepted
48H	Print or disk redirection paused
49H–4FH	Reserved
50H	File already exists
51H	Duplicate FCB
52H	Cannot make directory
53H	Fail on Int 24H (critical error)
54H	Too many redirections
55H	Duplicate redirection
56H	Invalid password
57H	Invalid parameter
58H	Network device fault
5AH	Required system component not installed

Handle service demonstration

The programs in Listings 9-3 and 9-4 demonstrate how to use the handle services to create a file, write data to it, reset the file pointer, and then read data from the file and close it. Each of the program's functions returns a value that the calling program can use to determine whether an error occurred. When an error does occur, the function places the code for the error in a global variable called *errorcode* that the program can test to determine the nature of the error. These demonstration programs do not implement error checking, but a real-world program, of course, would need to do so.

```
DECLARE FUNCTION CloseFile% (handle%)
DECLARE FUNCTION CreateFile% (filename$)
DECLARE FUNCTION ReadFile% (handle%, bytes%, array() AS INTEGER)
DECLARE FUNCTION SetFilePointer& (handle%, offset&, origin%)
DECLARE FUNCTION WriteRecord% (handle%, bytes%, source() AS INTEGER)

' $INCLUDE: 'QB.BI'

DEFINT A-Z

DIM SHARED inRegs AS RegTypeX, outRegs AS RegTypeX

' Declare a shared variable for error codes
DIM SHARED errorcode AS INTEGER

' Allocate two data arrays
DIM data1(100), data2(100)


' Begin execution

CLS

' Initialize one array with a sequence of numbers
FOR i = 0 TO 99
    data1(i) = i
NEXT i

' Display the data on the screen
PRINT "Original data:"
PRINT

FOR i = 0 TO 99 STEP 5
    PRINT data1(i), data1(i + 1), data1(i + 2), data1(i + 3), data1(i + 4)
NEXT i

PRINT "Press any key to continue"
WHILE INKEY$ = "": WEND
```

LISTING 9-3. *(continued)*
Demonstration of using the handle services for file manipulation in Basic.

LISTING 9-3. *continued*

```
' Create an ASCIIZ string for the filename. File will be
' in the current directory and on the current drive.

f$ = "handles.zzz" + CHR$(0)

' Create the file and save the handle in variable myfile
myfile = CreateFile(f$)

' Write the contents of one array to the file
result = WriteRecord(myfile, 200, data1())

' Set the file pointer to the beginning of the file
result& = SetFilePointer(myfile, 0, 0)

' Read the data into the second array
result = ReadFile(myfile, 200, data2())

' Close the file
result = CloseFile(myfile)

' Display the data on the screen
PRINT
PRINT "Data read from disk:"
PRINT

FOR i = 0 TO 99 STEP 5
    PRINT data2(i), data2(i + 1), data2(i + 2), data2(i + 3), data2(i + 4)
NEXT i

END

FUNCTION CloseFile (handle)
    ' Closes the file associated with the handle; returns 1 if successful,
    ' 0 if an error was encountered

    inRegs.ax = &H3E00
    inRegs.bx = handle

    ' Call Int 21H Function 3EH to close the file
    CALL INTERRUPTX(&H21, inRegs, outRegs)

    IF outRegs.flags AND 1 THEN
        errorcode = outRegs.ax
        CloseFile = 0
    ELSE
        CloseFile = 1
    END IF
END FUNCTION

FUNCTION CreateFile (filename$)
    ' Creates file filename$ with no special attributes
    ' Returns the handle, or 0 if an error was encountered
```

(continued)

LISTING 9-3. *continued*

```
    inRegs.ax = &H3C00
    inRegs.cx = 0
    inRegs.ds = VARSEG(filename$)
    inRegs.dx = SADD(filename$)

    ' Call Int 21H Function 3CH to create the file
    CALL INTERRUPTX(&H21, inRegs, outRegs)

    IF outRegs.flags AND 1 THEN
        errorcode = outRegs.ax
        CreateFile = 0
    ELSE
        CreateFile = outRegs.ax
    END IF
END FUNCTION

FUNCTION ReadFile (handle, bytes, array() AS INTEGER)
    ' Reads the specified number of bytes from the file or device
    ' associated with the handle
    ' Returns the number of bytes read, or 0 if an error was encountered

    inRegs.ax = &H3F00
    inRegs.bx = handle
    inRegs.cx = bytes
    inRegs.ds = VARSEG(array(0))
    inRegs.dx = VARPTR(array(0))

    ' Call Int 21H Function 3FH to read bytes from the file
    CALL INTERRUPTX(&H21, inRegs, outRegs)

    IF outRegs.flags AND 1 THEN
        errorcode = outRegs.ax
        ReadFile = 0
    ELSE
        ReadFile = outRegs.ax
    END IF
END FUNCTION

FUNCTION SetFilePointer& (handle, offset&, origin)
    ' Sets the file pointer of the file associated with the handle
    ' to the specified offset, relative to the origin, as follows:
    ' origin = 00H from start of file
    '        = 01H from current pointer position
    '        = 02H from end of file

    ' Returns a long integer that gives the new pointer position
    ' If an error was encountered, returns &HFFFFFFFF

    inRegs.ax = &H4200 + (origin AND &HFF)
    inRegs.bx = handle
```

(continued)

LISTING 9-3. *continued*

```
        inRegs.cx = offset& \ &H10000
        inRegs.dx = offset& AND &HFFFF

        ' Call Int 21H Function 42H to set the file pointer position
        CALL INTERRUPTX(&H21, inRegs, outRegs)

        IF outRegs.flags AND 1 THEN
            SetFilePointer& = &HFFFFFFFF
            errorcode = outRegs.ax
        ELSE
            SetFilePointer& = (outRegs.dx * &H10000) + outRegs.ax
        END IF
END FUNCTION

FUNCTION WriteRecord (handle%, bytes%, source() AS INTEGER)
    ' Writes the specified number of bytes from the array source%
    ' to the file or device associated with handle%
    ' Returns the number of bytes written, or 0 if an error
    ' was encountered

    inRegs.ax = &H4000
    inRegs.bx = handle%
    inRegs.cx = bytes%
    inRegs.ds = VARSEG(source(0))
    inRegs.dx = VARPTR(source(0))

    ' Call Int 21H Function 40H to write bytes to the file
    CALL INTERRUPTX(&H21, inRegs, outRegs)

    IF outRegs.flags AND 1 THEN
        WriteRecord = 0
        errorcode = outRegs.ax
    ELSE
        WriteRecord = outRegs.ax
    END IF
END FUNCTION
```

```c
/* Using the handle services */

#include <stdio.h>
#include <dos.h>

/* Declare the register unions */
union REGS inregs, outregs;
struct SREGS segregs;
```

LISTING 9-4. *(continued)*
Demonstration of using the handle services for file manipulation in C.

LISTING 9-4. *continued*

```c
/* Declare a global variable for error codes */
int errorcode;

/* Function prototypes */
int close_file(int handle);
int create_file(char _far *filename);
int read_file(int handle, int bytes, int _far *array);
long set_file_pointer(int handle, long offset, int origin);
int write_record(int handle, int bytes, int _far *array);
void clearscreen(void);

main()
{
    /* Declare an ASCIIZ string for the filename */
    char *filename = "testfile.xyz";

    /* Declare two data arrays */
    int data1[100], data2[100];

    int i, myfile, result;
    long new_ptr;

    clearscreen();

    /* Initialize one array with a sequence of numbers */
    for (i = 0; i < 100; i++)
        data1[i] = i;

    /* Display the data on the screen */
    puts("Original data:");

    for (i = 0; i < 100; i += 5)
        printf("\n%d\t%d\t%d\t%d\t%d", data1[i], data1[i+1], data1[i+2],
                data1[i+3], data1[i+4]);

    puts("\nPress any key to continue");
    getch();

    /* Create the file */
    myfile = create_file(filename);

    /* Write the contents of one array to the file */
    result = write_record(myfile, 200, data1);

    /* Set the file pointer to the beginning of the file */
    new_ptr = set_file_pointer(myfile, 0, 0);

    /* Read the data into the second array */
    result = read_file(myfile, 200, data2);
```

(continued)

LISTING 9-4. *continued*

```c
    /* Close the file */
    result = close_file(myfile);

    /* Display the data on the screen */
    clearscreen();
    puts("Data read from disk:");
    for (i = 0; i < 100; i += 5)
        printf("\n%d\t%d\t%d\t%d\t%d", data2[i], data2[i+1],
                data2[i+2], data2[i+3], data2[i+4]);
}   /* End of main() */

int close_file(int handle)
{
    /* Closes the file associated with the handle; returns 1 */
    /* if successful, 0 if an error was encountered */

    inregs.x.ax = 0X3E00;
    inregs.x.bx = handle;

    /* Call Int 21H Function 3EH to close the file */
    int86(0X21, &inregs, &outregs);

    if (outregs.x.cflag)
        {
        errorcode = outregs.x.ax;
        return(0);
        }
    else
        return(1);
}

int create_file(char _far *filename)
{
    /* Creates the file with name filename with no special attributes */
    /* Returns the file handle, or 0 if an error was encountered */

    inregs.x.ax = 0X3C00;
    inregs.x.cx = 0;
    segregs.ds = FP_SEG(filename);
    inregs.x.dx = FP_OFF(filename);

    /* Call Int 21H Function 3CH to create the file */
    int86x(0X21, &inregs, &outregs, &segregs);

    if (outregs.x.cflag)
        {
        errorcode = outregs.x.ax;
        return(0);
        }
```

(continued)

LISTING 9-4. *continued*

```c
        else
            return(outregs.x.ax);
}

int read_file(int handle, int bytes, int _far *array)
{
    /* Reads the specified number of bytes from the file or device */
    /* associated with the handle, and puts the data in array[] */
    /* Returns the number of bytes read, or 0 if an error was encountered */

    inregs.x.ax = 0X3F00;
    inregs.x.bx = handle;
    inregs.x.cx = bytes;
    inregs.x.dx = FP_OFF(array);
    segregs.ds = FP_SEG(array);

    /* Call Int 21H Function 3FH to read bytes from the file */
    int86x(0X21, &inregs, &outregs, &segregs);

    if (outregs.x.cflag)
        {
        errorcode = outregs.x.ax;
        return(0);
        }
    else
        return(1);
}

long set_file_pointer(int handle, long offset, int origin)
{
    /* Sets the file pointer of the file associated with the */
    /* handle to the specified offset, relative to the origin, */
    /* as follows: */
    /* origin = 00H from start of file
               = 01H from current pointer position
               = 02H from end of file */

    /* Returns a long integer that gives the new pointer position */
    /* If an error was encountered, returns &HFFFFFFFF */

    inregs.h.ah = 0X42;
    inregs.h.al = origin;
    inregs.x.bx = handle;
    inregs.x.cx = (offset >> 8);
    inregs.x.dx = (offset & 0XFFFF);

    /* Call Int 21H Function 42H to set the file pointer position */
    int86(0X21, &inregs, &outregs);
```

(continued)

LISTING 9-4. *continued*

```c
    if (outregs.x.cflag)
        {
        errorcode = outregs.x.ax;
        return(0XFFFFFFFF);
        }
    else
        return ((outregs.x.dx << 8) + outregs.x.ax);
}

int write_record(int handle, int bytes, int _far *array)
{
    /* Writes the specified number of bytes from the array */
    /* to the file associated with handle */
    /* Returns the number of bytes written, or 0 if an error */
    /* was encountered */

    inregs.x.ax = 0X4000;
    inregs.x.bx = handle;
    inregs.x.cx = bytes;
    inregs.x.dx = FP_OFF(array);
    segregs.ds = FP_SEG(array);

    /* Call Int 21H Function 40H to write bytes to the file */
    int86x(0X21, &inregs, &outregs, &segregs);

    if (outregs.x.cflag)
        {
        errorcode = outregs.x.ax;
        return(0);
        }
    else
        return(outregs.x.ax);
}

void clearscreen(void)
{
    int x;

    for (x = 0; x < 25; x++)
        printf("\n");
}
```

File Manipulation Service Reference

The reference for this chapter is divided into two sections. The first section covers the FCB services, and the second section covers the handle services.

FCB SERVICES

Int 21H   Function 0FH
Open file

Action: Opens an existing disk file and makes it available for reading from, writing to, or both

Call with: AH = 0FH
DS = segment of FCB (file control block)
DX = offset of FCB

Returns: On success:
AL = 00H
MS-DOS fills in the file control block as follows:

Offset in FCB	Contents
00H	Drive (1 = A, 2 = B, and so on)
0CH	Current block (00H)
0EH	Record size (80H)
10H	File size in bytes
14H	File date stamp
16H	File time stamp

On failure (file not found):
AL = FFH

Notes: This service obtains the file size, date, and time from the file's directory entry. For information about the formats of the date and time fields, see the discussion of date and time formats at the beginning of this chapter, in the section titled "File control blocks."

This service does not support pathnames. It is therefore limited to opening files in the current directory on the specified drive.

To use a record size other than the default 128 bytes, the program must place the desired record size in the FCB's record size field after the file is opened but before any other disk operations take place.

To perform random access reading or writing, the program must set the value of the relative-record number field in the FCB after opening the file.

Int 21H Function 10H
Close file

Action: Closes an open file and, if the file has been modified, updates the file's directory entry

Call with: AH = 10H
DS = segment of FCB (file control block)
DX = offset of FCB

Returns: On success:
AL = 00H

On failure (file not found):
AL = FFH

Notes: When this service closes a file, data in its buffers are written to the disk before the memory for the buffers is freed.

Int 21H Function 13H
Delete file

Action: Deletes the specified file(s) from the current directory

Call with: AH = 13H
DS = segment of FCB (file control block)
DX = offset of FCB

Returns: On success:
AL = 00H

On failure (file not found or file is read only):
AL = FFH

Notes: You can use the ? and * wildcard characters in the filename. If you do so, all matching files are deleted.

Int 21H   Function 14H
Sequential read

Action:	Reads the next record from the specified file and updates the file pointer
Call with:	AH = 14H DS = segment of FCB (file control block) of previously opened file DX = offset of FCB of previously opened file

Returns:	On success:
	    AL = 00H if read successful
	
	On failure:
	    AL = 01H if end of file
	        = 02H if segment overlapped in DTA (disk transfer area)
	        = 03H if partial record read at end of file

Notes:	The value in the FCB's record size field specifies the number of bytes read from the file. If this value and the location of the DTA buffer cause a segment overflow or overlap, the service fails and returns 02H. A combination of the FCB's current-block number field and current-record number field specifies the location in the file from which the data is read. This service updates these two fields. The service places the data read from disk in memory in the DTA. If this service reads a partial record at the end of the file, the data read is padded with zeros to the specified record length, and the service returns the value 03H.

Int 21H   Function 15H
Sequential write

Action:	Writes the next record to the file and updates the file pointer
Call with:	AH = 15H DS = segment of FCB (file control block) of previously opened file DX = offset of FCB of previously opened file

Returns: On success:
    AL = 00H if write successful

On failure:
    AL = 01H if disk is full
       = 02H if segment overlapped in DTA (disk transfer area)

Notes: This service writes the data logically (not necessarily physically) from the DTA to the disk.

The value in the FCB's record size field specifies the number of bytes written to the file. If this value and the location of the DTA buffer cause a segment overflow or overlap to occur, the service fails and returns 02H.

A combination of the FCB's current-block number field and current-record number field specifies the location in the file to which the data is written. This service updates these two fields.

Int 21H   Function 16H
Create file

Action: Creates a new file and opens it for read and write operations

Call with: AH = 16H
DS = segment of FCB (file control block)
DX = offset of FCB

Returns: On success:
    AL = 00H

MS-DOS fills in the file control block as follows:

Offset in FCB	Contents
00H	Drive (1 = A, 2 = B, and so on)
0CH	Current block (00H)
0EH	Record size (80H)
10H	File size in bytes
14H	File date stamp
16H	File time stamp

On failure:
    AL = FFH

Disks: Files and Records

Notes: This service obtains the file size, date, and time from the file's directory entry. For information about the formats of the date and time fields, see the discussion of date and time formats at the beginning of this chapter, in the section titled "File control blocks."

If a file with the specified name already exists, it is truncated to 0 (that is, all file contents are lost).

Call this service using an extended FCB to create a file that has special attributes (directory, hidden, and so on).

To use a record size other than the default 128 bytes, the program must place the desired record size in the FCB's record size field after the file is opened but before any other disk operations take place.

To perform random access reading or writing, the program must set the value of the relative-record number field in the FCB after creating the file.

Int 21H Function 17H
Rename File

Action:	Renames a file in the current directory of the specified drive
Call with:	AH = 17H DS = segment of special file control block (see "Notes") DX = offset of special file control block

Returns:	On success:
	    AL = 00H
	
	On failure (no matching files, or new filename already in use):
	    AL = FFH

Notes:	The special file control block has the drive code and the name and extension of the existing file in the usual positions (0 through 0BH), and the new filename starting 6 bytes after the end of the first name (at offset 11H). If the ? wildcard is included in the first filename, all matching files will be renamed. If one or more ? wildcard characters are included in the second filename, the corresponding letters in the original filename will be unchanged. Use this service with an extended FCB to rename a directory.

Int 21H   Function 1AH
Set DTA address

Action:	Specifies the starting address of the disk transfer area (DTA) to be used for future calls to FCB services
Call with:	AH = 1AH DS = segment of DTA DX = offset of DTA
Returns:	Nothing
Notes:	Use this service only to set up a DTA other than the default 128-byte DTA that MS-DOS sets up at offset 80H in the program segment prefix. It is the program's responsibility to ensure that the space allocated for the DTA is sufficient for any disk operations you want to perform.

Int 21H   Function 21H
Random read

Action:	Reads a selected record from a file
Call with:	AH = 21H DS = segment of FCB (file control block) of previously opened file DX = offset of FCB of previously opened file

Returns:	On success:
	    AL = 00H
	
	On failure:
	    AL = 01H if end of file
	        = 02H if segment overlap
	        = 03H if partial read at end of file

Notes:	The value in the FCB's record size field (default = 128 bytes) specifies the size of the record to be read. A combination of the FCB's relative-record number field and record size field specifies the file location from which the data is read.

The service reads the specified record into the DTA buffer. If the record size and the location of the DTA buffer cause a segment overflow or overlap to occur, the service fails and returns 02H.

This service does not update the FCB's relative-record number field automatically. To read successive records from a file, the application program must increment the relative-record number field between read operations.

If the service reads a partial record from the end of the file, the record is padded with zeros to fill the specified record length.

Int 21H Function 22H
Random write

Action:	Writes a single record to a file
Call with:	AH = 22H DS = segment of FCB (file control block) of previously opened file DX = offset of FCB of previously opened file

Returns:	On success:
	   AL = 00H
	
	On failure:
	   AL = 01H if disk full
	      = 02H if segment overlap

Notes:	The service writes the data logically (not necessarily physically) from the DTA (disk transfer area) to the disk. The value in the FCB's record size field specifies the number of bytes written to the file. If this value and the location of the DTA buffer cause a segment overflow or overlap to occur, the service fails and returns 02H. This service does not update the FCB's relative-record number field. To write successive records to a file, the program must increment the relative-record number field between write operations.

Int 21H   Function 23H
Get file size

Action:	Obtains the size of the specified file
Call with:	AH = 23H DS = segment of FCB (file control block) of unopened file DX = offset of FCB of unopened file
Returns:	On success: 　AL = 00H 　File size in FCB (see "Notes") On failure (file not found): 　AL = FFH
Notes:	Before calling this service, you must place a value in the FCB's record size field. On return, this service updates the FCB's relative-record number field to indicate the total number of records (of the specified size) in the file. The service rounds up this value, if necessary, to the next complete record. To find the number of bytes in the file, call this service with a record size of 1 in the FCB. Because record numbers are zero based, your program can use the value that this service returns (that is, the number of records) to position the file pointer at the end of the file.

Int 21H   Function 24H
Set relative-record number

Action:	Sets the relative-record number field in a file control block to correspond to the current file position
Call with:	AX = 24H DS = segment of file control block (FCB) of previously opened file DX = offset of FCB of previously opened file
Returns:	AL is destroyed; other registers not affected Relative record field in FCB updated

Notes: Before calling this service, the program must set all 4 bytes of the FCB's relative-record number field to 0. This field starts at offset 21H.

This service uses the contents of the record size, current-block number, and current-record number fields of the FCB to derive the corresponding value for the relative-record number field.

Use this service when switching from sequential to random access in a file.

Int 21H Function 27H
Random block read

Action:	Reads one or more sequential records from a file
Call with:	AH = 27H CX = number of records to read DS = segment of FCB (file control block) of previously opened file DX = offset of FCB of previously opened file

Returns:	AL = 00H if all requested records read
	    = 01H if end of file
	    = 02H if segment overlap
	    = 03H if partial read at end of file
	CX = number of records read

Notes:	A combination of the FCB's record size field and relative-record number field specifies the file location from which the records are read. This service reads the specified record(s) into the DTA buffer. If the record size, the number of records, and the location of the DTA buffer cause a segment overflow or overlap to occur, the service fails and returns 02H. This service updates the FCB's current-block number field, current-record number field, and relative record field to point to the file's next record. If the service reads a partial record at the end of the file, the record is padded with zeros to the specified record length.

Int 21H   Function 28H
Random block write

Action: Writes one or more sequential records to a file

Call with: AH = 28H
CX = number of records to write
DS = segment of FCB (file control block) of previously opened file
DX = offset of FCB of previously opened file

Returns: AL = 00H if all records written
   = 01H if disk full
   = 02H if segment overlap
CX = number of records written

Notes: This service writes the specified record(s) logically (not necessarily physically) from the DTA (disk transfer area) to the disk. If the record size, the number of records, and the location of the DTA buffer cause a segment overflow or overlap to occur, the service fails and returns 02H.

A combination of the FCB's record size field and relative-record number field specifies the file location from which the records are written.

This service updates the FCB's current-block number field, current-record number field, and relative-record number field to point to the file's next record.

If you call this service using CX = 0, the service writes no data. It adjusts the file size (that is, it extends or truncates the file) to the length that the FCB's relative-record number field and record size field specify.

Int 21H   Function 29H
Parse filename

Action: Parses a text string into the appropriate fields of a file control block

Call with: AH = 29H
AL = parsing control flags (see "Notes")
DS = segment of filename string
SI = offset of filename string
ES = segment of FCB (file control block)
DI = offset of FCB

Returns:	AL	= 00H if no wildcard characters encountered
		= 01H if parsed string contains wildcard characters
		= FFH if drive specifier invalid
	DS	= segment of first character after parsed filename
	SI	= offset of first character after parsed filename
	ES	= segment of formatted FCB of an unopened file
	DI	= offset of formatted FCB of an unopened file

Notes: The byte passed in AL controls certain aspects of the parsing procedure:

- Bit 3 = 1 if the extension field in the FCB will be modified only if the string to be parsed contains an extension.

  = 0 if the extension field in the FCB will be modified regardless; if the string to be parsed does not contain an extension, the FCB extension field will be filled with blanks.

- Bit 2 = 1 if the filename field in the FCB will be modified only if the string to be parsed contains a filename.

  = 0 if the filename field in the FCB will be modified regardless; if the string to be parsed does not contain a filename, the FCB filename field will be filled with blanks.

- Bit 1 = 1 if the drive identifier in the FCB will be modified only if the string to be parsed contains a drive.

  = 0 if the drive identifier in the FCB will be modified regardless; if the string to be parsed does not contain a drive, the FCB drive field will be set to 0 (the default drive).

- Bit 0 = 1 if leading separators will be ignored.

  = 0 if leading separators will not be ignored.

This service recognizes the following characters as separators:

: . ; , = + *tab space*

This service recognizes the following characters and all control characters as terminators, which specify the end of a filename:

: . ; , = + *tab space* < > ¦ / " []

If the string to be parsed does not contain a valid filename, the byte at location ES:DI + 1, upon return, points to an ASCII space character.

If the wildcard character * occurs in the filename to be parsed, that character and all following characters in the corresponding FCB field are set to ?.

Int 21H Function 2FH
Get DTA address

Action: Returns the starting address of the current DTA (disk transfer area)

Call with: AH = 2FH

Returns: ES = segment of DTA
BX = offset of DTA

Notes: The default DTA is 128 bytes at offset 80H in the program segment prefix.

HANDLE SERVICES

Int 21H Function 3CH
Create file

Action: Creates a new file and returns a handle for that file

Call with: AH = 3CH
CX = file attribute (00H if normal)

Bit(s)	Significance (if set)
0	Read only
1	Hidden
2	System
3	Volume label
4	Reserved (must be 0)
5	Archive
6–15	Reserved (must be 0)

DS = segment of ASCIIZ pathname (which can include drive, path, and filename)
DX = offset of ASCIIZ pathname

Returns: On success:
Carry flag = clear
AX = file handle

On failure:
Carry flag = set
AX = error code

Notes: If a file of the specified name exists, it is truncated to zero length, and all existing file data is lost.

This service fails if any of the following is true:

- Any element of the pathname does not exist.
- A file already exists that has the specified name and read-only attributes.
- The file is being created in the root directory, and the root directory is full.
- The program is running on a network, and the user has insufficient network access rights.

Int 21H   Function 3DH
Open file

Action:	Opens an existing file and returns a handle for that file
Call with:	AH = 3DH
	AL = file access mode:

Bit(s)	Meaning
0–2	00 = read access
	01 = write access
	010 = read and write access
3	Reserved (0)
4–6	Sharing mode (MS-DOS 3.0 and later)
	000 = compatibility mode
	001 = deny all
	010 = deny write
	011 = deny read
	100 = deny none
7	Inheritance flag (MS-DOS 3.0 and later)
	0 = child process inherits handle
	1 = child process does not inherit handle

DS = segment of ASCIIZ pathname (which can include drive, path, and filename)

DX = offset of ASCIIZ pathname

Returns: On success:
Carry flag = clear
AX = file handle

On failure:
Carry flag = set
AX = error code

Notes: When a file is opened, the file pointer is set to the beginning of the file (position 0).

This service fails if any of the following is true:

- Any element of the pathname does not exist.
- The file does not exist.
- The file is read only, and you try to open it using a write access mode.

Int 21H   Function 3EH
Close file

Action: Closes a file

Call with: AH = 3EH
BX = file handle

Returns: On success:
Carry flag = clear

On failure:
Carry flag = set
AX = error code

Notes: When passed the handle of an open file, this service writes all data in the internal buffers associated with the file to disk, closes the file, and releases the handle for reuse. If the file was modified, the service updates the time, date, and file size in the file's directory entry.

This service fails if passed an invalid handle.

Do not call this service using a zero handle. Doing so closes *stdin*, which breaks the connection between the keyboard and MS-DOS, making it impossible to use the keyboard. The only way to recover is to perform a cold boot by turning your machine off and then on again.

Int 21H   Function 3FH
Read file or device

Action: Reads data from an open file or device

Call with: AH = 3FH
BX = file handle
CX = number of bytes to read
DS = segment of buffer
DX = offset of buffer

Returns: On success:
    Carry flag = clear
    AX   = number of bytes read

On failure:
    Carry flag = set
    AX   = error code

Notes: This service reads the specified number of bytes from the file or device, places them in memory starting at DS:DX, and updates the file pointer position.

If the service returns the carry flag clear and AX contains the value 0, the file pointer was at the end of the file when the service was called.

If the service returns the carry flag clear and AX is less than CX, either a partial read was performed at the end of the file or an error occurred.

Int 21H   Function 40H
Write file or device

Action: Writes data to an open file or device

Call with: AH = 40H
BX = file handle
CX = number of bytes to write
DS = segment of buffer
DX = offset of buffer

Returns:	On success:	
	Carry flag	= clear
	AX	= number of bytes transferred
	On failure:	
	Carry flag	= set
	AX	= error code
Notes:	This service transfers the specified number of bytes from the buffer to the file or device and updates the file pointer position.	
	If CX equals 0, the file is extended or truncated to the current file pointer position.	
	If the service returns a clear carry flag but AX is less than CX, either a partial write or an error occurred. A partial write most often occurs when the disk being written to is full.	

Int 21H   Function 41H
Delete file

Action:	Deletes the specified file
Call with:	AH = 41H DS = segment of ASCIIZ pathname (which can include drive, path, and filename) DX = offset of ASCIIZ pathname

Returns:	On success:
	    Carry flag = clear
	On failure:
	    Carry flag = set
	    AX = error code

Notes:	Wildcard characters are not permitted in the pathname, so your program can delete only one file with each call to this service. This service deletes a file by replacing the first character in the file's directory entry with the ASCII character E5H and marking the file's clusters as "available" in the disk file allocation table. This service fails if any element of the pathname does not exist or if the specified file is read only.

Disks: Files and Records

Int 21H   Function 42H
Set file pointer position

Action: Sets the location of a file's pointer position

Call with: AH = 42H
AL = pointer movement method:
  00H= start move at start of file
  01H= start move at current file pointer position
  02H= start move at end of file

BX = file handle
CX = the 16 bits of the left half of offset (amount to move)
DX = the 16 bits of the right half of offset

Returns: On success:
  Carry flag = clear
  DX   = the 16 bits of the left half of new file pointer position
  AX   = the 16 bits of the right half of new file pointer position

On failure:
  Carry flag = set
  AX   = error code

Notes: The first byte of a file is at location 0. The last byte of an *n* byte file is at location *n–1*.

Regardless of the pointer movement method used, the new file pointer value that this service returns is relative to the start of the file.

To determine the length of a file, call this service using AL equal to 02H and an offset of 0. The file pointer that the service returns in AX and DX is 1 less than the file length in bytes.

If you call this service using pointer movement method 01H or 02H and a negative offset, it is possible to position the file pointer before the beginning of the file. The service will not report an error, but subsequent read or write attempts will cause an error.

Int 21H Function 43H
Get or set file attributes

Action:	Reads or sets the attributes of a file
Call with:	AH = 43H AL = 00H to get attributes = 01H to set attributes CX = new attributes (if AL = 01H):

Bit(s)	Significance (if set)
0	Read only
1	Hidden
2	System
3	Volume label
4	Directory
5	Archive
6–15	Reserved (must be 0)

DS = segment of ASCIIZ pathname (which can include drive, path, and filename)
DX = offset of ASCIIZ pathname

Returns:	On success:
	    Carry flag = clear
	    CX = file attribute (as above)
	On failure:
	    Carry flag = set
	    AX = error code

Notes:	You cannot use this service to change an existing file into a directory or a volume label, so bits 3 and 4 of CX must always be 0 when this service is called to set attributes.

Int 21H Function 45H
Duplicate handle

Action:	Creates a duplicate of an existing file handle
Call with:	AH = 45H BX = file handle to be duplicated

Disks: Files and Records

Returns: On success:
Carry flag = clear
AX = new file handle

On failure:
Carry flag = set
AX = error code

Notes: The handle contained in BX when this service is called must be the handle of a file or device that is currently open. The new handle has a different value than does the original handle, but it still refers to the same file or device and has the same file pointer position. Any operation that moves the file pointer for one of the handles moves the file pointer for the other handle as well.

You use a duplicate file handle primarily to flush the buffers and update the directory entry of an open file without actually closing the file. To do this, simply create a duplicate file handle and then close it. The original handle remains open for further read and write operations.

Int 21H   Function 46H
Redirect handle

Action: Makes one handle refer to the same file or device as a second handle

Call with: AH = 46H
BX = file handle
CX = file handle to be redirected

Returns: On success:
Carry flag = clear

On failure:
Carry flag = set
AX = error code

Notes: Given two handles, this service makes one handle refer to the same file or device as the second handle. The first (redirected) handle has the same file pointer position as the second handle.

If the handle passed in CX refers to an open file, the service closes that file before it redirects the handle.

You can use this service to redirect the standard output handle. For example, if you redirect *stdout* (handle 1) to *stdprn* (handle 4), information that would normally go to the screen goes to the printer instead.

Int 21H   Function 56H
Rename file

Action: Renames a file and/or moves it to a different directory on the same disk

Call with: AH = 56H
DS = segment of current ASCIIZ pathname (which can include drive, path, and filename)
DX = offset of current ASCIIZ pathname
ES = segment of new ASCIIZ pathname
DI = offset of new ASCIIZ pathname

Returns: On success:
    Carry flag = clear
On failure:
    Carry flag = set
    AX   = error code

Notes: This service does not permit the use of the wildcard characters * and ?.

This service fails if any of the following is true:

- The current and new pathnames refer to different disks.
- Any element of either pathname does not exist.
- A file that has the same pathname already exists.
- The file is being moved to the root directory, and the root directory is full.

Int 21H   Function 57H
Get or set file date and time

Action: Reads or modifies the date and time information in a file's directory entry

Call with: To read date or time:
    AH = 57H
    AL = 00H
    BX = file handle

To set date or time:
    AH = 57H
    AL = 01H
    BX = file handle
    CX = time:
        bits 0–4   = 2-second increments (0 through 29)
        bits 5–10 = minutes (0 through 59)
        bits 11–15 = hours (0 through 23)
    DX = date:
        bits 0–4   = day (1 through 31)
        bits 5–8   = month (1 through 12)
        bits 9–15 = year (relative to 1980)

Returns: On success:
    Carry flag = clear

If getting date and time:
    CX = time (in above format)
    DX = date (in above format)

On failure:
    Carry flag = set
    AX   = error code

Notes: The handle that is passed to this service must be associated with a file that has already been opened.

The date and time that this service sets are the ones assigned to the handle, even if the file is modified before the handle is closed.

If a file's 16-bit date field is set to 0, the file's date and time are not displayed in directory listings.

Int 21H   Function 5AH   [MS-DOS 3.0 and later]
Create temporary file

Action: On the specified drive and directory, creates and opens a new file that has a unique name

Call with: AH = 5AH
CX = attributes of new file:

Bit(s)	Significance (if set)
0	Read only
1	Hidden
2	System
3–4	Reserved (must be 0)
5	Archive
6–15	Reserved (must be 0)

DS = segment of ASCIIZ path (which can include drive and path)
DX = offset of ASCIIZ path

Returns: On success:
Carry flag = clear
AX = file handle
DS = segment of complete ASCIIZ pathname (which includes drive, path, and filename)
DX = offset of complete ASCIIZ pathname

On failure:
Carry flag = set
AX = error code

Notes: The buffer containing the ASCIIZ pathname that is passed to this service should have at least 13 extra bytes. The service uses this buffer to return the new file's complete pathname. This name includes the original pathname plus a backslash (if necessary) and the temporary filename.

This service fails if any element of the path does not exist or if you try to create a temporary file in a full root directory.

Files created using this service are not automatically deleted when the program terminates.

Int 21H   Function 5BH   [MS-DOS 3.0 and later]
Create new file

Action: Creates a new file only if the specified filename does not already exist

Call with: AX = 5BH
CX = attributes of new file:

Bit(s)	Significance (if set)
0	Read only
1	Hidden
2	System
3–4	Reserved (must be 0)
5	Archive
6–15	Reserved (must be 0)

DS = segment of ASCIIZ pathname (which can include drive, path, and filename)
DX = offset of ASCIIZ pathname

Returns: On success:
Carry flag = clear
AX = file handle

On failure:
Carry flag = set
AX = error code

Notes: Use this service to create a new file when you want to be sure not to truncate an existing file of the same name (as would happen if you used Int 21H Function 3CH).

The service fails if any of the following is true:

- Any element of the pathname does not exist.
- A file that has the same pathname already exists.
- You try to create the file in a root directory that is full.

Int 21H   Function 67H   [MS-DOS 3.3 and later]
Set handle count

Action: Sets the maximum number of handles available to the current program

Call with: AH = 67H
BX = desired number of handles

Returns: On success:
Carry flag = clear

On failure:
Carry flag = set
AX = error code

Notes: The default for the maximum number of handles available for one process is 20. This number includes the five standard handles (*stdin*, *stdout*, and so on) that MS-DOS opens when it loads the program. If you request fewer than 20 handles, MS-DOS uses 20 by default.

The service fails if you request over 20 handles and the available memory is insufficient.

If the number of handles requested exceeds the total number available on the system (as set using the FILES statement in CONFIG.SYS), this service returns no error. A later attempt to open or create a file or device will fail, however, if all the system's handles are in use (even if the program has not used all of its own handles).

Int 21H   Function 68H   [MS-DOS 3.3 and later]
Commit file

Action: Causes all data held in a handle's internal buffers to be physically written to the device; if the device is a file, causes the file's date, time, and size to be updated in the directory entry

Call with: AH = 68H
BX = file handle

Returns: On success:
Carry flag = clear

On failure:
Carry flag = set
AX = error code

Notes: Calling this service has the same effect as either closing and then reopening a file or creating a duplicate handle using Int 21H Function 45H and then closing the duplicate.

Writing the data in a file's internal buffers to disk guards against data loss in the event of a power failure or system crash.

Int 21H   Function 6CH   [MS-DOS 5.0]
Extended file open

Action: Opens, creates, or replaces a file in the specified disk and directory

Call with: AH = 6CH
BX = open mode:

Bit(s)	Meaning
0–2	000 = read access
	001 = write access
	010 = read and write access
3	Reserved (0)
4–6	Sharing mode
	000 = compatibility mode
	001 = deny all
	010 = deny write
	011 = deny read
	100 = deny none
7	Inheritance flag
	0 = child process inherits handle
	1 = child process does not inherit handle
8–12	Reserved (0)
13	Critical error handling
	0 = call Int 24H
	1 = return error to process
14	Write through
	0 = write operations can be buffered and deferred
	1 = data physically written at time of request
15	Reserved (0)

CX = attributes of file:

Bit(s)	Significance (if set)
0	Read only
1	Hidden
2	System
3–4	Reserved (must be 0)
5	Archive
6–15	Reserved (must be 0)

DX = open flag:

Bit(s)	Meaning
0–3	Action if file exists
	0000 = fail
	0001 = open file
	0010 = replace file
4–7	Action if file doesn't exist
	0000 = fail
	0001 = create file
8–15	Reserved (0)

DS = segment of ASCIIZ pathname (which can include drive, path, and filename)
SI = offset of ASCIIZ pathname

Returns: On success:
Carry flag = clear
AX = file handle
CX = action taken:
1 = file existed and was opened
2 = file did not exist and was created
3 = file existed and was replaced

On failure:
Carry flag = set
AX = error code

Notes: This service provides complete control over the process of opening and creating files. It combines the abilities of Int 21H Functions 3CH, 3DH, and 5BH.

The service fails if any of the following is true:

- Any element of the pathname does not exist.
- You try to create a file in a root directory that is full.
- You try to create a file that already exists and is read only.

CHAPTER 10

Disk Management and Directories

The previous chapter showed you how to use MS-DOS services to write data to and read data from disk files. That's certainly important, but there are also other disk-related tasks that you often need to perform. These tasks can be grouped under the general heading of *disk management*, and they are the subject of this chapter.

I use the term disk management to refer to certain disk-related tasks that are not connected directly to files or directories. These tasks include determining and changing the current drive, controlling the system's verify flag, and obtaining information about a disk drive. MS-DOS provides services for all of these tasks.

Determining and Changing the Current Drive

At any time, a PC has a single disk drive that is current. The *current drive* (also called the *default drive*) is where file operations occur by default—that is, if another disk drive is not specified. MS-DOS provides services that allow your programs to determine and change the current drive. For example, you can use MS-DOS services to determine what the current drive is when your program starts, change the current drive to suit your program's needs, and then return the current drive to the original setting before the program terminates.

You use Int 21H Function 19H to determine the current drive and Int 21H Function 0EH to change the current drive. The programs in Listings 10-1 and 10-2 illustrate how to use these two services.

```
DECLARE FUNCTION GetCurrentDrive$ ()
DECLARE FUNCTION SetCurrentDrive% (newdrive$)

' $INCLUDE: 'QB.BI'

DEFINT A-Z

DIM SHARED inRegs AS RegType, outRegs AS RegType


' Begin execution

CLS

PRINT "The current drive is "; GetCurrentDrive$
INPUT "Enter the letter of a new drive to make it current: ", x$
```

LISTING 10-1. *(continued)*
Demonstration of using MS-DOS services to determine and change the current drive in Basic.

LISTING 10-1. *continued*

```
    numDrives = SetCurrentDrive(x$)
    PRINT "Now the current drive is "; GetCurrentDrive$
    PRINT numDrives; "logical drives are available"

END

FUNCTION GetCurrentDrive$
    ' Returns the current drive as a two-character string that
    ' consists of the drive letter followed by a colon

    inRegs.ax = &H1900

    ' Call Int 21H Function 19H to get the current drive
    CALL INTERRUPT(&H21, inRegs, outRegs)

    ' Convert the drive code to a letter and add a colon
    GetCurrentDrive$ = CHR$((outRegs.ax AND &HFF) + 65) + ":"
END FUNCTION

FUNCTION SetCurrentDrive (newdrive$)
    ' Makes the drive specified by newdrive$ (a single-letter string
    ' specifying the drive) the current drive and returns the total
    ' number of logical drives available
    ' If the specified drive does not exist, no error occurs and no
    ' change is made

    inRegs.ax = &HE00

    ' Convert newdrive$ to a numeric code (A = 0, B = 1, etc.)
    inRegs.dx = ASC(UCASE$(newdrive$)) - 65

    ' Call Int 21H Function 0EH to set the current drive
    CALL INTERRUPT(&H21, inRegs, outRegs)

    ' Return the number of logical drives available
    SetCurrentDrive = outRegs.ax AND &HFF
END FUNCTION
```

```c
/* Using MS-DOS services to read and change the current drive */

#include <stdio.h>
#include <dos.h>

/* Declare the register unions */
union REGS inregs, outregs;
```

LISTING 10-2. *(continued)*
Demonstration of using MS-DOS services to determine and change the current drive in C.

LISTING 10-2. *continued*

```c
/* Function prototypes */
char get_current_drive(void);
int set_current_drive(char newdrive);
void clearscreen(void);

main()
{
    char newdrive;
    int num_drives;

    clearscreen();

    printf("\nThe current drive is %c:", get_current_drive());

    puts("\nEnter the letter of a new drive to make it current");

    newdrive = toupper(getchar());
    num_drives = set_current_drive(newdrive);

    printf("Now the current drive is %c:", get_current_drive());
    printf("\n%d logical drives are available.", num_drives);
}

char get_current_drive(void)
{
    /* Returns the ASCII code of the letter of */
    /* the current drive */

    inregs.x.ax = 0X1900;

    /* Call Int 21H Function 19H to get the current drive */
    int86(0X21, &inregs, &outregs);
    return(outregs.h.al + 65);
}

int set_current_drive(char newdrive)
{
    /* Makes the drive specified by newdrive (a single-letter string */
    /* specifying the drive) the current drive and returns the total */
    /* number of logical drives available */
    /* If the specified drive does not exist, no error occurs and no */
    /* change is made */

    inregs.x.ax = 0XE00;

    /* Convert newdrive to the drive code (A = 0, B = 1, etc.) */
    inregs.x.dx = newdrive - 65;

    /* Call Int 21H Function 0EH to set the current drive */
    int86(0X21, &inregs, &outregs);
```

(continued)

LISTING 10-2. *continued*

```
    /* Return the number of logical drives available */
    return(outregs.h.al);
}

void clearscreen(void)
{
    int x;

    for (x = 0; x < 25; x++)
        printf("\n");
}
```

Reading and Changing the Verify Flag

MS-DOS maintains a *verify flag* that determines whether MS-DOS performs read-after-write verification of information that it writes to disk. If the verify flag is off (the default), MS-DOS does not verify the data after it is written to disk. If the verify flag is on, after the data is written to disk MS-DOS reads it immediately to verify that it was written properly. Verification slows write operations, so you should use it only when writing critical data.

From the MS-DOS prompt, you can change the state of the verify flag by using the Verify command with the parameter *on* or *off*. From a program, you can use Int 21H Function 54H to read the state of the verify flag and Int 21H Function 2EH to change the flag state. Listings 10-3 and 10-4 demonstrate these services.

```
DECLARE SUB ClearVerify ()
DECLARE SUB SetVerify ()
DECLARE FUNCTION GetVerifyFlag% ()

DEFINT A-Z

' $INCLUDE: 'QB.BI'

DIM SHARED inRegs AS RegType, outRegs AS RegType


' Begin execution

CLS
```

LISTING 10-3. *(continued)*
Demonstration of reading and changing the state of the verify flag in Basic.

LISTING 10-3. *continued*

```
' Display the current verify flag setting
PRINT "The verify flag, which controls read-after-write verification"
PRINT "of data, is currently ";
IF (GetVerifyFlag = 0) THEN
    PRINT "OFF."
ELSE
    PRINT "ON."
END IF

' Offer the opportunity to change the verify flag setting
PRINT
PRINT "Enter 1 to set the verify flag or any other number to clear it."
INPUT answer

IF answer = 1 THEN
    CALL SetVerify
ELSE
    CALL ClearVerify
END IF

' Display the new verify flag setting
PRINT
PRINT "The verify flag is currently ";

IF (GetVerifyFlag = 0) THEN
    PRINT "OFF."
ELSE
    PRINT "ON."
END IF

END

DEFSNG A-Z
SUB ClearVerify
    ' Clears the verify flag

    inRegs.ax = &H2E00

    ' Set DX to 0 for MS-DOS version 2.0
    inRegs.dx = 0

    ' Call Int 21H Function 2EH to clear the verify flag
    CALL INTERRUPT(&H21, inRegs, outRegs)
END SUB

FUNCTION GetVerifyFlag%
    ' Returns the state of the verify flag
    ' 0 = clear, 1 = set

    inRegs.ax = &H5400
```

(continued)

LISTING 10-3. *continued*

```
    ' Call Int 21H Function 54H to get the state of the verify flag
    CALL INTERRUPT(&H21, inRegs, outRegs)
    GetVerifyFlag = outRegs.ax AND &HFF
END FUNCTION

SUB SetVerify
    ' Sets the verify flag

    inRegs.ax = &H2E01

    ' Set DX to 0 for MS-DOS version 2.0
    inRegs.dx = 0

    ' Call Int 21H Function 2EH to set the verify flag
    CALL INTERRUPT(&H21, inRegs, outRegs)
END SUB
```

```c
/* Using MS-DOS services to read and set the MS-DOS verify flag */

#include <stdio.h>
#include <dos.h>
#include <string.h>

/* Declare the register unions */
union REGS inregs, outregs;

/* Function prototypes */
void clearscreen(void);
void clear_verify(void);
void set_verify(void);
int get_verify_flag(void);

main()
{
    char ch, buf[4], *msg = "The verify flag is currently ";

    clearscreen();

    /* Display the current verify flag setting */
    if (get_verify_flag())
        strcpy(buf, "ON");
    else
        strcpy(buf, "OFF");

    printf("%s%s", msg, buf);
```

LISTING 10-4. *(continued)*
Demonstration of reading and changing the state of the verify flag in C.

LISTING 10-4. *continued*

```c
    /* Offer the opportunity to change the verify flag setting */
    puts("\nEnter s to set the verify flag or any other character
         to clear it.");
    ch = getchar();

    if (ch == 's')
        set_verify();
    else
        clear_verify();

    /* Display the new verify flag setting */
    if (get_verify_flag())
        strcpy(buf, "ON");
    else
        strcpy(buf, "OFF");

    printf("%s%s", msg, buf);
}

void clear_verify(void)
{
    /* Clears the verify flag */

    inregs.x.ax = 0X2E00;

    /* Set DX to 0 for MS-DOS version 2.0 */
    inregs.x.dx = 0;

    /* Call Int 21H Function 2EH to clear the verify flag */
    int86(0X21, &inregs, &outregs);
}

int get_verify_flag(void)
{
    /* Returns the state of the verify flag */
    /* 0 = clear, 1 = set */

    inregs.x.ax = 0X5400;

    /* Call Int 21H Function 54H to get the state of the verify flag */
    int86(0X21, &inregs, &outregs);
    return(outregs.h.al);
}

void set_verify(void)
{
    /* Sets the verify flag */

    inregs.x.ax = 0X2E01;
```

(continued)

LISTING 10-4. *continued*

```
    /* Set DX to 0 for MS-DOS version 2.0 */
    inregs.x.dx = 0;

    /* Call Int 21H Function 2EH to set the verify flag */
    int86(0X21, &inregs, &outregs);
}
void clearscreen(void)
{
    int x;

    for (x = 0; x < 25; x++)
        printf("\n");
}
```

Obtaining Information About Disk Drives

MS-DOS has several services that enable your programs to obtain information about a disk drive. Some of this information is technical—such as the number of bytes per sector and the number of sectors per cluster on the disk—and is rarely needed by an application program. Your programs more often need to determine the amount of available space on a disk drive. A program that stores large data files needs this information. By ensuring that enough disk space is available before trying to save the file, your program can avoid errors and inconvenience to the user.

The service Int 21H Function 1BH obtains information about the default disk drive, and Int 21H Functions 1CH and 36H obtain information about any disk drive. If you review the reference entries at the end of this chapter for these three disk information services, you'll notice that Int 21H Functions 1BH and 1CH differ in only one respect: whether the service obtains information about the default disk drive or about any disk drive. Both of these services return the *media descriptor byte*, which enables a program to distinguish between a hard disk and a floppy disk. Function 36H does not provide the media descriptor byte, but it is the only service that returns a value that shows the amount of free space on the disk drive. Listings 10-5 and 10-6 demonstrate using Int 21H Function 36H.

Both of the demonstration programs contain a function that calls Int 21H Function 36H, fills a data structure with disk information, and returns the amount of space available on the given disk. (You could modify the function so that it returns only the free-space information without placing other technical information in a data structure.) Because Int 21H Function 36H returns only the number of clusters available on the disk, and not the number of bytes available, the function calculates the number of available bytes by multiplying the number of available clusters by the number of sectors per cluster and the number of bytes per sector (both of which are also returned by the service).

```
DECLARE FUNCTION GetDriveSpace& (drive$)

' $INCLUDE: 'QB.BI'

DIM SHARED inRegs AS RegType, outRegs AS RegType

' Define a structure to hold disk data
TYPE Diskdata
    sectorsPerCluster AS INTEGER
    bytesPerSector AS INTEGER
    clusters AS INTEGER
    capacity AS LONG
END TYPE

DIM disk AS Diskdata


' Begin execution

CLS

PRINT "Enter letter of disk drive about which you would like information: "
INPUT drive$
PRINT

space& = GetDriveSpace(drive$)

IF space& < 0 THEN
    PRINT "Function failed for drive "; UCASE$(drive$)
ELSE
    PRINT "Drive "; UCASE$(drive$); ": available space ="; space&; "bytes"
    PRINT "Sectors per cluster ="; disk.sectorsPerCluster
    PRINT "Bytes per sector ="; disk.bytesPerSector
    PRINT "Total clusters ="; disk.clusters
    PRINT "Total capacity ="; disk.capacity; "bytes"
END IF

END

FUNCTION GetDriveSpace& (drive$)
    ' Obtains data about the drive whose letter is specified by
    ' drive$; places the drive data in a global structure of
```

(continued)

LISTING 10-5.
Demonstration of using Int 21H Function 36H to obtain information about a disk drive in Basic.

LISTING 10-5. *continued*

```
    ' type DiskData; on success, returns the total space available
    ' on the drive; on failure, returns a value less than 0

    SHARED disk AS Diskdata

    ' Convert the drive letter argument to a drive code
    ' (A = 1, B = 2, etc.)
    ' If an empty string was passed, use the default drive (code = 0)
    IF LEN(drive$) > 0 THEN
        inRegs.dx = ASC(UCASE$(drive$)) - 64
    ELSE
        inRegs.dx = 0
    END IF

    inRegs.ax = &H3600

    ' Call Int 21H Function 36H to get disk information
    CALL INTERRUPT(&H21, inRegs, outRegs)

    ' If the service failed, return an error code of -1
    IF outRegs.ax = &HFFFF THEN
        GetDriveSpace = -1
        EXIT FUNCTION
    END IF

    ' If the service succeeded, fill in the data structure
    disk.sectorsPerCluster = outRegs.ax
    disk.bytesPerSector = outRegs.cx

    ' To determine the total clusters, convert the unsigned integer
    ' that the service returns to the signed form that Basic uses
    IF outRegs.dx >= 0 THEN
        disk.clusters = outRegs.dx
    ELSE
        disk.clusters = outRegs.dx + 65536
    END IF

    ' Calculate the total disk capacity in bytes, performing the
    ' multiplication in two steps to avoid overflow
    disk.capacity = disk.clusters
    disk.capacity = disk.capacity * outRegs.ax
    disk.capacity = disk.capacity * outRegs.cx

    ' Calculate the available space in bytes, converting again
    ' from unsigned to signed integer
    IF outRegs.bx >= 0 THEN
        driveSpace& = outRegs.bx
    ELSE
        driveSpace& = outRegs.bx + 65536
    END IF
```

(continued)

LISTING 10-5. *continued*

```
        driveSpace& = driveSpace& * outRegs.ax
        driveSpace& = driveSpace& * outRegs.cx

        GetDriveSpace = driveSpace&
END FUNCTION
```

```c
/* Using MS-DOS services to obtain information about a disk drive */

#include <stdio.h>
#include <dos.h>

/* Declare the register unions */
union REGS inregs, outregs;

/* Define a structure to hold disk data */
struct diskdata {
    unsigned int sectors_per_cluster;
    unsigned int bytes_per_sector;
    unsigned int clusters;
    unsigned long capacity;
} disk;

/* Function prototypes */
void clearscreen(void);
long get_drive_space(char drive);

main()
{
    char drive;
    long space;

    clearscreen();

    puts("Enter letter of disk drive about which you would
        like information: ");
    drive = toupper(getchar());

    if ((space = get_drive_space(drive)) < 0)
        printf("\nFunction failed for drive %c", toupper(drive));
    else
        {
        printf("\nDrive %c: available space = %ld bytes",
            toupper(drive), space);
```

LISTING 10-6. *(continued)*
Demonstration of using Int 21H Function 36H to obtain information about a disk drive in C.

LISTING 10-6. *continued*

```c
            printf("\nSectors per cluster = %d", disk.sectors_per_cluster);
            printf("\nBytes per sector = %d", disk.bytes_per_sector);
            printf("\nTotal clusters = %d", disk.clusters);
            printf("\nTotal capacity = %ld bytes", disk.capacity);
            }
}

long get_drive_space(char drive)
{
    /* Obtains data about the drive whose letter is specified by the */
    /* parameter drive; places the drive data in a global structure of */
    /* type diskdata; on success, returns the total space available */
    /* on the drive; on failure, returns a value less than 0 */

    long space;

    /* Convert the drive letter argument to a drive code */
    /* (A = 1, B = 2, etc.) */
    inregs.x.dx = drive - 64;

    inregs.x.ax = 0X3600;

    /* Call Int 21H Function 36H to get disk information */
    int86(0X21, &inregs, &outregs);

    /* If the service failed, return an error code of -1 */
    if (outregs.x.ax == 0XFFFF)
        return(-1);

    /* If the service succeeded, fill in the data structure */
    disk.sectors_per_cluster = outregs.x.ax;
    disk.bytes_per_sector = outregs.x.cx;
    disk.clusters = outregs.x.dx;

    /* Calculate the total disk capacity in bytes */
    disk.capacity = (long)disk.clusters * outregs.x.ax * outregs.x.cx;

    /* Calculate the available space in bytes */
    space = (long)outregs.x.bx * outregs.x.cx;
    space *= outregs.x.ax;

    return(space);
}

void clearscreen(void)
{
    int x;

    for (x = 0; x < 25; x++)
        printf("\n");
}
```

Directory Operations

MS-DOS 2.0 introduced an important feature: the ability to divide a disk volume into subdirectories. Particularly on a hard disk, subdirectories are invaluable for organizing and keeping track of your program and data files. An application program frequently uses directories that the user creates and specifies in the MS-DOS command line that starts the program. It is often helpful, however, if a program can directly manipulate directories. MS-DOS provides several services that allow your programs to work with directories.

Determining and changing the current directory

As mentioned earlier in this chapter, each disk in your system has, at any given moment, a current, or default, directory. This directory is where disk operations take place if another directory is not specified. Each disk's current directory is initially the root directory (for example, C:\). You can determine the path of a disk drive's current directory by using Int 21H Function 47H, and you can change the current directory by using Int 21H Function 3BH.

Note that when you use Int 21H Function 47H to get the current directory, you must specify in the DL register which drive to access. When you change the current directory by using Int 21H Function 3BH, you can include a drive name when you specify the name of the directory. If the specified drive is different from the current one, the service changes the current directory of the specified drive but does not make the specified drive the current drive. For example, if the current drive is A: and you specify the pathname C:\TEMP in a call to Int 21H Function 3BH, the current directory of drive C: becomes TEMP, but the current drive remains A:.

The programs in Listings 10-7 and 10-8 demonstrate the use of these services. Before getting to the demonstrations, however, you need to know the method used to transfer directory names between MS-DOS services and the program. The MS-DOS directory services use ASCIIZ strings for this purpose. An ASCIIZ string is a string of normal ASCII characters that is terminated by a byte that has a value of 0. C normally stores strings in this way, so no special conversion is needed. In Basic, however, strings are not stored with a terminating zero byte. You must convert a normal Basic string to an ASCIIZ string before passing it to an MS-DOS directory service. This procedure is a simple one, requiring only that you use the concatenation operator (+) to tack on a zero byte at the end of the string, as shown in the following example:

```
ASCIIZstring$ = oldString$ + CHR$(0)
```

Typically, you would use Int 21H Function 47H to determine the current directory when the program starts and Int 21H Function 3BH to change the current directory as needed during program execution. Then you would restore the original current directory before exiting the program.

```basic
DECLARE FUNCTION GetDirectory$ (drive$)
DECLARE FUNCTION SetDirectory% (pathname$)

DEFINT A-Z

' $INCLUDE: 'QB.BI'

DIM SHARED inRegs AS RegTypeX, outRegs AS RegTypeX


' Begin execution

CLS

' Get the current directory on the default drive, and display it
oldpath$ = GetDirectory("")
PRINT "The current directory on the default drive is "; oldpath$

' Get a new path, and make it current
PRINT
INPUT "Enter the new directory name: ", pathname$

result = SetDirectory(pathname$)

' Check for an error, and display a message if the SetDirectory
' function failed
IF result = 0 THEN
    PRINT "Specified path not found"
END IF

' Display the current directory path
PRINT
PRINT "The current directory on the default drive is "; GetDirectory("")
PRINT

' Restore the original current directory
result = SetDirectory(oldpath$)

END

FUNCTION GetDirectory$ (drive$)
    ' Returns the path of the current directory
    ' If the function fails, it returns an empty string
```

LISTING 10-7. *(continued)*
Demonstration of using MS-DOS services to determine and change the current directory in Basic.

LISTING 10-7. *continued*

```
    ' Set up a buffer to hold the path
    buffer$ = STRING$(64, " ")

    ' Convert drive$ to a drive code (A = 1, B = 2, etc.)
    ' If no drive letter was passed, use code 0 for the default drive
    IF drive$ = "" THEN
        inRegs.dx = 0
    ELSE
        inRegs.dx = ASC(UCASE$(drive$)) - 64
    END IF

    inRegs.ax = &H4700

    ' Place the segment and offset of the buffer in DS:SI
    inRegs.ds = VARSEG(buffer$)
    inRegs.si = SADD(buffer$)

    ' Call Int 21H Function 47H to get the path of the current directory
    CALL INTERRUPTX(&H21, inRegs, outRegs)

    ' If the carry flag is set, return an empty string
    IF outRegs.flags AND 1 THEN
        GetDirectory$ = ""
        EXIT FUNCTION
    END IF

    ' Return the path, preceded by a backslash (\)
    GetDirectory$ = "\" + LEFT$(buffer$, INSTR(buffer$, " ") - 2)
END FUNCTION

DEFSNG A-Z
FUNCTION SetDirectory% (pathname$)
    ' Changes the current directory to pathname$ and returns 1 on
    ' success or 0 on failure (pathname not found)

    ' Convert pathname$ to an ASCIIZ string
    pathname$ = pathname$ + CHR$(0)

    inRegs.ax = &H3B00
    inRegs.ds = VARSEG(pathname$)
    inRegs.dx = SADD(pathname$)

    ' Call Int 21H Function 3BH to change the directory
    CALL INTERRUPTX(&H21, inRegs, outRegs)

    ' Test the carry flag
    IF outRegs.flags AND 1 THEN
        SetDirectory = 0
    ELSE
        SetDirectory = 1
    END IF
END FUNCTION
```

```c
/* Using MS-DOS services to get and change the current directory */

#include <stdio.h>
#include <dos.h>

/* Declare the register unions */
union REGS inregs, outregs;
struct SREGS segregs;

/* Function prototypes */
int get_directory(char drive, char _far *buf);
int set_directory(char _far *path);
void clearscreen(void);

main()
{
    char buf1[64], buf2[64];
    int result;

    clearscreen();

    /* Get the current directory on the default drive, and display it */
    if ((result = get_directory(' ', buf1)) != 0)
        printf("\nThe current directory on the default drive is \\%s", buf1);
    else
        puts("\nFunction failed");

    /* Get a new path, and make it current */
    puts("\n\nEnter the new directory name: ");
    gets(buf2);

    if ((result = set_directory(buf2)) == 0)
        puts("Specified path not found");

    /* Display the current directory path */
    if ((result = get_directory(' ', buf1)) != 0)
        printf("\nThe current directory on the default drive is \\%s", buf1);
    else
        puts("\nFunction failed");
}

int get_directory(char drive, char _far *buf)
{
    /* Places in buf the current directory of the specified drive */
    /* On success, returns 1; on failure, returns 0 */

    char temp[64];
```

LISTING 10-8. *(continued)*
Demonstration of using MS-DOS services to determine and change the current directory in C.

LISTING 10-8. *continued*

```c
        if (drive == ' ')
            inregs.x.dx = 0;
        else
            inregs.x.dx = toupper(drive) - 64;

    inregs.x.ax = 0X4700;
    inregs.x.si = FP_OFF(buf);
    segregs.ds = FP_SEG(buf);

    /* Call Int 21H Function 47H to get the path of the current directory */
    int86x(0X21, &inregs, &outregs, &segregs);

    /* If the carry flag is set, return 0 */
    if (outregs.x.cflag)
        return(0);

    /* Otherwise, return 1 */
    return(1);
}

int set_directory(char _far *path)
{
    /* Changes the current directory to path and returns 1 on */
    /* success or 0 on failure (pathname not found) */

    inregs.x.ax = 0X3B00;
    inregs.x.dx = FP_OFF(path);
    segregs.ds = FP_SEG(path);

    /* Call Int 21H Function 3BH to change the directory */
    int86x(0X21, &inregs, &outregs, &segregs);

    if (outregs.x.cflag)
        return(0);
    else
        return(1);
}

void clearscreen(void)
{
    int x;

    for (x = 0; x < 25; x++)
        printf("\n");
}
```

Creating and deleting directories

Most programs simply work with the directories that already exist on a disk. Some programs, however, might need to create new directories or delete existing directories. A database program, for example, might give the user the option of setting up a new subdirectory in which to store data. The ability to create directories is particularly important for a software installation utility—that is, a utility that installs a new program on a hard disk.

MS-DOS provides services to create and delete directories. When your programs use these services, they must specify the directory names using ASCIIZ strings, as explained earlier in this chapter. Int 21H Function 39H creates a directory, and Int 21H Function 3AH deletes a directory. Note that the service cannot delete a directory if it is the current directory, if it is not empty, or if the user is working on a network and has insufficient access rights. These two services allow you to specify the full pathname (which includes the drive name in addition to the path) for the directory you want to create or delete.

The programs in Listings 10-9 and 10-10 demonstrate how to use MS-DOS services to create and delete directories.

```
DECLARE FUNCTION DeleteDir% (path$)
DECLARE FUNCTION CreateDir% (path$)

DEFINT A-Z

' $INCLUDE: 'QB.BI'

DIM SHARED inRegs AS RegTypeX, outRegs AS RegTypeX


' Begin execution

CLS

INPUT "Enter the path and name of the directory to create: ", path$

result = CreateDir(path$)

IF result = 0 THEN
    PRINT "Directory "; path$; " could not be created."
    END
END IF

PRINT "Directory "; path$; "has been created."
PRINT "Enter D to delete the directory, or any ";
PRINT "other character to retain it: "
INPUT x$

IF UCASE$(x$) = "D" THEN
    result = DeleteDir(path$)
```

LISTING 10-9. *(continued)*
Demonstration of using MS-DOS services to create and delete directories in Basic.

LIISTING 10-9. *continued*

```
        PRINT "Directory deleted."
    END IF

END

DEFSNG A-Z
FUNCTION CreateDir% (path$)
    ' Creates the new directory specified by path$ and returns 1
    ' on success or 0 on failure (pathname not found)

    ' Convert path$ to an ASCIIZ string
    path$ = path$ + CHR$(0)

    inRegs.ax = &H3900

    inRegs.ds = VARSEG(path$)
    inRegs.dx = SADD(path$)

    ' Call Int 21H Function 39H to create the directory
    CALL INTERRUPTX(&H21, inRegs, outRegs)

    ' Check the carry flag, and return 0 on failure or 1 on success
    IF outRegs.flags AND 1 THEN
        CreateDir = 0
    ELSE
        CreateDir = 1
    END IF
END FUNCTION

DEFINT A-Z
FUNCTION DeleteDir% (path$)
    ' Deletes the directory specified by path$ and returns 1 on
    ' success and 0 on failure (for example, directory not found)

    ' Convert path$ to an ASCIIZ string
    path$ = path$ + CHR$(0)

    inRegs.ax = &H3A00

    inRegs.ds = VARSEG(path$)
    inRegs.dx = SADD(path$)

    ' Call Int 21H Function 3AH to delete the directory
    CALL INTERRUPTX(&H21, inRegs, outRegs)

    ' Check the carry flag, and return 0 on failure or 1 on success
    IF outRegs.flags AND 1 THEN
        DeleteDir = 0
    ELSE
        DeleteDir = 1
    END IF
END FUNCTION
```

```c
/* Using MS-DOS services to create and delete directories */

#include <stdio.h>
#include <dos.h>

/* Declare the register unions */
union REGS inregs, outregs;
struct SREGS segregs;

/* Function prototypes */
int delete_dir(char _far *path);
int create_dir(char _far *path);
void clearscreen(void);

main()
{
    char ch, newpath[64];
    int result;

    clearscreen();

    puts("Enter the path and name of the directory to create: ");
    gets(newpath);

    if ((result = create_dir(newpath)) == 0)
        {
        printf("\nDirectory %s could not be created.", newpath);
        exit(0);
        }

    printf("\nDirectory %s has been created.", newpath);
    puts("\nEnter D to delete the directory, or any other
        character to retain it.");
    ch = getchar();

    if (toupper(ch) != 'D')
        exit(0);

    if ((result = delete_dir(newpath)) == 0)
        puts("\nError deleting directory.");
    else
        puts("\nDirectory deleted.");
}
```

LISTING 10-10. *(continued)*
Demonstration of using MS-DOS services to create and delete directories in C.

LISTING 10-10. *continued*

```c
int create_dir(char _far *path)
{
    /* Creates the new directory specified by path and returns */
    /* 1 on success or 0 on failure (pathname not found) */

    inregs.x.ax = 0X3900;
    inregs.x.dx = FP_OFF(path);
    segregs.ds = FP_SEG(path);

    /* Call Int 21H Function 39H to create the directory */
    int86x(0X21, &inregs, &outregs, &segregs);

    /* Check the carry flag, and return 0 on failure or 1 on success */
    if (outregs.x.cflag)
        return(0);
    else
        return(1);
}

int delete_dir(char _far *path)
{
    /* Deletes the directory specified by path and returns 1 on */
    /* success or 0 on failure (for example, directory not found) */

    inregs.x.ax = 0X3A00;
    inregs.x.dx = FP_OFF(path);
    segregs.ds = FP_SEG(path);

    /* Call Int 21H Function 3AH to delete the directory */
    int86x(0X21, &inregs, &outregs, &segregs);

    /* Check the carry flag, and return 0 on failure or 1 on success */
    if (outregs.x.cflag)
        return(0);
    else
        return(1);
}

void clearscreen(void)
{
    int x;

    for (x = 0; x < 25; x++)
        printf("\n");
}
```

Disk Management and Directories Service Reference

Int 21H Function 0EH
Select disk drive

Action:	Specifies the drive to be the current, or default, drive and returns the total number of logical drives available
Call with:	AH = 0EH DL = drive code (0 = A, 1 = B, and so on)
Returns:	AL = number of logical drives
Notes:	For MS-DOS 3.0 and later, the value returned in AL is the number of logical drives. This value is either the one specified by the Lastdrive command (if any) in the CONFIG.SYS file or the number 5, which is the default value for the last drive. Drive codes can be in the range 0–25 (A–Z). If an invalid drive code is specified, no error occurs, and the current drive remains unchanged. Other Int 21H disk services use a different drive code, with 0 referring to the default drive and 1 = A, 2 = B, and so on.

Int 21H Function 19H
Get current disk drive

Action:	Returns the code of the current, or default, disk drive
Call with:	AH = 19H
Returns:	AL = drive code (0 = A, 1 = B, and so on)
Notes:	Other Int 21H disk services use a different drive code, with 0 referring to the default drive and 1 = A, 2 = B, and so on.

Int 21H Function 1BH
Get default drive data

Action:	Obtains information about the current, or default, disk drive
Call with:	AH = 1BH

Returns:	On success:
	  AL = sectors per cluster
	  CX = bytes per sector
	  DX = total clusters on drive
	  DS = sector of media descriptor byte
	  BX = offset of media descriptor byte
	
	On failure (invalid drive or other error):
	  AL = FFH

Notes:	The media descriptor byte contains one of the following values:
	  F8H Hard disk
	  F0H 1.44-MB, 18-sector, double-sided, 3.5-inch floppy disk or other, unidentifiable, types
	  F9H 720-KB, 15-sector, double-sided, 5.25-inch floppy disk or 1.22-MB, 9-sector, double-sided, 3.5-inch floppy disk
	  FAH 320-KB, 8-sector, single-sided, 5.25-inch floppy disk
	  FBH 640-KB, 8-sector, double-sided, 3.5-inch floppy disk
	  FCH 180-KB, 9-sector, single-sided, 5.25-inch floppy disk
	  FDH 360-KB, 9-sector, double-sided, 5.25-inch floppy disk
	  FEH 160-KB, 8-sector, single-sided, 5.25-inch floppy disk
	  FFH 320-KB, 8-sector, double-sided, 5.25-inch floppy disk
	
	The address that the service returns in DS:BX points to a copy of the media descriptor byte from the disk's FAT (file allocation table).
	
	Use Int 21H Function 1CH or 36H to obtain information about a drive other than the current drive.

Int 21H Function 1CH
Get drive data

Action:	Obtains information about any disk drive

Call with: AH = 1CH
DL = drive (0 = default, 1 = A, 2 = B, and so on)

Returns: On success:
AL = sectors per cluster
CX = bytes per sector
DX = total clusters on drive
DS = sector of media descriptor byte
BX = offset of media descriptor byte

On failure (invalid drive or other error):
AL = FFH

Notes: The address that the service returns in DS:BX points to a copy of the media descriptor byte from the disk's FAT (file allocation table).

For information about the media descriptor byte, see the entry in this reference section for Int 21H Function 1BH.

Int 21H Function 2EH
Set verify flag

Action: Sets or clears the verify flag, which, when set, causes MS-DOS to perform read-after-write verification of data

Call with: AH = 2EH
AL = 00H (to clear verify flag)
   = 01H (to set verify flag)
DL = 00H (MS-DOS versions 1.x and 2.x only)

Returns: Nothing

Notes: The setting of the verify flag affects all disk drives. If a particular disk's device driver does not support read-after-write verification, the verify flag's setting has no effect.

Int 21H   Function 36H
Get drive allocation information

Action:	Obtains information about a specified drive, including the amount of free space
Call with:	AH = 36H DL = drive (0 = default, 1 = A, 2 = B, and so on)
Returns:	On success: 　　AX = sectors per cluster 　　BX = number of free clusters 　　CX = bytes per sector 　　DX = total clusters on drive On failure (invalid drive or other error): 　　AX = FFFFH
Notes:	To calculate the amount of free space available on a drive (in bytes), multiply the value the service returns in BX by the values the service returns in AX and CX. Other Int 21H disk services use a different drive code, with 0 = A, 1 = B, and so on.

Int 21H   Function 39H
Create directory

Action:	Creates a new subdirectory using the specified pathname
Call with:	AH = 39H DS = segment of ASCIIZ pathname (which can include drive and path) DX = offset or ASCIIZ pathname
Returns:	On success: 　　Carry flag = clear On failure: 　　Carry flag = set 　　AX = error code

Notes: The following situations cause this service to fail:

- A directory with the same pathname already exists.
- Any element of the pathname to the new directory does not exist.
- The parent directory of the new directory is the root directory, and it is full.
- The program is running on a network, and the user has insufficient access rights.

Int 21H   Function 3AH
Delete directory

Action:	Deletes a specified subdirectory
Call with:	AH = 3AH DS = segment of ASCIIZ pathname (which can include drive and path) DX = offset of ASCIIZ pathname

Returns:	On success:
	    Carry flag = clear
	
	On failure:
	    Carry flag = set
	    AX = error code

Notes: The following situations cause this service to fail:

- The specified directory is the current directory.
- The specified directory is not empty.
- Any element of the pathname to the directory does not exist.
- The program is running on a network, and the user has insufficient access rights.

Int 21H Function 3BH
Set current directory

Action: Sets the current directory

Call with: AH = 3BH
DS = segment of ASCIIZ pathname (which can include drive and path)
DX = offset of ASCIIZ pathname

Returns: On success:
　　Carry flag = clear

On failure:
　　Carry flag = set
　　AX   = error code

Notes: This service fails if any element of the new pathname does not exist.

The ASCIIZ pathname that the program passes to the service can contain a drive specifier, such as C:\DATA. If the pathname contains this information and the specified drive is not the current one, the specified directory is made the current one on the drive, but MS-DOS doesn't change drives.

Int 21H Function 47H
Get current directory

Action: Obtains the current directory on the specified drive

Call with: AH = 47H
DL = drive code (0 = default, 1 = A, 2 = B, and so on)
DS = segment of 64-byte buffer
SI = offset of 64-byte buffer

Returns: On success:
　　Carry flag = clear
　　DS = segment of buffer containing path of the current directory
　　SI = offset of buffer containing the path of the current directory

On failure:
　　Carry flag = set
　　AX   = error code

Notes: This service fails if the drive code is invalid.

The path that this service returns does not include the drive letter or a leading backslash (\). Thus, if the root directory is current, the returned string will contain only a single byte (00H).

Other Int 21H disk services use a different drive code, with 0 = A, 1 = B, and so on.

Int 21H Function 54H
Get verify flag

Action: Returns the state of the verify flag, which, when set, causes MS-DOS to perform read-after-write verification of data

Call with: AH = 54H

Returns: AL = 00H if verify flag off
= 01H if verify flag on

CHAPTER 11

Serial and Parallel Ports

A *port* is an interface that allows a computer to exchange information with the outside world. On the PC, the interface consists of three parts: a physical connection from the computer to a peripheral device, a location in memory that contains information about the connection, and a buffer in memory that can store the information that will be or has been exchanged with the outside world.

Almost every PC has two types of ports: serial and parallel. This chapter explains how to use serial and parallel ports in your programs.

A serial port is so named because it sends individual bits of data sequentially, or serially, over a single wire. Serial ports are used for bidirectional communication between a computer and various peripheral devices such as external modems, certain printers and mice, pen plotters, local area networks, and even other computer systems. Serial ports operate at slow to moderate speed, and a direct connection from serial port to device is reliable over relatively long distances (up to 1000 feet in most cases).

A parallel port uses eight wires to transmit an entire byte at one time. Parallel ports transmit information much faster than do serial ports, but connections are limited to a maximum distance of about 50 feet. Although parallel ports have the capability for bidirectional data transfer, they are almost always used for output only—specifically, for transmitting data to printers.

Serial Ports

Most of today's PC systems have one or two serial ports, which are sometimes referred to as *communications ports*. The names of the ports are abbreviated as COM1 and COM2. In most cases, the physical connection to a serial port is a 9-pin or 25-pin connector on the rear panel of the system unit. From there, you can connect the port—by means of a special cable—to various peripheral devices that communicate by means of a serial port.

You might wonder why a serial port requires a 9-pin or 25-pin connector (which has a wire for each pin) if it uses only a single wire to transmit data. All of the pins in the 9-pin connectors are used, but only 10 to 12 of the pins in the 25-pin connectors are used in serial communications. At a minimum, a serial connection has three wires: a transmit wire, a receive wire, and a ground wire. Additional wires are used by the computer and the device to transmit *handshaking* signals, which manage the flow of information. Because a serial port is bidirectional, the devices on the two ends of the connection need to coordinate with each other to determine who's sending, who's receiving, and so on.

The serial port hardware handles the details of data transmission, handshaking, and the like. We'll look briefly at this hardware before getting to the main topic of this section, which is using serial ports in your programs.

The 8250 UART

At the heart of every serial port is a single chip, the 8250 UART on PCs and the 16450 UART on PC/ATs. The acronym UART stands for universal asynchronous receiver-transmitter. The two UART types are similar: The 16450 UART is an enhanced version of the 8250. In this chapter, I refer to the UART. All of the information included here applies to both the 8250 and the 16450.

The main job that the UART performs is converting data between the parallel form (8 bits in 1 byte) and the serial form (1 bit at a time). Within your computer, data is transmitted to and from the UART in parallel form. When you send data to another device via the serial port, the UART converts the parallel data to a stream of serial bits before transmitting it. Likewise, when you receive data via the serial port, the UART converts the serial bit stream to parallel form so that your program can use it.

The UART is not, however, automatically configured. Because a UART can operate at several different data transmission speeds, or *baud rates,* your program must specify the speed. Also, three configuration settings affect the way data is encoded in the serial stream: *parity checking,* number of *stop bits,* and *word length.* Parity checking, when used, makes use of 1 bit (the parity bit). The UART can use the value of that bit to check whether the data was sent successfully. Each set of bits that is sent contains 1 start bit and 1 or more stop bits that delimit the set. Communication programs most often use 1 stop bit. Use 2 stop bits only when you transmit at very slow transmission speeds. The word length specifies the number of bits that make up the data being sent. You can use a 7-bit word length if you are sending only ASCII characters, all of which can be represented in 7 bits. If, however, you want to send characters from the IBM extended character set, you must use an 8-bit word length. A typical configuration is 2400 baud, no parity checking, 8-bit word length, and 1 stop bit. For two devices to communicate successfully via a serial connection, the serial port (that is, the UART) at each end must be set to the same baud rate, parity, stop bits, and word length.

To be frank, the operating system's serial port services are rather limited. In particular, they limit the maximum communication speed that you can use. When you need maximum performance, you'll usually bypass the

MS-DOS and ROM BIOS serial port services and manipulate the UART hardware directly by using interrupt-driven routines that maximize the efficiency of data transfer. (Interrupt-driven serial communication uses interrupts to detect input at the serial port, allowing your program to perform other tasks while waiting for input.) These advanced topics are, however, beyond the scope of this book. John Campbell's book, *C Programmer's Guide to Serial Communications* (Howard Sams, 1987), is an excellent reference for these advanced topics.

If you need to write a program that uses the serial port, you should be aware that, in some cases, the serial port routines in your high-level language provide performance that is superior to the MS-DOS and BIOS services. For relatively undemanding tasks, however, the MS-DOS and BIOS services are often more than sufficient. The remainder of this chapter shows you how to use the relatively few serial port services that MS-DOS provides.

Int 21H serial port services

The MS-DOS serial port services that are available via Int 21H are limited for the most part to reading data from and writing data to a serial port. No Int 21H service is available for configuring a serial port—you must use either your high-level language or the ROM BIOS service described in the next section to set the transmission speed, parity, stop bits, and word length.

One method for reading from and writing to a serial port is using the handle-based services Int 21H Functions 3FH and 40H. Chapter 9 explained how to use these services to read and write files. Remember that one of the predefined handles in MS-DOS is AUX, handle number 3, which is associated with serial port COM1 by default. For information about these two services, see their reference entries in Chapter 9.

Note that using handle number 3 with Int 21H Functions 3FH and 40H works only with COM1. To use Int 21H Functions 3FH and 40H to access COM2, you must first use Int 21H Function 3DH to open COM2 and associate a handle with it. Chapter 9 also describes this service.

Two other Int 21H services allow a program to send and receive data, one character at a time, to and from COM1. The service Int 21H Function 03H reads one character from COM1, and Int 21H Function 04H sends one character to COM1.

MS-DOS translates calls to Int 21H Functions 03H and 04H into calls to the same device driver that the handle-based services use. Generally speaking, therefore, it is preferable to use the handle-based services because they allow your program to read and write multiple-character strings in a single call and access ports other than COM1.

Using either of the above input services to read data from a serial port has a significant disadvantage: These services do not check the status of the port to see whether one or more characters are waiting to be input. If your program requests input and no characters are ready, the program waits until a character is available. To check serial port status, you must use the service Int 21H Function 44H, which is the input/output control (IOCTL) service. Int 21H Function 44H has many subfunctions; the one of interest to us is Subfunction 06H, which checks input status. When you call this subfunction and pass to it the handle associated with a serial port, the subfunction returns a value that indicates whether data is ready at the port.

ROM BIOS serial port services

The ROM BIOS includes serial port services that are significantly more flexible than the Int 21H services. Like the Int 21H services, the ROM BIOS services are not interrupt driven and do not support high transmission speeds. They provide more capabilities than the Int 21H services, however, and are usually reliable at speeds of up to 2400 baud. The ROM BIOS services enable you to configure the serial ports and examine the status of a port. The four ROM BIOS serial port services and their descriptions are listed below:

Service	Description
Int 14H Function 00H	Initializes (configures) a serial port
Int 14H Function 01H	Writes a character to a serial port
Int 14H Function 02H	Reads a character from a serial port
Int 14H Function 03H	Gets the status of a serial port

The next section demonstrates how to write a perfectly usable, although basic, program that performs serial communications using these four ROM BIOS services.

A simple serial communications program

A serial communications program that sends to and receives from a remote computer must be able to operate in both *full duplex mode* and *half duplex mode*. In full duplex mode, every character that your communications program sends via the serial port is sent back, or echoed, by the remote computer's communications program. In half duplex mode, this echoing does not occur. Which duplex mode is used affects the way the communications program displays characters being sent.

- In full duplex mode, the program needs to display only the characters that it receives. Because of the full duplex echoing, this includes all characters that it sent to the remote computer.

- In half duplex mode, the program must display each character it sends in addition to each character it receives.

Communications programs more commonly use full duplex mode because it provides a built-in method of error checking. If you send some text and see it displayed on your screen correctly, you know that the remote computer has received it without error. Note that duplex mode is a feature of the communications software, not of the serial port.

You can choose from two general approaches to writing a serial communications program. One approach is interrupt driven. By using interrupts to detect input at the serial port, a program can maximize speed and efficiency. Commercially available communications programs are all interrupt driven. Because you must access the serial port hardware directly, such programming is quite complex and is beyond the scope of this book.

The other approach is called *polling*. A program that uses this approach checks, or polls, the serial port repeatedly to see if a character has been received. If so, the program retrieves and processes the character. The polling method presents one problem: The program can lose incoming characters if the characters are received faster than the program can poll the serial port. This problem is particularly likely to occur if the program needs to perform other tasks—such as scrolling the screen—between polls of the serial port.

Nevertheless, the polling method is relatively simple to program, and it can operate reliably at transmission speeds of up to 1200 baud (or even up to 2400 baud on faster computers). The demonstration programs in this chapter use the polling method. The general strategy for a program when you use the polling method is as follows:

1. See if the user has pressed a key. If so, read the character from the keyboard and transmit it. If using half duplex mode, display the character.

2. See if a character is waiting at the serial port. If so, retrieve it and display it.

3. Return to Step 1.

The programs in Listings 11-1 and 11-2 implement a simple serial communications program using polling. The programs first configure the serial port. As written, the parameters used are 1200 baud, even parity, 7-bit word length, and 1 stop bit. To use different settings, you can modify the configuration byte in the function that performs the configuration. You can also modify the function to allow the user to specify communications parameters.

The program next enters the loop described above. The loop continues executing until the user presses the F10 function key, which terminates the program. The program comments describe additional operation details.

```
DECLARE SUB GetPort ()
DECLARE SUB Transmit (char$)
DECLARE FUNCTION GetKey% ()
DECLARE SUB SetPort ()

' $INCLUDE: 'QB.BI'

' Constant defining which COM port to use
' Set to 0 for COM1, 1 for COM2, etc.
CONST PORT = 0

' Constants for half duplex mode and full duplex mode
CONST HALF = 1
CONST FULL = 0

' Constant defining the duplex mode used in the program
CONST DUPLEX = HALF

' Constants for true and false
CONST TRUE = 1
CONST FALSE = 0

DIM SHARED inRegs AS RegType, outRegs AS RegType


' Begin execution

CLS
PRINT "Press F10 to exit."

' Configure the serial port
SetPort

' This is the main loop. The function GetKey checks for keyboard
' input. If the user pressed a nonextended key, GetKey transmits
' the character by calling the Transmit subprogram, and if DUPLEX
' is set to HALF, it is also displayed on the screen. If the user
' pressed F10, GetKey returns FALSE, and the loop terminates. The
```

LISTING 11-1. *(continued)*
Demonstration of the implementation of a simple serial communications program in Basic.

LISTING 11-1. *continued*

```
' subprogram GetPort checks to see whether the serial port has
' received a character; if GetPort finds a character, it gets and
' displays it.

DO WHILE (1)
    IF (GetKey = 0) THEN EXIT DO
    CALL GetPort
LOOP

CLS

END

FUNCTION GetKey%
    ' Checks whether a character is waiting at the keyboard

    k$ = INKEY$

    IF k$ = "" THEN
        GetKey% = TRUE
        EXIT FUNCTION
    END IF

    ' If a character is waiting and its length isn't 2, it's a regular
    ' (nonextended) character. Transmit it, and if DUPLEX is set to HALF,
    ' echo it to the screen. If its length is 2, check to see whether F10
    ' was pressed (the second character's ASCII value is 68). Return FALSE
    ' if F10 was pressed and TRUE in all other cases.

    IF (LEN(k$) = 2) THEN
        keycode% = ASC(RIGHT$(k$, 1))
        IF keycode% = 68 THEN
            GetKey% = FALSE
            EXIT FUNCTION
        ELSE
            GetKey% = TRUE
            EXIT FUNCTION
        END IF
    ELSE
        CALL Transmit(k$)
        IF DUPLEX = HALF THEN PRINT k$;
        GetKey% = TRUE
        EXIT FUNCTION
    END IF
END FUNCTION

SUB GetPort
    ' Reads one character from the serial port (if a character is
    ' ready) and displays it on the screen
```

(continued)

LISTING 11-1. *continued*

```
    ' Check whether a character is ready
    inRegs.ax = &H300
    inRegs.dx = PORT
    CALL INTERRUPT(&H14, inRegs, outRegs)

    ' If a character is not ready, return
    IF (outRegs.ax AND &H100) = 0 THEN EXIT SUB

    ' If a character is ready, get it
    inRegs.ax = &H200
    inRegs.dx = PORT
    CALL INTERRUPT(&H14, inRegs, outRegs)

    ' Strip off the parity bit, and then use Int 21H Function 02H
    ' to display the character on the screen
    inRegs.dx = (outRegs.ax AND &H7F)
    inRegs.ax = &H200
    CALL INTERRUPT(&H21, inRegs, outRegs)
END SUB

SUB SetPort
    ' Initializes the serial port to 1200 baud, 7-bit word
    ' length, even parity, and 1 stop bit
    ' For these parameters, the initialization byte is binary
    ' 10011010, or 9AH

    inRegs.ax = &H9A
    inRegs.dx = PORT
    CALL INTERRUPT(&H14, inRegs, outRegs)
END SUB

SUB Transmit (char$)
    ' Transmits the character in char$ via the serial port

    inRegs.ax = 256 + ASC(char$)
    inRegs.dx = PORT
    CALL INTERRUPT(&H14, inRegs, outRegs)
END SUB
```

```
/* Simple serial communications program */

#include <stdio.h>
#include <dos.h>
```

LISTING 11-2. *(continued)*
Demonstration of the implementation of a simple serial communications program in C.

LISTING 11-2. *continued*

```c
/* Declare the register unions */
union REGS inregs, outregs;

/* Constants for true and false */
#define FALSE 0
#define TRUE !FALSE

/* Constant defining which COM port to use */
/* Set to 0 for COM1, 1 for COM2, etc. */
#define PORT 0

/* Constants for half duplex mode and full duplex mode */
#define HALF 1
#define FULL 0

/* Constant defining the duplex mode used in the program */
#define DUPLEX FULL

/* Function prototypes */
void set_port(void);
int get_key(void);
void transmit(char ch);
void get_port(void);
void clearscreen(void);

main()
{
    clearscreen();
    puts("Press F10 to exit.");

    /* Configure the serial port */
    set_port();

    /* This is the main loop. The function get_key() checks for
       keyboard input. If the user pressed a nonextended key,
       get_key() transmits the character by calling the Transmit()
       function, and if DUPLEX is set to HALF, it is also displayed
       on the screen. If the user pressed F10, get_key() returns
       FALSE, and the loop terminates. The function get_port() checks
       to see whether the serial port has received a character; if
       get_port() finds a character, it gets and displays it. */

    while(1)
        {
        if (!get_key())
            break;
        get_port();
        }

    clearscreen();
```

(continued)

LISTING 11-2. *continued*

```c
    }   /* End of main() */

void set_port(void)
{
    /* Initializes the serial port to 1200 baud, 7-bit word */
    /* length, even parity, and 1 stop bit */
    /* For these parameters, the initialization byte is binary */
    /* 10011010, or 9AH */

    inregs.h.ah = 0;
    inregs.x.dx = PORT;
    inregs.h.al = 0X9A;
    int86(0X14, &inregs, &outregs);
}   /* End of set_port() */

int get_key(void)
{
    char ch;

    /* Use Int 21H Function 0BH to check whether a character */
    /* is waiting at the keyboard */
    inregs.h.ah = 0XB;
    int86(0X21, &inregs, &outregs);

    /* If a character is waiting, get it; if not, return TRUE */
    if (outregs.h.al != 0)
        ch = getch();
    else
        return(TRUE);

    /* If the first character is not 0, it's a regular (nonextended) */
    /* character. Transmit it, and if DUPLEX is set to HALF, */
    /* echo it to the screen. */

    if (ch != 0)
        {
        transmit(ch);
        if (DUPLEX == HALF)
            putchar(ch);
        return(TRUE);
        }

    /* If the first character is 0, it's the first byte of a 2-byte */
    /* extended key code. Get the second byte, and see whether F10 was */
    /* pressed. If so, return FALSE. In all other cases, return TRUE. */

    if ((ch = getch()) == 68)
        return(FALSE);
    else
        return(TRUE);
}   /* End of get_key() */
```

(continued)

LISTING 11-2. *continued*

```c
void transmit(char ch)
{

    /* Transmits the character ch via the serial port */

    inregs.h.ah = 1;
    inregs.x.dx = PORT;
    inregs.h.al = ch;
    int86(0X14, &inregs, &outregs);
}   /* End of transmit() */

void get_port(void)
{
    /* Reads one character from the serial port (if a character */
    /* is ready) and displays it on the screen   */

    /* Check whether a character is ready */
    inregs.h.ah = 3;
    inregs.x.dx = PORT;
    int86(0X14, &inregs, &outregs);

    /* If a character is not ready, return */
    if (!(outregs.x.ax & 0X100))
        return;

    /* If a character is ready, get it */
    inregs.h.ah = 2;
    inregs.x.dx = PORT;
    int86(0X14, &inregs, &outregs);

    /* Strip off the parity bit, and then use Int 21H Function */
    /* 02H to display the character on the screen */
    inregs.h.dl = outregs.h.al & 0X7F;
    inregs.h.ah = 2;
    int86(0X21, &inregs, &outregs);
}   /* End of get_port() */

void clearscreen(void)
{
    int x;

    for (x = 0; x < 25; x++)
        printf("\n");
}   /* End of clearscreen() */
```

Parallel Ports

Because the parallel port is almost always connected to a printer, it is sometimes referred to as the *printer port*. All systems have at least a single parallel port, which is referred to logically as LPT1 or PRN. If needed, you can install additional parallel ports, and they are referred to as LPT2, LPT3, and so on.

Using a parallel port in your programs is quite a bit simpler than is using a serial port. With a parallel port, you're dealing only with sending information, rather than with both sending and receiving information. In addition, you need not configure a parallel port. The hardware fixes the data transmission speed and other parameters. Also, because the parallel port transmits entire bytes, you don't have to worry about start and stop bits and the conversion from parallel form to serial form.

To send data to a parallel port, use the handle-based service Int 21H Function 40H. Handle number 4 is MS-DOS's predefined handle for the standard printer, PRN. Using Int 21H Function 40H with the handle value 4, you can send multiple-character strings to the printer with a single call.

To send data to parallel ports other than LPT1, you must first use Int 21H Function 3DH to open the desired port (LPT2, LPT3, and so on) as a device and to get a handle for the port. Then pass its assigned handle to Int 21H Function 40H. Chapter 9 has more information about using these services.

You can also use Int 21H Function 05H to send data to the printer. This service transmits a single character to LPT1 and is sensitive to Ctrl-C.

The above Int 21H services have relatively slow throughput, although they are generally fast enough to keep up with a mechanical device such as a printer. A major disadvantage is that they do not allow the program to check the status of the printer, determining whether it is on line or off line or out of paper. For these reasons, printer output is better performed with the Int 17H ROM BIOS services. The three ROM BIOS parallel port services are listed below:

Service	Description
Int 17H Function 00H	Writes a character to a printer port and returns the port status
Int 17H Function 01H	Initializes a printer port and returns the port status
Int 17H Function 02H	Returns the port status

Both the handle-based services and the ROM BIOS services send ASCII characters to the printer. If you have a printer, such as an HP LaserJet and most dot matrix printers, that accepts ASCII characters for output, these services provide a simple way to output to the printer. However, if you have a printer, such as a PostScript printer, that requires you to send data to it in a special language, the only way to get output using these services is to send ASCII characters to the printer in that language. For example, to eject a page from an HP LaserJet, all you have to do is send a formfeed character (ASCII 12). To eject a page from a PostScript printer, you must send the eight letters of the command "showpage."

Printer demonstration

The programs in Listings 11-3 and 11-4 demonstrate how to use the ROM BIOS Int 17H parallel port services. The program first uses Int 17H Function 02H to obtain the printer status of the printer connected to LPT1. As you can see in the reference information at the end of this chapter, the status byte returned by this service contains a variety of information about the printer. We are interested in bit 4, which, when set, lets us know that the printer is on line and ready to print. You can, if you wish, modify the function that checks whether the printer is ready so that it returns more detailed information about the printer status—for example, informing the program if the printer is out of paper. For the demonstration, however, we simply want to know whether the printer is ready.

Next the program initializes the printer by calling Int 17H Function 01H. The service resets the printer to its startup state so that any special control codes that the printer received previously are canceled.

The program next prompts the user to enter three lines of text and prints the lines, using Int 17H Function 00H to send each character to the printer. At the end of each line, the program sends a carriage return character and a linefeed character to advance the printer to the start of the next line.

Finally the program sends a formfeed character to eject the page from the printer.

```
DECLARE SUB Printer (message$)
DECLARE SUB Formfeed ()
DECLARE SUB PrinterInit ()
DECLARE FUNCTION PrinterReady% ()

DEFINT A-Z
```

LISTING 11-3. *(continued)*
Demonstration of using ROM BIOS parallel port services for printer control in Basic.

LISTING 11-3. *continued*

```
' $INCLUDE: 'QB.BI'

DIM SHARED inRegs AS RegType, outRegs AS RegType

' Constants for printer control characters
CONST CR = &HD      ' Carriage return
CONST LF = &HA      ' Linefeed
CONST FF = &HC      ' Formfeed

' Begin execution

CLS

' Check whether the printer is ready
DO WHILE (PrinterReady = 0)
    PRINT "The printer is not ready; please correct, and then press any key."
    WHILE INKEY$ = "": WEND
LOOP

PRINT "Ready to print!"

' Initialize the printer
CALL PrinterInit

' Get three lines of text, and print them
PRINT "Enter three lines of text:"

FOR i = 1 TO 3
    LINE INPUT X$
    Printer (X$)
NEXT i

' Send a formfeed character to eject the page
CALL Formfeed

END

SUB Formfeed
    ' Send a formfeed character to LPT1

    inRegs.ax = FF
    inRegs.dx = 0
    CALL INTERRUPT(&H17, inRegs, outRegs)
END SUB

DEFSNG A-Z
SUB Printer (message$)
    ' Sends a string to LPT1

    length = LEN(message$)
```

(continued)

Serial and Parallel Ports

LISTING 11-3. *continued*

```
        ' Send each character in message$ to LPT1
        FOR i = 1 TO length
            inRegs.ax = ASC(MID$(message$, i, 1))
            inRegs.dx = 0
            CALL INTERRUPT(&H17, inRegs, outRegs)
        NEXT

        ' Send a linefeed and a carriage return at end of line
        inRegs.ax = LF
        inRegs.dx = 0
        CALL INTERRUPT(&H17, inRegs, outRegs)

        inRegs.ax = CR
        inRegs.dx = 0
        CALL INTERRUPT(&H17, inRegs, outRegs)
    END SUB

DEFINT A-Z
SUB PrinterInit
    ' Initializes the printer connected to LPT1

    inRegs.ax = &H100
    inRegs.dx = 0
    CALL INTERRUPT(&H17, inRegs, outRegs)
END SUB

DEFSNG A-Z
FUNCTION PrinterReady%
    ' Returns 0 if the printer connected to LPT1 is not ready
    ' or a nonzero character if it is ready

    inRegs.ax = &H200
    inRegs.dx = 0
    CALL INTERRUPT(&H17, inRegs, outRegs)

    ' Isolate bit 4 of register AH, which is set if the printer
    ' is ready
    PrinterReady = (outRegs.ax AND &H1000)
END FUNCTION
```

```
/* Demonstration of BIOS printer services */

#include <stdio.h>
#include <dos.h>
```

LISTING 11-4. *(continued)*
Demonstration of using ROM BIOS parallel port services for printer control in C.

LISTING 11-4. *continued*

```c
/* Declare the register unions */
union REGS inregs, outregs;

/* Constants for printer control codes */
#define CR 0X0D         /* Carriage return */
#define LF 0X0A         /* Linefeed */
#define FF 0X0C         /* Formfeed */

/* Function prototypes */
int printer_ready(void);
void formfeed(void);
void printer(char *ptr);
void printer_init(void);
void clearscreen(void);

main()
{
    int count;
    char buffer[80];

    clearscreen();

    /* Check whether the printer is ready */
    while (!printer_ready())
        {
        puts("The printer is not ready; please correct, and then
              press any key.");
        getch();
        }

    puts("Ready to print!");

    /* Initialize the printer */
    printer_init();

    /* Get three lines of text, and print them */
    puts("\nEnter three lines of text:");

    for (count = 1; count < 4; count++)
        {
        gets(buffer);
        printer(buffer);
        }

    /* Send a formfeed character to eject the page */
    formfeed();

}   /* End of main() */
```

(continued)

Serial and Parallel Ports   **327**

LISTING 11-4. *continued*

```c
void formfeed(void)
{
    /* Sends a formfeed character to LPT1 */

    inregs.h.ah = 0;
    inregs.h.al = FF;
    inregs.x.dx = 0;
    int86(0X17, &inregs, &outregs);
}   /* End of formfeed() */

void printer(char *ptr)
{
    /* Sends the string pointed to by ptr to LPT1 */

    int i;
    int length;

    length = strlen(ptr);

    /* Send each character in the string to LPT1 */
    for(i = 1; i <= length; i++)
        {
        inregs.h.ah = 0;
        inregs.h.al = *ptr++;
        inregs.x.dx = 0;
        int86(0X17, &inregs, &outregs);
        }

    /* Send a linefeed and a carriage return at end of line */
        inregs.h.ah = 0;
        inregs.h.al = LF;
        inregs.x.dx = 0;
        int86(0X17, &inregs, &outregs);

        inregs.h.ah = 0;
        inregs.h.al = CR;
        inregs.x.dx = 0;
        int86(0X17, &inregs, &outregs);
}   /* End of printer() */

void printer_init(void)
{
    /* Initializes the printer connected to LPT1 */

    inregs.h.ah = 1;
    inregs.x.dx = 0;
    int86(0X17, &inregs, &outregs);
}   /* End of printer_init() */
```

(continued)

LISTING 11-4. *continued*

```
int printer_ready(void)
{
    /* Returns 0 if the printer connected to LPT1 is not ready
    /* or a nonzero character if it is ready */

    inregs.h.ah = 2;
    inregs.x.dx = 0;
    int86(0X17, &inregs, &outregs);

    /* Isolate bit 4 of register AH, which is set if the printer */
    /* is ready */
    return(outregs.h.ah & 0X10);
}   /* End of printer_ready() */

void clearscreen(void)
{
    int x;

    for (x = 0; x < 25; x++)
        printf("\n");
}   /* End of clearscreen() */
```

Serial and Parallel Ports Service Reference

Int 14H Function 00H
Initialize serial port

Action:	Sets a serial port to a specified baud rate, parity, word length, and stop bits; also returns port status
Call with:	AH = 00H AL = initialization data (see "Notes") DX = serial port number (0 = COM1, 1 = COM2, and so on)
Returns:	AH = serial port status:

Bit	Meaning (if set)
0	Receive data ready
1	Overrun error detected
2	Parity error detected

Bit	Meaning (if set)
3	Framing error detected
4	Break detected
5	Transmit holding register empty
6	Transmit shift register empty
7	Time out

AL = modem status:

Bit	Meaning (if set)
0	Change in clear-to-send status
1	Change in data-set-ready status
2	Trailing edge ring indicator
3	Change in receive line signal detect
4	Clear to send
5	Data set ready
6	Ring indicator
7	Receive line signal detect

Notes: The initialization data consists of a single byte whose bits have the following meanings:

Bits 0–1 control word length:
    10 = 7-bit word
    11 = 8-bit word

Bit 2 controls stop bits:
    0 = 1 stop bit
    1 = 2 stop bits

Bits 3–4 control parity:
    00 = no parity
    10 = no parity
    01 = odd parity
    11 = even parity

Bits 5–7 control baud rate:
    000 = 110 baud
    001 = 150 baud
    010 = 300 baud
    011 = 600 baud
    100 = 1200 baud
    101 = 2400 baud
    110 = 4800 baud
    111 = 9600 baud

Int 14H Function 01H
Write character to serial port

Action:	Writes a single character to the specified serial port and returns the port status
Call with:	AH = 01H AL = ASCII character code DX = serial port number (0 = COM1, 1 = COM2, and so on)

Returns:	On success:
	    AH bit 7 = 0
	    AH bits 0–6 = serial port status:

Bit	Meaning (if set)
0	Receive data ready
1	Overrun error
2	Parity error detected
3	Framing error detected
4	Break detected
5	Transmit holding register empty
6	Transmit shift register empty

   AL = ASCII character code (unchanged)

   On failure (timed out):
   AH bit 7   = 1
   AL   = ASCII character code (unchanged)

Int 14H Function 02H
Read character from serial port

Action:	Reads a single character from a serial port and returns the port status
Call with:	AH = 02H DX = serial port number (0 = COM1, 1 = COM2, and so on)

Returns:	On success:
	    AH bit 7 = 0
	    AH bits 1–4 = serial port status:

Bit	Meaning (if set)
1	Overrun error detected
2	Parity error detected
3	Framing error detected
4	Break detected

AL = ASCII character code

On failure (timed out):
AH bit 7 = 1

Int 14H Function 03H
Get serial port status

Action: Returns the status of a serial port

Call with: AH = 03H
DX = serial port number (0 = COM1, 1 = COM2, and so on)

Returns: AH = serial port status
AL = modem status

Notes: For information about the serial port and modem status bytes, see the entry for Int 14H Function 00H.

Int 17H Function 00H
Write character to parallel port

Action: Sends one character to the specified parallel port and returns the status of the port

Call with: AH = 00H
AL = ASCII character code
DX = parallel port number (0 = LPT1, 1 = LPT2, and so on)

Returns: AH = parallel port status:

Bit	Meaning (if set)
0	Printer timed out
1	Unused
2	Unused
3	I/O error
4	Printer selected
5	Out of paper
6	Printer acknowledge
7	Printer not busy

Int 17H   Function 01H
Initialize parallel port

Action: Initializes the specified parallel port and returns its status

Call with: AH = 01H
DX = parallel port number (0 = LPT1, 1 = LPT2, and so on)

Returns: AH = parallel port status

Notes: For most printers, this service initializes the printer to its startup state.

For information about the parallel port status byte, see the entry for Int 17H Function 00H.

Int 17H   Function 02H
Get parallel port status

Action: Returns the status of the specified parallel port

Call with: AH = 02H
DX = parallel port number (0 = LPT1, 1 = LPT2, and so on)

Returns: AH = parallel port status

Notes: For information about the parallel port status byte, see the entry for Int 17H Function 00H.

Int 21H   Function 03H
Auxiliary input

Action:	Reads one character from the standard auxiliary device (by default, the serial port COM1)
Call with:	AH = 03H
Returns:	AL = ASCII character code
Notes:	This service is not buffered. If characters arrive at the serial port faster than the program reads them, some will be lost. If Ctrl-C is input from the keyboard, MS-DOS executes Int 23H.

Int 21H   Function 04H
Auxiliary output

Action:	Sends one character to the standard auxiliary device (by default, the serial port COM1)
Call with:	AH = 04H DL = ASCII character code
Returns:	Nothing
Notes:	If necessary, this service waits until the serial port receives a character. If Ctrl-C is input from the keyboard, MS-DOS executes Int 23H.

Int 21H   Function 05H
Parallel port output

Action:	Sends a single character to PRN (by default, LPT1)
Call with:	AH = 05H AL = ASCII character code

Returns:	Nothing
Notes:	If the printer is busy, this service waits until the character is accepted. If Ctrl-C is input from the keyboard, MS-DOS executes Int 23H.

Int 21H   Function 44H Subfunction 06H
Check input status

Action:	Determines whether a file or device associated with a handle has data available for input
Call with:	AH = 44H AL = 06H BX = handle of file or device

Returns:	On success:
	  Carry flag = clear
	  AL = 00H if device not ready or file pointer at end of file
	  AL = FFH if device ready or file pointer not at end of file
	On failure:
	  Carry flag = set
	  AX = error code

Notes:	Call with a value of 3 (the handle for AUX) in BX to check for a character at serial port COM1.

CHAPTER 12

Memory Management

The term *memory management* does not mean remembering your spouse's birthday before it happens (although that's not a bad idea!). Rather, it refers to methods your programs can use to make the best use of the memory installed in the computer. Many programs that work with small- to medium-sized amounts of data might not need active memory management. When a program is pushing the limits of the system's memory, however, good memory management techniques can mean the difference between a smooth-running, full-featured program and one that is compromised because of memory problems.

This chapter covers MS-DOS services for memory management, but before we get to that topic, let me tell you that I included only C demonstration programs in this chapter. Why? Despite the power of Microsoft QuickBasic, it (and all other versions of Basic) lack one powerful feature that is an integral part of the C language: pointers. A *pointer* is a special type of numeric variable that you use to manipulate memory addresses. Using pointers, a C program can easily read to and write from memory anywhere in the processor's address space. Without pointers, however, it is difficult or even impossible to accomplish this task in a Basic program. Even when a workaround can be devised in Basic, it is invariably so inefficient that it is hardly worth the effort.

Types of Memory

Before we discuss the techniques of memory management, let's take a look at the three types of memory that can be found on PCs: conventional, extended, and expanded.

Conventional memory

All PCs and all versions of MS-DOS can manage at least 1 megabyte of memory. This memory starts at address 00000H and extends to FFFFFH and is called *conventional memory*. Of course, not all computers have a full megabyte of conventional memory installed. Some early PCs might have only 256 KB or 512 KB of memory. Nevertheless, these systems could handle the addresses of a full megabyte of conventional memory if it were installed.

Only a part of conventional memory—the 640 KB that starts at 00000H and extends to 9FFFFH—is available for use by MS-DOS and your application programs. This portion of conventional memory is often called *user memory*. The memory above 640 KB (between 9FFFFH and FFFFFH) is reserved for video display memory, ROM hardware drivers, and the like.

The operating system occupies the lowest part of user memory, which starts at address 00000H. Located in this area are the interrupt vector table, the operating system proper (including associated tables and buffers), installable device drivers specified in your CONFIG.SYS file (if any), and the resident portion of COMMAND.COM.

The remainder of user memory is called the *transient program area,* or TPA (sometimes called the *memory arena*). Application programs are loaded in the TPA when they are executed. Memory-resident programs such as SideKick also use the TPA. The size of the TPA is equal to the total amount of user memory in your system (typically 640 KB) minus the memory that the operating system occupies. To determine the TPA size, enter the Chkdsk command from the MS-DOS prompt. (If you use MS-DOS 5, you can also use the Mem command.) The number of free bytes is the amount of memory available in the TPA. Figure 12-1 on the following page illustrates the structure of conventional memory.

You should note that the use of the term "conventional memory" is not standardized. Most often, the term is used as I have used it—to refer to the 1 megabyte of memory between the addresses 00000H and FFFFFH. Occasionally, however, the term is used to refer to the 640 KB of memory between the addresses 00000H and 9FFFFH—what I refer to as user memory. For example, the Mem command in MS-DOS 5 follows this latter convention. You need to stay alert to these different meanings of the term "conventional memory."

Extended memory

Memory at addresses above 1 megabyte (100000H) is called *extended memory*. Extended memory is available only on systems that use an 80286, 80386, or 80486 processor. As much as 15 megabytes of extended memory can be installed on 80286 systems, and 4095 megabytes on 80386 and 80486 processors. Most systems, though, have much less. Figure 12-2 on page 341 illustrates the location of extended memory in relation to conventional memory.

To understand extended memory, you must be familiar with the two CPU operating modes—*real mode* and *protected mode*—in which the 80286 (and higher) processors can operate. In real mode, an 80286 (and higher) processor is, in effect, a faster version of the 8088/8086 processor used in the original PC. These processors have full access to conventional memory in real mode but only limited access to extended memory. In protected mode, the full power of these processors is unleashed because they have the ability to access both conventional and extended memory.

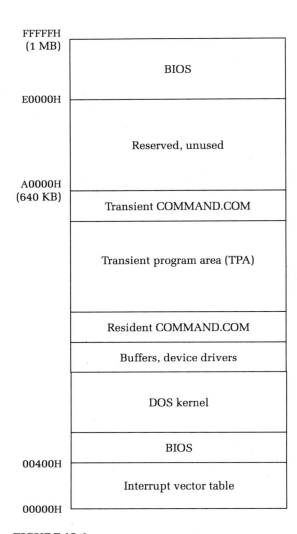

FIGURE 12-1.
The structure of conventional memory.

The mode in which a processor can operate is a function of the operating system in use. Protected mode operating systems, such as XENIX and OS/2, enable programs to have full access to extended memory. You can use both conventional and extended memory to hold program code and data. MS-DOS, however, runs in real mode. Under MS-DOS, you cannot ordinarily use extended memory to hold program code or data; for the most part, only conventional memory is available to programs.

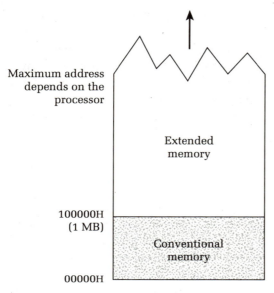

FIGURE 12-2.
Extended memory exists above conventional memory, starting at address 100000H.

Two ROM BIOS services, however, give a real mode program limited access to extended memory. These services—Int 15H Functions 87H and 88H—switch the processor from real mode to protected mode, perform a task, and then switch the processor back again. This is a relatively slow process that limits the usefulness of the services. These two ROM BIOS services are used frequently by utility programs that use extended memory to create a "RAM disk" or a print-spooler. For more information about these services, see the section "Managing Extended Memory" later in this chapter.

Expanded memory

Expanded memory is a type of memory that can be added to PCs to increase the amount of available memory. The specifications for its use were developed in 1985 by Lotus, Intel, and Microsoft. The 640 KB of conventional memory available under MS-DOS was more than sufficient for early PC applications. As applications and MS-DOS itself became larger and more powerful, however, this limit placed severe restrictions on program performance. Unlike extended memory, expanded memory is not limited to PCs that have 80286 (and higher) processors. You can use expanded memory on any PC, no matter what processor it uses. Expanded memory is officially defined in the Lotus/Intel/Microsoft Expanded Memory Specification, or LIM EMS for short.

At this writing, LIM EMS 4.0 is the latest version, although many systems still use version 3.2. Versions 3.2 and 4.0 permit access to as much as 8 and 32 megabytes of expanded memory, respectively. Expanded memory consists of two components: memory manager software and physical memory. The Expanded Memory Manager is a software driver that you install at boot time by including a Device statement in your CONFIG.SYS file. The physical memory consists of RAM chips installed on an add-in card or on your system motherboard. In many cases, the expanded memory is actually extended memory that the Expanded Memory Manager has configured as expanded memory. The Expanded Memory Manager serves as an interface between the physical memory and your program.

Programs cannot make use of expanded memory unless they're written specifically to do so. Most of today's commercial application programs can make use of expanded memory. Versions of MS-DOS prior to 4.0, however, are oblivious to the presence of expanded memory and take no part when an application program uses it. But MS-DOS versions 4.0 and later, as well as Microsoft Windows, are "EMS aware" and can use expanded memory when it is available. Note that the expanded memory interrupt calls described later in this chapter are calls to the Expanded Memory Manager software and not to MS-DOS or the ROM BIOS. The Expanded Memory Specification is, therefore, not a part of MS-DOS. Because the use of expanded memory is so common, and because being able to access it is useful in so many programming situations I felt justified in including this topic in a book about MS-DOS programming.

How can the Expanded Memory Manager make as much as 32 megabytes of memory available to a processor that can directly address a maximum of only 1 megabyte of conventional memory? It can do so using a technique called *bank switching*. Here's how it works.

Application programs access expanded memory through a 64-KB window called the *page frame*, which is located in conventional memory above 640 KB. The exact location of the page frame can be configured for each system, and it is always placed where it will not conflict with other special memory requirements (such as video display memory) that are located in the region of conventional memory between 640 KB and 1 megabyte. Because the page frame is located in conventional memory, 8088/8086 and 80286 (and higher) processors can address it directly when operating in real mode.

The physical expanded memory (whose actual address need not concern you) is divided into a number of *pages,* or *banks.* In LIM EMS versions 3.x, each page contains 16 KB of memory, so four pages can fit into the page frame in conventional memory. In LIM EMS version 4.0, a page can have a size other than 16 KB. Of course, the total number of pages available depends on the page size and the total amount of installed expanded memory.

The Expanded Memory Manager serves as an interface between application programs and expanded memory. When a program needs to write data to or read data from expanded memory, the manager ensures that the proper pages are mapped into the page frame and can be accessed, therefore, by the program. Figure 12-3 shows the relationships that exist among a program, the page frame, and expanded memory.

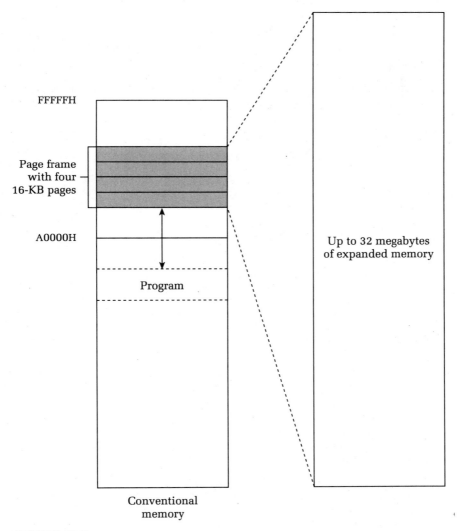

FIGURE 12-3.
The Lotus/Intel/Microsoft Expanded Memory Specification permits application programs to access multiple megabytes of memory through a 64-KB page frame in conventional memory.

Managing Conventional Memory

The management of conventional memory is the process by which a program controls the free area in the transient program area (TPA). MS-DOS allocates TPA memory in blocks called *arena entries;* each arena entry begins with a data structure called the *arena header.* The arena header, which a program must never modify directly, contains information about the arena entry: its size, whether it is allocated, and if allocated, who its "owner" is (that is, the program or process that is using the memory). A single arena entry can be as small as a single paragraph (16 bytes) or as large as the total TPA memory available.

The arena entries are found in sequential locations in memory. Each arena header begins immediately following the end of the previous arena entry. Because MS-DOS knows the size of each arena entry (each arena header contains this information), the arena headers are, in effect, chained together. Figure 12-4 illustrates this arrangement.

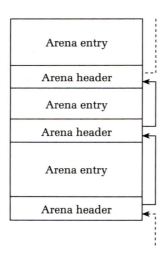

FIGURE 12-4.
Memory is organized into a series of arena entries; each arena entry is preceded by an arena header.

Memory management, then, consists of assigning arena entries when a program or other process requests memory and releasing the arena entries when they are no longer needed. Programs should do all memory management via MS-DOS interrupts and should never attempt to manipulate arena headers directly. MS-DOS has three memory allocation services, all of which are accessed via Int 21H:

Function 48H	Allocates an arena entry
Function 49H	Releases an arena entry
Function 4AH	Resizes an arena entry

When MS-DOS receives a request for memory allocation—for example, when loading a program to execute—it looks through the chain of arena entries to find a block of sufficient size. If MS-DOS finds a break in the arena header chain or some other anomaly, it generates an error. If MS-DOS encounters no problems, it uses one of three strategies to assign a block to the requesting process:

- First fit: MS-DOS allocates the lowest (first) arena entry on the chain that is large enough to fill the request.
- Best fit: MS-DOS allocates the smallest arena entry on the chain that is large enough to fill the request.
- Last fit: MS-DOS allocates the highest (last) arena entry on the chain that is large enough to fill the request.

The first fit strategy is the fastest because MS-DOS spends the least time looking through arena headers before allocating the memory. This strategy has one disadvantage, however: It can result in memory fragmentation. When a large enough arena entry is found, MS-DOS divides it into two entries—one that matches the memory allocation request exactly and one that contains the leftover memory. With this strategy, repeated memory allocation requests can fragment memory, resulting in relatively small blocks of allocated memory that are interspersed with blocks of free memory. You might, for example, have 200 KB of free memory, but a request for 50 KB will fail if that 200 KB is divided among ten separate 20-KB blocks.

You will probably rarely have problems with memory fragmentation in your programs. It can, however, be a serious issue for data-intensive programs that perform a lot of memory allocation and releasing. If you ever write a program that reports "Not enough memory" when you are sure enough is available, you might be running into a fragmentation problem. Unfortunately, MS-DOS does not perform any special memory cleanup (called *garbage collection*) to reclaim fragmented memory space by moving allocated blocks. Your program will have to take care of this task for itself. Garbage collection is beyond the scope of this book. Most books about programming algorithms give several methods for cleaning up memory.

Starting with MS-DOS 3.0, you can use Int 21H Function 58H to set the memory allocation strategy that MS-DOS uses. Earlier versions of MS-DOS always use the first fit method. Under versions 3.0 and later, first fit is the default, but you can use best fit or last fit when needed.

By selecting the memory allocation strategy judiciously, you can minimize fragmentation problems. The best fit method involves a speed penalty, but it lessens fragmentation by ensuring the best fit between the memory request and the allocated block. You can also specify last fit for relatively small allocation requests, keeping the worst of the fragmentation at the high end of free memory and retaining the low end of memory for larger requests.

Now that you understand the basics of conventional memory management, you might be wondering why and when memory management is needed. There are two primary situations in which the management of conventional memory is called for:

- When MS-DOS loads a program, MS-DOS itself uses the memory allocation services to set aside memory for the program's code and data needs.
- When a program that is executing needs to allocate memory dynamically for data storage.

It's the latter of these two situations that we are concerned with here. *Dynamic memory allocation* means that MS-DOS allocates memory space while the program is executing and not when the program is first loaded into memory. Let's look at an example.

Imagine that you're writing a program that—among its other data storage needs—requires space to store 1000 bytes, or characters, of data. In C, it is easy to declare an array of the appropriate type and size and then use standard array or pointer notation to write and read data as shown in the following example:

```
    ⋮
char data[1000];
    ⋮
data[1] = 'x';
    ⋮
```

If your program makes use of this array every time it runs, you have no problem. In some programs, however, data storage needs depend on circumstances that the programmer cannot foresee when writing the program. Perhaps that 1000-byte array will go unused at times, depending on the input that the program receives from the user. Even though unused, the array will still be allocated when the program is compiled, and the 1000 bytes of memory will be unavailable for other uses.

In such a situation, dynamic memory allocation comes to the rescue. Using the memory allocation services, your program can allocate a block (arena entry) of 1000 bytes only when and if it is needed. If the program never needs this storage, the memory remains available for other uses. If the storage is needed only temporarily, the memory can be freed when the program is finished with it, again making it available for other uses.

If you have a bit of experience in C programming, you probably know that *malloc()* and the related C standard library functions can perform dynamic memory allocation. Again, however, using the MS-DOS Int 21H services directly provides additional flexibility, particularly in regard to selecting the memory allocation strategy that MS-DOS uses. The program in Listing 12-1 shows you how to use the MS-DOS conventional memory allocation services in a C program.

```
/* Demonstrates using MS-DOS services for conventional memory allocation */

#include <stdio.h>
#include <dos.h>
#include <string.h>

/* Declare the register unions */
union REGS inregs, outregs;
struct SREGS segregs;

/* Define a macro to create a far pointer from a */
/* segment and an offset */
#define MK_FP(seg,off) ((void far *)(((unsigned long)(seg) << 16) \
    + (unsigned)(off)))

/* Define constants for the three MS-DOS */
/* memory allocation strategies */
#define FIRST_FIT 0
#define BEST_FIT 1
#define LAST_FIT 2

/* Declare a global variable for error codes */
int dos_error;

/* Function prototypes */
int get_alloc(void);
int set_alloc(int strategy);
void *mem_alloc(int paragraphs);
int mem_free(void * segment);
void clearscreen(void);
```

LISTING 12-1. *(continued)*
Demonstration of using the Int 21H conventional memory allocation services in C.

LISTING 12-1. *continued*

```c
main()
{
    char far *ptr1, far *ptr2;
    char buffer[80];
    int oldalloc;
    void *base1, *base2;

    clearscreen();

    /* Save the original memory allocation strategy */
    if((oldalloc = get_alloc()) == -1)
        {
        printf("\nError %d getting allocation strategy.", dos_error);
        exit(1);
        }

    /* Set the allocation strategy to last fit */
    if ((set_alloc(LAST_FIT)) == 0)
        {
        printf("\nError setting the memory allocation strategy.");
        exit(1);
        }

    /* Allocate 80 bytes (five paragraphs) of memory */
    if ((base1 = mem_alloc(5)) == 0)
        {
        printf("\nError %d allocating memory.", dos_error);
        exit(1);
        }

    /* Make a far pointer from the segment address */
    ptr1 = MK_FP(base1, 0);

    /* Get a string from the user */
    puts("Enter one line of text:");
    gets(buffer);

    /* Copy the string to the allocated memory */
    _fstrcpy(ptr1, (char far*)buffer);

    /* Change the allocation strategy to first fit */
    if ((set_alloc(FIRST_FIT)) == 0)
        {
        printf("\nError setting the memory allocation strategy.");
        exit(1);
        }
```

(continued)

LISTING 12-1. *continued*

```c
        /* Allocate another 80 bytes (five paragraphs) of memory */
        if ((base2 = mem_alloc(5)) == 0)
            {
            printf("\nError %d allocating memory.", dos_error);
            exit(1);
            }

        /* Make a far pointer from the segment address */
        ptr2 = MK_FP(base2, 0);

        /* Get a second string from the user */
        puts("Enter one line of text:");
        gets(buffer);

        /* Copy the string to the allocated memory */
        _fstrcpy(ptr2, (char far*)buffer);

        /* Copy the first line from the allocated */
        /* memory back to the buffer */
        _fstrcpy((char far*)buffer, ptr1);

        printf("\nFirst line: %s",buffer);

        /* Copy the second line from the allocated */
        /* memory back to the buffer */

        _fstrcpy((char far*)buffer, ptr2);

        printf("\nSecond line: %s",buffer);

        /* Free the two arena entries */
        if ((mem_free(base1)) == 0)
            {
            printf("\nError %d freeing memory.", dos_error);
            exit(1);
            }

        if ((mem_free(base2)) == 0)
            {
            printf("\nError %d freeing memory.", dos_error);
            exit(1);
            }

        /* Restore the original memory allocation strategy */
        if ((set_alloc(oldalloc)) == 0)
            {
            printf("\nError resetting memory allocation strategy.");
            exit(1);
            }
}       /* End of main() */
```

(continued)

LISTING 12-1. *continued*

```c
int get_alloc(void)
{
    /* Returns the code for the current MS-DOS memory allocation */
    /* strategy (0, 1, or 2) and returns -1 on error */

    inregs.h.ah = 0X58;
    inregs.h.al = 0X00;

    /* Call Int 21H Function 58H to get the allocation strategy */
    int86(0X21, &inregs, &outregs);

    if (outregs.x.cflag)
        {
        dos_error = outregs.x.ax;
        return(-1);
        }

    return(outregs.x.ax);
}

int set_alloc(int strategy)
{
    /* Sets the MS-DOS memory allocation strategy to the code */
    /* specified by the parameter strategy; returns 0 on */
    /* failure or 1 on success */

    inregs.h.ah = 0X58;
    inregs.h.al = 0X01;
    inregs.x.bx = strategy;

    /* Call Int 21H Function 58H to set the allocation strategy */
    int86(0X21, &inregs, &outregs);

    if(outregs.x.cflag)
        {
        dos_error = outregs.x.ax;
        return(0);
        }

    return(1);
}

void *mem_alloc(int paragraphs)
{
    /* Allocates an arena entry that contains the requested */
    /* number of paragraphs; returns the segment address */
    /* of the entry on success or 0 on failure */

    inregs.h.ah = 0X48;
    inregs.x.bx = paragraphs;
```

(continued)

LISTING 12-1. *continued*

```c
    /* Call Int 21H Function 48H to allocate an arena entry */
    int86(0X21, &inregs, &outregs);

    if (outregs.x.cflag)
        {
        dos_error = outregs.x.ax;
        return(0);
        }

    return((void *)(outregs.x.ax));
}
int mem_free(void * segment)
{
    /* Frees an arena entry allocated originally with Int 21H */
    /* Function 48H; returns 0 on failure or 1 on success */

    inregs.h.ah = 0X49;
    segregs.es = (int)segment;

    /* Call Int 21H Function 49H to free an arena entry */
    int86x(0X21, &inregs, &outregs, &segregs);

    if (outregs.x.cflag)
        {
        dos_error = outregs.x.ax;
        return(0);
        }

    return(1);
}
void clearscreen(void)
{
    int x;

    for (x = 0; x < 25; x++)
        printf("\n");
}
```

Managing Extended Memory

If your program runs on a system that has an 80286 (or higher) processor, a large amount of extended memory might be installed and available. If your program runs under MS-DOS, however, the processor operates in real mode, and any extended memory is not readily available. MS-DOS does provide two services, however, that permit a real mode program to have limited access to extended memory. Int 15H Function 88H determines the amount of extended memory available, and Int 15H Function 87H transfers data to and from extended memory. At the end of this chapter, you'll find reference entries for these services.

Determining the amount of extended memory by using Int 15H Function 88H is quite simple, but transferring data to and from extended memory by using Int 15H Function 87H is a bit more complex. Several shortcomings are associated with this service:

- Switching the processor to protected mode and then back to real mode is a relatively slow process, particularly on 80286 systems.

- Interrupts are disabled while the transfer service executes, possibly causing problems with certain programs that rely heavily on interrupts.

- The service provides no arbitration between two programs or drivers that might use the same region of extended memory. Your program and a RAM disk driver, for example, might write data to the same memory addresses. No error will be reported, but data will be lost.

Because of these shortcomings, I suggest that you do not attempt to use extended memory in your programs. Application programs can use extended memory safely and efficiently, but doing so requires complex programming that is beyond the scope of this book. If your programs need memory for data beyond that provided by conventional memory, you are much better off using expanded memory. MS-DOS 5 includes the EMM386 device driver, which enables systems with an 80386 processor to simulate expanded memory with extended memory. For more information about EMM386, see your MS-DOS 5 manual.

Managing Expanded Memory

When you want your program to use expanded memory, you must first determine whether an Expanded Memory Manager (EMM) driver is installed. Two methods are available to do so.

The first method uses Int 21H Function 3DH (which opens a file or a device) to attempt to open the EMM driver using its name, EMMXXXX0. If the service is successful, it means that an EMM driver is installed or that a disk file named EMMXXXX0 is present in the default drive and directory. Although this latter possibility might seem unlikely, you should rule it out by using a call to Int 21H Function 44H Subfunction 07H to verify that expanded memory is present. This subfunction checks the output status of a device associated with a handle. If you pass it the handle that was returned when you opened EMMXXXX0, it will return 00H if the device is actually a file (and EMM is not available) and FFH if the device is in fact an expanded memory manager. After verifying that an EMM driver is installed, use Int 21H Function 3EH to free the handle that the call to Int 21H Function 3DH returned. You do not need the handle to access expanded memory, and freeing it makes it available for another file or device.

The second method uses the address that is found in the Int 67H vector. Int 67H is the EMM driver interrupt, and the vector for Int 67H contains the address of the driver's location. By convention, the memory location at offset 0AH in the driver code's segment contains the driver name, EMMXXXX0. If this string is present at the indicated location, an EMM driver is installed.

The first method has the advantage of being "well behaved" because it relies solely on MS-DOS services. But because it opens a device, the first method involves more overhead than does the second. The second method, however, is less "well behaved" because it accesses memory that does not belong to the program. In almost all situations, you can use either method without a problem. The program in Listing 12-2 illustrates the second method of checking for an installed EMM driver. Later in this chapter, Listing 12-3 demonstrates the first method.

```
/* Demonstrates one method of checking for an installed */
/* Expanded Memory Manager */

#include <stdio.h>
#include <dos.h>

/* Define a macro to create a far pointer from a segment */
/* and an offset */
#define MK_FP(seg,off) ((void far *)(((unsigned long)(seg) << 16) \
    + (unsigned)(off)))

/* Declare the register unions */
union REGS inregs, outregs;
struct SREGS segregs;

/* Function prototypes */
int emm_avail(void);
void clearscreen(void);
```

LISTING 12-2. *(continued)*
Demonstration of checking for the presence of Expanded Memory Manager (EMM) software in C.

LISTING 12-2. *continued*

```c
main()
{
    clearscreen();

    if (emm_avail())
        puts("Expanded Memory Manager detected.");
    else
        puts("Expanded Memory Manager not found.");
}

int emm_avail(void)
{
    /* Returns 1 if Expanded Memory Manager found or 0 if not found */

    /* Declare pointers for the two strings; the pointer for the */
    /* name in the EMM driver must be a far pointer */
    char far *emmname;
    char *template = "EMMXXXX0";
    int count;

    /* Set up registers to get the Int 67H vector */
    inregs.h.ah = 0X35;
    inregs.h.al = 0X67;

    int86x(0X21, &inregs, &outregs, &segregs);

    /* Now the ES register contains the segment of the Int 67H vector */
    /* Make a far pointer from that using an offset of 0 */
    emmname = MK_FP(segregs.es, 0);

    /* Add 10 to the offset to move to the location of the driver name */
    emmname += 10;

    /* Compare 8 bytes; return 0 if a mismatch is found or 1 */
    /* if all 8 bytes match */
    for (count = 0; count < 8; count++)
        {
        if (*emmname++ != *template++)
            return(0);
        }

    return(1);
}

void clearscreen(void)
{
    int x;

    for (x = 0; x < 25; x++)
        printf("\n");
}
```

After your program verifies the presence of the Expanded Memory Manager, the program can work with the expanded memory via the manager's Int 67H service calls. As with the other interrupts you've seen in this book, you must place the function number in the AH register and the required parameters in other registers before calling the interrupt. The success or error status is returned in AH. Several dozen Int 67H EMM services are defined in EMS versions 3.2 and 4.0. Many of these services—particularly those introduced with EMS version 4.0—are intended primarily for more advanced programming tasks, such as creating an operating system or a memory-resident program that uses expanded memory. These services are rarely, if ever, needed when you write an application program. The remainder of this chapter limits discussion to those EMM services that are most likely to be of use to you.

EMM service error codes

The error codes that the EMM services return provide useful information about the cause of the error. The following table (Figure 12-5) lists the values and meanings of the error codes that are common to EMS versions 3.0, 3.2, and 4.0. The table does not include the EMS 4.0 error codes that are related to those EMM services used primarily for operating system and TSR (terminate-and-stay-resident) programming.

Code	Meaning
00H	Function successful
80H	Internal error in Expanded Memory Manager software
81H	Expanded memory hardware malfunction
82H	Expanded Memory Manager busy
83H	Invalid handle
84H	Invalid function requested
85H	No more handles available
86H	Error when saving or restoring mapping context
87H	Application requested more logical pages than are physically available; no pages allocated
88H	Application requested more logical pages than are logically available (i.e., some pages already allocated, so are not available); no pages allocated
89H	Zero pages requested; cannot be allocated
8AH	Logical page mapping request outside range of logical pages assigned to handle

(continued)

FIGURE 12-5.
EMM error codes.

FIGURE 12-5. *continued*

Code	Meaning
8BH	Illegal physical page request (that is, outside range 0–3)
8CH	Page-mapping, hardware-state save area full
8DH	Save of mapping context failed; save area already contains context associated with specified handle
8EH	Restore of mapping context failed; save area contains no context for specified handle
8FH	Subfunction parameter not defined

The steps to using expanded memory

Some of the terms in the Figure 12-5 might be puzzling to you now, but you'll learn more about them shortly. First let's take a look at the general procedure that an application program should follow to use expanded memory for data storage.

1. Verify that an Expanded Memory Manager is installed using one of the two methods described earlier in this chapter.

2. Check whether the Expanded Memory Manager and the physical memory are installed and operational by calling the service Int 67H Function 40H.

3. Obtain the Expanded Memory Specification version number by using Int 67H Function 46H. This step is necessary only if your program will call services that are not supported by all EMM versions.

4. Use Int 67H Function 41H to obtain the segment address of the page frame. This is the base address of the 64-KB segment that your program will use to read from and write to expanded memory.

5. Determine the total number of expanded memory pages available by calling Int 67H Function 42H.

6. Based on your program's memory needs and the information obtained in Step 5, allocate the required number of expanded memory pages by calling Int 67H Function 43H. If the service succeeds, it returns a handle that the program can use to refer to the allocated expanded memory pages.

7. Use Int 67H Function 44H to map a page of expanded memory into the physical page frame. It's the responsibility of the application program to keep track of what data is stored where in expanded memory.

8. After verifying that the proper page (or pages) of expanded memory is mapped into the page frame, the application program can use the standard data transfer methods to read from and write to the expanded memory via the page frame. Remember that the program must use far or huge pointers to access the page frame because the page frame is outside the default data segment.

9. Upon completion, the program should use Int 67H Function 45H to release its expanded memory pages. If it doesn't do so, these pages remain allocated even after the program has terminated and will be unavailable for use by other programs until the system is rebooted.

At the end of the chapter, you'll find reference entries for the most commonly used EMM services. These services are all that you need to use expanded memory in a wide variety of applications. For example, you could store database records in expanded memory by defining an array of structures in one or more expanded memory pages and then using pointers to access the actual data. You'll have to use far or huge pointers to access the page frame because it will always be outside the default data segment. I suggest that you review the reference material for these services and then look at Listing 12-3 to see how they're used.

C library functions for accessing expanded memory

The program in Listing 12-3 presents and demonstrates a basic set of functions that your program can use to access expanded memory. The program defines the following functions:

Function	Description
emm_avail()	Checks for the presence of Expanded Memory Manager software
emm_ok()	Verifies that the expanded memory software and hardware are present and functional
emm_pages()	Displays the total number of expanded memory pages and the number of unallocated pages
emm_frame()	Returns a pointer to the expanded memory page frame
emm_allocate()	Allocates a specific number of expanded memory pages and returns a handle to them
emm_map()	Maps a page of expanded memory into one of the four pages in the page frame
emm_read()	Transfers data from expanded memory to program memory
emm_write()	Transfers data from program memory to expanded memory
emm_release()	Releases the expanded memory associated with a handle

As you review the demonstration program in Listing 12-3, keep in mind that it takes the steps listed below. Also, the program makes use of a global variable named *emm_error*. If any of the expanded memory services fail, the program places the expanded memory error code in the variable and displays the error number. A more sophisticated program might use the error message to take corrective action, display an error message, and so on.

1. Checks whether an Expanded Memory Manager is installed
2. Verifies that expanded memory hardware and software are present and functioning properly
3. Determines and displays the total number of expanded memory pages and the number of unallocated pages in the system
4. Obtains and displays the segment address of the expanded memory page frame
5. Allocates eight pages of expanded memory
6. Maps expanded memory pages 0–3 into the four pages in the page frame
7. Writes data to each of the expanded memory pages 0–3
8. Maps expanded memory pages 4–7 into the page frame
9. Writes data to each of the expanded memory pages 4–7
10. Maps expanded memory pages 0–3 into the page frame
11. Reads and displays the data from expanded memory pages 0–3
12. Maps expanded memory pages 4–7 to the page frame
13. Reads and displays the data from expanded memory pages 4–7
14. Releases the expanded memory and then terminates

```
/* Demonstrates accessing expanded memory */

#include <stdio.h>
#include <dos.h>

/* Define a macro to create a far pointer from a segment */
/* and an offset */
#define MK_FP(seg,off) ((void far *)(((unsigned long)(seg) << 16) \
    + (unsigned)(off)))
```

LISTING 12-3. *(continued)*
Demonstration of expanded memory access in C.

LISTING 12-3. *continued*

```c
/* Declare the register unions */
union REGS inregs, outregs;

/* Declare global variables for expanded memory error codes and */
/* for the base address of the expanded memory page frame */
int emm_error;
char far *emm_base;

/* Function prototypes */
int emm_avail(void);
int emm_ok(void);
void emm_pages(void);
int *emm_frame(void);
int emm_allocate(int pages);
int emm_map(int emm_handle, int pf_page, int emm_page);
void emm_read(int pf_page, char *destination, int bytes);
void emm_write(int pf_page, char *source, int bytes);
int emm_release(int handle);
void clearscreen(void);

main()
{
    int emm_handle, *frame, count;
    char data[60];

    clearscreen();

    /* Check whether the EMM software is installed */
    if (emm_avail())
        puts("Expanded memory detected.");
    else
        puts("Expanded memory not found.");

    /* Check whether the EMM software and hardware are functional */
    if (emm_ok())
        puts("\nThe EMM software and hardware are functional.");
    else
        {
        puts("\nEMM hardware or software error.");
        printf("EMM error code %d.", emm_error);
        exit(1);
        }

    /* Display the number of total and unallocated EMS pages */
    emm_pages();

    /* Get the segment address of the page frame and display it */
    frame = emm_frame();
    printf("\nThe segment address of the EMS page frame is %u.\n\n", frame);
```

(continued)

LISTING 12-3. *continued*

```c
/* Make a far pointer to the page frame */
emm_base = MK_FP(frame, 0);

/* Allocate eight pages of expanded memory */
if ((emm_handle = emm_allocate(8)) == 0)
    {
    printf("\nError %d allocating expanded memory.", emm_error);
    exit(1);
    }

/* The next section writes a test string to each of the eight */
/* allocated pages of expanded memory. The first step is to */
/* map the expanded memory pages 0-3 to the four pages in the */
/* page frame. */

for (count = 0; count < 4; count++)
    {
    if ((emm_map(emm_handle, count, count)) == 0)
        {
        printf("\nError %d mapping the expanded memory pages.",
                emm_error);
        exit(1);
        }
    }

/* Create a string, and write it to expanded memory pages 0-3 */
for (count = 0; count < 4; count++)
    {
    sprintf(data, "STORED ON EXPANDED MEMORY PAGE %d.", count);
    emm_write(count, data, strlen(data)+1);
    }

/* Map expanded memory pages 4-7 to the four pages in the page frame */
for (count = 0; count < 4; count++)
    {
    if ((emm_map(emm_handle, count, count+4)) == 0)
        {
        printf("\nError %d mapping the expanded memory pages.",
                emm_error);
        exit(1);
        }
    }

/* Write test strings to expanded memory pages 4-7 */
for (count = 0; count < 4; count++)
    {
    sprintf(data, "STORED ON EXPANDED MEMORY PAGE %d.", count + 4);
    emm_write(count, data, strlen(data)+1);
    }
```

(continued)

LISTING 12-3. *continued*

```c
    /* Map expanded memory pages 0-3 to the four pages in the page frame */
    for (count = 0; count < 4; count++)
        {
        if ((emm_map(emm_handle, count, count)) == 0)
            {
            printf("\nError %d mapping the expanded memory pages.",
                    emm_error);
            exit(1);
            }
        }

    /* Read 40 bytes from each expanded memory page */
    for (count = 0; count < 4; count++)
        {
        emm_read(count, data, 40);
        printf("\nRetrieved from expanded memory page %d: %s", count, data);
        }

    /* Map expanded memory pages 4-7 to the four pages in the page frame */
    for (count = 0; count < 4; count++)
        {
        if ((emm_map(emm_handle, count, count + 4)) == 0)
            {
            printf("\nError %d mapping the expanded memory pages.",
                    emm_error);
            exit(1);
            }
        }

    /* Read 40 bytes from each expanded memory page */
    for (count = 0; count < 4; count++)
        {
        emm_read(count, data, 40);
        printf("\nRetrieved from expanded memory page %d: %s",
                count + 4, data);
        }

    /* Release the expanded memory */
    if ((emm_release(emm_handle)) == 0)
        {
        printf("\nError %d releasing the memory.", emm_error);
        exit(1);
        }
    else
        puts("\n\nExpanded memory was released successfully.");
}   /* End of main() */

int emm_avail(void)
{
    /* Returns FFH if Expanded Memory Manager found or 0 if not found */
```

(continued)

LISTING 12-3. *continued*

```c
        char *name = "EMMXXXX0";
        int handle, result;

        /* Attempt to open the file EMMXXXX0 in read-only mode */
        inregs.h.ah = 0X3D;
        inregs.h.al = 0;
        inregs.x.dx = (int)name;
        int86(0X21, &inregs, &outregs);

        /* If the open attempt was not successful, return 0 */
        if (outregs.x.cflag != 0)
            return(0);

        /* If the open attempt was successful, first save the handle and */
        /* then check to be sure it was the EMM and not a disk file */
        handle = outregs.x.ax;

        inregs.x.bx = handle;      /* Put handle in BX */
        inregs.h.ah = 0X44;
        inregs.h.al = 7;
        inregs.x.cx = 0;           /* Number of bytes to read */

        /* call Int 21H Function 44H Subfunction 7 to get output status */
        int86(0X21, &inregs, &outregs);

        /* Now the AL register contains 0 if the subfunction returned "not */
        /* ready," indicating that it is a file and not the EMM driver. */

        /* Save the value in the AL register and then close the file */
        result = outregs.h.al;

        inregs.h.ah = 0X3E;
        inregs.x.bx = handle;
        int86(0X21, &inregs, &outregs);   /* Close the file */

        /* Return FFH to the calling program if EMM was found or 0 if not */
        return(result);
}       /* End of emm_avail() */

int emm_ok(void)
{
        /* Returns a nonzero value if the EMM hardware and software are */
        /* present and functional or 0 if not */

        inregs.h.ah = 0X40;

        /* Call Int 67H Function 40H to get the EMM status */
        int86(0X67, &inregs, &outregs);
```

(continued)

LISTING 12-3. *continued*

```c
        if (outregs.h.ah == 0)
            return(1);
        else
            {
            emm_error = (int)outregs.h.ah;
            return(0);
            }
    }   /* End of emm_ok() */

void emm_pages(void)
{
    /* Displays the total number of EMM pages and the number of */
    /* unallocated pages. Returns a nonzero value on success or */
    /* 0 on failure */

    inregs.h.ah = 0X42;

    /* Call Int 67H Function 42H to get the number of EMM pages */
    int86(0X67, &inregs, &outregs);

    if (outregs.h.ah == 0)
        {
        printf("\nThe total number of EMS pages is %d.", outregs.x.dx);
        printf("\nThe number of unallocated EMS pages is %d.", outregs.x.bx);
        }
    else
        {
        printf("\nError %d getting the EMS pages.", outregs.h.ah);
        exit(1);
        }
}   /* End of emm_pages() */

int *emm_frame(void)
{
    /* Returns a pointer to the page frame segment or 0 on error */

    inregs.h.ah = 0X41;
    int86(0X67, &inregs, &outregs);

    if (outregs.h.ah == 0)
        return((int *)outregs.x.bx);
    else
        {
        emm_error = outregs.h.ah;
        return(0);
        }
}   /* End of emm_frame() */
```

(continued)

LISTING 12-3. *continued*

```c
int emm_allocate(int pages)
{
    /* Allocates the specified number of pages of expanded memory */
    /* and returns the associated handle; returns 0 on error */

    inregs.h.ah = 0X43;
    inregs.x.bx = pages;

    /* Call Int 67H Function 43H to allocate expanded memory pages */
    int86(0X67, &inregs, &outregs);

    if (outregs.h.ah == 0)
        return(outregs.x.dx);
    else
        {
        emm_error = outregs.h.ah;
        return(0);
        }
}   /* End of emm_allocate() */

int emm_release(int handle)
{
    /* Releases the handle and its associated expanded memory; */
    /* returns 0 on error or a nonzero value if no error occurs */

    inregs.h.ah = 0X45;
    inregs.x.dx = handle;

    /* Call Int 67H Function 45H to release expanded memory */
    int86(0X67, &inregs, &outregs);

    if (outregs.h.ah == 0)
        return(1);
    else
        {
        emm_error = outregs.h.ah;
        return(0);
        }
}   /* End of emm_release() */

int emm_map(int emm_handle, int pf_page, int emm_page)
{
    /* Maps the expanded memory page specified by emm_page to */
    /* the page frame page specified by pf_page. */

    inregs.h.ah = 0X44;
    inregs.h.al = pf_page;
    inregs.x.bx = emm_page;
    inregs.x.dx = emm_handle;
```

(continued)

LISTING 12-3. *continued*

```c
        int86(0X67, &inregs, &outregs);

    if (outregs.h.ah)
        {
        emm_error = outregs.h.ah;
        return(0);
        }
    else
        return(1);
}   /* End of emm_map() */

void emm_write(int pf_page, char *source, int bytes)
{
    /* Writes data to expanded memory */
    /* pf_page = expanded memory page (0-3) */
    /* source = pointer to data */
    /* bytes = number of bytes to write */

    char far *ptr;

    ptr = emm_base + pf_page * 0X4000;

    while (bytes-- > 0)
        *ptr++ = *source++;
}   /* End of emm_write() */

void emm_read(int pf_page, char *destination, int bytes)
{
    /* Reads data from expanded memory */
    /* pf_page = expanded memory page (0-3) */
    /* destination = pointer to destination for data */
    /* bytes = number of bytes to read */

    char far *ptr;

    ptr = emm_base + pf_page * 0X4000;

    while (bytes-- > 0)
        *destination++ = *ptr++;
}   /* End of emm_read */

void clearscreen(void)
{
    int x;

    for (x = 0; x < 25; x++)
        printf("\n");
}   /* End of clearscreen() */
```

Memory Management Service Reference

The following reference section is broken into three sections. Each section contains entries for the services used to manage one of the three types of memory: conventional, extended, and expanded.

CONVENTIONAL MEMORY SERVICES

Int 21H Function 48H
Allocate arena entry

Action:	Allocates an arena entry (a block of memory) and returns a pointer to the beginning of the entry
Call with:	AH = 48H BX = number of paragraphs of memory to allocate (one paragraph contains 16 bytes)

Returns:	On success:
	    Carry flag = clear
	    AX = segment address of arena entry
	
	On failure:
	    Carry flag = set
	    AX = error code
	    BX = size of largest available block (in paragraphs)

Notes:	Upon return from this service, the starting address of the arena entry is AX:0000. In a C program, the usual strategy is to create a far pointer from this information and then use the pointer to access the memory. By default, the memory allocation strategy used is first fit. For information about the memory allocation strategies and how to change the one MS-DOS uses, see the reference entry for Int 21H Function 58H.

Int 21H Function 49H
Release arena entry

Action:	Releases an arena entry (a block of memory), making it available for other uses

Call with:	AH = 49H ES = segment address of block to be released

Returns:	On success:
	     Carry flag = clear
	 On failure:
	     Carry flag = set
	     AX = error code

Notes:	Errors can result if either of the following occurs: ■ A program attempts to release a memory block that does not belong to it. ■ The segment address passed in ES is not a valid address for an existing memory block. This service assumes that the memory being released was allocated initially by a call to Int 21H Function 48H.

Int 21H Function 4AH
Resize arena entry

Action:	Decreases or increases the size of an allocated arena entry (memory block)
Call with:	AH = 4AH BX = new block size in paragraphs (one paragraph contains 16 bytes) ES = segment address of block to modify

Returns:	On success:
	     Carry flag = clear
	 On failure:
	     Carry flag = set
	     AX = error code
	     BX = maximum block size available (in paragraphs)

Notes:	This service assumes that the arena entry being modified was allocated initially by a call to Int 21H Function 48H. If the service fails when requesting an increase in block size, the value returned in BX gives the maximum possible size for the block.

Int 21H   Function 58H
Get or set memory allocation strategy

Action: Obtains or sets the memory allocation strategy for MS-DOS to use

Call with: To get allocation strategy:
            AH = 58H
            AL = 00H

To set allocation strategy:
            AH = 58H
            AL = 01H
            BX = strategy code:
                00H= first fit
                01H= best fit
                02H= last fit

Returns: On success:
            Carry flag = clear
            If getting strategy:
                AX = current allocation strategy code

On failure:
            Carry flag = set
            AX   = error code

Notes: The available memory allocation strategies are listed below:

- First fit: MS-DOS searches the available arena entries (memory blocks) from low address to high address and allocates the first entry it finds that is large enough.

- Best fit: MS-DOS examines all available arena entries and allocates the smallest block that will meet the request, regardless of its position.

- Last fit: MS-DOS searches the available arena entries from high address to low address and allocates the first block it finds that is large enough.

The default allocation strategy is first fit. If a program changes the memory allocation strategy, the program should restore the original strategy before termination.

EXTENDED MEMORY SERVICES

Int 15H   Function 87H
Transfer data from extended memory block

Action:	Transfers data between extended memory and user memory
Call with:	AH = 87H CX = number of words (2-byte pieces of data) to move ES = segment of Global Descriptor Table (see "Notes") SI = offset of Global Descriptor Table

Returns:	On success:
	   Carry flag = clear
	   AH = 00H
	
	On failure:
	   Carry flag = set
	   AH = status:
	      01H if RAM parity error
	      02H if exception interrupt error
	      03H if gate address line 20 (used in the transfer) failed

Notes:	You can use this service only on systems that have an 80286 (or higher) processor and installed extended memory. The Global Descriptor Table is a data area that contains 48 bytes that must be set up as shown in the table below. The ROM BIOS fills the reserved areas in the table before the processor is switched to protected mode. *Byte(s)* — *Contents* 00H–0FH — Reserved (should be 0) 10H–11H — Transfer length in bytes (at least 2 * CX – 1) 12H–14H — 24-bit source address 15H — Access rights (always 93H) 16H–17H — Reserved (should be 0) 18H–19H — Transfer length in bytes (at least 2 * CX – 1) 1AH–1CH — 24-bit destination address 1DH — Access rights (always 93H) 1EH–2FH — Reserved (should be 0) This service accesses extended memory by using 24-bit linear addresses in the range 000000H–FFFFFFH, with the least significant byte at the lowest address. It does not use segment:offset addresses.

When this service performs the memory transfer, it disables interrupts temporarily. As a result, this service might interfere with network drivers, communications programs, or other programs that require a prompt response to hardware interrupts.

Int 15H   Function 88H
Get extended memory size

Action:	Returns the amount of extended memory installed
Call with:	AH = 88H
Returns:	AX = amount of extended memory (in kilobytes)
Notes:	You can use this service only on systems that have an 80286 (or higher) processor.

EXPANDED MEMORY SERVICES

Int 21H   Function 44H Subfunction 07H
Get output status

Action:	Determines whether the device associated with a handle is ready to receive output.
Call with:	AH = 44H AL = 07H BX = handle

Returns:	On success:
	   Carry flag = clear
	   For a device:
	      AL = 00H if not ready
	         = FFH if ready
	   For a file:
	      AL = FFH
	On failure:
	   Carry flag = set
	   AX = error code

| Notes: | If the handle passed in BX is associated with a file, this service always returns FFH even if the disk is full or there is no floppy disk in the drive. |

Int 67H Function 40H [EMS 3.0 and later]
Get status

Action:	Determines whether the Expanded Memory Manager software and the expanded memory are installed and functional
Call with:	AH = 40H

Returns:	If EMM functional:
	  AH = 00H
	
	If EMM not functional:
	  AH = EMM error code (see Figure 12-5)

Notes:	Call this service only after you use one of the techniques presented earlier in this chapter to verify that Expanded Memory Manager software is present.

Int 67H Function 41H [EMS 3.0 and later]
Get page frame segment address

Action:	Returns the segment address of the page frame that the Expanded Memory Manager uses
Call with:	AH = 41H

Returns:	On success:
	  AH = 00H
	  BX = segment address of page frame
	
	On failure:
	  AH = error code (see Figure 12-5)

Notes:	The address that this service returns is the base (starting) address of a 64-KB page frame that can contain four 16-KB pages of expanded memory. A program can call this service either before or after the program has obtained a handle to expanded memory by using Int 67H Function 67H.

Int 67H Function 42H [EMS 3.0 and later]
Get number of pages

Action: Returns the total number of expanded memory pages in the system and the number of pages that are unallocated

Call with: AH = 42H

Returns: On success:
AH = 00H
BX = number of unallocated pages
DX = total number of pages

On failure:
AH = EMM error code (see Figure 12-5)

Notes: A program can call this service either before or after the program has obtained a handle to expanded memory by using Int 67H Function 67H.

Int 67H Function 43H [EMS 3.0 and later]
Allocate expanded memory handle and pages

Action: Allocates the specified number of expanded memory pages and returns a handle that the program uses to access those pages

Call with: AH = 43H
BX = number of 16-KB pages (must be greater than 0)

Returns: On success:
AH = 00H
DX = handle to expanded memory

On failure:
AH = EMM error code (see Figure 12-5)

Notes: This service will fail if the number of pages requested is greater than the number available or if no unused handles are available. If the former situation is the case, you can then use Int 67H Function 42H to determine the number of available pages.

You can change the number of pages associated with an existing handle by using Int 67H Function 51H.

Int 67H   Function 44H   [EMS 3.0 and later]
Map expanded memory page to page frame

Action: Maps a page of expanded memory onto one of the pages in the page frame

Call with: AH = 44H
AL = page number in page frame
BX = number of expanded memory page
DX = handle to expanded memory

Returns: On success:
AH = 00H

On failure:
AH = EMM error code (see Figure 12-5)

Notes: The number of the expanded memory page must be in the range 0 to *n*–1, where *n* is the number of logical pages that were allocated or reallocated to the handle by an earlier call to Int 67H Function 43H or 51H.

The page frame page number is 0, 1, 2, or 3.

Int 67H   Function 45H   [EMS 3.0 and later]
Release handle and expanded memory

Action: Unallocates the pages of expanded memory that are associated with a handle and then frees the handle for future use

Call with: AH = 45H
DX = handle to expanded memory

Returns: On success:
AH = 00H

On failure:
AH = EMM error code (See Figure 12-5)

Notes: A program must explicitly free its handle(s) to expanded memory before termination. Otherwise, the handles remain unavailable until the system is rebooted. A program that uses expanded memory should include its own Ctrl-C and critical error handlers (Interrupts 23H and 24H) to avoid termination without release of the handles.

Int 67H Function 46H　　　　　　　　　　[EMS 3.0 and later]
Get EMS version number

Action:	Returns the number of the EMS version that the Expanded Memory Manager supports
Call with:	AH = 46H
Returns:	On success: 　AH = 00H 　AL = version number (see "Notes") On failure: 　AH = EMM error code (see Figure 12-5)
Notes:	The version number is returned in binary-coded decimal format. The upper 4 bits of AL contain the integer portion of the version number, and the lower 4 bits contain the decimal portion. For example, a version number of 3.2 would be returned in AL as 32H.

Int 67H Function 51H　　　　　　　　　　　　　　　[EMS 4.0]
Reallocate pages for handle

Action:	Modifies the number of expanded memory pages that are associated with a handle
Call with:	AH = 51H BX = new number of pages DX = handle to expanded memory
Returns:	On success: 　AH = 00H 　BX = number of pages allocated to the EMM handle On failure: 　AH = EMM error code (see Figure 12-5)
Notes:	You can "allocate" zero pages to a handle. The handle remains active, and you can allocate pages to it at a later time. A handle that has zero allocated pages should still be released by using Int 67H Function 45H before the application terminates.

CHAPTER
13

Miscellaneous MS-DOS Services

T his chapter covers some of the miscellaneous MS-DOS services that can be important in writing a polished, robust program. You use the services that this chapter describes for manipulating the system date and time, obtaining equipment information, and handling errors.

Date and Time Services

All IBM-compatible PCs (those that have an 8088/8086 processor) have an internal clock that maintains the date and time. This clock—called the *system clock*—operates only when the computer is turned on. You can set the system date and time from the MS-DOS command prompt by using the Date and Time commands.

All IBM-compatible PC/ATs (those that have an 80286 and higher processor) have a system clock plus a separate, battery-operated clock that maintains the date and time when the computer is off. This clock is often called the *CMOS clock* because it is implemented in a special type of integrated circuit called CMOS. When a PC/AT is booted, the date and time are read from the CMOS clock to the system clock. The MS-DOS Date and Time commands reset both the system clock and the CMOS clock.

Note that some 8088/8086 PCs have a battery-operated clock in addition to a system clock. The battery clock might be a part of an option board that was installed in the computer, or it might be an extra feature on a PC clone system. Such optional clocks on PCs are generally not supported by MS-DOS and must be accessed using special software provided by the manufacturer.

MS-DOS has several services that permit a program to access the system clock. Use Int 21H Function 2AH to get the current date and Int 21H Function 2BH to set it. To get and set the current time, use Int 21H Functions 2CH and 2DH. The programs in Listings 13-1 and 13-2 show you how to use the date services to read and set the system date. Reading and setting the system time is an almost identical process and is left to you as a programming exercise. For more information about the services used here, see the reference section at the end of the chapter.

```
DECLARE FUNCTION SetDate% (d AS ANY)
DECLARE SUB GetDate (d AS ANY)

' $INCLUDE: 'QB.BI'

DEFINT A-Z

DIM SHARED inRegs AS RegType, outRegs AS RegType

' Define a structure for date information
TYPE Date
    year AS INTEGER
    month AS INTEGER
    day AS INTEGER
    weekday AS INTEGER
END TYPE

DIM SHARED today AS Date, mydate AS Date

' Declare an array for day names
DIM days$(7)


' Begin execution

CLS

' Fill the days array
days$(0) = "Sunday"
days$(1) = "Monday"
days$(2) = "Tuesday"
days$(3) = "Wednesday"
days$(4) = "Thursday"
days$(5) = "Friday"
days$(6) = "Saturday"

CALL GetDate(today)

PRINT "The current date is "; days$(today.weekday); ",";
PRINT today.month; "/"; today.day; "/"; today.year
PRINT

PRINT "Do you want to change the system date (y or n)? "
INPUT change$

IF (change$ = "y") THEN
    INPUT "Enter year (1980 - 2099): "; mydate.year
    INPUT "Enter month (1 - 12): "; mydate.month
    INPUT "Enter day of month (1 - 31): "; mydate.day
```

LISTING 13-1.
Demonstration of reading and setting the system date in Basic.

(continued)

LISTING 13-1. *continued*

```
        IF (SetDate(mydate) = 0) THEN
            PRINT "Error setting date."
        ELSE
            PRINT "Date successfully set to ";
            PRINT mydate.month; "/"; mydate.day; "/"; mydate.year
        END IF
    END IF

    IF (change$ = "y") THEN
        PRINT "Do you want to restore the original system date (y or n)?"
        INPUT restore$

        IF (restore$ = "y") THEN
            IF (SetDate(today) = 0) THEN
                PRINT "Error setting date."
            ELSE
                PRINT "Date successfully restored to ";
                PRINT today.month; "/"; today.day; "/"; today.year
            END IF
        END IF
    END IF

END

SUB GetDate (d AS Date)
    ' Fills structure d with the current system date

    inRegs.ax = &H2A00

    ' Call Int 21H Function 2AH to get the current date
    CALL INTERRUPT(&H21, inRegs, outRegs)

    d.year = outRegs.cx
    d.day = (outRegs.dx AND &HFF)
    d.weekday = outRegs.ax AND &HFF
    d.month = (outRegs.dx \ 256)
END SUB

FUNCTION SetDate (d AS Date)
    ' Sets the system date to the values in structure d
    ' Returns 0 on failure or a nonzero value on success

    inRegs.ax = &H2B00
    inRegs.cx = d.year
    inRegs.dx = (d.month * 256) + d.day

    ' Call Int 21H Function 2BH to set the date
    CALL INTERRUPT(&H21, inRegs, outRegs)

    SetDate = ((outRegs.ax AND &HFF) XOR &HFF)
END FUNCTION
```

```c
/* Demonstrates getting and setting the system clock   */

#include <stdio.h>
#include <dos.h>

/* Declare the register unions */
union REGS inregs, outregs;

/* Define a structure for date information */
struct date {
    int year;
    char month;
    char day;
    char weekday;
};

/* Function prototypes */
void get_date(struct date *d);
int set_date(struct date *d);
void clearscreen(void);

main()
{
    char change, restore;
    int result;
    struct date today, mydate;

    /* Declare an array of day names */
    char *days[] = {"Sunday","Monday","Tuesday","Wednesday",
                    "Thursday","Friday","Saturday"};

    clearscreen();

    get_date(&today);
    printf("The current date is %s, %i/%i/%i", days[today.weekday],
            today.month, today.day, today.year);

    puts("\n\nDo you want to change the system date (y or n)?");
    scanf("%s", &change);

    if (change == 'y')
        {
        printf("\nEnter year (1980 - 2099): ");
        scanf("%d", &mydate.year);
        printf("\nEnter month (1 - 12): ");
        scanf("%d", &mydate.month);
        printf("Enter day of month (1 - 31): ");
        scanf("%d", &mydate.day);
```

LISTING 13-2.
Demonstration of reading and setting the system date in C.

(continued)

LISTING 13-2. *continued*

```c
        if ((result = set_date(&mydate)) == 0)
            puts("Error setting the date.");
        else
            printf("Date successfully set to %s, %i/%i/%i.",
                    days[mydate.weekday], mydate.month, mydate.day,
                    mydate.year);
        }

    if (change == 'y')
        {
        puts("\n\nDo you want to restore the original system date
                (y or n)?");
        scanf("%s", &restore);

        if (restore == 'y')
            if ((result = set_date(&today)) == 0)
                puts("Error restoring the date.");
            else
                printf("Date successfully restored to %s, %i/%i/%i.",
                        days[today.weekday], today.month,
                        today.day, today.year);
        }
}    /* End of main() */

void get_date(struct date *d)
{
    /* Fills structure d with the current system date */

    inregs.h.ah = 0X2A;

    /* Call Int 21H Function 2AH to get the current date */
    int86(0X21, &inregs, &outregs);

    d->year = outregs.x.cx;
    d->month = outregs.h.dh;
    d->day = outregs.h.dl;
    d->weekday = outregs.h.al;
}    /* End of get_date() */

int set_date(struct date *d)
{
    /* Sets the system date to the values in structure d */
    /* Returns 0 on failure or a nonzero value on success */

    inregs.h.ah = 0X2B;
    inregs.x.cx = d->year;
    inregs.h.dh = d->month;
    inregs.h.dl = d->day;
```

(continued)

LISTING 13-2. *continued*

```c
    /* Call Int 21H Function 2BH to set the date */
    int86(0X21, &inregs, &outregs);
    return(!outregs.h.al);
}   /* End of set_date() */

void clearscreen(void)
{
    int x;

    for (x = 0; x < 25; x++)
        printf("\n");
}   /* End of clearscreen() */
```

Equipment Information Service

During the boot process, the boot code scans the system hardware and determines what peripheral equipment is installed. The boot code stores this information in the *hardware status word*, which is 2 bytes of data stored in memory. You can't change the equipment information after the boot process, but it is available to a program via Int 11H. A program can use this information to see whether the peripherals it requires are installed. The programs in Listings 13-3 and 13-4 illustrate the use of Int 11H. In these demonstrations, the programs use the service to determine the number of installed serial ports.

```
DECLARE FUNCTION NumSerialPorts% ()

DEFINT A-Z

' $INCLUDE: 'QB.BI'

DIM SHARED inRegs AS RegType, outRegs AS RegType


' Begin execution

CLS
PRINT "The program detected"; NumSerialPorts; "serial port(s)."

END
```

LISTING 13-3.
Demonstration of using Int 11H in Basic to determine the number of installed serial ports.

(continued)

LISTING 13-3. *continued*

```
FUNCTION NumSerialPorts
    ' Returns the number of serial ports reported by Int 11H

    CALL INTERRUPT(&H11, inRegs, outRegs)

    ' If the value in AX is so large that Basic translates it as
    ' a negative number, convert it to a positive long integer
    IF outRegs.ax < 0 THEN
        equip& = outRegs.ax + 65536
    ELSE
        equip& = outRegs.ax
    END IF

    ' The number of ports is in bits 9 through 11 of AX.
    ' To isolate the bits, divide the value in AX by 512
    ' to shift the bits right 9 digits, and then perform an AND
    ' operation with the result and 07H.

    NumSerialPorts = (equip& \ 512) AND &H7
END FUNCTION
```

```c
/* Demonstrates using Int 11H to obtain equipment information */

#include <stdio.h>
#include <dos.h>

/* Declare the register unions */
union REGS inregs, outregs;

/* Function prototypes */
int num_serial_ports(void);
void clearscreen(void);

main()
{
    clearscreen();
    printf("The program detected %i serial port(s).",
            num_serial_ports());
}

int num_serial_ports(void)
{
    /* Returns the number of serial ports reported by
    /* Int 11H */
```

(continued)

LISTING 13-4.
Demonstration of using Int 11H in C to determine the number of installed serial ports.

LISTING 13-4. *continued*

```
    int86(0X11, &inregs, &outregs);

    /* The number of ports is in bits 9 through 11 of AX.
    /* To isolate the bits, shift the value in AX right by
    /* 9 digits, and then perform an AND operation with
    /* the result and 07H. */

    return((outregs.x.ax >> 9) & 0X7);
}
void clearscreen(void)
{
    int x;

    for (x = 0; x < 25; x++)
        printf("\n");
}
```

Error Handling

Any robust program must be able to handle errors. If an error occurs when a program calls an MS-DOS service, the program must be able to obtain information about the error. Ideally, the program could determine the following:

- That an error occurred
- Where the error occurred
- The exact nature of the error
- What corrective action can be taken

Depending on the MS-DOS service that the program called and the nature of the error, MS-DOS makes some or all of this information available to the program. Unfortunately, MS-DOS error handling is rather confusing because MS-DOS uses four different methods for reporting errors. You've already seen all four of these methods earlier in this book in the discussions of various Int 21H services. We'll take a look at the four methods here.

Many of the older MS-DOS services—those introduced way back with MS-DOS versions 1.x—report error status in the AL register. After the service call, AL contains 0 if no error occurred or an error code if an error was detected. The error codes have no standard meaning; each service assigns its own meaning to specific codes. Int 21H services that use this method of error reporting are mostly the file management services and others in the range 00H through 2EH.

Miscellaneous MS-DOS Services

Certain MS-DOS services that were introduced with MS-DOS versions 2.0 through 4.0 use the second method of error reporting. On return from the service, a clear carry flag (equal to 0) indicates no error. A set carry flag (equal to 1) indicates that an error occurred, and register AX contains an error code. These error codes are called *extended error codes;* they are standardized for all services that use them and are listed in Figure 13-1.

Code	Meaning
01H	Function number invalid
02H	File not found
03H	Path not found
04H	Too many open files
05H	Access denied
06H	Handle invalid
07H	Arena entries destroyed
08H	Insufficient memory
09H	Arena entry address invalid
0AH	Environment invalid
0BH	Format invalid
0CH	Access code invalid
0DH	Data invalid
0FH	Disk drive invalid
10H	Attempted to remove current directory
11H	Not same device
12H	No more files
13H	Disk write protected
14H	Unknown unit
15H	Drive not ready
16H	Unknown command
17H	Data error (CRC)
18H	Bad request-structure length
19H	Seek error
1AH	Unknown media type
1BH	Sector not found
1CH	Printer out of paper
1DH	Write fault
1EH	Read fault

FIGURE 13-1. *(continued)*
MS-DOS extended error codes.

FIGURE 13-1. *continued*

Code	Meaning
1FH	General failure
20H	Sharing violation
21H	File-lock violation
22H	Disk change invalid
23H	FCB unavailable
24H	Sharing buffer exceeded
25H	Code page mismatched
26H	End of file
27H	Disk full
28H–31H	Reserved
32H	Unsupported network request
33H	Remote machine not listening
34H	Duplicate name on network
35H	Network name not found
36H	Network busy
37H	Device no longer exists on network
38H	NetBIOS command limit exceeded
39H	Error in network adapter hardware
3AH	Incorrect response from network
3BH	Unexpected network error
3CH	Remote adapter incompatible
3DH	Print queue full
3EH	Not enough space for print file
3FH	Print file deleted
40H	Network name deleted
41H	Network access denied
42H	Incorrect network device type
43H	Network name not found
44H	Network name limit exceeded
45H	NetBIOS session limit exceeded
46H	File sharing temporarily paused
47H	Network request not accepted
48H	Print or disk redirection paused
49H–4FH	Reserved

(continued)

FIGURE 13-1. *continued*

Code	Meaning
50H	File already exists
51H	Duplicate FCB
52H	Cannot make directory
53H	Fail on Int 24H (critical error)
54H	Too many redirections
55H	Duplicate redirection
56H	Invalid password
57H	Invalid parameter
58H	Network device fault
5AH	Required system component not installed

The first 20 error codes in this table are the most commonly used. No single service uses all of these codes, of course, but standardizing them makes it much easier for a program to handle errors. For example, you could create an array of strings in which each array element contained the text of the error message associated with a specific extended error code. When an error was detected, you could use the error code as an index to the array to display the appropriate message to the user.

The third MS-DOS error reporting method deals with *critical errors*. A critical error is a hardware error that takes place during a read or write operation and that requires immediate attention, such as trying to read from a floppy disk when the disk drive door is open. When a critical error occurs, MS-DOS calls Int 24H, which invokes the critical error interrupt handler and passes to it a code that describes the nature of the error. The code in the interrupt handler is responsible for displaying error messages, taking corrective action, and so on.

The default MS-DOS critical error interrupt handler is rudimentary. It is responsible for the infamous "Abort, Retry, Fail?" messages that we all see once in a while. Because it is so limited, this interrupt handler provides little flexibility for graceful recovery, data security, and the like. Most application programs replace the default critical error interrupt handler with one of their own so that programs can handle critical errors in a way that safeguards the user's data. This topic, however, is beyond the scope of this book. For information about techniques that you can use to write your own critical error interrupt handler, refer to books that cover such advanced programming topics.

The fourth method that MS-DOS uses to report errors was introduced with MS-DOS 3.0. This is via Int 21H Function 59H, which gets extended error information. When you call this MS-DOS service, it returns the following information:

- The extended error code (see Figure 13-1)
- The *error class*, which specifies the general type of error (for example, hardware failure, authorization problem, or locked file)
- The *error location*, which specifies the area in which the error occurred (for example, memory, serial device, or network)
- The *suggested action* to be taken (for example, retry, get new information from user, or ignore)

The information that this service returns is relevant to the error that occurred (if any) with the last Int 21H service call. For more information about the return values for this service, see the reference section at the end of this chapter. If no error occurred with the last MS-DOS service call, Int 21H Function 59H returns 0 in register AX.

Miscellaneous Service Reference

This reference is broken into three sections. Each section contains the reference entries for one of the topics discussed in this chapter: date and time, equipment information, and error handling.

DATE AND TIME SERVICES

Int 21H Function 2AH
Get system date

Action:	Reads the date from the system clock
Call with:	AH = 2AH
Returns:	CX = year (1980–2099) DH = month (1–12) DL = day (1–31) AL = day of week (0 = Sunday, 1 = Monday, and so on)
Notes:	The values that this service returns are in the same format as those required by Int 21H Function 2BH, which sets the date.

Int 21H Function 2BH
Set system date

Action:	Sets the date on the system clock
Call with:	AH = 2BH CX = year (1980–2099) DH = month (1–12) DL = day (1–31)

Returns:	On success:
	    AL = 00H
	On failure:
	    AL = FFH

Notes:	If the service returns FFH in register AL, most likely the program passed an invalid date (for example, DL = 99). If this situation occurs, the system date is not changed.

Int 21H Function 2CH
Get system time

Action:	Reads the time from the system clock
Call with:	AH = 2CH
Returns:	CH = hours (0–23) CL = minutes (0–59) DH = seconds (0–59) DL = hundredths of a second (0–99)
Notes:	Most PC system clocks do not have a resolution of $1/100$ second, so the values that this service returns in register DL are discontinuous and cannot be used for precision timing. The values that this service returns are in the same format as those used by Int 21H Function 2DH, which sets the time.

Int 21H Function 2DH
Set system time

Action:	Sets the time on the system clock
Call with:	AH = 2DH CH = hours (0–23) CL = minutes (0–59) DH = seconds (0–59) DL = hundredths of a second (0–99)

Returns:	On success:
	   AL = 00H
	On failure:
	   AL = FFH

Notes:	If the service returns FFH in register AL, most likely the program passed an invalid time (for example, CL = 99). If this situation occurs, the system time is not changed.

EQUIPMENT INFORMATION SERVICE

Int 11H
Get equipment information

Action:	Returns the ROM BIOS hardware status word
Call with:	Nothing
Returns:	AX = hardware status word (see "Notes")
Notes:	The bits in the hardware status word have the following meanings: *Bit(s)* *Meaning* 0 1 if floppy disk drive(s) installed 1 1 if math coprocessor installed 2 1 if pointing device installed (PS/2 only)

(continued)

Bit(s)	Meaning
2–3	Amount of system board RAM (PC and PC*jr* only): 00 = 16 KB 01 = 32 KB 10 = 48 KB 11 = 64 KB
4–5	Initial video mode: 00 = reserved 01 = 40x25 color text 10 = 80x25 color text 11 = 80x25 monochrome text
6–7	Number of floppy disk drives (if bit 0 set): 00 = 1 01 = 2 10 = 3 11 = 4
8	Reserved
9–11	Number of serial ports installed
12	1 if game adapter installed
13	1 if internal modem installed (PC and PC/XT only)
14–15	Number of printers installed

ERROR HANDLING SERVICE

Int 21H Function 59H
Get extended error information

Action: Returns detailed information about the error generated by the most recent Int 21H service call

Call with: AH = 59H
BX = 00H

Returns: AX = extended error code (see Figure 13-1)
BH = error class (see "Notes")
BL = recommended action (see "Notes")
CH = error location:
   01H = unknown
   02H = block device (disk or disk emulator)
   03H = network
   04H = serial device
   05H = memory

If extended error code = 22H (invalid disk change):
ES = segment of ASCIIZ string that gives volume label of disk to insert
DI = offset of ASCIIZ string that gives volume label of disk to insert

Notes: Calling this service after any Int 21H service call returns an error status. If this service is called when the previous service call had no error, 0000H is returned in AX.

You'll find this service useful when a file control block service signals an error by returning FFH in register AL or when a file handle service signals an error by setting the carry flag.

In addition to changing the registers that it uses to return results, this service modifies registers CL, DX, SI, DI, ES, BP, and DS.

The possible error class values returned in the BH register have the following meanings:

Value	Meaning
01H	Out of resource (such as storage or handles)
02H	No error, but a temporary situation (such as a locked region in a file) that is expected to end
03H	Authorization problem
04H	Internal error in system software
05H	Hardware failure
06H	Software failure not caused by the active program
07H	Application program error
08H	File or item not found
09H	File or item of invalid format or type
0AH	File or item locked
0BH	Wrong disk in drive, bad spot on disk, or storage medium problem
0CH	File or item already exists
0DH	Unknown error

The possible values for the recommended actions returned in BL have the following meanings:

Value	Meaning
01H	Retry immediately
02H	Retry after a delay
03H	Get new values from the user; current values are bad
04H	Terminate after cleaning up
05H	Terminate immediately without cleaning up
06H	Ignore the error
07H	Prompt the user to fix the problem and then retry

APPENDIX A

MS-DOS and BIOS Interrupt Services

The following two tables list the MS-DOS and BIOS interrupt services that are described in this book. The first table lists them by category, with each category corresponding to a chapter in the book. The second table lists them in numeric order.

Services by Category

Service	Description	Page number
Keyboard Services		
Int 16H Function 00H	Read character from keyboard	74
Int 16H Function 02H	Read keyboard flags	74
Int 16H Function 03H	Set keyboard repeat	75
Int 16H Function 05H	Place character and scan code	76
Int 16H Function 12H	Get enhanced keyboard flags	77
Int 21H Function 01H	Character input with echo	78
Int 21H Function 06H	Direct I/O without echo	78
Int 21H Function 07H	Direct character input without echo	79
Int 21H Function 08H	Character input without echo	79
Int 21H Function 0AH	Read line from *stdin*	79
Int 21H Function 0BH	Check input status	80
Int 21H Function 0CH	Flush input buffer and then input a character	81
Int 21H Function 33H	Get or set break flag	81
Mouse Services		
Int 33H Function 00H	Reset mouse and get status	136
Int 33H Function 01H	Show mouse cursor	137
Int 33H Function 02H	Hide mouse cursor	138
Int 33H Function 03H	Get mouse cursor position and button status	138
Int 33H Function 04H	Set mouse cursor position	139
Int 33H Function 05H	Get button press information	139
Int 33H Function 06H	Get button release information	140
Int 33H Function 07H	Set horizontal limits for mouse cursor	141
Int 33H Function 08H	Set vertical limits for mouse cursor	141
Int 33H Function 09H	Set graphics mode cursor shape	142
Int 33H Function 0AH	Set text mode cursor shape	143

Service	Description	Page number
Int 33H Function 0BH	Read mouse motion counters	143
Int 33H Function 0CH	Set user-defined mouse event handler	144
Int 33H Function 0DH	Enable light-pen emulation	145
Int 33H Function 0EH	Disable light-pen emulation	145
Int 33H Function 0FH	Set mickeys-to-pixels ratio	145
Int 33H Function 10H	Set mouse cursor exclusion area	146
Int 33H Function 13H	Set double-speed threshold	146
Int 33H Function 15H	Get buffer size for saving mouse driver state	147
Int 33H Function 16H	Save mouse driver state	147
Int 33H Function 17H	Restore mouse driver state	148
Int 33H Function 1AH	Set mouse sensitivity	148
Int 33H Function 1BH	Get mouse sensitivity	149
Int 33H Function 1CH	Set mouse driver interrupt rate	149
Int 33H Function 1DH	Set mouse cursor display page	150
Int 33H Function 1EH	Get mouse cursor display page	150
Int 33H Function 21H	Reset mouse driver	150
Int 33H Function 2AH	Get cursor hot spot	151

Display Services

Service	Description	Page number
Int 10H Function 00H	Set display mode	195
Int 10H Function 01H	Set cursor appearance	195
Int 10H Function 02H	Set cursor position	196
Int 10H Function 03H	Get cursor position	197
Int 10H Function 05H	Set active display page	197
Int 10H Function 06H	Clear or scroll window up	198
Int 10H Function 07H	Clear or scroll window down	198
Int 10H Function 08H	Read character and attribute at cursor position	199
Int 10H Function 09H	Write character and attribute at cursor position	199
Int 10H Function 0AH	Write character at cursor position	200
Int 10H Function 0EH	Write character, update cursor position	201
Int 10H Function 0FH	Get display mode	202
Int 10H Function 12H	Get configuration information	202
Int 10H Function 1AH	Get or set display hardware information	203

(continued)

Service	Description	Page number
Int 11H	Get equipment information	204
Int 21H Function 02H	Character output	204
Int 21H Function 06H	Direct I/O without echo	205
Int 21H Function 40H	Write characters to file or device	205
File Management Services—FCB Services		
Int 21H Function 0FH	Open file	254
Int 21H Function 10H	Close file	255
Int 21H Function 13H	Delete file	255
Int 21H Function 14H	Sequential read	256
Int 21H Function 15H	Sequential write	256
Int 21H Function 16H	Create file	257
Int 21H Function 17H	Rename file	258
Int 21H Function 1AH	Set DTA address	259
Int 21H Function 21H	Random read	259
Int 21H Function 22H	Random write	260
Int 21H Function 23H	Get file size	260
Int 21H Function 24H	Set relative record number	261
Int 21H Function 27H	Random block read	262
Int 21H Function 28H	Random block write	263
Int 21H Function 29H	Parse filename	263
Int 21H Function 2FH	Get DTA address	265
File Management Services—Handle Services		
Int 21H Function 3CH	Create file	265
Int 21H Function 3DH	Open file	266
Int 21H Function 3EH	Close file	267
Int 21H Function 3FH	Read file or device	268
Int 21H Function 40H	Write file or device	268
Int 21H Function 41H	Delete file	269
Int 21H Function 42H	Set file pointer position	270
Int 21H Function 43H	Get or set file attributes	270
Int 21H Function 45H	Duplicate handle	271
Int 21H Function 46H	Redirect handle	272
Int 21H Function 56H	Rename file	273
Int 21H Function 57H	Get or set file date and time	273

Service	Description	Page number
Int 21H Function 5AH	Create temporary file (MS-DOS 3.0 and later)	274
Int 21H Function 5BH	Create new file (MS-DOS 3.0 and later)	275
Int 21H Function 67H	Set handle count (MS-DOS 3.3 and later)	276
Int 21H Function 68H	Commit file (MS-DOS 3.3 and later)	277
Int 21H Function 6CH	Extended file open (MS-DOS 5.0)	278

Disk Management and Directory Services

Int 21H Function 0EH	Select disk drive	303
Int 21H Function 19H	Get current disk drive	303
Int 21H Function 1BH	Get default drive data	304
Int 21H Function 1CH	Get drive data	304
Int 21H Function 2EH	Set verify flag	305
Int 21H Function 36H	Get drive allocation information	306
Int 21H Function 39H	Create directory	306
Int 21H Function 3AH	Delete directory	307
Int 21H Function 3BH	Set current directory	308
Int 21H Function 47H	Get current directory	308
Int 21H Function 54H	Get verify flag	309

Serial and Parallel Port Services

Int 14H Function 00H	Initialize serial port	329
Int 14H Function 01H	Write character to serial port	331
Int 14H Function 02H	Read character from serial port	331
Int 14H Function 03H	Get serial port status	332
Int 17H Function 00H	Write character to parallel port	332
Int 17H Function 01H	Initialize parallel port	333
Int 17H Function 02H	Get parallel port status	333
Int 21H Function 03H	Auxiliary input	334
Int 21H Function 04H	Auxiliary output	334
Int 21H Function 05H	Parallel port output	334
Int 21H Function 44H Subfunction 06H	Check input status	335

Memory Management Services—Conventional Memory

Int 21H Function 48H	Allocate arena entry	366
Int 21H Function 49H	Release arena entry	366

(continued)

MS-DOS and BIOS Interrupt Services

Service	Description	Page number
Int 21H Function 4AH	Resize arena entry	367
Int 21H Function 58H	Get or set memory allocation strategy	368
Memory Management Services—Extended Memory		
Int 15H Function 87H	Transfer data from extended memory block	369
Int 15H Function 88H	Get extended memory size	370
Memory Management Services—Expanded Memory		
Int 21H Function 44H Subfunction 07H	Get output status	370
Int 67H Function 40H (EMS 3.0 and later)	Get status	371
Int 67H Function 41H (EMS 3.0 and later)	Get page frame segment address	371
Int 67H Function 42H (EMS 3.0 and later)	Get number of pages	372
Int 67H Function 43H (EMS 3.0 and later)	Allocate expanded memory handle and pages	372
Int 67H Function 44H (EMS 3.0 and later)	Map expanded memory page to page frame	373
Int 67H Function 45H (EMS 3.0 and later)	Release handle and expanded memory	373
Int 67H Function 46H (EMS 3.0 and later)	Get EMS version number	374
Int 67H Function 51H (EMS 4.0)	Reallocate pages for handle	374
Miscellaneous Services		
Int 11H	Get equipment information	387
Int 21H Function 2AH	Get system date	385
Int 21H Function 2BH	Set system date	386
Int 21H Function 2CH	Get system time	386
Int 21H Function 2DH	Set system time	387
Int 21H Function 59H	Get extended error information	388

Services in Numeric Order

Service	Description	Page number
Int 10H Function 00H	Set display mode	195
Int 10H Function 01H	Set cursor appearance	195
Int 10H Function 02H	Set cursor position	196
Int 10H Function 03H	Get cursor position	197
Int 10H Function 05H	Set active display page	197
Int 10H Function 06H	Clear or scroll window up	198
Int 10H Function 07H	Clear or scroll window down	198
Int 10H Function 08H	Read character and attribute at cursor position	199
Int 10H Function 09H	Write character and attribute at cursor position	199
Int 10H Function 0AH	Write character at cursor position	200
Int 10H Function 0EH	Write character, update cursor position	201
Int 10H Function 0FH	Get display mode	202
Int 10H Function 12H	Get configuration information	202
Int 10H Function 1AH	Get or set display hardware information	203
Int 11H	Get equipment information	204, 389
Int 14H Function 00H	Initialize serial port	329
Int 14H Function 01H	Write character to serial port	331
Int 14H Function 02H	Read character from serial port	331
Int 14H Function 03H	Get serial port status	332
Int 15H Function 87H	Transfer data from extended memory block	369
Int 15H Function 88H	Get extended memory size	370
Int 16H Function 00H	Read character from keyboard	74
Int 16H Function 02H	Read keyboard flags	74
Int 16H Function 03H	Set keyboard repeat	75
Int 16H Function 05H	Push character and scan code	76
Int 16H Function 12H	Get enhanced keyboard flags	77
Int 17H Function 00H	Write character to parallel port	332
Int 17H Function 01H	Initialize parallel port	333
Int 17H Function 02H	Get parallel port status	333
Int 21H Function 01H	Character input with echo	78

(continued)

Service	Description	Page number
Int 21H Function 02H	Character output	204
Int 21H Function 03H	Auxiliary input	334
Int 21H Function 04H	Auxiliary output	334
Int 21H Function 05H	Parallel port output	334
Int 21H Function 06H	Direct I/O without echo	78, 205
Int 21H Function 07H	Direct character input without echo	79
Int 21H Function 08H	Character input without echo	79
Int 21H Function 0AH	Read line from *stdin*	79
Int 21H Function 0BH	Check input status	80
Int 21H Function 0CH	Flush input buffer and then input a character	81
Int 21H Function 0EH	Select disk drive	303
Int 21H Function 0FH	Open file	254
Int 21H Function 10H	Close file	255
Int 21H Function 13H	Delete file	255
Int 21H Function 14H	Sequential read	256
Int 21H Function 15H	Sequential write	256
Int 21H Function 16H	Create file	257
Int 21H Function 17H	Rename file	258
Int 21H Function 19H	Get current disk drive	303
Int 21H Function 1AH	Set DTA address	259
Int 21H Function 1BH	Get default drive data	304
Int 21H Function 1CH	Get drive data	304
Int 21H Function 21H	Random read	259
Int 21H Function 22H	Random write	260
Int 21H Function 23H	Get file size	261
Int 21H Function 24H	Set relative record number	261
Int 21H Function 27H	Random block read	262
Int 21H Function 28H	Random block write	263
Int 21H Function 29H	Parse filename	263
Int 21H Function 2AH	Get system date	387
Int 21H Function 2BH	Set system date	388
Int 21H Function 2CH	Get system time	388
Int 21H Function 2DH	Set system time	389
Int 21H Function 2EH	Set verify flag	305

Service	Description	Page number
Int 21H Function 2FH	Get DTA address	265
Int 21H Function 33H	Get or set break flag	81
Int 21H Function 36H	Get drive allocation information	306
Int 21H Function 39H	Create directory	306
Int 21H Function 3AH	Delete directory	307
Int 21H Function 3BH	Set current directory	308
Int 21H Function 3CH	Create file	265
Int 21H Function 3DH	Open file	266
Int 21H Function 3EH	Close file	267
Int 21H Function 3FH	Read file or device	268
Int 21H Function 40H	Write characters to file or device	205, 268
Int 21H Function 41H	Delete file	269
Int 21H Function 42H	Set file pointer position	270
Int 21H Function 43H	Get or set file attributes	271
Int 21H Function 44H Subfunction 06H	Check input status	335
Int 21H Function 44H Subfunction 07H	Get output status	370
Int 21H Function 45H	Duplicate handle	271
Int 21H Function 46H	Redirect handle	272
Int 21H Function 47H	Get current directory	308
Int 21H Function 48H	Allocate arena entry	366
Int 21H Function 49H	Release arena entry	366
Int 21H Function 4AH	Resize arena entry	367
Int 21H Function 54H	Get verify flag	309
Int 21H Function 56H	Rename file	273
Int 21H Function 57H	Get or set file date and time	273
Int 21H Function 58H	Get or set memory allocation strategy	368
Int 21H Function 59H	Get extended error information	390
Int 21H Function 5AH	Create temporary file (MS-DOS 3.0 and later)	274
Int 21H Function 5BH	Create new file (MS-DOS 3.0 and later)	275
Int 21H Function 67H	Set handle count (MS-DOS 3.3 and later)	276
Int 21H Function 68H	Commit file (MS-DOS 3.3 and later)	277
Int 21H Function 6CH	Extended file open (MS-DOS 5.0)	278

(continued)

Service	Description	Page number
Int 33H Function 00H	Reset mouse and get status	136
Int 33H Function 01H	Show mouse cursor	137
Int 33H Function 02H	Hide mouse cursor	138
Int 33H Function 03H	Get mouse cursor position and button status	138
Int 33H Function 04H	Set mouse cursor position	139
Int 33H Function 05H	Get button press information	139
Int 33H Function 06H	Get button release information	140
Int 33H Function 07H	Set horizontal limits for mouse cursor	141
Int 33H Function 08H	Set vertical limits for mouse cursor	141
Int 33H Function 09H	Set graphics mode cursor shape	142
Int 33H Function 0AH	Set text mode cursor shape	143
Int 33H Function 0BH	Read mouse motion counters	143
Int 33H Function 0CH	Set user-defined mouse event handler	144
Int 33H Function 0DH	Enable light-pen emulation	145
Int 33H Function 0EH	Disable light-pen emulation	145
Int 33H Function 0FH	Set mickeys-to-pixels ratio	145
Int 33H Function 10H	Set mouse cursor exclusion area	146
Int 33H Function 13H	Set double-speed threshold	146
Int 33H Function 15H	Get buffer size for saving mouse driver state	147
Int 33H Function 16H	Save mouse driver state	147
Int 33H Function 17H	Restore mouse driver state	148
Int 33H Function 1AH	Set mouse sensitivity	148
Int 33H Function 1BH	Get mouse sensitivity	149
Int 33H Function 1CH	Set mouse driver interrupt rate	149
Int 33H Function 1DH	Set mouse cursor display page	150
Int 33H Function 1EH	Get mouse cursor display page	150
Int 33H Function 21H	Reset mouse driver	150
Int 33H Function 2AH	Get cursor hot spot	151
Int 67H Function 40H (EMS 3.0 and later)	Get status	371
Int 67H Function 41H (EMS 3.0 and later)	Get page frame segment address	371
Int 67H Function 42H (EMS 3.0 and later)	Get number of pages	372

Service	Description	Page number
Int 67H Function 43H (EMS 3.0 and later)	Allocate expanded memory handle and pages	372
Int 67H Function 44H (EMS 3.0 and later)	Map expanded memory page to page frame	373
Int 67H Function 45H (EMS 3.0 and later)	Release handle and expanded memory	373
Int 67H Function 46H (EMS 3.0 and later)	Get EMS version number	374
Int 67H Function 51H (EMS 4.0)	Reallocate pages for handle	374

APPENDIX B

The ASCII and IBM Extended Character Sets

ASCII	Dec	Hex	Ctrl		ASCII	Dec	Hex	Ctrl
	0	00	NUL	(Null)	<space>	32	20	
☺	1	01	SOH	(Start of heading)	!	33	21	
☻	2	02	STX	(Start of text)	"	34	22	
♥	3	03	ETX	(End of text)	#	35	23	
♦	4	04	EOT	(End of transmission)	$	36	24	
♣	5	05	ENQ	(Enquiry)	%	37	25	
♠	6	06	ACK	(Acknowledge)	&	38	26	
•	7	07	BEL	(Bell)	'	39	27	
◘	8	08	BS	(Backspace)	(	40	28	
○	9	09	HT	(Horizontal tab)	)	41	29	
◙	10	0A	LF	(Linefeed)	*	42	2A	
♂	11	0B	VT	(Vertical tab)	+	43	2B	
♀	12	0C	FF	(Formfeed)	,	44	2C	
♪	13	0D	CR	(Carriage return)	-	45	2D	
♫	14	0E	SO	(Shift out)	.	46	2E	
☼	15	0F	SI	(Shift in)	/	47	2F	
►	16	10	DLE	(Data link escape)	0	48	30	
◄	17	11	DC1	(Device control 1)	1	49	31	
↕	18	12	DC2	(Device control 2)	2	50	32	
‼	19	13	DC3	(Device control 3)	3	51	33	
¶	20	14	DC4	(Device control 4)	4	52	34	
§	21	15	NAK	(Negative acknowledge)	5	53	35	
▬	22	16	SYN	(Synchronous idle)	6	54	36	
↨	23	17	ETB	(End transmission block)	7	55	37	
↑	24	18	CAN	(Cancel)	8	56	38	
↓	25	19	EM	(End of medium)	9	57	39	
→	26	1A	SUB	(Substitute)	:	58	3A	
←	27	1B	ESC	(Escape)	;	59	3B	
∟	28	1C	FS	(File separator)	<	60	3C	
↔	29	1D	GS	(Group separator)	=	61	3D	
▲	30	1E	RS	(Record separator)	>	62	3E	
▼	31	1F	US	(Unit separator)	?	63	3F	

ASCII	Dec	Hex	Ctrl	ASCII	Dec	Hex	Ctrl
@	64	40		`	96	60	
A	65	41		a	97	61	
B	66	42		b	98	62	
C	67	43		c	99	63	
D	68	44		d	100	64	
E	69	45		e	101	65	
F	70	46		f	102	66	
G	71	47		g	103	67	
H	72	48		h	104	68	
I	73	49		i	105	69	
J	74	4A		j	106	6A	
K	75	4B		k	107	6B	
L	76	4C		l	108	6C	
M	77	4D		m	109	6D	
N	78	4E		n	110	6E	
O	79	4F		o	111	6F	
P	80	50		p	112	70	
Q	81	51		q	113	71	
R	82	52		r	114	72	
S	83	53		s	115	73	
T	84	54		t	116	74	
U	85	55		u	117	75	
V	86	56		v	118	76	
W	87	57		w	119	77	
X	88	58		x	120	78	
Y	89	59		y	121	79	
Z	90	5A		z	122	7A	
[	91	5B		{	123	7B	
\	92	5C		¦	124	7C	
]	93	5D		}	125	7D	
^	94	5E		~	126	7E	
_	95	5F		△	127	7F	DEL

ASCII	Dec	Hex	ASCII	Dec	Hex	ASCII	Dec	Hex	ASCII	Dec	Hex
Ç	128	80	á	160	A0	└	192	C0	α	224	E0
ü	129	81	í	161	A1	┴	193	C1	β	225	E1
é	130	82	ó	162	A2	┬	194	C2	Γ	226	E2
â	131	83	ú	163	A3	├	195	C3	π	227	E3
ä	132	84	ñ	164	A4	─	196	C4	Σ	228	E4
à	133	85	Ñ	165	A5	┼	197	C5	σ	229	E5
å	134	86	ª	166	A6	╞	198	C6	μ	230	E6
ç	135	87	º	167	A7	╟	199	C7	τ	231	E7
ê	136	88	¿	168	A8	╚	200	C8	Φ	232	E8
ë	137	89	⌐	169	A9	╔	201	C9	Θ	233	E9
è	138	8A	¬	170	AA	╩	202	CA	Ω	234	EA
ï	139	8B	½	171	AB	╦	203	CB	δ	235	EB
î	140	8C	¼	172	AC	╠	204	CC	∞	236	EC
ì	141	8D	¡	173	AD	═	205	CD	φ	237	ED
Ä	142	8E	«	174	AE	╬	206	CE	ε	238	EE
Å	143	8F	»	175	AF	╧	207	CF	∩	239	EF
É	144	90	▒	176	B0	╨	208	D0	≡	240	F0
æ	145	91	▓	177	B1	╤	209	D1	±	241	F1
Æ	146	92	▓	178	B2	╥	210	D2	≥	242	F2
ô	147	93	│	179	B3	╙	211	D3	≤	243	F3
ö	148	94	┤	180	B4	╘	212	D4	⌠	244	F4
ò	149	95	╡	181	B5	╒	213	D5	⌡	245	F5
û	150	96	╢	182	B6	╓	214	D6	÷	246	F6
ù	151	97	╖	183	B7	╫	215	D7	≈	247	F7
ÿ	152	98	╕	184	B8	╪	216	D8	°	248	F8
Ö	153	99	╣	185	B9	┘	217	D9	•	249	F9
Ü	154	9A	║	186	BA	┌	218	DA	·	250	FA
¢	155	9B	╗	187	BB	█	219	DB	√	251	FB
£	156	9C	╝	188	BC	▄	220	DC	η	252	FC
¥	157	9D	╜	189	BD	▌	221	DD	²	253	FD
₧	158	9E	╛	190	BE	▐	222	DE	■	254	FE
ƒ	159	9F	┐	191	BF	▀	223	DF		255	FF

INDEX

Note: Page numbers in *italics* refer to figures.

Special Characters

8088/8086 processors, 376
   memory processing, 18
8250 UART, 313
16450 UART, 313
80286 processors, 339, 376
   extended memory, 351
   memory processing, 19
80386 processors, 19

A

active display page, 160
   setting, 197–98
address
   disk transfer area, 230, 259, 265
   handler, 26
AH register, 22, *23*
   accessing, 37, *37*
alias, 217
allocation units, 212–13
AL register, 22, *23*
   accessing, 37, *37*
ANSI.SYS file, 8
   controlling screen display with, 180–81, *181–82,* 183–85
      in Basic, 183–84
      in C, 184–85
application programs, 2, *10*
   disk data accessing process, 210, *211*
   expanded memory, 342, 343, *343,* 356–57
   memory allocation, 346
   relationship with MS-DOS, 2–4, *3*
   switching between, 6–7
   transient program area, 339
arena entries, 344, *344*
   allocating, 366
   releasing, 366–67
   resizing, 367

arena headers, 344, *344,* 345
ASCII characters
   extended character set, 405–8
   parallel port services, 323–24
ASCIIZ strings, 30–31, 243
   handle services, 222
   specifying directory names, 294, 299
attribute bytes
   control, 165
   file, 227
   meanings of individual bits in, 217, *217*
   text mode, *156,* 156–58
AUTOEXEC.BAT file, 10, 213
AUX handle, 314
auxiliary input, 334
auxiliary output, 334
AX register, 22, *23,* 35
   accessing, 36–37, *37*

B

Backspace key, function, 48
banks
   expanded memory, 342
   switching, 342
base-2 system, 16
base-10 system, 16
base-16 system, *17,* 17–18
base pointer (BP) register, 23
basic input/output system. *See* BIOS
Basic programming language. *See also specific interrupt services*
   calling interrupts from, 27–32
   INTERRUPT and INTERRUPTX subprograms, 28
   lack of pointers, 338
   Produce Debug Code option, 46
   RegType and *RegTypeX* data structures, 28–31

Basic programming language, *continued*
   text mode cursor position, 161
   versions, 28
baud rates, 313, 314, 316, 329–30
best fit, memory allocation, 345, 346
BH register, 22, *23*
binary notation, 16
   hexadecimal notation related to, *17,* 17–18
BIOS, 7–8, *10,* 19, 210. *See also* ROM BIOS
   character input, 52–55
   keyboard flags, 62
   services, 26
   text (*see* text display services)
   text mode cursor position, 161
   video portion, structure, 185–86
BIOS parameter block (BPB), 211
bits
   attribute bytes, meanings, 217, *217*
   blink, 156
   cursor mask and screen mask, 113–14, *114*
   extracting from register, 30
   intensity, 156
   stop, 313, 314, 329–30
blink bit, 156
BL register, 22, *23*
   accessing, 37, *37*
bootable disks, root directory, 218
boot code, 381
booting
   cold and warm, 212
   procedure, 212–13
   sequence, 212
boot sector, 210–11, *214*
bootstrap routine, 211, 212–13
   disk, 211, 213
Borland Turbo C compiler, calling interrupts from, 40
BPB (BIOS parameter block), 211
BP (base pointer) register, 23
break flags, querying and setting, 48–52, 81
buffers
   disk, 19
   display, 154
   input (*see* input buffer)
   refresh, 154

buffers, *(continued)*
   storing mouse driver state, 147
   video, 154
BX register, 22, *23*
   accessing, 36–37, *37*
BYTEREGS, 36–37, *37,* 40
bytes
   attribute (*see* attribute bytes)
   high, 22, *23*
   low, 22, *23*

C

C programming language. *See also specific interrupt services*
   calling interrupts from, 33–40
   portability, 12
   versions, 34
carry flag, 24, 37, 38, 166, 384
   handle services, 243
   testing, 30
central processing unit (CPU)
   memory addressing, 18–21, *20*
   registers, *21–22,* 21–24
cflag, 37, 38
CGA (Color Graphics Adapter), 155, 159, *159*
   detecting, 186
CGA/MDA BIOS, 185, 186
character cells
   mouse cursor position, 86–87
   text modes, screen display, 155–56
characters
   ASCII character set, 406–7
   IBM extended character set, 408
   parallel port services, 323–24
   placing in keyboard buffer, 71–74, 76–77
   reading, 47–55, 74, 199
      with echo, 78
      without echo, 78–79
      Int 16H Function 00H, 53–55
   writing, 199–201, 204–5
char type, 36
CHKDSK program, 11
CH register, 22, *23*
ClearButtons routine, 92
clearing, windows, 174–80, 198–99
clocks, system, 376

CL register, 22, *23*
clusters, 212–13, 215–16
   assignment codes, 215, *215*
   starting, 218
CMOS clock, 376
code segment (CS) register, 22, 24, 37
cold boot, 212
Color Graphics Adapter (CGA), 55, 155
   detecting, 186
      in Basic, 186–90
      in C, 190–94
color text modes, 156, *157*
   attribute bytes, 158
columns, converting pixels to, 86–87
COM1 port, 312, 314
COM2 port, 312, 314
COMMAND.COM file, 9–10, 213, 339
   replacing, 10
command processor, 9–10, *10*
commands, 210
   recalling, 7
command tail, 228–29, *229*
communications ports. *See* serial ports
communications program, serial ports, 315–22
   in Basic, 317–19
   in C, 319–22
compiler, 3–4
CONFIG.SYS file, 8, 10, 210, 213, 339, 342
   FILES statement, 241
   installing ANSI.SYS in, 180
control flags, 24
control services, mouse, 85, *85–86*
conventional memory, 338–39, *340*, *344*, 344–51, 366–68, 397–98. *See also* user memory
   arena entry, 344, *344*
      allocating, 366
      releasing, 366–67
      resizing, 367
      getting and setting memory allocation strategy, 368
CP/M-86, 4
CPU (central processing unit)
   memory addressing, 18–21, *20*
   registers, *21–22*, 21–24
critical errors, 386

critical errors, *(continued)*
   codes, *244*
CS (code segment) register, 22, 24, 37
Ctrl-Break key combination, 45–46
   checking for, 46–47
Ctrl-C key combination, 45, 46, 166
current drive, 282
cursor mask, 89–90, 113–14, *114*
cursors
   control, display services, 165
   mouse (*see* mouse cursor)
   text mode
      appearance, 160, 195–96
      position, 160–61, 196–97, 201
CX register, 22, *23*
   accessing, 36–37, *37*

D

data loss, Ctrl-Break and Ctrl-C, 46
data segment (DS) register, 22, 23, 37
date, getting and setting, 273–74, 376–81, 387–88
   in Basic, 377–78
   in C, 379–81
date field, 225
   coding, 218, *218, 226*
/D compiler switch, 47
DEBUG program, 11
decimal notation, 16
default disk transfer area, 229, *229*
default drive, 282
default file control blocks, 229, *229,* 230
delay rate, keyboard, 67–70
destination index (DI) register, 23
device drivers, 210, 339. *See also* mouse driver
   Expanded Memory Manager, 352–65
   installable, 8
   resident, 7–8
devices
   reading, 268
   writing, 268–69
DEVICE statement, 210, 342
DH register, 22, *23*
directories, 209, 294–302, 397
   creating and deleting, 298–302, 306–7
      in Basic, 299–300
      in C, 301–2

determining and changing, 294–98, 308–9
   in Basic, 295–96
   in C, 297–98
  parent, 217
  root, 216–18, *216–18*
DI (destination index) register, 23
disk bootstrap routine, 211, 213
disk buffers, 19
disk drives, 281–93, 397
  current, 282
  determining and changing, 303
  determining and changing current drive, 282–85, 303–4
  obtaining information about, 289–93, 304–5, 306
   in Basic, 290–92
   in C, 292–93
  reading and changing verify flag, 285–89, 305, 309
   in Basic, 258–87
   in C, 287–89
disk operating system, 2. *See also* MS-DOS; MS-DOS 5; PC-DOS
disk read services, 230
disks, 207–19
  bootable, root directory, 218
  boot sector, 210–11, *214*
  diversity, 209
  file allocation table, 212–13, *215*, 215–16
  files area, 219
  logical devices, 209–10, *211*
  mechanical devices, *208*, 208–9
  RAM, 19, 341
  root directory, 216–18, *216–18*
disk transfer area (DTA), 227–30
  address, 230, 259, 265
  program segment prefix, 228–29, *229*
disk write services, 230
display adapters, 154–55
  configuration information, 202
  detecting, 185–94
   in Basic, 186–90
   in C, 190–94
display buffer, 154
display flag, displaying and hiding mouse cursor, 87–88

display modes, 158–59, *159*
  getting, 159, 160, 202
  setting, 159, 194
display pages, 159–60, 165
  active, 160, 197–98
  changing, 160
  mouse cursor, 150
  multiple, 160
  text mode, cursor control in, 160–61
display services, 395–96
DL register, 22, *23*
doserrno, 35, 37, 38
DOS.H, 35, 36, 37, 38
DOS kernel, 8–9, *10*, 19, 26
DOSKEY, 7
drive identifier field, 224, *224*
drives. *See* disk drives
DS (data segment) register, 22, 23, 37
DTA (disk transfer area), 227–30
  address, 230, 259, 265
  program segment prefix, 228–29, *229*
DX register, 22, *23*
  accessing, 36–37, *37*
dynamic memory allocation, 346–47

E

echo
  character input with, 78
  character input without, 78–79
EDLIN, 7
EGA. *See* Enhanced Graphics Adapter
EGA BIOS, 185, 186
86-DOS, 4
EMM. *See* Expanded Memory Manager
EMM386 device driver, 352
Enhanced Graphics Adapter (EGA), 55, 155
  detecting
   in Basic, 186–90
   in C, 190–94
enhanced keyboard, 42, *44*, 71
environment block, 228, *229*
equipment information service, 381–83, 389–90
error codes
  critical errors, *244*
  expanded memory, *355*, 355–56, 358

error codes, *continued*
   extended, 384, *384–86*
errors, 383–84, *384–86*, 386–87
   carry flag signaling, 24, 37, 38, 166
   class, 387
   critical, *244,* 386
   detection, 31
   doserrno, 35 37, 38
   file control block services, 232, 233
   full duplex mode, 316
   getting extended error information, 390–91
   handle services, 243, *243–45*
   location, 387
   memory allocation, 345
   standard, 165–66
escape sequences, 180–84
   controlling screen display with
      in Basic, 183–84
      in C, 184–85
   supported by ANSI.SYS, *181–82*
ES (extra segment) register, 22, 23, 37
expanded memory, 19, 341–43, *343,*
      352–65, 370–74, 398
   accessing, 357–65
   allocating handle and pages, 372
   banks, 342
   error codes, *355,* 355–56, 358
   getting EMS version number, 374
   getting number of pages, 372
   getting output status, 370–71
   getting page frame segment address, 371
   getting status, 371
   mapping expanded memory page to page
      frame, 373
   physical, 342
   releasing handle and expanded memory, 373
   steps to using, 356–57
Expanded Memory Manager (EMM),
      342–43, 352–65
   error codes, 355, *355–56*
extended characters
   scan codes, 47
   set, IBM, 408
extended error codes, 384, *384–86,* 387
extended file control block, *226,* 226–27, *227*

extended keys
   codes, 43
   reading, 53
extended memory, 19, 339–41, *341,*
      351–52, 369–70, 398
   getting size, 370
   transferring data from, 369–70
extension field, *224,* 224–25
external hardware interrupts, 25
extra segment (ES) register, 22, 23, 37

F

far pointer, 233
FAT (file allocation table), 209, 212–13, *215,*
      215–16
FCBs. *See* file control blocks
fields
   extended file control block, *226,* 226–27
   file allocation table, *215,* 215–16
   normal file control block, 224–25, *224–26*
   root directory, 216, *216*
file access methods, 231
file allocation table (FAT), 209, 212–13, *215,*
      215–16
file attribute byte, 227
file attributes, getting and setting, 271
file control blocks (FCBs), 222, 223–40, *227,*
      254–65
   default, 229, *229,* 230
   disk transfer area, 227–30
   error handling, 232
   extended, *226,* 226–27, *227*
   file manipulation procedure, 231–32
   normal, 224–25, *224–26*
   read and write methods, 231
   services in Basic, 232, 233–36
   services in C, 233, 237–40
file create service, 225
file handles, 165–66, 222, 240–53, *241, 242,*
      265–79
   duplicate, creating, 271–72
   error handling, 243, *243–45*
   file manipulation procedure, 242–43
   number in use, 241–42
   number open, 241
   redirecting, 272

file handles, *continued*
  services
    advantages and disadvantages, 223, 241
    in Basic, 246–49
    in C, 249–53
file management services, 396–97
  file control block, 223–40, 254–65, 396
  handle, 240–53, 265–79, 396–97
  overview, 222–23
filename, parsing, 263–64
filename field, 224, *224*
  meanings of first byte in, 217, *217*
file open service, 225
file pointer, 241
  setting position, 270
files, 222
  closing, 255, 267
  committing, 277
  creating, 257–58, 265–66, 274–76, 278–79
  deleting, 255, 269
  getting size, 261
  opening, 254, 266–67, 278–79
  pointer, 241
  reading, 268
    random, 259–60
    random block read, 262
    sequential, 256
  renaming, 258, 273
  replacing, 278–79
  temporary, creating, 274–75
  writing, 268–69, 277
    random, 260
    random block write, 263
    sequential, 256–57
files area, 219
file size field, 218, *224,* 225
FILES statement, 241
first fit, memory allocation, 345, 346
flags, 40
  break, querying and setting, 48–52, 81
  carry, 24, 37, 38, 166, 384
    handle services, 243
    testing, 30
  control, 24
  display, displaying and hiding mouse cursor, 87–88

keyboard, 62–67, 74–75, 77
  status, 24
  verify, reading and changing, 285–89, 305, 309
flags register, 24
FORMAT program, 11
FP_OFF macro, 233
FP_SEG macro, 233
full duplex mode, 315, 316
function dispatcher, 228, *229*

G

garbage collection, 345
general-purpose registers, 22, *23*
  accessing, 36–37, *37*
Global Descriptor Table, 369
graphics modes
  mouse programming, 84–85, 112–35, *113*
    in Basic, 115–25
    in C, 125–35
  screen output, 158–59, *159*
ground wire, 312

H

half duplex mode, 315, 316
handle count, setting, 276–77
handshaking signals, 312
hardware, *10*
  initialization, 213
  video, getting and setting information, 203–4
hardware cursor, 88
  appearance, 89
  position, 88–89
hardware status word, 381
help, 7
Hercules Graphics Card, 155
Hercules Graphics Card Plus, 155
Hercules InColor Card, 155
hexadecimal notation, *17,* 17–18
  binary notation related to, *17,* 17–18
  memory addressing, 18
hexadecimal scan codes, keyboard, 42–43, *44*
hidden files, 8
high byte, 22, *23*
high memory, 6
HIMEM.SYS file, 8
hot spot, mouse cursor, 114, 151

I–J

IBM, 4
IBMBIO.COM file, 8, 213, 218
IBMDOS.COM file, 9, 213, 218
IBM extended character set, 405–8
IBM hardware compatibility, BIOS display
    services, 165
#include directive, 34, 38
$INCLUDE metacommand, 28, 31
initialization, 8
    hardware, 213
    parallel ports, 333
    serial ports, 329–30
initialization module, of COMMAND.COM
    file, 10
input buffer
    flushing, 59–62, 81
    placing characters in, 71–74, 76–77
input redirection, 45
input status, checking, 56–59, 80, 335
inregs argument, 28, 37–38
installable device drivers, 8
instruction pointer (IP) register, 23
Int 09H, 43
Int 10H, 165
    Function 00H, 159, 195
    Function 01H, 195–96
    Function 02H, 160, 161, 169, 170, 196
    Function 03H, 160, 161, 197
    Function 05H, 160, 197–98
    Function 06H, 198
        in Basic, 175–77
        in C, 177–80
    Function 07H, 198–99
        in Basic, 175–77
        in C, 177–80
    Function 08H, 199
        in Basic, 175–77
        in C, 177–80
    Function 09H, 169–74, 199–200
        in Basic, 170–71
        in C, 172–74
    Function 0AH, 169–74, 200–201
        in Basic, 170–71
        in C, 172–74
    Function 0EH, 201

input buffer, *(continued)*
    Function 0FH, 159, 160, 202
    Function 12H, 186, 202
    Function 1AH, 186, 203
Int 11H, 186, 204, 381–83, 389–90
    in Basic, 381–82
    in C, 382–83
Int 14H
    Function 00H, 315, 329–30
    Function 01H, 315, 331
    Function 02H, 315, 331–32
    Function 03H, 315, 332
Int 15H
    Function 87H, 341, 352, 369–70
    Function 88H, 341, 352, 370
Int 16H, 45
    Function 00H, 52–55, 74
        in Basic, 53–54
        in C, 54–55
        drawbacks, 53
    Function 02H, 62–67, 74–75
        in Basic, 63–65
        in C, 65–67
    Function 03H, 67–70, 75–76
        in Basic, 68–69
        in C, 69–70
    Function 05H, 71–74, 76–77
        in Basic, 71–72
        in C, 72–74
    Function 12H, 62, 63, 77
Int 17H
    Function 00H, 324–29, 332–33
        in Basic, 324–26
        in C, 326–29
    Function 01H, 324–29, 333
        in Basic, 324–26
        in C, 326–29
    Function 02H, 324–29, 333
        in Basic, 324–26
        in C, 326–29
Int 21H, 31, 38, 165, 213, 243, 278–79
    error handling, 383–84, *384–86*, 386–87
    Function 01H, *47*, 78
    Function 02H, 166, 204
        in Basic, 166–67
        in C, 167–69

Int21H, *continued*
  Function 03H, 314, 315, 334
  Function 04H, 314, 315, 334
  Function 05H, 323, 334–35
  Function 06H, *47,* 78, 166, 205
  Function 07H, *47,* 79
  Function 08H, *47,* 48–52, 56, 79
    in Basic, 48–50
    in C, 50–52
  Function 0AH, 56, 79–80
  Function 0BH, 56, 80
    in Basic, 57
    in C, 58–59, 319–22
  Function 0CH, 59–62, 81
    in Basic, 60
    in C, 61–62
  Function 0EH, 282–85, 303
    in Basic, 282–83
    in C, 283–85
  Function 0FH, 225, 232, 254
  Function 10H, 232, 255
  Function 13H, 255
  Function 14H, 256
  Function 15H, 256–57
  Function 16H, 225, 232, 257–58
  Function 17H, 258
  Function 19H, 282–85, 303
    in Basic, 282–83
    in C, 283–85
  Function 1AH, 230, 232, 259, 315
  Function 1BH, 292, 304
  Function 1CH, 292, 304–5
  Function 21H, 231, 259–60
  Function 22H, 231, 260
  Function 23H, 261
  Function 24H, 231, 261–62
  Function 27H, 231, 262
  Function 28H, 231, 263
  Function 29H, 263–64
  Function 2AH, 376–81, 387
    in Basic, 377–78
    in C, 379–81
  Function 2BH, 376–81, 388
    in Basic, 377–78
    in C, 379–81
  Function 2CH, 376, 388

Int21H, *continued*
  Function 2DH, 376, 389
  Function 2EH, 285–89, 305
    in Basic, 285–87
    in C, 287–89
  Function 2FH, 230, 265
  Function 30H, 32, 38–39
  Function 33H, 48–52, 81
    in Basic, 48–50
    in C, 50–52
  Function 36H, 289–93, 306
    in Basic, 290–92
    in C, 292–93
  Function 39H, 299, 306–7
    in Basic, 299–300
    in C, 300–302
  Function 3AH, 299, 307
    in Basic, 299–300
    in C, 300–302
  Function 3BH, 294, 295, 308
    in Basic, 295–96
    in C, 297–98
  Function 3CH, 243, 265–66
  Function 3DH, 243, 266–67, 314, 323, 352, 353, 358–65
  Function 3EH, 243, 267, 353
  Function 3FH, 243, 268, 314
  Function 40H, 165, 166–69, 181, 205, 243, 268–69, 314, 323
    in Basic, 166–67
    in C, 167–69
  Function 41H, 269
  Function 42H, 243, 270
  Function 43H, 271
  Function 44H, 315
    Subfunction 06H, 315, 335
    Subfunction 07H, 352–53, 358–65, 370–71
  Function 45H, 271–72
  Function 46H, 272
  Function 47H, 294, 295, 308–9
    in Basic, 295–96
    in C, 297–98
  Function 48H, 345, 366
    in C, 347–51
  Function 49H, 345, 366–67
    in C, 347–51

Int21H, *continued*
   Function 4AH, 345, 367
   Function 54H, 285–89, 309
     in Basic, 285–87
     in C, 287–89
   Function 56H, 273
   Function 57H, 273–74
   Function 58H, 346, 368
     in C, 347–51
   Function 59H, 232, 243, 387, 390–91
   Function 5AH, 274–75
   Function 5BH, 243, 275–76
   Function 67H, 276–77
   Function 68H, 277
   Function 6CH, 243, 278
   functions for calling, 35–36
   input redirection, 45
   memory allocation, in C, 347–51
   serial port, 314–15
Int 23H, 45, 46
Int 24H, 386
Int 33H, 84, 85, *85–86,* 151
   Function 00H, 87, 91, 136–37
   Function 01H, 87, 90, 137–38
   Function 02H, 87, 138
   Function 03H, 89, 138
   Function 04H, 139
   Function 05H, 89, 139–40
   Function 06H, 89, 140–41
   Function 07H, 90, 141
   Function 08H, 90, 141–42
   Function 09H, 113, 114, 142
     in Basic, 115–25
     in C, 125–35
   Function 0AH, 88–89, 89–90, 143
   Function 0BH, 90, 143
   Function 0CH, 91, 144–45
   Function 0DH, 145
   Function 0EH, 145
   Function 0FH, 145–46
     in Basic, 115–25
     in C, 125–35
   Function 10H, 88, 90, 146
   Function 13H, 146–47
   Function 15H, 147
   Function 16H, 147

Int21H, *continued*
   Function 17H, 148
   Function 1AH, 148
   Function 1BH, 149
   Function 1CH, 149
   Function 1DH, 150
   Function 1EH, 150
   Function 21H, 87, 150–51
   Function 2AH, 88, 136, 151
Int 67H, 353–55
   Function 40H, 356–57, 358–65, 371
   Function 41H, 356–57, 371
   Function 42H, 356–57, 358–65, 372
   Function 43H, 356–57, 358–65, 372
   Function 44H, 356–57, 373
   Function 45H, 357, 358–65, 373
   Function 46H, 356–57, 374
   Function 51H, 374
int86() function, 25, 34–35, 40
int86x() function, 25, 34, 35, 38, 40
intdos() function, 25, 35–36, 40
intdosx() function, 25, 35–36, 38, 40
intensity bit, 156
internal interrupts, 25
interrupt handler, 24
interrupt rate, mouse driver, 149
interrupts, 9, 24–26
   calling from Basic, 27–32
   calling from C, 33–40
   categories, 25
   mechanism, 26
interrupt service routine (ISR), 24
interrupt services. *See also specific interrupt services*
   listed by category, 394–98
   listed in numeric order, 399–403
INTERRUPT subprogram, 25, 28, 31
interrupt vector table, 26
INTERRUPTX subprogram, 25, 28, 31
intnum argument, 28
int type, 36
IO.SYS file, 8, 213, 218
IP (instruction pointer) register, 23
ISR (interrupt service routine), 24
jump instruction, 211, 212

K

keyboard, 41–81, 394
  checking input status, 56–59
  Ctrl-Break and Ctrl-C, 9, 45–47, 166
  delay and repeat rate, 67–70, 75–76
  enhanced, 42, *44,* 71
  flags, 62–67, 74–75, 77
  flushing input buffer, 59–62, 81
  Int 16H Function 00H (BIOS character input), 52–55
  Int 21H character input services, *47,* 47–52
  line input, 56
  overview, 42–43, *44*
  PC/AT, 42, *44,* 71
  PC/XT, 42, *44*
  placing characters in buffer, 71–74, 76–77
  redirection, 45
  scan codes, 42–43, *44*
  services, 74–81
key combinations, detecting, 62

L

last fit, memory allocation, 345, 346
libraries
  link, 28
  Quick, 28
library functions, 34–35
light-pen emulation, enabling and disabling, 145
LIM EMS (Lotus/Intel/Microsoft Expanded Memory Specification), 341–42
line input, reading, 56, 79–80
link libraries, 28
Loadhigh command, 19
locate(), 58
LOCATE statement, 89, 161
Lotus/Intel/Microsoft Expanded Memory Specification (LIM EMS), 341–42
low byte, 22, *23*
LPT1 port, 323
LPT2 port, 323

M

machine language code, 4
macros, FP_OFF and FP_SEG, 233

malloc() function, 347
MCGA (Multi-Color Graphics Array), 155, 159, *159*
  detecting
    in Basic, 186–90
    in C, 190–94
MDA (Monochrome Display and Printer Adapter), 155
media descriptor byte, 215, *215*
megabyte, 18
memory, 337–74
  conventional (*see* conventional memory; user memory)
  DTA size, 230
  expanded (*see* expanded memory)
  extended (*see* extended memory)
  fragmentation, 345–46
  high, 6
  organization, 19–20, *20*
  user (*see* conventional memory; user memory)
memory addressing, 18–21, *20,* 22
  segmented, 19–21
memory allocation, 345–51
  dynamic, 346–47
memory allocation strategy, getting and setting, 368
memory arena, 339
memory mapping, 154, *156,* 156–58, *158*
memory-resident programs, 43, 53, 339
mickeys, 90
  ratio to pixels, 115–35
  setting, 145–46
Microsoft mouse driver, 84
Monochrome Display and Printer Adapter (MDA), 155
  detecting
    in Basic, 186–90
    in C, 190–94
monochrome text modes, 156, *157*
  attribute bytes, 157
MORE program, 11
mouse, 83–151, *85–86,* 394–95
  graphics mode programming, 84–85, 112–35, *113*
  in Basic, 115–25

mouse, *continued*
  in C, 125–35
    light-pen emulation, enabling and disabling, 145
    motion counters, 143
    movement, 90
      speed, 146–47
    resetting and getting status, 91, 136–37
    sensitivity
      getting, 149
      setting, 148
    text mode programming, 84–85, 91–112
      in Basic, 92–101
      in C, 101–12
    three-button, 136
    user-defined event handler, 91
mouse cursor
  appearance, 89–90, 113–14, *114*, 142–43
  button press information, 139–40
  button release information, 140–41
  displaying and hiding, 87–88, 137–38
  display page, 150
  exclusion area, 90
  graphics mode cursor definition, 113–14, *114*
  hot spot, 114, 151
  movement, 90, 141–42, 146
  position, 86–87, 139
  position and button status, 138
  text mode cursor types, 88–89
mouse driver, 84, 136
  buffer for storing state, 147
  Microsoft, 84
  resetting, 150–51
  restoring state, 148
  saving state, 147
  setting interrupt rate, 149
mouse event handler, user-defined, 91, 144–45
mouse inquiry services, 85, *85–86*
MS-DOS, 2–13
  backward compatibility, 4
  components, 7–11, *10*
  expanded memory, 342
  functions, 2–3
  history, 4–6, *5*
  obtaining version number, 31–32, 38–39
  programming and, 3–4, 11–12

MS-DOS, *continued*
  release dates and enhancements of major versions, 4–6, *5*
  services, 11–13
    (*see also specific interrupt services*)
  text display services (*see* text display services)
  visual shell, 6–7
MS-DOS 5
  EMM386 device driver, 352
  enhancements, 6–7
MSDOS.SYS file, 9, 213, 218
Multi-Color Graphics Array (MCGA), 155
  detecting
    in Basic, 186–90
    in C, 190–94
multitasking, *56,* 56–59

N–O

near pointer, 233
normal file control block, 224–25, *224–26*
notation
  binary, 16
  decimal, 16
  hexadecimal, *17,* 17–18, *18*
OEM (original equipment manufacturer) information, 211
offset registers, 19–20, 23–24
original equipment manufacturer (OEM) information, 211
OS/2, 340
output, standard, 165, 166
output functions, 45
outregs argument, 28, 37–38

P

page frame, 342, 343, *343*
  mapping extended memory to, 373
pages, expanded memory, 342
parallel ports, 323–29, 397
  getting status, 333
  initializing, 333
  output, 334–35
  ROM BIOS services for, 323
  writing characters to, 332–33

parent directory, 217
parity checking, 313, 314, 329–30
PC/AT
   CMOS clock, 376
   keyboard, 42, *44,* 71
PC-DOS, 4
   IBMBIO.COM file, 8, 213, 218
   IBMDOS.COM file, 9, 213, 218
PC/XT keyboard, 42, *44*
pixels, 86, 154
   bits in mask and, 113–14, *114*
   converting to rows and columns, 86–87
   mouse cursor position, 86–87
   pattern, 156
   ratio of mickeys to, 115–35
      setting, 145–46
   video adapters, 154–55, 158
pointers
   far, 233
   file, setting position, 270
   importance, 338
   near, 233
polling, 25, 91
   communications program, 316–22
      in Basic, 317–19
      in C, 319–22
pop-up programs, 43, 53, 339
portability, MS-DOS services and, 12
ports, 312. *See also* parallel ports; serial ports
POST (power-on self test), 212
power-on self test (POST), 212
printer ports. *See* parallel ports
printf() function, 161
print-spooler, 341
PRINT statement, 161
PRN port, 323
process termination handler, 228, *229*
Produce Debug Code option, 46
program segment prefix (PSP), 228–29, *229,* 230
prompt, 2
protected mode, 339–41
PSP (program segment prefix), 228–29, *229,* 230
p-System, 4
puts() function, 161

Q

QB.BI file, 28, 29, 31
QB.LIB file, 28
QB.QLB file, 28
QBX.BI file, 28, 29, 31
QBX.LIB file, 28
QBX.QLB file, 28
QEMM386, 19
Quick library, 28

R

RAM (random access memory)
   memory mapping, 154, *156,* 156–58, 158
   video, 154, 159–60, 174, 175–80
RAM chips, 342
RAM disks, 19, 341
random access memory (RAM)
   memory mapping, 154, *156,* 156–58, 158
   video, 154, 159–60, 174, 175–80
random block access, 231
random record access, 231
read-write head, 208
real mode, 339–41, 351–52
receive wire, 312
records, 222, 231
   relative record number, 261–62
refresh buffer, 154
registers, 19, *21–22,* 21–24
   accessing, 29–30, 36–37, *37*
   extracting individual bits from, 30
   flags, 24
   general-purpose, 22, *23*
   offset, 19–20, 23–24
   segment, 19–21, 22, 37
REGS argument, 34, 36–38, *37,* 38, 40
RegType data structure, 28–31
RegTypeX data structure, 28–31
repeat rate, keyboard, 67–70
resident device drivers, 7–8
resident module, COMMAND.COM file, 9
ROM BIOS, 8
   keyboard interrupt service, 43
   real mode programs, 341
ROM bootstrap routine, 212–13
root directory, 216–18, *216–18*
rows, converting pixels to, 86–87

S

SADD statement, 166
saving, mouse driver state, 147
scan codes
    extended characters, 47
    keyboard, 42–43, *44*
    placing in keyboard buffer, 76–77
    reading, 74
scan lines
    mouse cursor appearance, 89
    text mode display cursor appearance, 160, 195–96
screen display, 153–205
    BIOS display services, 161–64
        in Basic, 162–63, 170–71
        in C, 163–64, 172–74
    controlling with ANSI.SYS, 180–81, *181–82,* 183–85
        in Basic, 183–84
        in C, 184–85
    detecting video hardware, 185–94
        in Basic, 186–90
        in C, 190–94
    display pages, 159–60
        text mode, cursor control in, 160–61
    getting and setting hardware information, 203–4
    graphics modes, 158
    MS-DOS display services, 165–69
        in Basic, 166–67
        in C, 167–69
    PC display modes, 158–59, *159*
    pixels, 154
    reading data from video RAM, 174
    scrolling and clearing windows, 174–80
        in Basic, 175–77
        in C, 177–80
    text modes, 155–58, *156, 157*
        cursor control in, 160–61
    video adapters, 154–55
screen masks, 89–90, 113–14, *114*
    designing
        in Basic, 115–25
        in C, 125–35
scroll() function, 177–80
scrolling, windows, 174–80, 198–99
Scroll subprogram, 175–77
Seattle Computer Products, 4
sectors
    logical, 209–10
    physical, 208, *208,* 209–10
segmented memory addressing, 19–21
segment registers, 19–21, 22
    altering, 37
segregs argument, 37–38
sequential access, 231
serial ports, 312–22, 397
    21H services, 314–15
    communications program, 315–22
        in Basic, 317–19
        in C, 319–22
    configuring, 314
    getting status, 332
    initializing, 329–30
    reading characters from, 331–32
    ROM BIOS serial port services, 315
    UART, 313–14
    writing characters to, 331
SI (source index) register, 23
software cursor, 88–89
    appearance, 89–90
software interrupts. *See* interrupts; *specific interrupts*
SORT program, 11
source index (SI) register, 23
SP (stack pointer) register, 23, 24
SREGS argument, 35, 37–38, 38, 40
SS (stack segment) register, 22, 23, 24, 37
stack pointer (SP) register, 23, 24
stack segment (SS) register, 22, 23, 24, 37
standard error, 165–66
standard output, 165, 166
status flags, 24
stdin, 45
    reading line input from, 56, 79–80
stdout, 45
stop bits, 313, 314, 329–30
StringOut subprogram, 181
strings, displaying, 169–74
subdirectories, 294. *See also* directories
SuperVGA, 158

/? switch, 7
SYSINIT, 213
system clock, 376
system context, 26
system services, 9, 11–13
   advantages, 11–12
   limitations, 12
   MS-DOS vs. BIOS, 26

T

terminate-and-stay-resident (TSR) programs, 43, 53, 339
text
   output position, 88–89
   reading, 48–52, 74
      Int 16H Function 00H, 53–55
text display services
   BIOS, 161–64, 165, 169–74
      in Basic, 162–63, 170–71
      in C, 163–64, 172–74
   MS-DOS, 165–69
      in Basic, 166–67
      in C, 167–69
text editor, 7
text modes
   cursor position, 196–97, 201
   mouse cursor types, 88–89
   mouse programming, 84–85, 91–112
      in Basic, 92–101
      in C, 101–12
   screen output, 155–58, *156, 157*
      cursor control, 160–61
      monochrome and color, 156, *157,* 158
time, getting and setting, 273–74, 376, 388–89
time field, 225
   coding, 218, *218, 225*
TPA (transient program area), 339, 344
tracks, 208, *208*
transient module, COMMAND.COM file, 10
transient program area (TPA), 339, 344
transmit wire, 312
TSR (terminate-and-stay-resident) programs, 43, 53, 339
Turbo C, calling interrupts from, 40
type-ahead buffer, flushing, 59–62

U

UART (universal asynchronous receiver-transmitter), 313–14
UMBs (upper memory blocks), 6
union, 36
universal asynchronous receiver-transmitter (UART), 313–14
upper memory blocks (UMBs), 6
user memory, 338–39. *See also* conventional memory
   used by MS-DOS 5, 6
utility programs, 11

V

VARPTR statement, 166, 232
VARSEG statement, 232
verify flag, reading and changing, 285–89, 305, 309
   in Basic, 285–87
   in C, 287–89
VGA. *See* Video Graphics Array
VGA/MCGA BIOS, 185–86
video adapters, 154–55. *See also* screen display
   configuration information, 202
   modes, 154–55
video buffer, 154
Video Graphics Array (VGA), 55, 155, 158
   detecting
      in Basic, 186–90
      in C, 190–94
video RAM, 154
   display pages, 159–60
   reading data from, 174, 175–80
virtual screen, 86
   size, 136
      for graphics modes, 113, *113*

W–X

WaitClick routine, 92
warm boot, 212
windows, 174
   scrolling and clearing, 174–80, 198–99
word length, 313, 314, 329–30
WORDREGS, 36–37, *37,* 40
XENIX, 340

Peter G. Aitken

Peter G. Aitken has been programming PCs since they were first introduced 10 years ago. He is an experienced microcomputer author, with nine books and over 60 magazine articles to his credit. Among his books are several on C and Basic programming. Aitken is a member of the faculty at Duke University Medical Center, where he uses PCs extensively in his research on the nervous system.

The manuscript for this book was prepared and submitted to Microsoft Press in electronic form. Text files were processed and formatted using Microsoft Word.

Principal editorial compositor: Barb Runyan

Principal proofreader: Shawn Peck

Principal typographers: Lisa Iversen and Katherine Erickson

Interior text designer: Peggy Herman

Principal illustrator: Lisa Sandburg

Cover illustrator: Don Baker

Cover color separator: Color Services

Text composition by Microsoft Press in Melior Regular with display type in Melior Bold, using the Magna composition system and the Linotronic 300 laser imagesetter.

Printed on recycled paper stock.

Essential References from Microsoft Press

MICROSOFT® MS-DOS® PROGRAMMER'S REFERENCE
Microsoft Corporation

This is Microsoft's official reference to the MS-DOS operating system—an absolute necessity for every DOS* programmer. This comprehensive resource is updated to version 5 and provides easy access to essential information about the structure of MS-DOS and its programming interface. The heart of this book is a comprehensive reference to hundreds of MS-DOS system interrupts and functions. There are details on syntax and usage along with information on special notes, warnings, and version compatibility. The coverage of Interrupt 21h functions is indispensable to assembly language programmers. If you do any DOS programming, you need the MICROSOFT MS-DOS PROGRAMMER'S REFERENCE.
472 pages, softcover $24.95 ($32.95 Can.)

*DOS as used herein refers to the MS-DOS and PC-DOS operating systems

MICROSOFT® MOUSE PROGRAMMER'S REFERENCE, 2nd ed.
Microsoft Press and the Hardware Division of Microsoft Corporation

This is the official documentation for programming the Microsoft Mouse. It provides all the software and how-to information you need to incorporate a sophisticated mouse interface for MS-DOS operating system-based programs. Fully updated to cover Microsoft BallPoint mouse and the mouse driver version 8, this edition includes: sample programs that demonstrate mouse programming in six PC programming languages; a complete reference to all mouse function calls; an overview of mouse programming; detailed information about writing and using mouse menu programs; comprehensive index; and much more. The two 5¼-inch companion disks include sample mouse menus, MOUSE.LIB and EGA.LIB, and a collection of valuable programming examples in interpreted Basic, Microsoft QuickBasic, Microsoft C, Microsoft QuickC, Microsoft Macro Assembler, FORTRAN, and Pascal.
352 pages, softcover, with two 5¼-inch disks $34.95 ($44.95 Can.)

THE PROGRAMMER'S PC SOURCEBOOK, 2nd ed.
Reference Tables for IBM® PCs, PS/2,® and Compatibles; MS-DOS® and Windows™
Thom Hogan

This reference book saves you the frustration of searching high and low for key pieces of technical data. Here is all the information culled from hundreds of sources and integrated into convenient, accessible charts, tables, and listings. The first place to turn for immediate, accurate information about your computer and its operating system, THE PROGRAMMER'S PC SOURCEBOOK covers MS-DOS through version 5, IBM personal computers (and compatibles), including the PS/2 series, and Windows 3. Among the subjects covered are DOS commands and utilities, interrupts, mouse information, EMS support, BIOS calls and support services, memory layout, RAM parameters, keyboards, the IBM extended character set, and more.
808 pages, softcover   8½ x 11 $39.95 ($54.95 Can.)

*Microsoft Press books are available wherever quality computer books are sold.
Or call **1-800-MSPRESS** for ordering information or placing credit card orders.**
*Please refer to **BBK** when placing your order. Prices subject to change.*

---

* In Canada, contact Macmillan Canada, Attn: Microsoft Press Dept., 164 Commander Blvd., Agincourt, Ontario, Canada M1S 3C7, or call (416) 293-8141.

In the U.K., contact Microsoft Press, 27 Wrights Lane, London W8 5TZ.

More Great Resources from Microsoft Press

DAN GOOKIN'S PC HOTLINE
Dan Gookin

Deleted your root directory? Virus corrupted your system? Error messages driving you nuts? Need some PC support—now? Dan Gookin's PC HOTLINE has quick-fix, on-the-money solutions—along with candid advice on preventing future computer trauma and making your computer system purr. His straightforward advice and humorous approach make him a welcome computerside adviser for any PC user. Discover how to optimize your system under Windows, purchase hardware safely via mail order, deal with interrupt conflicts and common hard disk problems, and lead a more trouble-free computer life. Dozens of great batch files included.
256 pages, softcover   6 x 9 $14.95 ($19.95 Can.)

THE MICROSOFT® GUIDE TO MANAGING MEMORY WITH DOS 5
Dan Gookin

"Now you can get your full dollar's worth out of all that memory in your computer."
From the Introduction

One of the most significant features of DOS 5 is its ability to effectively use extended and expanded memory to shatter the 640K barrier. This official guide provides clear information on how this is done. Beginning to intermediate DOS 5 users will find out how memory works and how to install it, how it is purchased, and how it is configured. The author walks you through the simple steps necessary to convert, configure, and optimize memory with DOS 5.
208 pages, softcover $14.95 ($19.95 Can.)

The Waite Group's
MICROSOFT QUICKBASIC™ BIBLE
Mitchell Waite, Robert Arnson, Christy Gemmell, and Harry Henderson

Covering Microsoft QuickBASIC through version 4.5, this is the definitive reference, the cornerstone—indeed, the "bible"—on Microsoft QuickBASIC. The MICROSOFT QUICKBASIC BIBLE is a gold mine of comprehensive, up-to-date information, superb program examples, and expert advice. This book features detailed information on every QuickBASIC keyword, function, and feature compatability information for eight other versions of BASIC, in addition to hundreds of instructive and useful programming examples and tutorials.
960 pages, softcover $27.95 ($36.95 Can.)

---

*Microsoft Press books are available wherever quality computer books are sold. Or call **1-800-MSPRESS** for ordering information or placing credit card orders.**
*Please refer to **BBK** when placing your order. Prices subject to change.*

---

* In Canada, contact Macmillan Canada, Attn: Microsoft Press Dept., 164 Commander Blvd., Agincourt, Ontario, Canada M1S 3C7, or call (416) 293-8141.

In the U.K., contact Microsoft Press, 27 Wrights Lane, London W8 5TZ.